RELIGION
AND
SOCIETY
IN INTERACTION

PRENTICE-HALL SOCIOLOGY SERIES
Neil J. Smelser, *Editor*

RELIGION AND SOCIETY IN INTERACTION

The Sociology of Religion

RONALD L. JOHNSTONE
Central Michigan University

PRENTICE-HALL, INC., *Englewood Cliffs, N.J.*

Library of Congress Cataloging in Publication Data

JOHNSTONE, RONALD L.
　　Religion and society in interaction.

　　Includes bibliographical references and index.
　　1. Religion and sociology. I. Title.
BL6.J63　　　301.5′8　　　74–30049
ISBN　0–13–773085–3

To
Margaret and Ross
and
my wife, Arline

© 1975 by PRENTICE-HALL, INC.
Englewood Cliffs, New Jersey

Printed in the United States of America

10　9　8　7　6　5

Prentice-Hall International, Inc., *London*
Prentice-Hall of Australia, Pty. Ltd., *Sydney*
Prentice-Hall of Canada, Ltd., *Toronto*
Prentice-Hall of India Private Limited, *New Delhi*
Prentice-Hall of Japan, Inc., *Tokyo*

Contents

Part II
RELIGION AND THE INDIVIDUAL

Part III
RELIGION IN SOCIETY

Part V
SOCIOLOGICAL PROJECTIONS

Preface

This introductory text to the sociology of religion follows an outline that with ongoing modifications has worked successfully in over ten years of teaching courses variously titled Religion and Society, Sociology of Religion, and Religion in Contemporary Society. The book is intended primarily for a first college-level course in the sociology of religion, taken preferably by students who have had at least an introductory course in sociology.

Yet in writing the text, I also have kept in mind those persons who from time to time have asked me what the sociology of religion is all about. They seem to come primarily from the ranks of organized religion and include seminary professors and denominational administrators as well as laymen in local congregations. This book will be an aid to them in their quest for insight and information not only about an academic subject but also about the relationship of religion to the society in which they live.

The book consists of five parts. Part I is an introduction to the sociological perspective on religion; it grapples with the problem of defining religion and considers the fascinating but ultimately frustrating question of the origins of religion. Part II treats the relationship of religion to the individual: Who is religious? How does religion affect people? How do people become religious? In Part III we concentrate on the major focus of the sociology of religion in an analysis of the place of religion in society and a discussion of the interactive, reciprocal relationship of religion to other institutions within society. In Part IV we look specifically at some of the major features of religion in the United States—the social environment and experience of a majority of the readers of this text. In a final chapter that constitutes Part V, we consider several theoretical perspectives with an eye to projecting the future of religion in society.

In this progression the reader will experience firsthand some of the problems inherent in the enterprise we call the sociology of religion and will become involved and somewhat expert in the process of applying the sociological perspective. He also will develop an insight into and understanding of the place of religion in society that will supplement his prior understanding, whether gained from the inside as a believer or from the outside as a serious, or even casual, observer of religious phenomena.

As always in producing any written words, one's debts to others are both many and monumental. I must single out two former teachers in particular: David Schuller who convinced me of the relevance of the sociological perspective in understanding the world around us, and Gerry Lenski who introduced me both to the sociology of religion as an important subfield within sociology and to the far-reaching relevance of social stratification as a sociological variable.

Without question my wife Arline deserves the epitome of gratitude for patience and endurance that in many ways exceeded my own. Finally, my special thanks to Lois Dunn who typed the final manuscript with not only dispatch and accuracy but good humor as well.

R. L. J.

THE SOCIOLOGICAL PERSPECTIVE ON RELIGION

Part I

1

The
Sociological
Perspective

Religion is a social phenomenon and is in an interactive relationship with the other social units that constitute a society. This seemingly obvious assertion, which lies at the very foundation of the sociology of religion, is actually not nearly so simple as it may seem. Nor is it so readily accepted as one might expect.

Many people, particularly the religiously committed, think of religion in an entirely different way. Some prefer to see religion as the context of man's communion with the supernatural, and religious experience as something outside ordinary experience, while others see religion as an expression of man's instinctual reaction to cosmic forces. Still others see religion as an explicit set of messages from a deity. These viewpoints certainly deemphasize, or ignore, or even reject the sociological dimensions of religion. Nevertheless, whether we're talking about religion in general, or a particular religious family such as Christianity or Buddhism, or a specific religious group such as the Four Square Gospel Tabernacle, the phenomenon of religion will be seen to interact with other social institutions and forces in society, to follow and illustrate sociological principles and laws.

In other words, whatever else it is (or isn't), religion is indisputably a social phenomenon and as such is in a continual reciprocal, interactive

3

relationship with other social phenomena. That, in brief, is what the sociology of religion is all about; and this book is basically concerned with the specification and elaboration of this point in a variety of dimensions and on a number of levels.

CHARACTERISTICS OF THE SOCIOLOGY OF RELIGION

Asserting that religion is a social phenomenon suggests several things. In the first place the statement has a *nonevaluative intent*. Thus we are not going to be able nor even want to speak about the truth or falsity of religion. Speaking of religion in terms of the Good, the True, and the Beautiful may be worthwhile and even stimulating for philosophers and theologians—or anyone, for that matter (even sociologists); but such considerations have nothing to do with sociology. Sociology that claims to accurately describe reality demands that its practitioners approach their subjects—religion no less than any other (and perhaps more than most)—with all the neutrality and objectivity they can muster.

Of course, no sociologist can always (if ever) be perfectly neutral and objective with regard to his subject, let alone one so value-laden and emotionally charged as religion. Recent studies in the sociology of knowledge, as well as honest discussions that have punctured the myth of a "value-free" sociology, have been sufficient to discourage any such pretentions. Nonetheless, a conscious, deliberate striving for neutrality and objectivity must be present—indeed, it should be evident—in any sociological investigation.

The sociology of religion is also *empirical*: it can only study and reach conclusions about phenomena that are observable. In order to confirm or refute any particular theory, the sociologist must test that theory with relevant empirical observations: *data*. And since data are by their nature limited to the observable, the measurable, the quantifiable, whatever elements of religion are spiritual or supernatural, in the sense that they cannot be seen with the eye or otherwise measured or recorded, are by definition beyond the purview of sociology.

Our characterization of the sociology of religion so far, as objective and empirical, can be summed up by stating that the sociology of religion is conducted according to the *scientific method*: the systematic search for verifiable data ("facts") firmly rooted in prior knowledge and theoretical formulations, requiring evidence as opposed to hearsay, opinion, intuition, or common sense and involving procedures that others can verify and replicate (reproduce under essentially identical conditions).

It is at this point that the sociologist of religion encounters probably the most strenuous objection from the religiously committed, which usually runs something like this: Since religion relates primarily to the supernatural—that is, to forces that are usually unseen—and involves matters of the heart as well, anything the sociologist can say about religion, limited as he is to describing the observable, will be at best superficial and unimportant, at worst false and misleading. J. Milton Yinger has supplied some useful imagery in speaking to this issue. He frames the objection to the empirical study of religion with the question: "How is it possible to see a stained-glass window from the outside?"[1] That is, the beauty and the message or picture of a church's stained-glass window is visible only when one is *inside* and can see the sunlight shining through. Professor Yinger goes on to note, however, that the view from the inside constitutes only part of what can be learned about the window. Only from the outside, for example, can the viewer appreciate the exterior framework or context within which that window exists. Furthermore, there are, as Yinger suggests, pieces of information potentially important to understanding the significance of the window that have nothing to do with viewing it from the inside (or from the outside, for that matter): who built it, who installed it, who provides for its repair, who goes in to view it from the inside. We can also consider the reason it was installed, what "outsiders" think of it, how it resembles or differs from other windows, whether the style of newer windows is the same or is changing, and so on.

Rather than belabor the obvious parallel we are suggesting between this situation and the study of religion, it is enough to note that questions like these can be answered empirically, that they are important questions, and that the answers to them amplify our understanding. Granted, empirical data do not constitute the only information of any importance about religion. Nor can we claim that empirical or observable measures of religion reveal its "essence." Studying religion empirically places a certain restriction on our enterprise—but no more severe a restriction than is placed on the position of those who claim religion to be strictly concerned with spiritual matters and therefore off-limits to empirical investigation. Each "side" of this issue can contribute to an understanding of the total phenomenon.

CENTRAL SOCIOLOGICAL ASSUMPTIONS

Having established that the scientific study of religion is a legitimate endeavor, it remains for us to indicate why, for the sociologist, it is an

---

[1] J. Milton Yinger, *The Scientific Study of Religion* (New York: Macmillan, 1970), p. 2.

important one—that is, how it furthers sociology's task of attempting to understand the dynamics of people living in groups. For this purpose it will be helpful to identify some of the central assumptions of sociology, whether applied to the study of religion, the family, the class system, the division of labor, or any other social phenomenon.

The Sociological Perspective

In the first place, what exactly *is* sociology? Very briefly stated, sociology is the study of the interaction of human groups and of their influence on society's institutions (including other groups) and on behavior in general. Thus sociology has a twofold goal: (1) understanding the dynamics of group life—what groups are, how they function, how they change, how they differ from one another; and (2) understanding the influence of groups on individual and collective behavior. One fundamental assumption of sociology implied by this is that all human activity is influenced by groups. Throughout a person's lifetime groups impinge on his biological "raw material," shaping it, modifying it, influencing it—*socializing* it, to use the sociologists' term. This process begins with the family and proceeds through the hundreds of educational, associational, peer, and work groups that a person participates in and has contact with throughout his lifetime.

In both fundamental senses of the sociological enterprise—explaining group dynamics and explaining group influence—religion qualifies perfectly as a field of sociological study and analysis. Leaving aside for now the question of whether religion is also (or even primarily) an individual phenomenon, it is obviously at least a group phenomenon. Thus to the extent that religions organize themselves into groups—congregations, denominations, dioceses, cells, fellowships, and so on—an important task for sociology is the study of the structure and functioning of these groups simply *as groups*. In other words, we want to determine how and to what extent religious groups follow sociological laws governing group life in general. In what ways does a congregation, for example, operate like any other voluntary association—like, say, the League of Women Voters? Or how and to what degree do major religious denominations function like other large bureaucracies—like, say, the Chrysler Corporation, or the United States Army?

Insofar as religion is organized into groups it exerts influences not only on its members, but also on nonmembers and on other groups and institutions. The second dimension of our preliminary definition of sociology—as a study of group influence—thus suggests that religious groups have at least the potential for influencing people just as do groups that center around one's family, peers, or workplace. The question is not so much *whether* such influence exists but *to what degree, in what ways,* and *how it can be measured.*

The Nature of Man

A number of assumptions in sociology center around the definition of man's nature. Here we shall emphasize three.

First, and perhaps most obviously, man is a *biological organism,* a creature with physiological drives, needs, potentials, and limitations. The socializing influence of groups is thus both directed at and limited by biological factors. Religion is of course among those socializing agents that attempt to influence or modify man's biological nature. For example, different religious groups have different approaches to and provide or allow different outlets for sexual drives. And insofar as people in fact internalize these different emphases—whether they be permissive, compensatory, restrictive, or whatever—to that extent people will have different personalities and evidence different values and attitudes. In short, although the sociological perspective rejects notions of biological determinism, it recognizes as openly as possible that the human being has potentialities and limitations that are biologically provided.

Another sociological assumption regarding man's nature that is worth mentioning is his apparently unique *ability to symbol.* By this we mean man's ability arbitrarily to attach specific meanings to things, sounds, words, acts—meanings which are not intrinsic to the items themselves but which he has created. By establishing consensus on these meanings groups are able to communicate and to accumulate knowledge. Using language, his prime symbolic mechanism, man can deal with abstract concepts and emotions such as love, justice, and equality as easily as he can ask someone to pass the potatoes at the dinner table.

The ability to express meanings symbolically is primarily responsible for the variety of groups, cultures, ideologies, and technologies throughout history. There is no activity in which man is engaged that does not involve acts of symbolizing—whether lecturing, voting, making love, or "being religious." Religion in fact consists entirely of symbols and of activities that are interpreted and mediated by symbols. This is true whether the symbols have empirical referents or not. God, hell, salvation, star of David, nirvana, guru, mana—all have meaning to those initiated into a particular symbolic system. The meaning of each of these is not inherent in the word itself, in the combination of sounds, but is supplied by the believer. Even if divine truths have been revealed to man by a supernatural being, those truths have been expressed in human language, or immediately get translated into human language—otherwise the message would have no meaning for people.

Yet another primary sociological assumption about human nature is that *people become human only in groups*—admittedly, a dramatic way of stating that the influence of groups on the human organism through socialization is crucial and far-reaching. We do not propose to debate the academic question of whether the newborn babe is in fact human. The point is simply that the newborn infant isn't yet very much of what it's going to become, and that what it does become will be largely attributable to socializing influences. One of those socializing influences is religion, which in fact affects everyone, whether or not they are born into a "religious" family, or attend Sunday school, or are married by a clergyman, and so on. For religion also exerts an indirect influence on people, if only in an inverse way as a negative reference group or through its influence on secular institutions.

Human Action Is Directed Toward Problem Solving

A fundamental assumption of sociology is that *every human action is in some form and to some degree a problem-solving act or mechanism.* Whether he is working at a job, getting married, planning a party, or genuflecting, the human being is engaged in the process of solving or resolving some existing (present) or anticipated (future) problem. The problem may be how to satisfy a biological need for nourishment, how to achieve victory on the athletic field, or how to get God to help you pass an exam this afternoon. In any case, the person perceives a problem that he must solve, either now or, if he fails to take appropriate action, in the future.

Religious behavior is problem-solving like any other social activity. Praying, attending church services, observing religious laws, and experiencing (or even recounting) "mountaintop experiences," for example, are all religious activities that contribute in some way (at least from the perspective of the religious participant) toward solving a problem, either existing or anticipated. Note that we are not suggesting (or denying) that religion in fact either solves problems or creates them. Rather, our point is that people often engage in religious activities *in the belief* that this can solve problems. Lest there be any misunderstanding, once again we shall emphasize that throughout this book no attempt is made to determine or question the truth or falsity, the efficacy or inefficacy, of religion in general, of any specific religion in particular, or of anyone's personal religious beliefs. Engaged as we are in sociological investigation, we are concerned solely with what can be observed, including what people *believe* exists and happens.

All Social Phenomena Are Interrelated

The final sociological assumption that we need to clarify before delving in detail into the sociology of religion is that *all social phenomena within a given group or society are interrelated.* That is, all social phenomena are continually interacting with one another. Most important for our purposes, religion interacts—is in a dynamic reciprocal relationship—with every other social phenomenon and process: religion both influences them and is influenced by them; religion both acts and reacts, is both an independent variable and dependent variable, both cause and effect. This principle—of the continual dialectic involving religion and other social phenomena—is a central theme of this book, for determining the nature and extent of these mutual influences are key tasks in the sociology of religion.

DEVELOPMENT OF THE SOCIOLOGY OF RELIGION

A clearly identifiable interest in a formalized sociological study of religion goes back barely a hundred years, roughly coincident with the beginning of formalized sociology in general near the midpoint of the last century. The stimulus for sociological interest in religion seems to have been the reports of anthropologists during the early and middle nineteenth century who encountered and studied "primitive" societies in Africa and Oceania. Two significant observations made by these social scientists were (1) the existence everywhere of some form of religion, and (2) the fascinatingly wide variety of religious forms and behaviors.[2] In other words, religion was observed to be as diverse as it was widespread.

Such had always been true, of course. But as long as societies remained relatively isolated, the diversity and universality of religion was not fully appreciated. The advent of European colonialism and the consequent increase in world trade and commercial intercourse after the Middle Ages raised the frequency and intensity of intersocietal contacts and eventually led to ethnographical investigations by social scientists. As a result more and more people began taking an interest in understanding and explaining the worldwide diversity of religion.

The reaction within Western society to revelations of such religious

[2]This pair of observations and the four responses that follow are suggested by J. Milton Yinger in *Sociology Looks at Religion* (New York: Macmillan, 1961), pp. 11–12.

diversity was varied. Many from within the ranks of the Christian church concluded rather quickly that all these other religious systems are wrong, misguided, benighted: Ours is the only correct one. Ours is Godgiven. Therefore, we must try to point out the others' errors, convert to Christianity the people who believe differently, and prevent the spread of these other, erroneous religious systems. Extensive missionary efforts that had begun in the 1700s were intensified in the nineteenth century. These far exceeded anything since the last of the Crusades in the thirteenth century.

Others responded to the newly discovered religions by maintaining that all religions are to be understood as sincere efforts to struggle with perplexing human problems and that therefore each should be considered as good as any other so long as its adherents are satisfied. That is, despite such variation, the essence of religion is common to all of them.

A third reaction, essentially the opposite of the above one, was that the various claims to religious truth are mutually exclusive and contradictory. Therefore, all are erroneous and should be dispensed with if possible. A variant on this theme was the prediction that as science progressed and eliminated superstition, religion would be increasingly rejected and finally relegated to the status of a relic from prescientific days.

A fourth response was that while each of the various religions has valuable aspects, no one of them is perfect. Therefore, we need to pick and choose the best elements from each for the particular society and age in which we live. Christian Science, Bahai, and various modern Buddhist cults still hold this view. In fact, each of these points of view has its contemporary advocates. But as we have tried to make clear in the first part of this chapter, none of these positions is appropriate for the social scientist, since each involves value judgments of one sort or another.

Following the initial flurry of social scientists' interest in religion initiated by early anthropologists, sociological interest in and research on religion, with a few notable exceptions, lay somewhat dormant until fairly recently. David Moberg has suggested several reasons for this. (1) Some sociologists, discouraged by the close historical association of religion with philosophy and metaphysics, decided that religion couldn't be fruitfully studied empirically. (2) Other sincerely interested sociologists yielded to the opposition against sociological research on religion that came from many religious groups. (3) Those teaching in state universities were fearful of jeopardizing their positions if they should somehow overstep the boundary separating church and state. (4) Others, convinced that religion was definitely on its way to extinction anyway, preferred not to waste their time. (5) Still others who had personally rejected religion were reluctant to maintain any contact with it—even if only of a research nature.[3]

The notable exceptions included some of the early sociological giants, such as Emile Durkheim, Georg Simmel, and Max Weber, who devoted a significant portion of their scholarly energies to analyzing the role of religion in society. After Weber's publication of his *Sociology of Religion* in 1921, however, little research or theoretical development occurred in the sociology of religion until after World War II, when there was a dramatic upsurge in religious activity, particularly in the United States. Significant increases in church membership and attendance at religious services, extensive building programs, and the establishment of hundreds of new congregations each year engendered serious talk of a religious revival.

Sociologists became interested. Here was a social phenomenon to be explored and explained, a development that was particularly intriguing in that many social scientists had long been predicting the eventual and even precipitous demise of religion, particularly in its institutional form. The sociologists' new research interest in religion that began in the late 1940s and early 1950s has continued essentially unabated to the present. One reason for this is that these new developments in religion, which clamor for investigation and explanation, have continued at a rapid pace. Furthermore, the persistence of religion in its various forms has finally forced sociologists to renew the effort, initiated by early fathers of sociology like Durkheim and Weber, of attempting to understand the nature and function of religion. For both these reasons this book concentrates on systematizing sociological research and theoretical efforts that have appeared during the past twenty years or so—not because the newest efforts are necessarily the best ones, but simply because most of the empirical work in the field is of relatively recent vintage. Indeed, it appears that social scientists are beginning to fulfill the prophecy of the anthropologist James Frazer, who predicted a half-century ago that the time would come when the religions of the world would no longer be regarded in terms of their truth or falsehood, but simply as phenomena to be studied like any other expression of humanity.[4]

[3]David O. Moberg, *The Church as a Social Institution* (Englewood Cliffs, N.J.: Prentice-Hall, 1962), p. 13.
[4]James Frazer, *The Gorgon's Head* (London: Macmillan, 1927), pp. 281–82.

2

A Sociological Definition of Religion

Everyone "knows" what religion is. For our purposes, however, such knowledge needs to be systematized. We need to achieve some consensus on the boundaries of our subject matter, which we all recognize as having great diversity, before we can proceed to analyze it. Without denying the validity of any individual's private definition, we need to establish some ground rules that we can follow throughout this text. Clearly there is nothing absolute about a definition: no definition, of any phenomenon, religion included, is inherent in the phenomenon itself. What we require, then, is a *working definition* of religion—specifically, a definition that we can be fairly sure includes the major ideas of this concept, a definition that is moreover flexible and responsive to changing conditions and new evidence—so that we can communicate fairly sensibly not only among ourselves but with others as well. Although we shall not include everything that anyone has ever thought religion might be, we shall try to isolate the core or essential elements.

THE CHARACTERISTICS OF RELIGION

The English word *religion* has a Latin root, that much is certain. But there is disagreement over whether the Latin root word is *religare*, meaning "to bind together" (suggesting possibly the concept of a group or fellowship) or *relegere*, meaning "to rehearse, to execute painstakingly," referring probably to the repetitive nature of liturgy. Either word makes sense as a root, and each taps a dimension of religion that we'll include in our definition. Yet it is clear that etymology by itself will not provide us with an ultimate answer to our problem of definition.

Religion Is a Group Phenomenon

Let's start with the concept occasionally suggested by the Latin word *religare*—that of the group or fellowship. The assertion that religion is a group phenomenon is significant both for what it says and for what it fails to say, for what it excludes. What it excludes is of course the individual aspect. Certainly religion is an individual matter in any number of ways: in that it involves personal emotions and thoughts; or insofar as one's religion is purely a matter of personal beliefs; or insofar as individuals are free to commit themselves to whichever religious system they prefer. Still, it would not make sense to expect that one could somehow systematically study every individual's personal religious beliefs. Sociology, being committed to systematic study of group behavior has no such problem in concentrating on the group dimension of religion.[1]

Throughout history and in every corner of the globe people have engaged in religious behavior: congregations, ceremonial gatherings, denominations, prayer meetings, family pilgrimages, ecumenical councils—all are examples of religious activity. Even when a lone figure is acknowledged to have experienced visions or received supernatural dispensations, he frequently attracts others—that is, he becomes a leader (perhaps even a prophet) with a following, often whether he seeks it or not. True, we also see occasional isolated mystics and religious hermits in mountaintop seclusion. Even most of these, however, belong to some subgroup of a major religion (such as Catholicism or Buddhism) which may encourage or even structure and coordinate such activity.

Elaborating our admittedly arbitrary division of religion into its personal and group dimensions, J. Paul Williams suggests that there are at least four types or levels of religiousness: (1) the *secret* level, which a person keeps to himself and does not divulge or discuss; (2) the *private*,

---

[1]This is not to ignore the fact that sociologists, particularly social psychologists, also study the behavior of individuals. For example, the current considerable sociological interest in the nature of religious commitment and in the process of religious socialization and internalization of religious concepts and values obviously necessitates careful attention to individual behavior. Nevertheless, the purpose of such research with individuals is to be able to generalize to larger groups and categories of people.

which he divulges or discusses with only a few carefully chosen intimates; (3) the *denominational,* which the individual shares with many others in a large group; and (4) the *societal,* which he shares with the members of society at large.[2] Williams's first two categories will occupy very little of our time—not because they fail to involve religion (they obviously do), but simply because of the reasons already mentioned for narrowing our range of coverage, and also, to some extent, because solid sociological research into individual aspects of religion has only recently begun. Not that we shall ignore the individual dimension entirely. For example, Chapter 6, while it does not deal with precisely what Williams means by "secret" religiousness, focuses on what we might call the social-psychological dimension of religion—the process of individual internalization of religion. Our primary attention, however, will be on what Williams identifies as denominational and societal religion, with particular emphasis on the former—again reflecting the fact that most research in the sociology of religion has been in this area.

For the purpose of further clarifying our definition of *religion,* we may refer to the extremely important contribution to this subject made by W. C. Smith, who stresses the role of individual experience and faith in religion. Smith in fact prefers not to use the term *religion* at all, and instead emphasizes the concept of religious *tradition,* which he defines as the cumulative repository of the past religious experiences and expressions of a people, both as individuals and in groups. *Faith,* according to Smith, is based on the religious experiences of people as they individually relate to the transcedent.[3] Smith's prime emphasis, then, is on the individual nature of faith and of religious experiences, which in turn contribute to the ever-expanding cumulative religious tradition. Certainly this emphasis can be useful for studying religion in some other context; but insofar as our approach here is sociological the focus of this text is necessarily on the group aspect of what Smith defines as the cumulative religious tradition. Thus we shall focus on religion as a group phenomenon not because it lacks an individual dimension, but because the group level is where the sociologist is best able to begin studying it.

So much for what is excluded by our characterization of religion as a group phenomenon. Now we may ask: What is *included* in this aspect of our definition? Answering this question requires that we specify exactly what a group is; in this regard, fortunately, sociologists are very explicit. According to one definition that most sociologists would accept, a

2J. Paul Williams, "The Nature of Religion," *Journal for the Scientific Study of Religion* 2, no. 1 (1962): 8.
3Wilfred C. Smith, *The Meaning and End of Religion* (New York: Macmillan, 1962).

group has six major features. The first and most basic is that *a group is composed of two or more people (members) who have established certain patterns of interaction* (including communication) with one another. Such interaction does not necessarily take place continually, or even daily. Nor does every member of a group interact with every other member. Nor is this interaction necessarily face-to-face. The point is simply that the people who constitute a group—group members—are *aware* of one another (perhaps even know one another) and have established patterns of interaction characteristic of their group.

The second major feature of a group, according to our definition, is that *group members share certain common goals*—in fact, this is the reason they came together in the first place (although they may not have known it then). The process of forming a group thus involves the fundamental sociological concept, introduced in Chapter 1, that all human behavior consists of some sort of problem-solving activity. Saying that a group has common goals implies that individuals who are confronted with common problems have made contact and have agreed to work together toward the goal of solving those problems. Imagine, for example, five individuals, each deeply concerned about industrial-waste pollution in a certain trout stream, who through casual conversation (perhaps while trying to fish the stream) "discover" one another and subsequently form a group called STEP (Save Trout from Environmental Pollution), whose primary goal is reducing pollution in this and other trout streams. Thus what was originally the separate concern of five individuals has become a group concern, which in turn implies a certain common goal or set of goals.

Third, as a result of the above, *a group is guided by shared norms.* For once a group defines its goals, it then determines how to reach them: that is, the group specifies that such and such is what its members will do, as well as when, where, and how. All such specifications are norms—more or less formal expectations concerning appropriate behavior by one or all members of the group.

Fourth, *every group member has a role*, or set of functions, to fulfill. As such, a role consists of a set of specific norms the group wants carried out. The development of different roles within the group gives rise to what is known as *the division of labor*. Thus whenever a member leaves the group or adopts a new role, the group may need to keep the division of labor in balance by recruiting someone else—either another member or an outsider—for that particular role.

Fifth, *a group functions collectively in accordance with a status system*, a hierarchy in which different amounts of power, authority, and prestige are accorded to different roles and to the individuals in those roles. Different groups of course have different criteria for establishing status rankings. Roles involving group coordination, decision making, and interpretation, for example, which inherently carry the greatest authority and prestige, are very often assigned to those individuals who are believed to perform these tasks most ably, although such other factors as seniority, wealth, and kinship can also be influential.

Sixth, *group members feel and express a sense of identification with the group*: "I belong" . . . "This is my group" . . . "Yes, I'm an active member of STEP." The degree of group commitment, dedication, and identification varies from member to member, and most groups are able to tolerate some such variability. But without a certain minimum amount of identification and commitment on the part of its members, a group will soon disintegrate.

These six characteristic features of a group obviously apply to religious groups no less than to any other kind. Thus in studying religion as a group phenomenon we already know many things to expect and even some questions to ask: How does a given religious group differ from all others in terms of these six aspects? What, for example, are the religious group's goals? its norms? its roles? its status criteria?

Religion Is Concerned with the Sacred and Supernatural

A second characteristic that we wish to include in our definition of *religion* is its involvement with what Durkheim identified as the "sacred," with what Rudolf Otto termed the "holy" or the "wholly other."[4] There is a universal tendency for religion to express awe, reverence, and fear with regard to certain things, beings, or situations and to distinguish them from the ordinary, the mundane—or, as Durkheim defines it, the "profane." Old Testament Jews removed their sandals upon entering the temple, many Christians make the sign of the cross when praying to God, Hindus give cows the right of way, Muslims undertake pilgrimages to Mecca, American Indians avoided disturbing holy plots of ground. All such behavior expresses the recognition of a sacred place or situation. In each instance people acknowledge being in the presence of something special—something above and beyond them that demands adopting special attitudes, performing certain actions, and perhaps articulating special words as well.

For many people—for whole religious systems, for the matter—that "something special," the *sacred*, in fact involves the *supernatural*, a

[4]Emile Durkheim, *The Elementary Forms of the Religious Life*, trans. Joseph Ward Swain (New York: Collier, 1961), p. 52; Rudolf Otto, *The Idea of the Holy*, trans. John W. Harvey (London: Oxford University Press, 1936), pp. 8–41.

power or being not subject to the laws of the observable universe. Such a power may be personified by Jesus, by Vishnu, by Allah, or by any number of gods, devils, goblins, or spirits. Or perhaps it is simply a vague and diffuse power, such as that identified by the Polynesian term *mana* (which we shall discuss shortly).

In these beliefs a dichotomy of reality is being expressed. On the one hand there are the "profane" (ordinary) events and the visible environment of the routine workaday world. On the other hand there is the invisible, largely uncontrollable, out-of-the-ordinary realm. To a greater or lesser degree people can control and predict familiar everyday situations—the choice of daily tasks, conversations with others, the acts of eating and copulating, the seeking of nightly rest, and so on. But most people seem to believe that there is more to life than such ordinary situations and events. What about the big bang in the sky last week and the twisting dagger of light that preceded it? What about my friend who dropped dead while running beside me? What about that place in the swamp where a whole hunting party was swallowed up in the mud? Such things are out of the ordinary; they can't be taken for granted; they elicit fear, awe, respect. We are here in the presence of Otto's "wholly other"— an entirely different order of existence.

It should be emphasized that the experiences that people define as sacred vary considerably and the objects of their awe and reverence are infinitely diverse. Yet every society has its list of such awesome and mysterious things and events. Religion deals with them. Religion provides explanations and answers; religion prescribes methods of placation and of expressing appropriate reverence. The sacred, the holy, the supernatural, together with man's relationship to them, thus constitute the prime subject matter of religion.

Although the term *sacred* may occasionally connote little more than "deserving or demanding respect," with no necessary thought of a supernatural power being involved, it is usual for the two concepts to go together. That which is considered sacred is so precisely because some supernatural force or activity arouses the feeling of awe that surrounds the sacred object, person, place, or situation. While they are not strictly synonymous concepts, the sacred and the supernatural are in most societies so intimately related that we can regard them as inseparable for the purposes of our definition of religion.

Some theorists, however, prefer not to use the concept of the supernatural, and perhaps even that of the sacred, in their definitions of religion. J. Paul Williams, for example, proposes that a primary feature of any religion is the belief-attitude that an Ultimate of some kind exists and that certain aspects of life depend in some way and to some degree upon that Ultimate (whatever it is and however it is defined). Moreover, Williams argues, a religion need not view the Ultimate as supernatural or even sacred, but simply as somehow final or basic—such as the concept of "natural law," or that of the "order of the universe."[5] Williams's approach has the advantage of allowing us to define as *religious* systems certain *thought* systems that exclude the supernatural, such as Jainism, Ethical Culture, early Buddhism, and early Confucianism. (Of course, if we choose to view the reverence for life which these groups espouse as acknowledging the existence of the sacred, then they seem to qualify as religions anyway).

Using Williams's criterion of the Ultimate would of course mean categorizing as religions such political ideologies as communism and fascism and such intellectual systems as scientism and humanism. Whether they should be so defined is an important question that we shall discuss near the end of this chapter.

Religion Involves a Body of Beliefs

A third characteristic of religion, one that is much more straightforward and easy to describe, is that it invariably includes or implies a body of beliefs. This characteristic proceeds directly from the foregoing considerations of the sacred and the supernatural. For in the act of endeavoring to deal with or justify these phenomena and experiences, religious groups develop explanations, work out rationales, and discover "facts" that are eventually systematized into a body of beliefs.

Every major religion has its sacred book or books that spell out or at least provide the basis for determining the beliefs the group holds: the Bible, the Koran, the Book of Mormon, the Bhagavad-Gita, *Science and Health with a Key to the Scriptures*. Furthermore, every major religion has beliefs *in addition* to those contained in such "official" or basic writings: the interpretations and extensions of lesser prophets and of other successors to the founder(s) of the religion, for example. Then, too, there is in every religion—and not just in those of preliterate societies—the oral tradition: unwritten explanations, in the form of myths, sagas, and proverbs, handed down to each new generation by word of mouth.

Here, of course, we are dealing with a characteristic not unique to religious groups, for groups of any kind have beliefs. Although we can view beliefs as attitudes or opinions so far as the individual is concerned, group beliefs properly fall under the heading of the norms established or accepted by the group. Norms, in other words, specify not only

[5]Williams, "The Nature of Religion," p. 9.

how a group's members are expected to behave but also what they are expected to believe, how they are to interpret and relate to things and events. The distinctiveness of religious groups so far as beliefs and norms are concerned rests simply with the subject matter of those beliefs. The beliefs of religious groups specifically concern the sacred and most likely also the supernatural.

Religion Involves a Set of Practices

A fourth characteristic of religion is that it universally involves specific practices—again in response to normative expectations. One of the most obvious features of any religion—obvious because it consists of behavior rather than beliefs or attitudes or perspectives—is the performance of ritual and the host of other activities generated by its beliefs. The gathering to worship, the rain dance, the sacrifice of animal or person, the ceremonial foot washing, the immersing in water at baptism, the vigil—all these are examples of what we are referring to.

It is important to understand that there is nothing intrinsically religious in a given act; an act or practice becomes religious only when the group defines it as such. Thus the act of eating a meal may be no more than a means of gaining sustenance—or it may be an *agape* ("love feast") of the first-century Christians, or a ceremonial enactment of the Last Supper. One may wear a robe solely to fend off the cold or (in medieval Europe) to indicate one's academic rank—or to indicate that one is a holy man or messenger of God. Journeying to a distant town may be for the purpose of conducting business, or taking in the sights—or it may be fulfilling the religious obligation of making a pilgrimage to a holy city at least once during one's lifetime.

Other Characteristics

Although only one of the characteristics of religion discussed above is unique to religious groups, these are probably the four most important ones (or the five most important, if we distinguish the sacred from the supernatural). Now we shall briefly mention two other characteristics of religion that have been suggested, each of which is worth considering.

Perhaps the most frequently cited characteristic of religion other than those discussed is its moral implications. Another way of saying this is that a religion deliberately exerts influence on its adherents in an attempt to make them behave in prescribed ways everywhere, all the time, and in all situations. Of particular significance here is that religion is unique in claiming a "higher" source or basis for its morality: You should do such and so or refrain from such and so because God wills it, or because it is in tune with cosmic forces—not simply because our group says so or only because it's the only natural, logical, sensible, or humane thing to do. In other words, religion ultimately invokes the sacred or the supernatural in order to influence the behavior of individuals.

It has also been asserted that religion is strictly a matter of the emotions. The philosopher-theologian Friedrich Schleiermacher, for example, contended that the essence of religion lies, not in the intellect, nor in the sphere of behavior such as reflected by ethics, but in the realm of emotions or "feelings."[6] The issue here is one of "reductionism" —of trying to distill the nature of a phenomenon (in this case, religion) into a single characteristic. And in this regard, although emotion definitely plays an important part in religion, several other aspects, including the intellect and behavior, are important as well.

A FORMAL DEFINITION OF RELIGION

In attempting to formally define religion we shall go no further than to gather together the ingredients we have discussed. Our definition is thus perhaps less elegant than some, yet more inclusive than many. Sociologically viewed, then, and in terms of what will come under review in this book, *religion* can be defined as *a system of beliefs and practices by which a group of people interprets and responds to what they feel is supernatural and sacred.*

Let it be clearly understood that by employing this definition we are, for purposes of sociological investigation at least, adopting the position of the hard-nosed relativist and agnostic. That is, we are neither affirming nor denying the existence of the supernatural; nor are we stating whether what a group defines as sacred is or is not in fact sacred. We *are* asserting, however, that people in groups do in fact believe in the supernatural and identify certain beings, events, etc. as sacred. These beliefs and the attitudes and behavior stemming from them thus become the subject matter of the sociology of religion.

It should also be clear by now that the above definition is to be understood as neither the final nor the best definition of religion; rather, it is a pragmatic one—one, moreover, that is reasonably in tune with what the majority of people consider religion to be. This latter point is particularly important, for it is unnecessary, and would even be unwise, deliberately to define religion in a manner too different from the way most people understand it.

[6]Friedrich Schleiermacher, *Speeches on Religion* (London: K. Paul, Trench, Trubner, 1893), p. 36.

APPLICATION OF THE DEFINITION

Before ending our formal treatment of the definition of *religion* (in a real sense, the remainder of this book represents an elaboration and explication of our definition), two serious questions require discussion. One concerns the application of our definition, particularly with regard to whether we should include or exclude certain ways of life and thought when speaking of religion. The other involves the issue of whether there is a distinction to be made between religion and magic (not stage magic, of course, but magic in the original sense of using charms and spells to control supernatural forces)—and if there is, where to draw the line—or whether the two are really a single concept.

Should the Various "Isms" Be Called Religions?

With respect to the former question, there has been much discussion about whether the various "isms," such as communism, fascism, scientism, and humanism, should be included under the heading of religion.

Proponents of this viewpoint are particularly fond of citing the characteristics of communism to support their argument, pointing out its "religious" elements—its prophets, its emphasis on orthodox beliefs, its rituals, its sacred shrines, the missionary zeal and unquestioning commitment of its adherents. And those who argue that scientism qualifies as a religion find similar patterns: a system of beliefs about the utility of scientific endeavors, a set of practices (the scientific method), prophets of old (the founding fathers of modern science), sacred places (the laboratory, the computer room), supreme loyalty and commitment of its adherents, the missionary zeal, if you will, with which proponents try to win others to share their faith in science.

Although we do not take such analogies terribly seriously, no one can deny the existence of certain striking parallels between such ideologies and thought systems, on the one hand, and religion as we have defined it on the other. If we want to be precise, however, our characterization of religion as involving the sacred and the supernatural quite clearly places these ideologies and thought systems outside the realm of religion. Before leaving the subject, however, it is only fair to make the observation—and the point can hardly be overstressed—that certain pronounced elements in ideologies like communism are unlike anything else *outside* religion. Certainly the tenets of communism, for example, are held "religiously," and its adherents frequently exhibit "religious" zeal in pursuing group goals. The importance of this observation is that it helps us understand the behavior of such systems' organizations and adherents. Nevertheless, sticking by our definition, we shall not include such thought systems in our discussion of religions in the following chapters.

It should be emphasized that more than a technicality is involved here. If we made our definition of religion progressively broader and our criteria more inclusive, we would soon reach the point where *everything* could be defined as religion. Then *nothing* would be religion, inasmuch as there would be no alternative categories. Subsuming all (or even nearly all) human behavior in a definition of religion would be much like saying that all human behavior is sexual or that all human behavior is economic. In a certain sense such assertions say something important: they draw attention to the profound fact that sexuality, economics, and religion are pervasive phenomena which touch almost every form of human activity to at least some degree. However, to reduce all human activity to any one of the categories requires stretching that category to absurd dimensions and is ultimately counterproductive. A more reasonable solution (at least this is the consensus within sociology) is to draw somewhat narrower boundaries around one's subject matter, thereby facilitating more intensive study and analysis of a more manageable body of data.

The Relationship of Religion and Magic

Resolving the issue of the relationship between religion and magic is in some ways more difficult. By way of introduction, let us consider the concept of *mana* (a Polynesian term), which is common in "primitive" religions, and vestiges of which appear in the religious systems of industrial societies as well. Purnell Benson notes, for example, that mana appears in numerous religions under various names: in Hinduism it is *darshan*; in Christianity it is *divine grace*; among American Indians it was called *manito* by the Algonquins, *wakanda* by the Sioux, *orenda* by the Iroquois, and *maxpe* by the Crow.[7]

Mana is a prime ingredient in magic. To those who believe in it there exists in the world, everywhere, and in everything, an elemental force, a primary energy—mana. Mana even exists—it floats, so to speak— in the very air we breathe. Often it is just *there*, not directly attached to anything, simply waiting to be grasped, harnessed, used. Though mana is in people, in things, in animals, in plants, and in the atmosphere, it is impotent until someone or something, or a spirit perhaps, activates it by discovering the secret key that unlocks its energies.

[7]Purnell H. Benson, *Religion in Contemporary Culture* (New York: Harper & Brothers, 1960), p. 136.

Enter magic, which attempts to exercise power over people and things by controlling the ubiquitous mana. The practice of magic is thus not an expression of ignorance, as is commonly supposed, but a conscious, deliberate attempt to circumvent what might normally be expected to occur. That is, magic is typically used to undercut the predictable by marshalling sufficient mana—elemental force—to change what otherwise would be inevitable.

In those societies where magic is most likely to be practiced and condoned (the more "primitive" societies), people make little if any distinction between magic and religion—nor for that matter among scientific knowledge, religious knowledge, common-sense knowledge, and magic. Knowledge is knowledge, be it scientific, religious or whatever. This lack of categories of course makes the task of distinguishing between magic and religion a bit more difficult.

We may begin, however, by noting the similarities and the differences or contrasts that have been suggested in the long debate over the relationship of religion and magic. First some similarities: (1) both are serious attempts to deal with and solve the basic problems people face; (2) both are based on faith in the existence and efficacy of powers that cannot be seen and can only be inferred by results; (3) both involve ritual activity, traditionally prescribed patterns of behavior; and (4) both are bona fide elements of the group's larger culture.

Some differences or contrasts: (1) religion more often centers on such overarching issues as salvation and the meaning of life and death, whereas magic is more likely to be employed in grappling with current, concrete problems (counteracting a viper's bite, bringing rain, defeating the enemy, for example); (2) religion is more often future-oriented, while magic is primarily concerned with the here and now (or at least the very near future); (3) religion's orientation toward supernatural powers tends to be one of obeisance and supplication, involving sacrifice and prayer (such as asking the appropriate deity or spirit to act on one's behalf), whereas magic is more manipulative, more often suggestive of pride then of humility (the magician seeks direct control over things and events, even at times seeking to trick the deity or defeat him in a contest if he can control enough mana); and (4) religion is characteristically a group activity, with groups of people collectively engaged in rituals and worship, while magic is typically an individual affair—the magician against the world, so to speak. Of course it is important to recognize that the magician conducts his work within a group (his society), and that in a real sense it is the group that *allows* him to work. Thus even though the magician works alone, his work is group-sanctioned.

Are religion and magic, then, different phenomena, or two aspects of the same phenomenon? Or is one a subpart of the other? The last alternative is probably the most helpful way to see their relationship. Recalling our definition of religion, we find that magic fulfills each of our criteria: magic consists of beliefs and practices; it very clearly is concerned with the sacred and the supernatural; and it is practiced within a group—in a sense it is "possessed" by a group, although practiced by an individual. In fact, the relationship of magic to religion is virtually a classic example of specialization, for magic is typically practiced where the religious system considers it a legitimate and useful activity and encourages or at least allows its use. Thus magic is probably best seen neither as a competitor with religion nor as an alternative to it, but as a specialized subunit of religion. In fact, rarely is religion without at least some magical elements, just as magic is seldom practiced entirely apart from a larger religious system that legitimates it.

FINAL REFLECTION ON THE DEFINITION OF RELIGION

As the reader reflects a moment on the discussion in this chapter, he or she very likely senses considerable ambivalence at this point. If so, we have achieved one of our purposes in this chapter. Frankly, as we write this text, we face a dilemma which cannot be resolved to the satisfaction of all. The dilemma resides in (1) the recognition that our definition of religion (the five characteristics) is not inclusive of all phenomena that may in some sense be "religious," and it tends to be "conservative" in the sense that the focus is inevitably upon what has been traditionally recognized as religious—the religious institution in society, and, (2) that such traditional institutional forms of religion do happen to be a prominent feature of societies and as such merit analysis and understanding.

Thus we have opted in this introductory text to concentrate on what is commonly regarded as religion and seems to fall fairly cleanly within our definition (a fantastically broad array of data and developments as it is). But we recognize and draw attention to the fact that there is likely more that can legitimately be called religion than this. Thus, in one sense we conclude this chapter deliberately leaving the issue of defining religion somewhat open-ended. Yet we also proceed from a closed-ended approach as we pragmatically attempt to cover a manageable subject. That is, we shall spend most of our time in this text discussing religion as included in our definition. But we strongly assert that when the discussion is ended we shall have only begun to talk about what from other perspectives or definitions could have been included.

3

The Sources
of Religion

We now approach what is admittedly a highly speculative but at the same time a highly fascinating issue in the sociology of religion: the question of the origins and sources of religion. When we realize that the question is phrased not so often as "From where does religion come?" but "Why is man religious?" we see that the question of origins and sources is a relatively common one—one that has intrigued philosophers throughout the centuries and scientists more recently. The answers have been many and varied, although we'll soon discover that they can be fairly conveniently organized into relatively few categories.

The question of religion's origin per se is no longer pursued by social science, for any evidence of an origin or origins has been lost in prehistory. Attempts to reconstruct origins by examining contemporary preliterate societies have in fact served only to delay slightly the admission that such evidence, if it ever existed, is lost in antiquity. It is important to recognize that the scientific method is limited in this regard; in fact, it is incapable of establishing absolutely verifiable conclusions about past events on the basis of present or even past realities. Thus even when substantial evidence appears to support an attractive theory, any hypothesis regarding religion's origins is doomed to remaining forever tentative. More on this problem later in the chapter.

Yet despite such limitations in the pursuit of religion's origins, we

propose to explore the question briefly. We do this because of the historical value and intellectual stimulation such a look at the past provides;
but more important, such an exploration will serve to introduce us to
several relevant contemporary issues in the sociology of religion that we'll
discuss more fully later. These are such issues as the functional view of
religion, the nature and extent of social influences upon religion, and to
some extent the conflict between theology and sociology regarding an
analysis of religion.

With regard to prehistoric man, it seems reasonable to assume on
the basis of available evidence that he seldom had questions about the
sources of his religious beliefs and practices. They were such an integral
part of his culture and normative system that he most likely saw them
simply as "in the nature of things." Things were that way and always
had been. Therefore, there was little likelihood that questions of religious
origins would occur to him. There often existed myths and tales of the
origin of man or of one's society, but seeing religion as something distinct from the rest of one's beliefs and practices in society was not likely.

REVELATION AS ORIGIN

With the beginning of both Christianity and, before that, of Judaism,
part of the answer was extremely simple: God was the originator of their
religions. God created man and the world; he already in the Garden of
Eden established some general principles and laws; he later spoke through
selected prophets, and they recorded God's words and their own God-
inspired commentary. God himself was at work instructing his people,
and in the process was creating religion through the process of revelation.

Nor is this hypothesis or explanation of the origin of religion
unique to Judaism and Christianity. Even Gautama Buddha, the founder
of Buddhism, reports having experienced revelation of a sort as he sat
under the Bo-tree, practically at the end of his rope in his quest for
truth. The insight around which he developed his religious system hit
him out of the blue, so to speak; he had a "revelation." The revelation
that inspired Mormonism was in the form of golden plates buried in the
hill called Cumorah in New York State. Muhammad reported receiving
visions (revelation) from the angel Gabriel in a cave near Mecca.

All such cases report the belief that either God himself or some
other cosmic, supernatural force intervened in history, altered the normal
course of events, and deliberately added to what had been previously
known. Whether by personal contact with the divine power, an experience with an intermediary, sudden inspired insight, discovery of secret

written messages, or whatever, it is the direct intrusion of a supernatural power with new knowledge and insight for man.

It is important to realize, of course, that such revelational explanations for the origins of religion concern what believers consider to be the only "true" religion—i.e., their own. Proponents of the revelation hypothesis refer only to their religion as the one revealed by God. Other religions may exist, but their source is something else, an inferior source, although it is likely that other religions are intimately bound up in trying to find the very truth that God has given only to "us."

THE "NATURAL-KNOWLEDGE-OF-GOD" EXPLANATION

Christian theologians, claiming direct revelation from God for their gift of "true" religion, have always been intrigued by the existence of other religions. If God revealed himself directly only to the Chosen People of Israel, they asked themselves, how did the religions of other peoples arise? The answer they finally settled on, based on scattered verses from the Bible, was the "natural-knowledge-of-God" concept: every human being is born with a fundamental awareness of the divine, a rudimentary knowledge that God or some power is ultimately responsible for what he sees around him. All other religions, then, are the result of man's striving to build on this fundamental awareness and make some sense out of it. The great diversity of religious systems is then relatively easy to explain. Because the initial awareness of God is so vague and diffuse, men are forced to call upon their imagination and experience in developing these systems. And since the imagination and experience of people is so diverse, the religious systems they evolve consequently differ.

Associated with the natural-knowledge-of-God idea is the "witness-of-nature" concept: the wonder and complexity of nature reinforces people's innate knowledge of the divine and motivates them to seek explanations. What I see around me—the cycle of seasons, the wonder of the flora and fauna, the majesty of the mountains, the splendor of the sun by day and the moon and stars at night—must have been brought into existence by someone or some power, some god or gods. And perhaps that god has helpers and supervisors of specific spheres and activities such as the oceans, farming, lovemaking, war, and so on. Eventually a complex system evolves from an original "seed of divine awareness."

Sociologists can obviously neither confirm nor refute such an hypothesis. Note, however, that except for the idea of inherent initial awareness, this attempt to explain the origins of religion is basically in harmony with modern sociological concepts. That is, there is a recognition that man himself creates his norms and beliefs and thought systems in response to his experiences and surroundings, and that a fundamental factor in such experiences is his contact with the physical environment. But more on such sociological views later in this chapter.

THE ANTHROPOLOGICAL EXPLANATION

We now turn from the explanations of theologians to those of the social scientists, who have attempted to explain the sources or origins of religion on the basis of empirical observations. We first focus on the anthropologists, particularly those of the nineteenth century who were so instrumental in stimulating investigation of religion from the perspective of social science.

The views of the early anthropologists on this subject are too diverse to even summarize here. It is worth noting, however, that many believed that religion somehow arose in response to man's experiences. As primitive man encountered awesome, mysterious, even terrifying events—thunder and lightning, earthquakes, tidal waves and floods, illness, birth and death—he felt the need to understand their causes. Religious systems thus gradually evolved out of man's need to assign causes for so-called natural phenomena and other recurrent experiences.

Some differences in emphasis and focus among early anthropologists are also worth noting. Max Müller, for example, is a representative of the "naturistic" school, which emphasized the role of physical acts of nature—natural events like storms, sunrises, tides.[1] Prehistoric man was fearful and almost completely defenseless and at the mercy of these events: Why do they happen and why to me in particular? Müller suggests that since prehistoric man saw other people cause events—pushing rocks, throwing stones, shooting arrows, felling trees, and so on—he reasoned that preliterate people likely thought that *everything* that happens must be caused either by man or manlike agents. What evolved then was the belief in spirits—invisible beings much like men in the sense that they possessed wills and abilities to bring about effects by their actions. It is these spirits who *cause* natural events. Thus prehistoric man might suggest that a spirit crashes giant cymbals and produces thunder; that a fire-breathing spirit spits out lightning; that a spirit heaves itself out of the bowels of the earth and causes an earthquake; that a spirit takes the sun out of its basket and puts it on a shelf in the sky each morning; and so on.

[1]See F. Max Müller, *Anthropological Religion* (London: Longmans Green, 1892); idem, *Lectures on the Origin and Growth of Religion* (London: Longmans, 1878).

Early anthropologists discovered among the "primitive" peoples they studied an apparently universal belief in such spirits, a phenomenon termed *animism*: the belief that all sorts of inanimate objects as well as living, growing things and moving creatures possess souls. Rocks, trees, animals, and people have spirits in them, whereas some spirits are freewheeling and unattached to things. All spirits, however, are conceived of in a thoroughgoing anthropomorphic fashion. That is, they have shape, mind, feelings, and will, though they are invisible beings. They are much like people in that they are amenable to sound arguments or placating gifts, particularly when they are in a good mood. They can also be quarrelsome, nasty, and dangerous when upset or angry. They like flattery, loyalty, and deference, and so one must be continually vigilant to stay on their right side.

Thus when a coconut fell on his head, prehistoric man is less likely to have said, "The coconuts are ripe; it's coconut season again," and more likely to have asked, "Who threw it? What did I do now to make a spirit angry?" Or tripping over a root in his path he may be less likely to curse his clumsiness and more likely to ask why the root's spirit reached out and grabbed him: Was it only a playful jest, or a warning that worse may happen if I don't shape up in some way?

Whereas Müller emphasized the external events of nature, Edward Tylor, who represents the "animistic" school, focused on such personal experiences as dreams, and seeing one's reflection in the water.[2] When I dream of sexual conquest, or felling the enemy on the field of battle, or running from a tiger, what is happening is that the spirit that resides in me (my soul) is out for the night—having a ball, displaying his valor, or running into a bit of trouble. My image in the stream? Why it's none other than my spirit looking up at me. See, when I smile, it smiles; when I frown, it frowns.

Another representative anthropologist, Robert Lowie, focused on those experiences that generated a sense of "mystery and weirdness" in man. For Lowie, religion is not simply a matter of identifying spirits or distinguishing body and soul. Rather, religion only arose when one's emotions became involved and a sense of mystery pervaded one's observations of the activities that spirits engage in.[3]

Many more hypothesis developed by anthropologists could be cited, but the above examples are enough to make the point that what we are calling the anthropological explanation for the origin of religion focuses primarily on man's belief in spirits and in what these spirits do. Such beliefs arise essentially from prehistoric man's need to explain natural

---

[2]See Edward B. Tylor, *Primitive Culture* (London: Murray, 1871).
[3]Robert Lowie, *Primitive Religion* (New York: Boni & Liveright, 1924), p. xvi.

events in his physical environment as well as his own experiences. In a real sense this is a need for rationality of a sort, for a means of making coherent the many things one has no control over.

THE PSYCHOLOGICAL EXPLANATION

Another broad area of explanation, the psychological perspective, in general treats the origins of religion in terms of man's emotional needs —in other words, not so much like Müller and Tylor, who emphasized man's cognitive needs to explain the mysterious, but more in terms of man's need to resolve and adjust emotionally to the mysterious and the disastrous, more like Lowie's emphasis. In this view, man seeks to maintain emotional stability in the face of danger, insecurity, and disruption, particularly as he encounters illness, accident, and death: How can I keep going as my world (health, personal relationships, etc.) crumbles about me? Why do disasters happen to me and to those I love? Can I make any sense out of it all? How can I find strength to go on?

Man finds a solution for such frustration, so a common psychological explanation would suggest, by fitting his experience into the larger framework of a divine plan with a long-range perspective: All things work out for good for those who love God. Things will be better in the by and by. He died because God needed him more than we did. God is testing me to see if I am worthy. My sins have caught up with me and I'm being punished.

Psychologist Walter Houston Clark has borrowed W. I. Thomas's idea that man basically has "four wishes" or drives—for security, response, recognition, and new experience—and contends that these are reasonably comprehensive for understanding the psychological need and appeal of religion.[4] This leads us beyond the idea of emotional adjustment just expressed, although we are still dealing quite specifically with emotional needs that the individual strives to fulfill—specifically, according to Clark's approach, through religion.

Another psychologist, George S. Spinks, agrees with Clark by speaking of religion as actively fulfilling fundamental human needs, but takes this idea a step further by emphasizing the uncertainties and terrors that continually threaten to overwhelm the individual.[5]

Sigmund Freud, the "father of psychoanalysis," sees religion stem-

---

[4]Walter Huston Clark, *The Psychology of Religion* (New York: Macmillan, 1958), p. 67. William I. Thomas, *The Unadjusted Girl*, (Boston: Little, Brown, 1923), pp. 4ff.

[5]George S. Spinks, *Psychology and Religion* (Boston: Beacon Press, 1963), pp. 46–47.

ming primarily from a sense of guilt derived at least partly from the Oedipus complex and the attempts by the male to reconstruct a father image after his "love affair" with his mother and his ritual killing of his father. Thus for Freud religion is a mechanism that allows people to sublimate many primitive instincts that society represses.[6] In general, then, from the psychological point of view religion serves an adjustment function. That is, it helps people survive frustration in trying to fulfill or serve drives and needs and adapt to the frightening experiences that threaten their emotional integrity.

THE SOCIOLOGICAL VIEW

We now turn to the sociological treatment of the issue of religion's sources or origins. Actually, to continue using the term *origins* would be misleading. Certainly contemporary sociologists no longer use the term; nor did the early representatives of sociology that we shall soon cite. A more appropriate term is *social correlates* (or simply *correlates*) of religion—that is, associations between various events and features on the one hand and religious forms and expressions on the other. As shall be evident throughout this text, one of the central concerns of contemporary sociology of religion is tracing the interaction of social factors and religion, not pretending or even hoping to discover "origins," but only influences on and modifiers of religion. In an important sense it makes little difference to the social scientist whence religion came originally anyway. The fact that it exists is sufficient to merit our attention and analysis.

As we might expect, sociologists who seek to discover the "influences" on and "correlations" of religion focus on the various processes involved in social interaction and group life. Theirs is not so much the anthropologists' emphasis on personal experiences with the physical environment, or the psychologists' emphasis on personal emotional adjustment, but an emphasis on models of what transpires in group interaction processes.

In elaborating the sociological position we shall first consider the contribution of the pioneering social theorist Georg Simmel. Patterns of social interaction that are themselves nonreligious, Simmel asserted, exert a prime influence on religion. Many feelings and patterns of expression commonly termed "religious" are also found in other areas of life and in fact are basic ingredients of social interaction in general: exaltation, commitment, fervor, love, and so on are common to all forms of human

[6]Sigmund Freud, *The Future of an Illusion* (New York: Liveright, 1928).

experience and relationships. Faith, for example, is a common ingredient in relationships between individuals. Most of our interactions with people are founded on faith: faith that an approaching stranger will not shoot me as I reach out to shake his hand; faith that the pilot of the plane knows how to fly, is not on a suicide mission, and is sober; faith that the cook at the drive-in has not laced the hamburger relish with arsenic; and so on. *Religious* faith, then (to continue the example), is a supreme form of a prime factor in everyday interaction. "In faith in a deity," Simmel writes, "the highest development of faith has become incorporate, so to speak; has been relieved of its connection with its social counterpart."[7]

Implicit in what Simmel says here is a crucial sociological assumption concerning religious "origins"—namely, that the models for many if not all religious sentiments, expressions, and beliefs reside originally in society at large, in its patterns of interaction. In other words, society precedes religion: before religion can develop, there must first exist general patterns of social interaction—i.e., a society—that can serve as a model.

Another pioneer, and Simmel's contemporary, Emile Durkheim, devoted much of his theoretical and research energies to studying religion and was particularly intrigued by the question of religion's origins and social correlates. Durkheim emphasized religion's role in influencing and reinforcing societal integration—in legitimating society's values and norms by providing divine sanctions for behavior that society defines as normative and by periodically bringing people together for ritual activities that strengthen their feeling of unity. Like Simmel, Durkheim believed that general patterns of social interaction provide models and precursors for religion. But Durkheim goes further in asserting (quite dramatically) that society's norms, roles, and social relationships are so closely reflected by religion that the latter is nothing more than these characteristics expressed in somewhat different form. The extreme of this position is Durkheim's contention that the real object of veneration in any religion is society itself: that which is venerated may be *called* "God," but it is in reality society.[8]

Durkheim, then, concentrates on the functional aspect of religion. That is, religion performs a beneficial function within society, for all religious acts (in Durkheim's view) tend to reaffirm society's legitimacy and bind its members more closely together. Durkheim thus introduces and applies to the study of religion the approach called *functionalism,* which we shall discuss further in Chapter 8.

[7]Georg Simmel, "A Contribution to the Sociology of Religion," *American Journal of Sociology* 11, no. 3 (1905); 366–67.
[8]Emile Durkheim, *The Elementary Forms of the Religious Life,* trans. Joseph Ward Swain (New York: Collier, 1961).

More recently Guy E. Swanson has adopted Durkheim's basic position and modified it somewhat in conducting a monumental piece of research. Starting with the basic sociological assumption that all human ideas arise from man's experience with his environment,[9] both physical and social, Swanson attempted to discover examples of specific human experiences giving rise to certain forms of religious belief. In his 1960 study *The Birth of the Gods* Swanson focused on religion's preoccupation with the supernatural in an attempt to determine the origin of this concept. Like the early anthropologists, Swanson noted the predominance of spirits and of the concept of mana in "primitive" religious systems. What are the sources of the belief in such phenomena? Swanson suggests that spirits, which he defines as "organized clusters of purposes" having a personal identity and access to mana, grow out of, and consequently stand for, social patterns already present in the society.[10] That is, as Durkheim and Simmel both maintained earlier, society serves as the model for religion.

Furthermore, Swanson then asks to what social relationships do the experiences with spirits correspond. He suggests four conditions or types of social patterns or groups: (1) social relationships in which there is an evident connection between cause and effect, associated with the belief that spirits have a purpose and a will; (2) relationships regarded as persisting over the generations, which relates to the belief that spirits are immortal; (3) particular groups that are the source of particular spirits, which means that every spirit has a specific identity; and (4) groups that have distinctive purposes, associated with the fact that spirits differ in purpose and role.[11]

Using this general orientation to the source or basis of belief in spirits, Swanson analyzed data drawn from preliterate and early historical societies in order to trace the relationship between certain kinds of belief (such as monotheism, polytheism, and the beliefs in ancestral spirits, in reincarnation, in the immanence of the soul, and in the efficacy of witchcraft) and various social conditions and relationships. That is, he sought correlations between religious beliefs and practices, on the one hand, and, on the other, such social factors as the society's source of food, its amount of food production, the degree of danger of attack from alien societies, size of the population, the degree of private-property ownership, the emphasis on communal vs. noncommunal specialities within the society, social stratification, the nature and frequency of unlegitimated contacts with members of other societies, the variety and kinds of social

---

[9] Guy E. Swanson, *The Birth of the Gods* (Ann Arbor: University of Michigan Press, 1960), p. 1.
[10] Ibid., p. 18.
[11] This typology is summarized from ibid., pp. 19–20.

organizations, and so on. In some cases Swanson found a surprisingly high correlation between a set of social factors and a particular religious belief or practice—that is, an instance where a particular belief, say, was always (or almost always) present *only if* certain social factors were *also* present, and always (or nearly always) absent *only when* the same factors were absent. In all cases, he found fascinating and highly suggestive correlations, whether of high magnitude or not. For example, the belief and practice of witchcraft, Swanson discovered, tends to occur in societies where people must interact with one another on important matters with no clear norms, controls, and structures to guide them.[12] Thus people resort to witchcraft apparently as a substitute, as a compensatory device for attempting to explain and above all to control what happens to them. Or to take another example: The belief in reincarnation is more likely to appear in societies where the pattern of settlement is dominated by "small hamlets, compounds of extended families, small nomadic bands, scattered rural neighborhoods, or other units smaller than a village."[13] The apparent logic underlying this is that there is a greater probability that a person will be regarded as living on through reincarnation where there are intimate, highly interdependent, long-lasting relationships within a relatively small but fairly independent social unit—where, in other words, the social unit is thought to survive the members who constitute it at any given time. The individual and his idiosyncrasies within such groups are of considerable interest and importance. As Swanson points out: "The particular potentialities of each member are appreciated as limiting or facilitating the lives of all the others, and those effects persist after a member dies."[14] These effects are such things as "his technological inventiveness, his habits of shirking work, his fecundity, or the qualities of his voice in the ceremonial songs [that] have shaped adaptations of his fellows ... [and that] continue after his death."[15] In other words, "the memory lingers on." Moreover, the social relationships and structure of the group provide a "model" for the development of a belief in personal reincarnation.

While Swanson himself admits that even strong positive correlations do not conclusively establish cause-and-effect relationships between social factors and religious beliefs, his achievement lies in having shown that certain beliefs are extremely unlikely to occur and be accepted unless certain social factors, conditions, or relationships are present. For example, it is extremely unlikely that a society lacking a certain degree

[12]Ibid., chapter 8.
[13]Ibid., p. 113.
[14]Ibid., p. 112.
[15]Ibid.

and type of organizational complexity will accept belief in a monotheistic "high god" (one considered responsible for creating the world) even if the belief is suggested by a member of the group, revealed by a deity, or diffused from another society. Specifically, societies that accept that belief have a hierarchical arrangement of three or more "sovereign groups" (groups having ultimate decision-making authority over specified areas of life).[16] Although Swanson stops short of asserting any causal relationship here and would simply affirm that this social structure is likely the model for the emergence of monotheism much of the time, the relationship is strong enough to at least tempt the reader to begin thinking of talking about necessary and sufficient conditions for the development of that particular belief.

CONCLUSION

Although the origins and ultimate sources of religion can never be known with certainty, research and speculation on these subjects has not been fruitless. The hypotheses we have summarized—the anthropological theories that emphasize man's interaction with nature; the psychological theories that stress man's fears, frustrations, and emotional needs; and the sociological theories that focus on the social context in which religion exists—at the very least contribute to our understanding of what religion is, why it has come about, and perhaps also why it persists.

In summary, then, it seems reasonable to advance the following propositions concerning the forces that sustain religion, if not give rise to it: (1) People are continually and universally threatened with failure, frustration, and injustice. (2) Religion becomes man's attempt in groups to "relativize" such threats to his wholeness by placing them within a context of a larger system or plan and by "explaining" much that happens in terms of supernatural intervention into and control over earthly events. (3) At the same time, threats similar to those experienced by individuals also affect social relationships—and, in fact, society itself. (4) Religion arises as an attempt by society to cushion such threats (both to itself and to its members) by bringing people into a ritual fellowship of common belief. Religion is thus a response to both individual and group needs. (5) The characteristic form of religious belief and interpretation in a given society is significantly conditioned by the type and complexity of existing social patterns and relationships.

[16]Ibid., pp. 62–65.

RELIGION
AND
THE INDIVIDUAL

Part

4

The Measurement
of Religiosity

"Why yes, she's a very religious person!" "As for him, he's about as irreligious as you can get." "They are the most religious couple I've ever
met." How many times have you either said something like that about a
person or heard someone else observe and evaluate someone in a similar
manner? A fairly common occurrence, certainly. But what do such statements mean? What is a religious person? What is an irreligious (or nonreligious) person? What criteria do people use in making such judgments
and evaluations? Are there common understandings regarding these criteria? And do such assertions ultimately make any sense at all? That is,
how do we decide if or to what degree a person is religious?

MEASURING RELIGION:
A PROBLEM FROM VARIOUS PERSPECTIVES

The question of distinguishing the religious from the nonreligious is one
that occurs in many contexts. Certainly individuals who are committed
to a particular religious system are concerned about whether they meet
their group's criteria for being religious: Am I a true believer? Have I
committed the unpardonable sin? Are there any signs and indications
that tell me whether I measure up or not?

Christian theologians talk about "marks" of Christianity, and theologians of every belief pore over sacred scriptures trying to distill the essential characteristics and behavior that sets the true believer apart from all others. "Do you believe in Jesus Christ as your only Savior?" "Do you bow toward Mecca at the specified five times daily?" "Do you belong to the Catholic Church and attend mass at least the minimum prescribed number of times a year?"

Denominational administrators seek "indicators" of religiosity for the purpose of evaluating their programs. If, for example, certain congregations in their jurisdiction participate in a "Religious Enrichment Seminar" and consequently increase their contributions to the denomination's general fund, administrators may reason that this is a program to be urged on all the other congregations. Or if people who attended the denomination's parochial schools now attend church more often, contribute higher proportions of their income, and participate in the organizational life of the congregation more extensively than those who did not attend such schools, then such schools are most likely regarded as accomplishing their religious purpose.

Researchers in the sociology of religion also continually search for valid ways of defining the concept of "being religious"—what we'll be calling religiosity from now on. Sociologists are specifically interested in identifying what constitutes religiosity for the purpose of measuring it in relation to other factors: Is the religious person different from a non-religious person in any other respects? And if so, how? Is the religious person more humanitarian or less so? Is he more prejudiced or less? More economically successful or less? More likely to be politically liberal? Better "adjusted"? And so on.

One place to start in our attempt to define religiosity is the definition of religion that we arrived at in Chapter 2: a set of beliefs and practices, centered around a belief in the supernatural and an orientation toward the sacred, that are shared by members of a group. Thus we could say that anyone who is a member of a religious group, who believes certain things about the supernatural and the sacred, and who engages in certain activities associated with these beliefs is a religious person, and that everyone else is not. Would that it were so simple!

Some religious groups have approximated this approach in trying to distinguish the religious from the irreligious person. Historically, the Roman Catholic Church has maintained that any member who participated in a specified minimum number of ritual activities was a saved member of Christ's church, and that all others were not. Lutherans tended toward this approach also, identifying the true church and its members wherever the Word of God was taught and preached in purity and wherever the sacraments were correctly administered.

Such neat definitions, however, leave several questions unanswered. Should any distinction be made, for example, between those who evidence maximum participation in the group's ritual activities and those who just "get by" with minimal participation? Or are such extremes to be considered equally religious when compared with others who do not participate in these activities at all? And what about the person who occasionally participates in the ritual but has not made a membership commitment? Is he therefore not religious? Or what about the person who participates occasionally, and who is a member, but actually is a disbeliever or at least doubts some of the group's central beliefs? Some people are more sincere in their religious beliefs than others; some are more enthusiastic in their ritual participation than others. Some "leave their religion at the church door," while others attempt to apply it in all life situations. Are all of these people religious? And if so, are they equally religious? And what about the person—to return to an issue left over from Chapter 2—who shares a group's belief but prefers to meditate and worship on his own?

Our definition of religion is less helpful than we might hope in determining people's religiosity because of a fundamental principle of sociology—namely, that most any characteristic that can be attributed to a given social phenomenon exists at some point on a *continuum*. That is, such characteristics typically are neither totally present nor totally absent, but exist to a greater or lesser degree along a range from high to low. For example, among business organizations classified as bureaucracies some organizations are more highly bureaucratized than others. Bureaucratic organizations may therefore be ranked from high to low along a continuum called "bureaucracy." Nations, to take another example, can be arranged along a continuum called "industrialization." Or people along continua called "authoritarianism," "prejudiced," "self-motivating," and so on.

Similarly it is likely that people, if not organizations, may be located at various points on a continuum called "religiousness" or "religiosity." People intuitively assume this when they make statements and comparisons such as those that begin this chapter. Our problem here, however, is how to *operationalize* the concept of religiosity—how to translate such feelings into terms of observable characteristics that will permit us to make meaningful comparisons among people. Realize, of course, that we embark on this process not in order to make invidious comparisons among people or to judge them, but solely in order to be able to determine the impact of such differences. The latter question is the focus of the next chapter, where we look specifically at the effects of religion on behavior. But first we must establish means of measuring different levels of religiosity.

SOCIOLOGICAL DEFINITIONS OF RELIGIOSITY:
THE ORGANIZATIONAL APPROACH

Sociologists take two basic approaches to defining religiosity and applying it to their research. The first approach centers on people's affiliations with religious organizations or groups, according to which sociologists attempt to predict and observe differences in people's behavior and attitudes. Technically this approach focuses not so much on religiosity (which involves something going on inside the individual) as it does on the organization itself. The net effect is similar in the sense that whenever we talk about the effect of religion on people's behavior we are assuming a religious group's influence somewhere along the line.

The second approach to identifying religiosity deals with individuals and tends to disregard religious affiliations except as a possible control variable. Various approaches under this heading will be discussed toward the end of this chapter.

The Member/Nonmember Dichotomy

Typologies of religiosity that begin and end with the organization (as opposed to the individual) are basically three in number. The first is the member/nonmember dichotomy. The underlying assumption here is that if religion has an impact on people's behavior, then we should be able to observe differences between those who are members of religious groups ("religious" persons) and those who are not ("nonreligious" persons). Obviously this is a very gross or general measure inasmuch as it combines a wide diversity of people within the categories member/nonmember and believer/nonbeliever. Certainly the range of intensity, commitment, and sincerity within the member category is great. And the nonmember category includes not only aggressive antireligionists, but also some persons who hold many if not all the beliefs held by religious group members but who have simply not formally affiliated with a religious group. Despite such limitations, such an approach can be useful for beginning the research process of trying to understand the impact of religion on people and social structures.

Major Religious Families

The second approach is slightly more sophisticated in that it subdivides all those who belong to religious groups into major categories such as Protestant, Catholic, and Jewish (in Western societies), or Hindu,

Muslim, Buddhist, and Christian (in Asian societies), or any number of other relevant sets of affiliations. Extensive research using such religious distinctions has been fruitful in showing different attitudes and behavior among such major groupings. For example, whereas 62 percent of the Catholics polled in one survey reported attending religious services at least once a week, only 25 percent of the Protestants polled and 12 percent of the Jews polled so reported.[1] And whereas 83 percent of Catholics and 76 percent of Protestants in the same survey reported that they regarded religion as "very important" in their lives, only 47 percent of Jews so reported.[2] In Lenski's 1959 survey in Detroit he found that while 42 percent of Jews had positive attitudes toward work, the proportions for white Protestants, black Protestants, and white Catholics were only 30 percent, 24 percent, and 23 percent respectively.[3] The same study revealed that only 11 percent of Jews, but 34 percent of white Protestants, 38 percent of black Protestants, and 66 percent of white Catholics felt that divorce was always or usually wrong.[4] Questions about political party preference from the same survey revealed that the Republican party was preferred by 54 percent of white Protestants, 30 percent of white Catholics, 13 percent of black Protestants, and 3 percent of Jews.[5] These are only a few of the almost endless list of research findings documenting differences in attitude, behavior, and commitment among major religious groupings.

Denominational Affiliation

By the early 1960s, however, many sociologists began to point out that while research showing differences among such major groupings as Protestants, Catholics, and Jews may be revealing, it also tends to hide almost as much as it reveals, for these categories are still so broad that they obscure significant internal diversity. Primary objection focused on the Protestant category, which includes fundamentalists and other extremely conservative groups as well as theologically liberal groups that reject much of traditional Christian doctrine. Similar problems were seen to exist for the Catholic and Jewish categories as well: there are both liberal and conservative Catholics, and there are Reform, Conservative, and Orthodox Jews.

[1]Will Herberg, *Protestant-Catholic-Jew* (Garden City, N.Y.: Doubleday, 1956), p. 236. (Originally in "Do Americans Go to Church?" *Catholic Digest* (December, 1952); 5.

[2]Ibid. (Originally in "How Important Religion Is to Americans," *Catholic Digest* (February, 1953); 8.

[3]Gerhard E. Lenski, *The Religious Factor* (Garden City, N.Y.: Doubleday, 1961), p. 84.

[4]Ibid., p. 150.

[5]Ibid., p. 125.

Moreover, in surveys even fairly large (and expensive) samples do not include enough members of, say, the various subcategories of Protestantism to make meaningful comparisons. For example, suppose you wanted to analyze social differences among various religious groups in the United States and at some point decided to make specific comparisons between Unitarians and Mennonites—two groups nearly at opposite extremes on a continuum called "Protestantism." Suppose you had been able to afford to survey a fairly large sample of one thousand persons representative of the United States population. Suppose also that your sampling techniques had worked perfectly and you had picked a truly proportionate representative sample. You would then find when you went to your sample, theoretically at least, exactly eight-tenths of one Unitarian and nine-tenths of one Mennonite. You would also get only one-and-eight-tenths Seventh Day Adventists, nine Mormons, and eleven members of the United Church of Christ—hardly a sufficient number of any of these groups (not to mention a host of other small religious groups) to reach valid conclusions about any of them.

Mainline Protestant church bodies, however, such as Presbyterians, Methodists, Lutherans, Baptists, and Episcopalians, each have many more members; consequently they can provide sufficient numbers in national or area samples of a thousand or more persons to justify making comparisons among them. Thus evolved the third typology or stage of utilizing religious affiliations as an independent variable when major subcategories of Protestants began to be studied. The research team of Charles Glock and Rodney Stark of the University of California at Berkeley, who were among the first to use this approach extensively, found significant differences among major Protestant denominations that one might have thought existed only among smaller groups which tend to hold more extreme views. For example, Glock and Stark discovered that on such a fundamental doctrinal question as the divinity of Jesus the proportion of members of major Protestant bodies who accept without reservation the traditional view—namely, that Jesus is the Son of God—and admit to having no personal doubts about it are as follows: 40 percent of Congregationalists, 54 percent of Methodists, 59 percent of Episcopalians, 72 percent of Presbyterians, 74 percent of Disciples of Christ, 74 percent of American Lutherans, 76 percent of American Baptists, 93 percent of Missouri Synod Lutherans, and 99 percent of Southern Baptists.[6] Differences among the same Protestant groups on the question of miracles is even more dramatic. The proportion of those who believe that miracles actually happened as described in the Bible are: 28 percent of Congregationalists, 37 percent of Methodists, 41 percent of Episcopalians, 58

---

[6]Charles Y. Glock and Rodney Stark, *Christian Beliefs and Anti-Semitism* (New York: Harper & Row, 1966), p. 7.

percent of Presbyterians, 62 percent of the Disciples of Christ, 62 percent of American Baptists, 69 percent of American Lutherans, 89 percent of Missouri Synod Lutherans, and 92 percent of Southern Baptists.[7] Or consider the somewhat less dramatic but still significant differences in proportion of persons who agree with the statement, "The races would probably get along just fine in this country if Communists and other radicals didn't stir up trouble": 33 percent of Congregationalists, 36 percent of Methodists and Disciples of Christ, 45 percent of both Episcopalians and American Baptists, 46 percent of Presbyterians, 50 percent of Missouri Synod Lutherans, 56 percent of American Lutherans, and 70 percent of Southern Baptists.[8] Religious affiliation among subdenominations within Protestantism apparently makes a difference.

It is perhaps becoming obvious that we are straying from a strict definition or understanding of religiosity. What we have been doing—and will continue to do in the rest of this chapter—is indicating some of the major ways in which researchers have attempted to operationalize the concept of religiosity in order to assess its effect or impact on people's behavior. The three types of measurement we have already looked at are in reality all subtypes of the affiliation measure, which focuses on the religious group a person belongs to. How do we know whether a person is religious? We consider him religious if he professes to be a Protestant, a Catholic, a Jew, or whatever. Thus, we are more likely to find differences among groups than to show the effects of differences in personal religiosity. We may want to talk about the religiosity of people but wind up focusing on the general or central tendencies of groups and differences among those groups—an important focus indeed, but hardly the whole package. At most, the focus on group differences measures the effect of formal religious differences among groups, primarily differences in belief and doctrine. What we lack are measures of differentiation in intensity or sincerity of belief and degree of religious interest. Such ideas are closer to the concept of religiosity, which presupposes a difference of degree of commitment and interest in religious ideas, religious answers or solutions, and religious participation.

SOCIOLOGICAL DEFINITIONS OF RELIGION: THE INDIVIDUAL APPROACH

We now turn to focus on major attempts by sociologists to measure religiosity more narrowly defined as the degree and type of commitment to

[7]Ibid., p. 10.
[8]Ibid., p. 168.

religious values and norms, with the ultimate aim in the next chapter of discovering how such differences affect behavior.

Although it has not always been recognized, there is great diversity within each group category discussed above, a fact illustrated by the historical development of the attempts to measure differences related to religious group affiliation. Thus one doesn't have to labor long at distinguishing religious group members from nonmembers before becoming aware that not all members are alike in their beliefs, commitment, or behavior. And while the task of contrasting the major categories of Protestants, Catholics, and Jews exposed numerous differences, such broad and inclusive categories were soon recognized to be just that—inclusive of a great deal of internal diversity within each category, as numerous studies, including those by Glock and Stark, have documented. Implicit in the data from such studies, though not always discussed, are great differences within each of the subgroups as well. For example, although only 28 percent of Congregationalists but 92 percent of Southern Baptists believe in miracles, there nevertheless exists within each of these groups internal differentiation, which is even more obvious within the other Protestant groups that fall between the Congregationalists and Southern Baptists as reported earlier in this chapter. In other words, although 72 percent of Congregationalists do *not* believe in miracles, 28 percent *do* believe in them; although 42 percent of Presbyterians do not believe in miracles, 58 percent believe in them; and so on. How do we explain such internal diversity? Why do some members of a group accept one point of view, belief, practice, or social perspective while other members do not?

Measures of Individual Ritual Participation

Such questions have led some researchers to ignore at least temporarily formal group differences and regroup—or more accurately, recategorize—people on other bases, such as types of commitment, intensity of belief, and so on. An early attempt along these lines, one which has subsequently been widely used, is based on *ritual participation*, the frequency with which people attend the formal religious services of their religious group. Thus those who report attending weekly or nearly every week might be categorized as demonstrating a "high" degree of religiosity; those attending once or twice a month would perhaps be categorized as showing a "moderate" degree; and those attending less often would be classed "low" on this scale. Refinements of this measure into a five-point scale (with the addition of "moderately high" and "moderately low" categories) and even a seven-point scale have been used. Other factors such as frequency of participation in other activities sponsored by the religious group have been included by some researchers. Commonly, when Protestants and Catholics are major components in the study, frequency of attendance at the sacrament of Communion or the Lord's Supper is used as a measure of religiosity. Quite obviously such measures attempt to assess variations in the intensity of commitment and the importance of religion to the individual.

But many researchers have objected that such a procedure does not really measure religiosity, that attendance statistics tell us nothing about how a given individual *feels* about his attendance. A person's regular attendance may be simply a result of habit and mean relatively little to him personally. Or his regular attendance may be due to family or other group pressures: he may not want to disappoint his grandmother, or to give his employer cause to question his morality. Or perhaps he attends regularly because he looks forward to the opportunity to socialize after services.

Measures of Individual Prayer Life

Such objections have spurred attempts to measure religiosity by other means. One method has been to ask people about their prayer life —focusing again, however, as with church attendance, on frequency. The reasoning here is that if a person reports engaging frequently in personal, private prayer (where "frequently" is usually defined as at least daily), then his religion is likely more meaningful and important to him than it is to the person who prays only occasionally or the person who never prays except in groups, as in formal religious services.

Church attendance, other ritual and organizational participation, and personal prayer have all been viewed as "objective" measures of religious involvement and commitment in the sense that they are all activities fairly easily measurable in terms of frequency. Important here is the common assumption that people are in fact aware of the frequency of their participation and that they tend to be fairly honest in reporting such "objective" data about themselves.

Measures of Importance of Religion to Individuals

Other, more "subjective" measures of religiosity rely on respondents' ability, in interviews and questionnaires, to categorize themselves in terms of their personal commitment to religion and to evaluate how important religion is to them personally. These measures, occasionally composites or indexes based on more than one question, vary from one study to another, but usually are based on questions such as, "How important would you say religion is in your life—very important, somewhat important, not very important, or not at all important?" Or: "All in all, how important would you say your church membership is to you?"

Evaluation of Individual Measures of Religiosity

All the attempts to operationalize the concept of religiosity that we've mentioned have in common the fact that each relies on a single measure or single set of measures (e.g., combining frequency of church attendance with frequency of Communion attendance, frequency of personal prayer, and extent of involvement in the total organizational life of a congregation). As we'll report in some detail in Chapter 5, such measures of religiosity have revealed significant differences among people. For example, a 1960 survey revealed that among white southern college students those who attended church were somewhat more prejudiced against blacks than those who never attended—although there were also strong indications that among the churchgoers those who attended more frequently were less prejudiced than infrequent churchgoers.[9] Or to cite another brief example: among American middle-class men those who attend church more regularly tend to be more upwardly mobile.[10]

Differences of this sort, however, have not been so great or so consistent as some researchers had anticipated. The primary reason, according to recent research, seems to be that religiosity is not a one-dimensional phenomenon. That is, not all people are religious in the same way. A person may rank high in religiosity on one dimension or measure but low on another or several others. Thus if certain behavior is positively correlated with a high score on one scale of religiosity but not on another, then entirely different conclusions would be reached concerning the impact of religion on that behavior depending upon which measure of religiosity was used.

SOCIOLOGICAL MEASURES OF RELIGIOSITY: MULTIDIMENSIONAL MEASURES

Several researchers taking a multidimensional view of religion, have either combined several specific measures into a composite of some kind or utilized several discrete measures. The rationale for such approaches is that

[9]R. K. Young, W. M. Benson, and W. H. Holtzman, "Changes in Attitudes Toward the Negro in a Southern University," *Journal of Abnormal and Social Psychology* 60, no. 1(1960); 131–33.
[10]Lenski, *The Religious Factor*, p. 103.

religion is not a single, uniform entity that can be apprehended by any single measure; rather, people can "be religious" in various ways. Although the following discussion does not touch on every such multidimensional measure, we'll proceed essentially chronologically.

In works published in 1951 and 1954 Joseph Fichter distinguished four ways in which a person could be a Catholic.[11] Based on attendance at mass, participation in confession, sending children to parochial school, other involvement in church subgroups, and expressed religious interest, Fichter constructed the typology of *nuclear Catholic, modal Catholic, marginal Catholic,* and *dormant Catholic.* Nuclear Catholics go beyond minimal requirements of membership, are active in parish life, and attend Holy Communion at least weekly. Such "ideal" members in Fichter's second (1954) sample were found to comprise only 5.7 percent of all Catholics.[12] Modal Catholics comprised about 70 percent of the membership and were described by Fichter as follows:

> *Since the modal parishioner holds a position midway between the nuclear and the marginal Catholic, he may be said to live up to his religion in a "middling sort of way." He generally observes the Friday abstinence and knows the difference between Advent and Lent. His name is likely to be on the roster of the Holy Name Society at some time during his life, but he hardly ever attends a meeting. He attends Sunday Mass most of the time but has difficulty "catching Mass" when holy days of obligation occur during the working week. His children fill the parochial schools, and he has a kind of aloof respect for priests and nuns.*[13]

The marginal Catholic (about 20 percent of Catholics) considers himself to be a member of the Catholic church and tends to be so considered by the church itself, yet may not have attended mass during the past year, may not have received Holy Communion or participated in confession, and, although he has the opportunity, does not send his children to a Catholic parochial school.[14] The dormant Catholic is one who was born into a Catholic family, baptized as a Catholic, may have been married by a priest, and perhaps asks for a priest's services as death approaches, yet is not a formal member of a Catholic congregation.[15]

Fichter's work was pioneering research. If asked why something seemingly so obvious had not been done before, we can only simply say that it hadn't been done. If the reader recalls that in Chapter 1 we noted

---

11Joseph Fichter, *Southern Parish* (Chicago: University of Chicago Press, 1951); idem, *Social Relations in the Urban Parish* (Chicago: University of Chicago Press, 1954).
12Ibid., p. 24.
13Ibid., p. 41.
14Ibid., pp. 61–62.
15Ibid., p. 69.

that empirical research in the sociology of religion is a relatively recent undertaking, he will now appreciate what "recent" means in this context.

It should be fairly clear from earlier comments that Fichter's typology is a simple one in the sense that his measure of religiosity essentially involves only ritual and formal participation in a religious organization. Excluded are several dimensions we have hinted at earlier and others we'll be identifying as we proceed. Yet his typology made an important contribution, particularly in that it stimulated others to expand and improve on his work.

Not long after publication of Fichter's research, Charles Glock suggested that religion could be thought of as consisting of four dimensions, which he identified as the *experiential*, the *ritualistic*, the *ideological*, and the *consequential*.[16] The experiential dimension attempts to measure the degree of emotional attachment to the supernatural. The ritualistic is the by-now-familiar dimension that includes church attendance and prayer life.[17] The ideological dimension refers to the degree of commitment a person expresses in the religious beliefs of his group; and the consequential dimension refers to the impact of religious commitment and involvement on general behavior.

In 1961, Yoshio Fukuyama, employed then as research director of the Congregationalist Christian Churches and using data gathered from 4,095 members of that denomination, conducted an empirical test of Glock's dimensions, reformulating them as the *cognitive*, the *cultic*, the *creedal*, and the *devotional*. Fukuyama's cognitive dimension, not included in Glock's fourfold typology, refers to what people know about religion, how well informed they are about the Bible and religious matters generally, and how much satisfaction they get from listening to sermons and participating in religious discussions. The cultic is equivalent to Glock's ritualistic dimension. The creedal dimension refers to what a person believes as distinguished from what he knows or how he expresses his religion; this is essentially Glock's ideological dimension. The devotional dimension approximates Glock's experiential measure—religious

---

[16]Charles Y. Glock, "The Religious Revival in America," in *Religion and the Face of America*, ed. Jane Zahn (Berkeley: University Extension, University of California, 1959), pp. 25–42.

[17]Stark and Glock have subsequently subdivided the ritualistic into two parts: *ritual* and *devotion*. Ritual includes such formal religious activities as attending religious services and taking Communion—what can be called public activities. Devotion includes such behavior as praying and studying sacred books and religious writings. (Rodney Stark and Charles Y. Glock, *American Piety: The Nature of Religious Commitment* [Berkeley: University of California Press, 1968].) Nudelman believes this added distinction makes sense both theoretically and empirically. (Arthur E. Nudelman, "Dimensions of Religiosity: A Factor-Analytic View of Protestants, Catholics, and Christian Scientists," *Review of Religious Research* 13, no. 1 [1971]; 42–56.)

feelings and emotions in contrast to abstract creedal statements and beliefs.

Fukuyama found a variety of differences in characteristics and attitudes of church members that were related to these four types. For example, men are more likely than women to score high on the cognitive dimension, less likely to score high on the other three. Age is also a factor in that the older people are the more likely they are to score high on the creedal and the devotional dimensions. Education is important also: the higher one's educational level the more likely it is that he will score high on the cognitive dimension and lower on the devotional dimension. In terms of attitudes, traditional responses are more likely to come from those for whom the creedal and devotional dimensions of religion are important, more liberal attitudes from those with a cognitive or cultic orientation.[18]

In the same year that Fukuyama's study appeared, 1961, Gerhard Lenski published his pathbreaking work *The Religious Factor*, based on data from a sample of adults in the Detroit metropolitan area. Lenski also used four measures of religiosity: *associational involvement*, as reflected by frequency of church attendance and participation in subgroups of the religious organization; *communal involvement*, the degree to which people's primary relations (relationships with relatives and friends) are restricted to persons of one's own religious group (incidentally, Lenski found only an extremely small relationship between these first two measures[19]); "*doctrinal orthodoxy*," referring to the dimension of belief and distinguishing between those who agree with the prescribed doctrines of their religious group (the orthodox) and those who do not (the heterodox); and *devotionalism*, the importance people place on personal contact or communion with God, a concept which Lenski operationalized as frequency of prayer and seeking to determine God's will when important decisions have to be made.

The data collected by Lenski in order to test these measures led him to an important discovery that has since been confirmed by several other researchers:

> *Especially valuable was the demonstration that orthodoxy and devotionalism are not merely two alternative measures of "religiosity" as is so often imagined. On the contrary, they are separate and independent orientations, and each has its own peculiar consequences for the behavior of individuals.*[20]

[18]Yoshio Fukuyama, "The Major Dimensions of Church Membership," *Review of Religious Research* 2, no. 4 (1961); 154–61.
[19]Lenski, *The Religious Factor*, p. 22.
[20]Ibid., p. 24.

Lenski's data quite clearly demonstrated that it is possible to "be religious" on one or two dimensions but not necessarily on all. That is, one person is religious in one way, another in some other way. Thus, convincing evidence was beginning to mount that any unidimensional measure of religiosity is bound to be misleading—if not false in a strict sense of the term, then at least serving to obscure many important differences among people concerning what they mean by religiosity and how they express their attachment and commitment to a religious group and its ideological system.

We earlier described Glock's fourfold typology and described (in a footnote) how he and Stark later subdivided the ritualistic dimension into ritual and devotion. Glock also later added a fifth major dimension—the intellectual, which measures the degree to which a person is knowledgable about the formal beliefs of his religion.[21]

In 1966, Joseph Faulkner and Gordon DeJong reported their development of sets of questions for measuring each of Glock's dimensions of religiosity.[22] We include two of these sets to give the reader an idea of how these concepts have been operationalized in research.

Ideological scale: (1) Agreement with the statement: "Do you believe that the world will come to an end according to the will of God?" (2) Agreement with the statement: "I believe in a Divine God, creator of the universe, who knows my innermost thoughts and feelings, and to whom one day I shall be accountable," rather than statements that refer to the Deity as "a power greater than myself, which some people call God and some people call Nature," or deny or doubt the existence of a supreme being altogether. (3) Agreement with the statement: "Do you believe that it is necessary for a person to repent before God will forgive his sins?" (4) Agreement with the statement: "God has and continues to act in the history of mankind." (5) Agrees that the Bible is God's word and is completely true or at least contains only some human errors while its basic moral and religious teachings are true.

Experiential scale: (1) Strongly agrees with the question: "Would you say that one's religious commitment gives life a certain purpose which it could not otherwise have?" (2) States that at least occasionally "There are particular moments (I) feel 'close' to the Divine." (3) Agrees with the question: "Would you say that religion offers a sense of security in the face of death which is not otherwise possible?" (4) Agrees with the statement: "Religion provides the individual with an interpretation of his existence which could not be discovered by reason alone." (5) Agrees with the statement: "Faith, meaning putting full confidence in the things we hope for and being certain of things we cannot see, is essential to one's religious life."

[21]Charles Y. Glock, "On the Study of Religious Commitment," *Religious Education* 62, no. 4 (1962); 98–110.
[22]Joseph E. Faulkner and Gordon F. DeJong, "Religiosity in 5-D: An Empirical Analysis," *Social Forces* 45, No. 2 (1966); 246–54.

So far, the culmination of the multidimensional approach is to be found in the factor-analytic studies of church members conducted in the late 1960s by Morton King and Richard Hunt, who collated and, where necessary, elaborated the measures developed by Glock, Fukuyama, Lenski, and others.[23] King and Hunt identified eleven possible ways of "being religious" and constructed multiple questions and statements to measure each. Questionnaires were then administered to several samples of church members and the results subjected to factor analysis (research technique that brings together several variables under a common heading and shows their relationship to yet other variables) in order to find correlations among questions and measures and to make distinctions among measures. The result was to identify six primary measures of religiosity, some consisting of two or more relatively independent submeasures:

I. Creedal Assent (to traditional Christian doctrines)
II. Devotionalism (prayer life)
III. Congregational Involvement
    A. Church Attendance
    B. Organizational Activity
    C. Financial Support
IV. Religious Knowledge (knowledge of Bible, church history, and denominations)
V. Orientation to Religion
    A. Growth and Striving (reading the Bible and religious literature and trying to learn, understand, and apply religion)
    B. Extrinsic (religious involvement as utilitarian in social life)
VI. Salience
    A. Behavior (sharing and talking about religion and "witnessing")
    B. Cognition (conscious awareness of the relevance of religion for life)[24]

The advantage of this typology is not only that it combines the best insights of most of the previous attempts to measure religiosity, but also that it specifies sets of measures for each dimension. One is hard put to think of other important ways in which one can be religious, at least within traditional Christianity. We must be careful of course to specify that not only was this typology developed within the context of traditional Christianity, but it applies well only there also. Quite as-

[23]Morton B. King and Richard A. Hunt, *Measuring Religious Dimensions,* Studies in Social Science no. 1 (Dallas, Texas: Southern Methodist University, 1972).
[24]Ibid., pp. 103–6.

suredly this set does not include every possible dimension of religiosity relevant for those outside Christianity in other contexts, whether "non-religious" Westerners or people with non-Western religious traditions.

SOCIOLOGICAL DEFINITIONS OF RELIGIOSITY:
THE INTRINSIC-EXTRINSIC DISTINCTION

Another typology of religiosity, the intrinsic-extrinsic distinction, is only a dichotomy, but it has generated considerable discussion and research. The distinction between intrinsic and extrinsic religious orientations was initially made in 1950 by the psychologist Gordon Allport in *The Individual and His Religion,* although at that point they were not named as such or clearly defined. By 1960 Allport had defined these dimensions as follows:[25]

> *Extrinsic religion is a self-serving utilitarian, self-protective form of religious outlook, which provides the believer with comfort and salvation at the expense of outgroups. Intrinsic religion marks the life that has interiorized the total creed of his faith without reservation, including the commandment to love one's neighbor. A person of this sort is more intent on serving his religion than on making it serve him.*

In other words, "the extrinsically motivated person *uses* his religion, whereas the intrinsically motivated *lives* his religion."[26]

Working with Allport's intrinsic-extrinsic concept, Hunt and King proposed the existence of five primary components, which they described as follows:

Universal-Parochial: *Brotherhood and love of neighbor vs. ethnocentrism and exclusion of those unlike oneself.*

Unselfish-Selfish: *Effort to transcend self-centered needs vs. self-serving, protective use for own ends.*

Relevance for all of life: *Floods whole life with motivation and meaning vs. compartmentalized, non-integrated into one's way of life.*

Ultimate-Instrumental: *End vs. means; master motive vs. utilitarian uses.*

Associational-Communal: *Involved for religious fellowship and deeper values vs. affiliation for sociability and status.*[27]

25Gordon W. Allport, *Personality and Social Encounter* (Boston: Beacon Press, 1960), p. 257.
26Gordon W. Allport, "The Religious Context of Prejudice," *Journal for the Scientific Study of Religion* 5, no. 3 (1966); 447–57.
27Richard A. Hunt and Morton King, "The Intrinsic-Extrinsic Concept: A Review and Evaluation," *Journal for the Scientific Study of Religion* 10, no. 4 (1971); 343.

Numerous other studies have sought to operationalize and refine this dichotomy. However, a major problem is that although the implicit assumption has been that a continuum is involved, the continuum is multidimensional, not unidimensional, and therefore is very difficult to utilize effectively in research. Hunt and King point out that nearly all studies that have employed this typology have documented its multidimensionality. That is, the concepts refer to several, not two, distinctive measures of religiosity. Quite possibly they are not even poles on a continuum but distinctive measures themselves.[28] They conclude that although the typology has served a useful purpose and has generated helpful research and theoretical discussion, it should be abandoned, and that attention should now be given to labels, ideas, and scales of greater specificity.[29]

SOCIOLOGICAL DEFINITIONS OF RELIGIOSITY:
THE OPEN-ENDED "ULTIMATE CONCERN" APPROACH

Other researchers who have recently probed into the phenomenon of religiosity have sought to bypass institutionally related factors by defining religion in terms of theologian Paul Tillich's "ultimate concern" and then attempting to determine what people are concerned about "ultimately" and how "ultimate" and intense is their concern. This approach deliberately seeks to avoid definitions of religiosity that are closely tied to the concepts of membership and participation in traditional religious organizations and the activities that such groups encourage.

In preliminary work along these lines J. Milton Yinger has devised open-ended questions designed to steer people's thinking out of traditionally understood institutional religion and belief systems and to probe their "basic" religious feelings. For example, Yinger seeks to discover people's fundamental religious concern by posing questions like the following to his respondents:

> *In your most reflective moments, when you are thinking beyond the immediate issues of the day—however important—beyond headlines, beyond the temporary, what do you consider the most important issue mankind has to face? Or, to put the question another way, what do you see as the basic, permanent question for mankind?*[30]

We might even suggest here that religiosity could be measured in terms of whether people think at all about such fundamental questions and

---

[28]Ibid., pp. 351–52.
[29]Ibid., p. 354.
[30]J. Milton Yinger, "A Structural Examination of Religion," *Journal for the Scientific Study of Religion* 8, no. 1 (1969); 93.

issues and/or in terms of what questions *are* fundamental for them. Conceivably people might be more or less "religious" depending upon whether their "fundamental question" was, "How can I become economically successful in the shortest possible time?" or, "What can I do to help attain world peace and brotherhood?" or, "How can I get into tune with the ultimate divinity?"

Quite clearly Yinger is trying to get beyond understandings and definitions of religion centered around affiliation with and simple formal participation in highly institutionalized religious organizations. He is trying to get back to "basics"—to the essence of religion which may exist within institutions and may well exist outside traditional religious forms. It should be observed, however, that Yinger does not seek to define religion in strictly individualistic terms. He still pursues the group dimension. One of the questions he presents to respondents, for example, is:

> *Are you a participant in or member of some group, whether large or small, for which the "basic, permanent question" and the beliefs connected with it are the focus of attention and the most important reasons for its existence? If so, please characterize the group briefly.*[31]

Certainly an approach like Yinger's consciously tries to get at something different, at something that previous research into religiosity has not been able to pinpoint. Such research certainly shows great promise for pushing forward the understanding of religiosity. On the other hand, it should be pointed out that such research, while it may take us well beyond our current understanding of religion and religiosity, need not invalidate research findings that relate differences in behavior to differences in people's relationships to traditional religious organizations.

SUMMARY EVALUATION

We have now examined several attempts at operationalizing the concept of religiosity. That is, how do we measure what religion is and means to people? Implicit in such attempts is the search for commonalities among people in terms of religious meanings and feelings. Because the religiosity of each individual is most likely of a unique sort—in the sense that no two people share the exact same religious feelings, experiences, ideas, beliefs, and commitments—the sociologist searches for measures that will allow him to group a number of people into meaningful categories and to use those categories to arrive at valid conclusions. That is, are some

---

[31]Ibid., p. 93.

people religious in a general way that is similar to the way some others are religious? Do others manifest other combinations of characteristics? And so on. All of the typologies we have presented make just such attempts to identify major dimensions of religiosity or ways of being religious. They then group or categorize people around those dimensions or expressions of religiosity.

The ultimate point of it all is that people can be and are religious in different ways. What we have considered in this chapter are some of these ways. Considerable research continues to try to refine what has already been developed. To date the typologies developed by Glock and Stark and by King and Hunt appear to constitute the most inclusive ones, particularly for Western religions and for persons affiliated with formal religious organizations like churches.

At this point there is consensus that religiosity is multidimensional. Thus a person may score high on one dimension and be termed "very religious," yet score low on one or more other measures and be identified as only "slightly religious" or even "irreligious." For example, a person may know his religious teachings or doctrines inside and out, yet seldom or never attend religious services, never engage in devotional activities, disbelieve what he knows intellectually about his religion, and evidence no effect of his religious knowledge on his behavior. Obviously it is important to specify what our dimension or measuring device is when we reach conclusions about people's level or degree of religiosity. It would be convenient if one or two measures correlated highly with all the others, if one or two indicators predicted fairly accurately one's performance or commitment in terms of other indicators. Unfortunately the intercorrelations of the indicators are not high at all. For example, the fact that a person believes in and is committed to orthodox doctrine does not necessarily mean that he engages in an active devotional life, possesses extensive intellectual knowledge of his religious system, or shows any effect of his faith on his daily life.

We must exercise extreme caution as social scientists when making judgments about the religiosity of people. Although we are reluctant to advise readers how to interact with other people, this principle would seem to apply when judging the religiosity of others in ordinary social situations. Our concern here, however, is of course primarily in confronting and evaluating research and rhetoric about religion, whether it appears from the scientific or the theological point of view. That is, we must always be careful to check the researchers' operational definitions. How is *religious* defined? Is it unidimensional or multidimensional? What specific measures are used?

In brief, then, sociologically speaking there is no single "correct" definition of religiosity. Religious commitment is multidimensional—there are several, probably many, ways to "be religious"—and is therefore much too complex to be measured in only one way. The research task of the future, so far as measuring religiosity is concerned, is not finding a single measure, but isolating the various ways in which people evidence religious commitment and deriving precise measuring instruments to distinguish them.

5

The Effects
of Religion
on Behavior
and Attitudes

From Chapter 4's discussion of various ways in which people can "be religious," we now turn to a summary of some of the effects of religion (as measured in various ways) on the behavior and attitudes of people. If people can be seen as understanding, feeling, or being touched by religion differently, it follows logically that we should be able to observe in people the differential effects resulting therefrom. In a real sense this chapter provides some documentation for the assertion that "religion makes a difference." A more precise way of saying this is that religion, whether measured in terms of personal religiosity, affiliation, frequency of participation, or whatever, is one of the many independent variables at work in society that influences the attitudes and behavior of people.

In this chapter we shall be applying some of the fundamental principles of sociology outlined in Chapter 1. In particular we are going to document many of the ways in which religion as a group phenomenon affects individual group members. In the process we shall be utilizing some of the typologies of religiosity discussed in Chapter 4, providing data that show differences in attitudes and behavior that are affected in some way and to some degree by religious group membership and by type of attachment to religious groups and ideologies. It should be noted that we shall be touching fleetingly on a wide variety of topics, some of which will be treated in greater detail in later chapters. Although our primary interest at the moment is demonstrating the variety of ways in which religion affects behavior, each of these is important in its own right and could well be pursued at greater length. Readers may wish to do so either on their own or with the help of the instructor later in the course as theory and data shed additional light on a discrete subject area.

THE PROBLEM OF MEASUREMENT

The reader should be aware at the outset that clear and direct cause-and-effect relationships among variables will be difficult if not impossible to establish. Essentially we'll be working with correlations and associations between measures of religion and religiosity on the one hand, and various measures of attitudes, belief, commitment, and behavior on the other. Although (as pointed out in Chapter 3 with respect to the question of the origins of religion) absolute proof of causal relationships cannot be made, if the connection between measures of religiosity and various attitudes and behavior are at least fairly substantial and "make sense," we shall infer that religion does affect attitudes and behavior in certain ways. The observations and conclusions that follow, based as they are on sound empirical data, should satisfy most people. Yet the reader is urged to keep in the back of his mind the inherent problem involved in making cause-and-effect statements in research—namely, there is no way, technically speaking, to prove cause-and-effect relationships beyond any shadow of doubt. As in research of any kind we seek data evidencing such a high degree of consistency with theoretical predictions and rationales that we are encouraged to make what amounts to a "leap of faith" and to assert that a projected relationship between variables actually exists—or more precisely, *probably* exists. This is what we mean by relationships among variables "making sense." That is, the connections between variables and our conclusions about them should be logical and consistent with theoretical predictions that were made before data were gathered as well as with prior research findings on the subject (always being open, of course, to the possibility that new findings that contradict old ones are in fact correct). For example, should we find data that show that persons who hold conservative theological beliefs are more likely to be politically conservative as well—are more likely to vote, say, for George Wallace, Barry Goldwater, or Richard Nixon for president than for George McGovern, Edward Kennedy, or Hubert Humphrey—we would be justified in feeling we had discovered a connection between religion and politics. Certainly other factors are likely involved. And perhaps a third, key factor is ultimately responsible for at least some people being both religiously and politically conservative. Even then, however, we could say that some connection that seems to "make sense" exists between religious and political conservatism.

THE EFFECT OF RELIGION ON SOCIAL VALUES

One important area in which religious differences are observed to have differential influences is in the realm of *social values*—attitudes regarding human rights, political processes, international relations, and so on. In sum we are referring here to peoples' fundamental stances with respect to society and to the obligations, rights, privileges, and responsibilities of the members of that society, as well as of outsiders.

Some data from Lenski's study that we referred to in the last chapter show important differences in the social values of white Protestants, black Protestants, (white) Catholics, and Jews. Respondents in this study were asked whether the First Amendment guarantee of freedom of speech in the U.S. Constitution applies to criticizing the president, making speeches attacking religion, and making speeches in favor of fascism or communism. As the data in Table 5–1 show, among members of the four groups white Protestants are most likely to give a liberal interpretation of First Amendment guarantees, black Protestants the least likely. The average proportions reported in the last column of the table show

TABLE 5–1

Proportion of Middle-Class Detroiters Expressing Belief That Various Practices Are Protected by The Constitution, by Religious Affiliation of Respondents

	Criticism of President	Attacks on Religion	Fascist Speeches	Communist Speeches	N*	Mean
White Protestants	88%	65%	53%	46%	117	63%
Jews	89	53	47	37	19	57
White Catholics	77	52	43	34	92	52
Black Protestants	77	54	23	23	13	44

Source: Adapted from Gerhard E. Lenski, *The Religious Factor* (Garden City, N.Y.: Doubleday, 1961), p. 145.
  N = number of respondents.

this most clearly. Other studies, however, such as those by Samuel Stouffer, indicate that Jews are more liberal than Protestants in this respect.[1] Lenski's data may in fact be somewhat misleading in view of the small numbers of Jews and black Protestants in his sample. Nevertheless, it is safe to conclude that some differences exist among Protestants, Catholics, and Jews in terms of social values.

We have additional and more dramatic differences from Lenski's study in Table 5–2.

Note that Jews are relatively uncritical of all five forms of behavior listed, though more critical of gambling than Catholics and more critical of birth control than white Protestants. Protestants, both white and black, are more strongly opposed to gambling and drinking than either Catholics or Jews. And Catholics expressed greater opposition than did members of the other three groups to birth control, divorce, and conducting business on Sunday.

Two important summary observations need to be made here: (1) these data supply added evidence for differences in attitudes among religious groups; and (2) care must be exercised in making generalizations, bcause the specific issue being investigated becomes important. It would be fallacious for example, to conclude that Lenski's data demonstrate that Jews take the most liberal position on traditional moral issues, Protestants a moderate position, and Catholics the most conservative stance. The stance taken depends on the issue in question.

It should also be noted that Lenski's study, published in 1961, is

TABLE 5–2

Proportion of Middle-Class Detroiters Expressing the View That Various Practices Are Always or Usually Wrong from the Moral Standpoint, by Religious Affiliation of Respondents

	Gambling	Moderate Drinking	Birth Control	Divorce	Sunday Business	N
White Protestants	50%	21%	8%	34%	58%	117
White Catholics	17	10	63	66	63	92
Jews	32	5	21	11	17	19
Black Protestants	77	23	25	38	54	13

Source: Adapted from Lenski, The Religious Factor, p. 150.

[1]See, e.g., Samuel A. Stouffer, Communism, Conformity, and Civil Liberties (Garden City, N.Y.: Doubleday, 1955), p. 143.

TABLE 5–3

Clergymen Agreeing with the Statement, "The Government Is Providing Too Many Services That Should Be Left to Private Enterprise," by Denominational Affiliation and Theological Orientation

	Methodist	Episco-palian	Presby-terian	American Baptist	American Lutheran	Missouri Synod Lutheran
Fundamentalist	68%	*	76%	70%	75%	88%
Conservative	55	47%	56	62	62	63
Neoorthodox	32	34	24	33	40	25
Liberal	27	26	22	14	26	*

Source: Adapted from Jeffrey K. Hadden, The Gathering Storm in the Churches (Garden City, N.Y.: Doubleday, 1969), p. 79.
   *Number of cases too small to compute statistically reliable proportions.

based on data that were gathered in 1958 and thus are not necessarily representative today. Probably the biggest change would be in a reduction in the proportion of both Protestants and Catholics who morally disapprove of birth control (not including abortion). For example, Stokes found in 1968 that 74 percent of Catholics (compared with 96 percent of Protestants) approved of practicing some method of birth control, and 63 percent of Catholics admitted actually using a method unacceptable according to Catholic doctrine (compared with 95 percent of Protestants).[2] On the other hand, the 1969 Knudsen and Rich study of church members in Columbus, Ohio, included data on attitudes toward gambling and drinking that, though not strictly comparable to Lenski's 1958 data, suggest fairly high congruence with the latter.[3]

Using a large sample of clergymen (nearly seven thousand) Jeffrey Hadden found striking differences in attitudes on selected social issues according to both denominational affiliation and type of theological commitment or conviction. Tables 5–3 and 5–4 show these differences. The differences related to theological position are strikingly dramatic —in some denominations more than 50 percentage points separate the fundamentalist-oriented and liberal clergy. Differences by denominational affiliation of the clergymen are not so great, yet they too exist. For example, among the fundamentalists note the 20 percentage points differ-

[2]C. Shannon Stokes, "Religious Differentials in Reproductive Behavior," Sociological Analysis 33, no. 1 (1972): 30.
[3]Dean D. Knudsen and Pamela J. Rich, Religion and Modern Life: Beliefs and Practices of Church Members (Lafayette, Ind.: Institute for the Study of Social Change, Purdue University, 1971), pp. 41–42.

ence between Methodists and Missouri Synod Lutheran clergymen on the question of government services vs. free enterprise. (Table 5–3).

Such differences exist, it has been shown, not only among denominations but within what are often called denominational families. For example, Lawrence Kersten found that great differences exist among clergymen in the four major Lutheran groups in the United States— four groups which correspond somewhat closely in expressed theological position to the designations used by Hadden: fundamentalistic (Wisconsin Synod), conservative (Missouri Synod), neoorthodox (American Lutheran Church), and liberal (Lutheran Church in America). In Table 5–5 one again sees dramatic differences in social attitudes and orientation that are related to membership in a particular religious group. Religious factors are certainly not the only ones influencing these clergymen to espouse their positions. Yet it would seem much more than coincidence that the official statements, theological positions, and devotional writings of these groups closely match the expressed views of their representative clergymen.

Kersten has also researched the attitudes of laymen in the same four Lutheran groups and discovered that the dramatic differences among clergymen are here either reduced or disappear entirely as shown in Table 5–6 (which uses the same questions as in Table 5–5). Thus affiliation with religious groups of fairly different theological persuasion and emphasis does not seem to produce differences among lay members.

Using a different index, Glock, Ringer, and Babbie reached similar conclusions with respect to Episcopalian laymen. The authors used a composite measure of member involvement that included frequency of ritual

TABLE 5–4

Proportion of Clergymen Agreeing with the Statement, "Most People Who Live in Poverty Could Do Something About Their Situation if They Really Wanted To," by Denominational Affiliation and Theological Orientation

	Methodist	Episco-palian	Presby-terian	American Baptist	American Lutheran	Missouri Synod Lutheran
Fundamentalist	61%	*	53%	52%	51%	60%
Conservative	40	54%	26	39	37	36
Neoorthodox	22	16	12	17	19	14
Liberal	19	16	11	14	23	*

Source: Adapted from Hadden, The Gathering Storm, p. 80.
*Number of cases too small to compute statistically reliable proportions.

TABLE 5–5

Proportion of Clergymen Expressing Attitudes Favorable to Social Welfare, by Branch of Lutheranism

	LCA	ALC	MS	WS
1. Agree with statement, "The federal government ought to help provide medical care for all age groups."	56%	30%	31%	33%
2. Agree with statement, "I would be willing to pay more taxes so that low-income families could get low-rent public housing."	87	69	61	33
3. Disagree with statement, "The government is providing too many services that should be left to private enterprise."	54	39	23	7
4. Respond "Not enough" to question, "In connection with problems such as housing, unemployment, education, and so on, would you say that on the whole what the government is doing is too much, about the right amount, or not enough?"	64	42	28	0

Source: Adapted from Lawrence K. Kersten, *The Lutheran Ethic* (Detroit: Wayne State University Press, 1970), p. 63, by permission of Wayne State University Press.

Note: LCA = Lutheran Church in America; ALC = American Lutheran Church; MS = Missouri Synod; WS = Wisconsin Synod.

involvement (church attendance and Holy Communion participation), extent of organizational involvement (informal subgroups of church guilds and clubs), and intensity of intellectual involvement (measured by proportion of one's personal magazine reading that is church-related). They found that degree of involvement is not significantly related to the social points of view of Episcopalian parishioners.[4]

Such data certainly raise serious questions about how much impact religion has on people. We stated at the beginning of this chapter that religion does make a difference. We have now been looking at the area of social attitudes and find that although differences among denominations exist, they are modest. If we are focusing on members of a single denomination or denominational family, there seem to be no significant differences among laymen, although clergymen exhibit significant differences that are related to their theological position. Although we need data from additional denominations to add substantiation, our tentative conclusion at this point is that although religion makes a difference or has some effect on people's attitudes toward selected social issues, the differences are greatest among clergy, and then not so much by denomination as by relative theological conservatism/liberalism of the clergymen.

[4] Charles Y. Glock, Benjamin B. Ringer, and Earl R. Babbie, *To Comfort and to Challenge* (Berkeley: University of California Press, 1967), p. 165.

TABLE 5–6

Proportion of Laymen Expressing Attitudes Favorable to Social Welfare (Regarding the Statements in Table 5–5), by Branch of Lutheranism

	LCA	ALC	MS	WS
Statement 1 (agree)	47%	42%	44%	41%
Statement 2 (agree)	41	42	33	37
Statement 3 (disagree)	32	34	29	30
Statement 4 (responding "NOT ENOUGH")	31	33	29	25

Source: Adapted from Kersten, The Lutheran Ethic, p. 63, by permission of Wayne State University Press.
Note: LCA = Lutheran Church in America; ALC = American Lutheran Church; MS = Missouri Synod; WS = Wisconsin Synod.

Differences among laymen become evident only when groups representing considerably different theological positions and heritages are compared.

In short, religion has an effect on the social attitudes of representatives of particular religious groups. But the relationship and effect is not quite so great as some might suppose.

THE EFFECT OF RELIGION ON RACIAL ATTITUDES

A social phenomenon that has attracted much attention and research is that of race relations—in particular, the attitudes and behavior of whites toward blacks and the degree of support of whites for the civil rights movement that flowered in the 1960s. Some fairly dramatic differences in attitudes toward various aspects of the civil rights movement have been related to measures of religiosity and religious affiliation. Kenneth W. Eckhardt, for example, found that dramatic differences in white student support for civil rights were related to the students' religiosity (defined as degree of commitment to selected traditional religious beliefs and practices). Having established five categories of religiosity—"very religious," "somewhat religious," "moderately religious," "not very religious," and "not at all religious"—Eckhardt found that the proportions of students who militantly supported civil rights increased from 16 percent for those in the two categories of strongest religiosity to 36, 39, and 67 percent respectively for the moderately religious, those not very religious, and those not at all religious.[5]

[5]Kenneth W. Eckhardt, "Religiosity and Civil Rights Militancy," Review of Religious Research 11, no. 3 (1970); 199.

Hadden reports similar differences among Protestants, Catholics, and Jews with respect to civil rights issues. Only 33 percent of the Protestants and 43 percent of the Catholics in his sample agreed with the statement, "I am basically sympathetic with Northern ministers and students who have gone to the South to work for civil rights," while 70 percent of Jews expressed agreement.[6] Given the statement, "Martin Luther King, Jr., is an outstanding example of making Christianity relevant and meaningful for our day," 27 percent of Protestants, 30 percent of Catholics, and 59 percent of Jews expressed agreement.[7]

Lenski had earlier found parallel differences in his Detroit study, which revealed that 58 percent of Catholics would be disturbed or unhappy if a black with a comparable education and income moved into their neighborhood, and only slightly fewer Protestants (53 percent) would feel disturbed. Only 19 percent of Jews, however, would object.[8] In his summary comments, Lenski stated that approximately two-fifths of both white Catholics and Protestants gave answers which indicated a negative image of blacks, while only one-eighth of Jews did so.[9]

Differences in race relations attitudes among various Protestant denominations are reported by Glock and Stark, though the differences are not particularly great nor entirely consistent for denominations from one measure or question to another.[10] The group that particularly distinguishes itself in expressing attitudes apparently prejudicial toward blacks is the (white) Southern Baptists. The case for making a connection between religion and racial attitudes here is undoubtedly seriously jeopardized by the fact that a high proportion of Southern Baptists are residents of southern states. What is the principal influence on their racial attitudes: region or religion? Differences between Protestants as an inclusive category and Catholics are slight and inconsistent.

Among the four Lutheran groups, Kersten found no differences among lay members on a battery of five questions related to civil rights for blacks. However, there were significant differences among Lutheran clergymen on two questions. For example, the proportion of clergymen agreeing with the statement, "I basically disapprove of the Negro civil rights movement in America," were as follows: 11 percent for Lutheran Church in America (LCA), 4 percent for American Lutheran Church

---

[6]Jeffrey K. Hadden, *The Gathering Storm in the Churches* (Garden City, N.Y.: Doubleday, 1969), p. 139.
[7]Ibid., p. 137.
[8]Gerhard Lenski, *The Religious Factor* (Garden City, N.Y.: Doubleday, 1961), p. 65.
[9]Ibid., p. 66.
[10]Charles Y. Glock and Rodney Stark, *Christian Beliefs and Anti-Semitism* (New York: Harper & Row, 1966), p. 168.

(ALC), 20 percent for Missouri Synod, 39 percent for Wisconsin Synod.[11]

We can thus conclude that religion (religious affiliation) also makes a difference in whites' attitudes regarding blacks and the question of race relations in general. These differences tend to be most evident among broad religious categories such as Protestants, Catholics, and Jews, but decrease in magnitude and consistency when subgroups within the Protestant category are compared, except perhaps among clergymen. The latter suggestion, however, is little more than a guess except for Lutheran clergymen—the only ones for whom we have available relevant data.

THE EFFECT OF RELIGION ON ANTI-SEMITISM

Another closely related issue of social concern for which religious variables make a difference is the centuries-old issue of anti-Semitism. Glock and Stark's extensive study of the relationship between Christianity and anti-Semitism (from which we have already reported other data) presents evidence of a relationship between the denominational affiliation of respondents and certain negative reactions to Jews. Although we may question the validity of some of the questions they used to measure anti-Semitism, Glock and Stark's overall conclusion—that anti-Semitism varies by denomination—appears to be supported. For example, they found that whereas 26 percent of Congregationalists, Methodists, and Catholics could be classed as non-anti-Semites, only 5 percent of Southern Baptists, 8 percent of sect members, and 13 percent of American Baptists could be so exonerated.[12] At the opposite pole, 26 percent of sect members, 24 percent of Southern Baptists, and 23 percent of Missouri Synod Lutherans were classified as "high" on the anti-Semitic scale, while only 7 percent of Congregationalists, 9 percent of Methodists, and 11 percent of Catholics were so categorized.[13]

Kersten found that laymen of the four branches of Lutheranism do not differ in terms of anti-Semitism (approximately a third in each of the four groups scored "high" on his index), but that Lutheran clergymen in the four groups vary significantly. For example, only 10 percent of LCA and 8 percent of ALC clergymen evidenced high anti-Semitism, but 26 percent of Missouri Synod and 31 percent of Wisconsin Synod clergymen scored high.[14] It should be noted that although differences are

[11]Lawrence K. Kersten, *The Lutheran Ethic* (Detroit: Wayne State University Press, 1970), p. 72.
[12]Glock and Stark, *Christian Beliefs and Anti-Semitism*, p. 129.
[13]Ibid., p. 129.
[14]Kersten, *The Lutheran Ethic*, p. 79.

greater among the clergy than among the laymen, Lutheran clergymen as a whole are less likely to be anti-Semitic than their lay counterparts.

Although it is somewhat tangential to the focus of this book, we do need to mention that the issue of anti-Semitism is a complex one that demands a high level of research ingenuity. This is so in great part because Jewishness is a phenomenon that exists on several levels. There is ethnic Jewishness, which is evidenced as the attempt among Jews to maintain not only continuity with their long and rich heritage but also a measure of present distinctiveness that comes through preserved customs, endogamy, intragroup economic assistance, contiguous residence, and the like—all of which may be quite apart from religious concerns or motivation. This can be called the secular Jewish pattern, which may well be a prime focus of the anti-Semetic feelings of some non-Jews who resent the economic and occupational success of many Jews and Jews' practice of protecting their own, which Jews regard as a moral commandment but anti-Semites perhaps view as exclusivity.

There is also what we might call nationalistic Jewishness, which many Jews express as sympathy (even identity) with the state of Israel, some longing to return to the ancient homeland, some granting financial or at least moral support. Some non-Jews construe such orientations as divided loyalty and conclude that Jews cannot be trusted wholeheartedly and unquestioningly to support the government of the United States (or of any other nation of which Jews are citizens). Such sentiments and conclusions also are expressions of anti-Semitism.

A third manifestation of Jewishness is that of religious identification. (Most Jews maintain some sense of identification with religious Judaism in one of its three contemporary forms—Orthodox, Conservative, and Reform.) It is in this area that much of what is called anti-Semitism occurs. But it is precisely here that the sources become difficult to sort out. That is, a conservative Protestant Christian who believes that a personal faith in Jesus Christ is necessary for eternal life will also believe that Jews must renounce their religion if they are to be forgiven the sins that they and all people are guilty of. That is, he believes that Jews must be converted to Christianity—no less than Buddhists, Muslims, Hindus, Unitarians, Mormons, and perhaps even Catholics. Such a belief then becomes construed as a type of anti-Semitism, yet is undoubtedly different from anti-Semitism that is in reaction to Jews in a political, economic, or social sense.

Very likely all types of anti-Semitism are related in various ways, yet also distinct in other ways. The importance of the purely religious or theological factor here is maintained by Melvin Tumin in his appraisal of research on American anti-Semitism. He points out that religious dif-

ferences such as those between Jews and conservative Protestants tend
to assume great importance and salience unless they are somehow consciously prevented from doing so. This is to be expected if we realize
that for many people, religious differences represent fundamental differences in values and points of view.[15]

THE EFFECT OF RELIGION ON MARRIAGE AND THE FAMILY

Another area of human behavior in which research has documented differences related to religious influence is that of marriage and the family.
Perhaps the greatest amount of popular attention in this regard has been
focused on attitudes regarding family size and birth control. Among the
major religions in the United States, Catholics traditionally have been
known to have the largest families, Protestants the next largest, and Jews
the smallest. And among the three groups Catholics have been the least
likely to favor or use birth control techniques—except the "rhythm"
method sanctioned by the Catholic hierarchy. Research clearly documents
such differences in the past. Notestein found in the 1930s that at each
class level Catholics had larger families than Protestants.[16] A study in
Indianapolis found that the Catholic birthrate was 25 percent greater
than the Protestant rate and that Jews had the lowest birthrate of all,
18 percent below the Protestant rate.[17] More recently Freedman, Whelpton, and Smit reported that although there has been some exaggeration
of fertility differences among the three major religious groups and that
from some points of view the similarities are more striking than the differences, Catholic families are nonetheless larger than Protestant families,
and both are larger than Jewish families.[18]

There is evidence, however, that historic differences, particularly
between Catholics and Protestants, are evening out. Freedman, Whelpton, and Campbell's 1959 study reported that Catholic wives had given
birth to almost exactly the same number of children as had Protestant
wives.[19] This finding is slightly misleading in that Catholic women

[15]Melvin M. Tumin, An Inventory and Appraisal of Research on Anti-Semitism
(New York: Freedom Books, 1961), p. 144.
[16]Frank W. Notestein, "Class Differences in Fertility," Annals of the American
Academy of Political and Social Science, Nov. 1936, p. 33.
[17]P. K. Whelpton and C. V. Kiser, "Social and Psychological Factors Affecting
Fertility," in The Household Survey in Indianapolis (New York: Millbank Memorial Fund, 1946), 1: 6–8.
[18]Ronald Freedman, Pascal K. Whelpton, and John W. Smit, "Socio-Economic
Factors in Religious Differentials in Fertility," American Sociological Review 26,
no. 4 (1961): 614.
[19]Ronald Freedman, Pascal K. Whelpton, and Angus Campbell, Family Planning, Sterility, and Population Growth (New York: McGraw-Hill, 1959), pp. 278–
79.

marry on the average of one-and-a-half years later than do Protestant women, thus shortening their childbearing potential. This means that if Catholic and Protestant women who married at the same age are compared, then Catholic women are found to be slightly more fertile. Thus religion continued to have some slight effect on fertility, even though the net effect, because of other factors such as age at marriage, was one of no great difference in family size between Protestants and Catholics.

Paul Glick's study of U.S. Census Bureau data for 1957 supports this observation. Glick concluded that the fertility rate for Catholic married women of childbearing age throughout the United States was on the average not significantly different from Protestant married women of the same age categories.[20] This is so even though urban Catholic women have higher fertility rates than urban Protestant women. The fact that a higher proportion of Protestant women are rural residents who register higher fertility rates generally tends to counterbalance the higher fertility rate for urban Catholic women. Glick also found that the fertility rate for Jewish women was only about three-fourths as large as that for Protestants and Catholics. Even taking into account the high proportion of Jewish women who are city dwellers, their fertility rate is still 14 percent below that of Protestant and Catholic urban women.[21]

In short, fertility rates among the major religious groups in the United States appear to be converging, with the possible exception that the Jewish rate continues to be lower than the two other groups. Undoubtedly contributing to this convergence are developments in a directly related aspect of marriage and family interaction—namely, attitudes and practices regarding birth control. It is now clear from both indirect and direct evidence that even a majority of Catholics occasionally if not regularly use "artificial" means to prevent pregnancy.

Another feature of marriage and the family is that many American marriages become dissolved. Does religious affiliation or commitment make a difference so far as marital stability or dissolution are concerned? Yes, but again differences are small. From a composite of several studies involving over twenty-four thousand cases, Salisbury in 1967 reported divorce rates of 5 percent for both Catholics and Jews and 8 percent for Protestants. These compare with 18 percent for persons with no religious preference.[22] Apparently religion "makes a difference"—not so much from one religious group to another as in terms of members of religious

---

[20]Paul G. Glick, "Intermarriage and Fertility Patterns Among Persons in Major Religious Groups," *Eugenics Quarterly* 7, no. 1 (1960); 36–37.
[21]Ibid., p. 37.
[22]W. Seward Salisbury, *Religion in American Culture* (Homewood, Ill.: Dorsey Press, 1964), p. 424.

groups versus nonmembers. More recent research seems to confirm the earlier research reported above. Christiansen and Barber found in Indiana that after four years of marriage (analysis conducted in 1964 on 1960 marriages) that the divorce rate was only slightly higher for Protestants than for Catholics.[23] Burchinal and Chancellor made similar observations but added that the differences between homogamous (both partners of the same religion affiliation) Catholic and homogamous Protestant marriages so far as survival is concerned "cannot be considered as representing important differences."[24]

THE EFECT OF RELIGION ON RELIGIOUS VALUES

Another area we wish to examine in demonstrating the existence of and, in a limited way, the diversity of ways that religion affects the behavior and attitudes of people is what we might call religious values. In a sense we shall be describing differences among religious groups on religious issues. That is, we intend to demonstrate differences in the commitments, beliefs, and attitudes of members of various religious groups and show that a knowledge of peoples' religious affiliation enables us to make some fairly reliable predictions of how they differ from others.

For example, in the responses to a question regarding belief in God —which Christians until quite recently would probably have considered impertinent—we find considerable variation among Christian groups today, as demonstrated by the data gathered by Glock and Stark reported in Table 5–7. One of course cannot with complete satisfaction determine whether the religious group with its theology, preaching, and teaching is solely responsible for producing these differences. For example, perhaps the factor of self-selection entered in—in the sense that persons who do not accept traditional beliefs may affiliate themselves with groups congenial to their philosophy. But at least one can observe significant differences among the members of various denominations. That is although religious affiliation and exposure to the teachings of a particular denomination may not have made all the difference, religious affiliation tells us something about the affiliates and shows differences among them.

How important religion is to people is another dimension on which people vary. In fact, this variable has been used as a measure of the

[23]Harold Christiansen and Kenneth E. Barber, "Interfaith Versus Intrafaith Marriage in Indiana," *Journal of Marriage and Family Living* 29, no. 3 (1967), 467.
[24]Lee B. Burchinal and Loren E. Chancellor, "Survival Rates Among Religiously Homogamous and Interreligious Marriages," *Social Forces* 41, no. 4 (1963); 361.

TABLE 5–7

Proportion of People Accepting the Statement, "I know God Really Exists and I Have No Doubt About It," by Denominational Affiliation

Congregational	41%	American Baptist	78%
Methodist	60	Missouri Lutheran	81
Episcopalian	63	Southern Baptist	99
Disciples of Christ	76	Sects	96
Presbyterian	75	Total Protestant	71
American Lutheran	73	Roman Catholic	81

Source: Adapted from Rodney Stark and Charles Y. Glock, American Piety: The Nature of Religious Commitment (Berkeley: University of California Press, 1968), table 2, p. 28.

religiosity of people. That is, almost by definition those who say religion is of little or no importance to them are evidencing a low level of religiosity or commitment to what we understand religion to be. In data gathered by the author from a representative sample of American adults aged eighteen and over in 1970, we find some variation in the degree of importance people attach to religion, although the clear tendency within all religious groups in this country is for a majority of people to speak of religion as "very important" to them personally. Baptists, members of small denominations and sects, and Catholics are more likely than other major Protestant denominations and Jews to say that religion is very important to them (78.4 percent of Baptists, 79.5 percent of sects, and 70.1 percent of Catholics, compared with e.g., 56.3 percent of Episcopalians and 56.7 percent of Presbyterians).[25]

Catholics far outdistance members of other groups in church attendance, 62.5 percent attending weekly or nearly that often, while only 8.3 percent of Jews and 42.1 percent of Protestants attend that often. There are differences among Protestants, too, though not so great as the differences among the major groupings of Protestants, Catholics, and Jews. Among Protestants who report attending religious services weekly or nearly every week the range is from 53.8 percent for members of sects and small Protestant denominations to a low of 34.4 percent for Episcopalians.[26]

Another measure of differences among religious groups is Stark and Glock's "ethicalism index," which attempts to differentiate among respondents in terms of the degree of importance they attach to the necessity of "doing good for others" and "loving thy neighbor" for gaining

[25]Survey conducted by the National Opinion Research Center for the Lutheran Council in the U.S.A., 1970.
[26]Ibid.

salvation. Respondents could view one or both items as "absolutely necessary," as of "probable help," or of "no effect." Table 5–8 shows the differences by denomination on this index. Note particularly the column headed "Low (those seeing neither—or at most one—of the ingredients in the index as affecting one's salvation). All groups except the Lutherans and Baptists are extremely unlikely to reject these items. That is, with the exception of Baptists and Lutherans, all groups are very likely to score medium or high on the "ethicalism index"—to view ethical actions as important for salvation. Baptists and Lutherans are more likely than the others to reject the necessity of such behaviors (as high as 40 percent of the Southern Baptists). The Lutherans and Baptists are of course reflecting a theological emphasis on "grace alone," "Christ alone" as the criterion for salvation. It is interesting to speculate as an application of these data whether Baptists and Lutherans are in fact less likely than members of the other religious groups to "do good for others" and "love their neighbors." The data do not provide an answer.

Complementing the above measure is the "particularism index," devised by the same authors, which includes two questions designed to measure the degree to which persons believe that only people who believe in Jesus can be saved and who identify Christians as God's chosen people today. Overall, a total of 64 percent of Protestants think a person who does not accept Jesus cannot be saved, while only 29 percent of Catholics feel the same way. More Protestants than Catholics (although both in lower proportions) think of Christians as God's chosen people today (35

TABLE 5–8
Distribution of Church Members on the "Ethicalism Index"

	High	Medium	Low
Congregational	52%	42%	6%
Methodist	51	45	4
Episcopalian	51	45	4
Disciples of Christ	60	40	0
Presbyterian	43	46	11
American Lutheran	41	43	16
American Baptist	43	41	16
Missouri Lutheran	37	41	22
Southern Baptist	33	27	40
Sects	61	32	7
Mean of All Protestant Groups	48	42	10
Roman Catholic	53	45	2

Source: Adapted from Stark and Glock, *American Piety*, p. 72.

TABLE 5-9

Achieved Factors in Worldly Success, by Religious Group (Whites Only)

	$2000 or More Median Income	Self- Employed	In High- Status Occupation	Median School Year Completed	In 3 or More Formal Groups
Catholic	27%	7%	19%	10.0	14%
Episcopalian	35	9	42	12.5	42
Lutheran	30	6	28	12.2	17
Calvinist	35	11	37	12.5	21
Methodist	32	8	27	12.3	23
Baptist	21	6	15	9.8	8
Small sects	16	11	17	9.5	9
No denomination	29	11	26	12.0	17
Semi-Christian	24	15	39	12.4	19
Jewish	42	41	62	12.5	45
Eastern Orthodox	35	15	13	9.3	8
No preference	23	9	28	10.0	7

Source: Adapted from Albert J. Mayer and Harry Sharp, "Religious Preference and Worldly Success," *American Sociological Review* 27, no. 2 (1962): 224.

percent versus 21 percent respectively).[27] Dramatic differences are evident even among Protestants when the "particularism index" is used: 56 percent of sect members and 51 percent of Southern Baptists scored high, while only 29 percent of United Presbyterians and 23 percent of Congregationalists did so. As might be expected, no Unitarians score high.[28]

Dramatic differences among denominations have been observed in terms of what Mayer and Sharp call "worldly success." As Table 5-9 shows, Jews and Episcopalians clearly outdistance other groups such as Baptists, small sects, and Catholics in terms of income, occupational status, and extent of formal education. If we compare only Protestants and Catholics, however, such differences decrease considerably. In fact, Glenn and Hyland report that on many measures Catholics surpassed Protestants in "worldly success."[29] It must be observed too that the reason for differential success in the past was not so much religious ideology as the more recent immigrant status of Catholics and the "circu-

[27]Rodney Stark and Charles Y. Glock, *American Piety: The Nature of Religious Commitment* (Berkeley: University of California Press, 1968), pp. 66, 68.
[28]Ibid., p. 68.
[29]Norval D. Glenn and Ruth Hyland, "Religious Preference and Worldly Success: Some Evidence from National Surveys," *American Sociological Review* 32, no. 1 (1967): 73–85.

lation of WASP elites" which severely limited economic opportunities for those who were not white Anglo-Saxon Protestants.

THE EFFECT OF RELIGION ON POLITICAL PARTY AFFILIATION

The popularly held view that members of different religious groups tend to prefer one or the other major political party has in fact been documented in recent nationally representative data gathered by the author. Only among Jews (66.7 percent), Baptists (63.1 percent), and Catholics (54.6 percent) do a majority of members indicate Democratic party preference. By way of contrast, 25 percent of Episcopalians, 26.9 percent of Presbyterians, and 31.7 percent of Lutherans identify with the Democratic party.[30] Again, these differences cannot be attributed solely to religion. As we observed in the preceding section, there are characteristic differences among religious groups in economic, occupational, and educational terms. These variables and a host of others affect political views and political party identity. Yet the differences due to religious affiliation remain regardless of other influences.

That is the point of this chapter: religion makes *some* difference with regard to attitudes and behavior. Certainly not all the difference in the world. But some. That is, religion qualifies as a sociological variable that must be taken into account in order to understand and explain differences in people's attitudes and behavior. Yet we also observe from data in this chapter that assessing the impact of religion is complicated by the presence of other influential factors.

[30]National Opinion Research Center survey (see footnote 25).

6

Becoming Religious

We now turn to the process by which people become religious and learn to express religious convictions and perspectives. This refers implicitly first of all to the fundamental social process called socialization. Thus we are working with the simple but basic observation that religion is a group phenomenon and that a member of a religious group is either born into it or joins it at some later stage in the life cycle; in either case he is taught the norms of the group. In this process the group socializes (it teaches and trains), and the individual internalizes the norms (he learns). Throughout this chapter we shall move back and forth between these two foci of the socialization or learning process.

ELEMENTS IN RELIGIOUS SOCIALIZATION

We begin with the group and the desire to socialize new members. That is, the group desires to bring a person (a member) into a committed, functional relationship with other members of the group so that the new member knows what the group stands for, can fill a role within the group, and can further the aims of the group and help it reach its goals. Some of this process is nonstructured and occurs through informal contacts and interactions with other members; much of it is structured and formal, channeled through educational agencies and processes.

77

In "primitive" societies (that is, preliterate and/or prehistoric societies usually with a hunting and gathering economy), religious socialization, as with nearly all socialization, is primarily informal. The child gradually learns the beliefs and understandings of the group through conversation and by hearing his elders recount the sagas and tales passed down through the generations. In a similar manner, the child learns practices associated with and growing out of religious beliefs. As indicated in Chapter 3, religious socialization is seldom distinguishable from general socialization in "primitive" societies, inasmuch as their members seldom distinguish the religious from other spheres of thought or knowledge.

There is nevertheless some degree of organization and planning in the socialization of "primitive" religion. For example, Wallace distinguishes two forms, in addition to individual expression, in which "primitive" religion is manifested: the shamanic and the communal. A shaman (such as a witch doctor or medicine man) is one who is believed to possess greater access to and control over mana and who performs service rituals for people. Obviously, viewing shamanic activity is a learning experience for the neophyte. Similarly with the communal form of religious expression, conducted both by natural subcommunities (such as nuclear families, larger kinship groups, and affinity groups such as those determined by age or sex) and by the total community acting in concert, there are rites of passage from one stage in the life cycle to another (such as puberty rites), for example, or tribal totem celebrations in which everyone gathers around the symbol or symbols of their common origin and loyalty in order to reaffirm their unity as well as their common past.[1] Certainly a great deal of socialization and learning take place at all these levels of "primitive" religion.

Although informal socialization still exists and remains influential in agrarian and industrial societies, with the greater specialization of roles and differentiation of activities religious socialization becomes more formalized. Religious teachers deliberately teach neophytes specifically religious norms, and formalized religious ceremonies are conducted during which neophytes learn about religious activities and gradually begin to participate in them.

The socializing or educative intent of religious groups is summarized in a classic manner by Jesus: "Go therefore and make disciples of all nations, ... *teaching* them to observe all things whatsoever I have commanded you."[2] This refers to socialization pure and simple: transmitting

---

[1]Anthony F. C. Wallace, *Religion: An Anthropological View* (New York: Random House, 1966), pp. 86–91.

[2]Matthew 28:19–20 (Revised Standard Version). Emphasis added.

knowledge as well as training in appropriate activities. Most religious groups view this process as a lifelong one. Worship services in the Western tradition are in significant part of a socializing nature, extending or expanding on what is already known. A sermon, for example, expounds and explains, not simply exhorts and directs. The various communal ceremonies of most religious groups, in fact, are fundamentally socializing experiences: in addition to recognizing the deity through giving praise and thanksgiving and performing rituals believed to please the god or gods, joint activities perform a reinforcement function, reminding participants of their beliefs and of how they are to conduct themselves before the deity.

Worship services and ceremonial gatherings may also bring about the conversion or full commitment of newcomers, another aspect of socialization. When a person hears something or learns something that moves him to attach himself to the group, socialization has begun; now formal educational processes take over. The person's commitment is also reinforced through new informal socialization contacts.

Thus several things are involved in religious socialization. First the group convinces the newcomer to make a commitment to the group and what it stands for, often on the basis of very little knowledge or contact. (By newcomer we mean either a potential convert or the child of a group member.) Second, there is the core process of building on that commitment through teaching the newcomer the norms of the group—its beliefs and appropriate behaviors and rituals. (Note that these stages are interchangeable—that is, a person may be involved in the process of learning norms for some time before being converted or committing himself.) Third, the group tries to extend its influence over the person to those situations where he is not in direct contact with the group or its members. That is, the group tries to influence *all* the individual's values; this is essentially the morality dimension that many suggest is an integral feature of religion. Finally, there is the reinforcement and encouragement aspect of continuing socialization. One reason religious groups encourage their members to continue participating in ceremonies, attending education classes, and listening to sermons after having learned the "basics" of the religion is to "strengthen" and reinforce the members' commitment.

METHODS OF RELIGIOUS SOCIALIZATION ∕

Formal Methods

We have already touched on the socialization methods of religious groups. At this point we need merely to systematize them. There is first the formal mechanism that most religious groups establish—in a strict sense of the term, the educational system. All groups establish explicit teaching activities, which may take the form of a guru gathering a few persons around him, an evangelist on a tree stump or a soapbox, a Bar Mitzvah preparatory class, or a Sunday sermon. The teaching function has been an integral and important part of religion from the beginning. Certainly the founder of any religion or religious group teaches as he tries to get across his message and vision. Once established, the religious group uses diverse methods, both formal and informal, to get across its ideas and the body of its knowledge, beliefs, and practices to the neophyte member. The effectiveness of such socialization is a major topic of this chapter and is discussed at several points in the chapters that follow.

Informal Methods

Another way in which socialization takes place is informally—through interaction with the members of a religious group. Such socialization or learning from others occurs in all kinds of groups, of course. The general socialization of children into the society that occurs through interaction with peers, for example, is of primary importance and well documented. And it is popular knowledge that what you learn from associates in a work group through casual conversation is at least as important—if not more so—than the socialization that occurs through participating in formal orientation programs or by studying job descriptions.

Interestingly, many religious groups recognize the importance of informal socialization and consequently often deliberately encourage it. A term frequently used by religious groups in this connection is *fellowship*: members of religious groups are encouraged "to fellowship" with fellow members. Such formal mechanisms as religious youth groups, men's clubs, ladies' auxiliaries, and senior citizens groups are organized in great part with the hope and expectation that members of the larger organization—for example, the congregation—will develop friendships and maintain ties outside formal religious contexts. What is involved here is recognition of the importance of reinforcement: through continued and frequent contact with others of your religious group, the formal norms and beliefs you have been taught and have accepted will be reinforced and, as it's often expressed, "your faith will be strengthened."

Considerable empirical evidence has been gathered that tends to support this strategy, though it is difficult to determine which is cause and which effect—whether such contact strengthens one's faith, or whether those of strong faith seek out fellowship in the first place. Thus studies have shown that the person whose close personal friends are mainly members of his religious group tends to be more orthodox in his beliefs, a more regular participant in religious ceremonies, and a heavier contributor of time and money to his religious organization. Glock and Stark, for example, constructed an index of "religious experience," based on whether respondents were certain of having "a feeling [of being] somehow in the presence of God," "a sense of being saved in Christ," and " a feeling of being punished by God for something you had done." Almost invariably, regardless of Christian denomination, respondents with a greater number of best friends also members of their congregation scored higher on this index.[3]

An intensive extension of the fellowship mechanism for religious socialization occurs through marriage. Religious groups urge endogamy—i.e., marriage within the group—assuming (rightly) that a marriage between two persons from the same religious group will encourage both persons to participate and remain with the group. Intermarriage with a person of another religious group introduces the risk of losing your member to the other group, and may reduce the level of participation and commitment of your member even if he or she does not defect. There is of course the possibility of gaining a new member through intermarriage of one of your members with an outsider. Some groups in fact appear to be net gainers through this process. Yet few groups wish to advocate such an approach because of the risks involved. Thus religious groups have traditionally forbidden (or all but forbidden) interfaith marriage. Until very recently Roman Catholics, for example, could not be married by a priest in church if the non-Catholic partner refused to join the Catholic Church or would not sign a statement agreeing that any children born of the marriage would be socialized as Catholics. Many Orthodox Jewish families ostracize children who marry Gentiles. In the face of high rates of interfaith marriage, most groups have been relenting on this issue, although the official stance of discouraging interfaith marriage remains.

THE EFFECTIVENESS OF RELIGIOUS SOCIALIZATION

The Impact of Attendance at Worship Services

We now turn to the question of the impact or effectiveness of mechanisms, primarily the formal ones, that religious groups use to socialize their members. One major subject of sociological investigation has been the impact within Western industrial societies of the formal instruction and inspiration that takes place in the regular religious cere-

---

[3]Charles Y. Glock and Rodney Stark, *Religion and Society in Tension* (Chicago: Rand McNally, 1965), p. 164.

mony—the classic example being the weekly (Sunday or Saturday morning) worship service. Many studies have focused on differences among the regular attenders at such services, on the one hand, and less regular attenders, infrequent attenders, and nonattenders on the other. We had occasion to refer to such studies in Chapter 4 as we looked at attempts by sociologists to define and measure religiosity. Here we are interested in the same or similar data from another perspective. That is, if effective socialization in fact takes place in formal religious services, then we should find differences along a continuum of attendance at (or at least exposure to) such services. Specifically, we would expect to find evidence of greater knowledge, firmer belief, stauncher commitment, and a greater sense of morality among those more often exposed.

Before attempting to validate this hypothesis it should be pointed out that in the United States there is considerable religious illiteracy even among members of religious groups. Schroeder and Obenhaus, for example, reach pessimistic conclusions about the level of biblical knowledge and of cognitive understanding of the Christian faith in Corn City (the fictitious name of a real town in Iowa). They note that of the town's church members who are of above-average intellectual ability and reasonably strongly committed to and involved in church life ("nuclear" and "modal" members) less than half were able to relate a reasonably accurate version of the story of the good Samaritan.[4]

In my own study of Lutheran young people, only 8.7 percent of those sampled who attended church services regularly and also attended a parochial school could correctly identify Nathanael as one of Jesus' disciples, and only 25 percent correctly identified Enoch as the Old Testament character who is described as never experiencing physical death.[5]

In a nationwide survey of adults in the United States conducted in 1970, only 15 percent correctly identified five prominent biblical figures (Moses, Daniel, Jonah, Peter, Paul). In fact, a greater number of respondents (17.5 percent) were unable to identify even a single figure, and less than half (46.4 percent) were able to identify at least three.[6]

These and similar studies indicate that such a high rate of religious illiteracy exists among even regular church members that we should not expect the impact of regular participation in formal religious activities on behavior to be particularly dramatic. If concepts and knowledge do

[4]W. W. Schroeder and Victor Obenhaus, *Religion in American Culture* (New York: Free Press, 1964), p. 117.

[5]Ronald L. Johnstone, *The Effectiveness of Lutheran Elementary and Secondary Schools as Agencies of Christian Education* (St. Louis: Concordia Seminary Research Center, 1966), p. 100.

[6]Ronald L. Johnstone (project director), national survey data gathered by the National Opinion Research Center for the Lutheran Council in the U.S.A., 1970.

not "sink in," then we can hardly expect them to exert much measurable influence.

With this caution in mind, we can proceed to examine how exposure to the religious group and its teachings influences beliefs and behavior. The data in Table 6–1 indicate some fairly clear and consistent correlations between frequency of church attendance and likelihood of (1) accepting certain traditional conservative Christian beliefs, and (2) exhibiting superior biblical biographical knowledge. Keep in mind, of course, that these are correlations and not necessarily cause-and-effect re-

TABLE 6–1

Percentage of Church Members Agreeing with Selected Biblical Doctrines and Evidencing Knowledge of Biblical Biography, by Frequency of Church Attendance

	Frequency of Church Attendance			
	Weekly or nearly so	*About once a month*	*Seldom*	*Never*
"The Devil actually exists and is an active and evil influence in the world."				
Definitely agree‡	65%†	48%	39%	38%
Definitely disagree	12	16	28	27
"Jesus will actually return to the earth someday and the world will be destroyed after he has separated the believers from the nonbelievers."				
Definitely agree‡	58	48	39	39
Definitely disagree	11	15	22	31
"A child is already sinful when it is born."				
Definitely agree‡	37	19	12	18
Definitely disagree	44	60	72	72
"The real purpose of religion should be to help people with their problems and needs rather than help them to get to heaven."				
Definitely agree	26	44	40	45
Definitely disagree‡	27	17	17	14
"He was in a lion's den."				
Correctly identifies Daniel	66	57	51	53

TABLE 6–1 (continued)

	Frequency of Church Attendance			
	Weekly or nearly so	About once a month	Seldom	Never
"A voice spoke to him from a burning bush."				
Correctly identifies Moses	48	36	33	26
"He was swallowed by a great fish or whale."				
Correctly identifies Jonah	73	62	65	57
"He is the disciple who denied Jesus three times."				
Correctly identifies Peter	41	34	25	19
"He wrote many letters or epistles That are in the New Testament."				
Correctly identifies Paul	46	21	18	18
Total N*	652	273	394	74

*Excluded from the total sample of 1490 persons are the 96 (6.4 percent) who reported no religious membership or preference.

†Note that only the "definitely agree" and "definitely disagree" responses are reported. This explains the facts that percentages listed do not total 100 percent and differ in totals from one question to another.

‡The responses marked with a double dagger (‡) are those generally considered the more orthodox or traditional responses to the question. It should be noted, however, that there is definite disagreement among various traditions within Christianity on the third and fourth questions, and between Christians and Jews on all four questions.

Source: Ronald L. Johnstone (project director), national survey data gathered by the National Opinion Research Center for the Lutheran Council in the U.S.A., 1970.

lationships. Many other factors besides church attendance affect religious beliefs and knowledge. Also, it is even possible that holding certain traditional beliefs is part of what makes people attend church regularly. Further, there is no control in these data for respondent relative liberalism or denominational affiliation: religious liberals are combined here with conservatives, Protestants with Catholics. Nonetheless, the evident correlation between frequency of church attendance and conservative beliefs connotes at least some influence of the former on the latter.

If we single out for study two generally conservative denominations (Baptists and Lutherans), the relationships observed in Table 6–1 become more dramatic and lend greater support to our hypothesis—that is, the data (see Table 6–2) show higher correlations between church attendance (in this case, at relatively conservative churches) and conservative doctrinal views. Table 6–2's data clearly show that the more frequent a respondent's church attendance (at a conservative church), the more likely he is to give conservative doctrinal responses and the greater is likely to be his biblical knowledge. Three additional observations can be made by comparing or combining data in the two tables: (1) The conservative subsample of Baptists plus Lutherans (of Table 6–2) is both more doctrinally conservative and more biblically knowledgeable than the total sample (of Table 6–1). (2) Respondents, regardless of theological orientation or frequency of church attendance, are more familiar with the Old Testament characters than with the New Testament characters. (3) The differences between those who seldom and those who never attend church are small (and in fact the "nevers" are even more likely than the "seldoms" to expect the return of Jesus and to believe that a child is born sinful). Probably one should not expect large differences between two categories of church members both of whom evidence low involvement. Further, the number of those making up the category of members who never attend

TABLE 6–2

Baptists and Lutherans Agreeing with Selected Orthodox Christian Doctrines and Evidencing Knowledge of Biblical Biography, by Frequency of Church Attendance

	Frequency of Church Attendance			
	Weekly or nearly so	About once a month	Seldom	Never
Definitely agree that the Devil exists and is active in the world	82%	62%	52%	48%
Definitely agree that Jesus will return to earth someday	80	60	50	57
Definitely agree that a child is already sinful at birth	53	26	11	24
Definitely disagree that the purpose of religion is to help people with problems not help them get to heaven.	16	35	39	43
Correctly identifies Daniel	76	64	53	52
Correctly identifies Moses	51	35	31	29
Correctly identifies Jonah	77	62	65	62
Correctly identifies Peter	59	39	24	14
Correctly identifies Paul	52	21	16	14
Total N	189	117	124	21

Source: Ronald L. Johnstone (project director), national survey data gathered by the National Opinion Research Center for the Lutheran Council in the U.S.A., 1970.

conservative churches (Table 6–2) is quite small, and therefore conclusions based on percentages in that category tend to be less reliable than otherwise.

The Impact of Parochial Schools

One primary socializing agent for several religious groups which has attracted considerable research and journalistic attention in recent years is the parochial school: elementary, secondary, and college. Historically these schools illustrate the full-blown socializing intent of religious groups more fully than any other agency or mechanism. Not only is there usually daily formal instruction in religious beliefs and ritual (especially in elementary parochial schools), but there are over thirty hours a week (i.e., school time) of "fellowship" with members of one's religious group. Also, the system increases the likelihood of marrying within the religious group, particularly if it's a parochial high school or college under discussion. Religious groups have established such schools with very specific intentions of preserving pure doctrine, encouraging maximum participation in religious activities, improving religious character, developing a rich devotional life, and particularly for Jewish schools, preserving a traditional lifestyle.

The question is then, how effective are parochial schools? That they aid in the religious socialization process is clear, though the success is not unequivocal. Three relatively recent studies bear on the subject: one on Catholic education (Greeley and Rossi), one on Lutheran parochial school education (Johnstone), and one on fundamentalist schools (Erickson). Each study is replete with data and observations, but we shall make only a few comments based on their findings as they relate to our concern in this chapter with religious socialization.

The Greeley-Rossi study found that education in Catholic schools had a measurable impact on those who experienced it. In general, the greater the number of years a person attended a Catholic school (including elementary, secondary, and college levels) the higher his religious performance and knowledge of doctrine. However, it was also noted that the most significant positive correlation between religious education and religious behavior was among those who had devout parents and later married a devout Catholic mate. The authors' comment on these findings emphasizes such reinforcement:

> *Something of a pattern begins to emerge: Religious education does indeed have an impact on the adult lives of its students, but only when the social context of childhood or adulthood supports and emphasizes the values*

learned in the school. Religious education apparently works when there is constant reinforcement from outside the school.[7]

In my study of Lutheran adolescents, the data concerning proportion of total education in Lutheran parochial schools lead one to conclude that parochial school education had a significant impact on doctrinal knowledge, biblical knowledge, and religious activities. However, many (though not all) differences apparently related to parochial schooling wash out if we apply a control variable for type of family background the student had experienced—that is, if we take into account how much family and home reinforcement there is for religious values and practices. If the family was what we termed an "ideal" or "nuclear" Lutheran family or even (in most cases) an "average" or "modal" Lutheran family, the parochial school training did not seem to add significantly to what a student brought with him from home so far as measures of religiosity are concerned. The parochial school education of those from "marginal" Lutheran families, on the other hand, produced marked results, in the sense of significantly increased levels of religious knowledge and participation in religious activities.[8]

Erickson's study of 212 elementary-school-age students from fundamentalist churches in the Midwest and Southwest resulted in findings that "lend no support to the view that sectarian [parochial school] education is more conducive to religious development than is public education."[9] Erickson reaches this conclusion, it should be noted, after controlling for the religiousness of parents, congeniality in the home (communicative relationships with parents), and level of student church involvement.

Attempting to integrate these three studies represents a challenge inasmuch as the sample in the first consists of adults, in the second of adolescents, and in the third of children. Further, different research instruments and analytic tools were used, and different foci were intended. All of which helps explain why their conclusions disagree at important points. Yet if we consider differences in the samples and speculate on what future research might reveal, we can make what we might call a predictive conclusion—a possible resolution of the difficulty of harmonizing the conflicting findings. If we can for the moment assume that Greeley and Rossi's adult sample is accurate for adults who had Catholic parochial school experience and may also be true of adults who attended

[7]Andrew M. Greeley and Peter H. Rossi, *The Education of Catholic Americans* (Chicago: Aldine, 1966), p. 101.
[8]Johnstone, *Effectiveness of Lutheran Schools*, ch. 5 and 10.
[9]Donald A. Erickson, "Religious Consequences of Public and Sectarian Schooling," *School Review* 72, no. 1 (1964); 29.

any group's parochial schools, then we can distinguish between long- and short-term effects of parochial school education. Thus significant short-term effects would be minimal for those with a strong family religious background and fairly dramatic for those with weak ones. In the long run, however, attendance at a parochial school and a strong family religious background may combine to form adults who are more religiously committed, informed, and active than those who lack one or the other ingredient. Such projections would go far in reconciling the differences among the three bodies of data cited above. However, only longitudinal studies can answer the question definitely. For the moment we have to settle for indications that parochial school training appears to have some religious impact—how much is not yet certain. On the other hand, all three studies document the crucial impact of the family's religious character. In fact, on the basis of these and other data presently available, we would have to conclude that home and family influence on religious socialization is paramount.

INTERNALIZATION OF RELIGION

We have been focusing on the agents and processes of religious socialization, and in assessing the effectiveness of such socialization we have focused on the group. We now turn in our discussion of socialization to the obverse of socialization—namely, internalization. What are some of the processes involved, stages of development, and differences in outcome for individuals who are being socialized?

In considering the process of the internalization of religion we are immediately required to distinguish between those who internalize the religious concepts and practices of a group from birth and those who undergo a conversion experience at some later point in life. We first look at the most common pattern—that of "growing up religious" within a particular religious context.

"Growing Up Religious"

A fundamental observation is that an individual internalizes the religion of his group essentially the same way he learns the language of his culture, or his sex role, or the life-style of his social class. The process is intimately tied up with the development of his personality and the evolution of his concept of self. A person internalizes—makes a part of himself—what he hears, sees, and both consciously and subconsciously considers applicable to himself. He hears words, is introduced to concepts, and is confronted with various phenomena at the intellectual, or cognitive, level. But he also—especially intially or primarily—emulates or imitates what he sees. In a sense he absorbs many patterns, norms, and values through the experience of seeing them exemplified by parents, peers, and others long before he confronts them intellectually.

Just as a child learns to talk before he is exposed to the rules of grammar and spelling, so he attains an orientation toward the supernatural (and, if he is a Christian, perhaps a concept of self as a sinner) long before he confronts such issues in the form of religious doctrines and propositions.

This orientation fits into the broad framework of the development of the self—a process in which religion plays a part. Early in the process of this development the child becomes aware of himself not simply as an "I" or subject—the center of the universe, so to speak—but also as a "me," an object with certain characteristics that others react to and interact with. He begins to learn how others expect him to behave if he is to interact successfully as well as satisfy his personal needs. He begins to see himself from various perspectives and in his various roles—male or female, son or daughter, friend or stranger, American or foreigner, and so on. As he is exposed to religious influences in the family and in the family's religious group, he also acquires the rudiments of a religious self. He begins to regard himself as related not only to the so-called natural and social worlds of things and people that he sees and interacts with, but also as related to an unseen world of the supernatural. He begins to have an orientation toward the sacred, however that is defined by his group. He begins to see himself in relation to that other world and expands his image of himself.

At this point, depending on the specific religious group context, great diversity may appear. One child begins to see himself as a worthless sinner utterly helpless in the face of the supernatural, while another sees himself as a special object of creation with great worth and potential. For most, a combination of both perspectives applies. In any case, the individual becomes aware of unseen powers. To some extent this may be comforting knowledge, a convenient way of explaining much that is incomprehensible. To some extent it may be frightening, particularly as one considers or learns the ways in which he can incur the wrath of those supernatural powers and even be punished by them.

In short, then, what a child is learning about himself from religious group sources supplements what he is learning about himself from interaction with playmates, television, siblings, and so on. Initially this learning is almost exclusively through informal observing and intuiting, only later to be supplemented by more formal cognitive learning. Most children in any society in fact derive some of their self-concept from religious sources, even if they are born into families which espouse no formal religious group affiliation. For everyone is at least indirectly influenced by religion through contact with other people and institutions.

It will be obvious to some readers that the foregoing description of the process of internalizing religion leans heavily on the symbolic interaction perspective in sociology, a basic premise of which is that people relate to things, events, and other people on the basis of the meanings they assign to them. These meanings in turn develop for and within the person during the process of social interaction. The religious expressions of other people and the religious institutions themselves contribute to the construct of meanings people develop. Obviously the particular set of observations and interactions that a given individual makes and experiences have a crucial influence on whatever religious meanings develop within him.

Gaining Religious Identity

Although religious socialization primarily aims at providing a person with an appropriate stance in relation to the supernatural and instructs him in the nature and function of that supernatural, another important socialization process involves teaching the child his religious identity. David Elkind has conducted research which indicates that even this process is complex. Children, Elkind contends, proceed through certain stages in learning who they are religiously. Thus a child of five who says, "I am a Catholic," understands that identification differently from a child of nine or a child of twelve. Elkind found that from the age of five or six most children know their religious identity and will freely admit they are, say, Protestant, or Catholic, or Jewish. But such an identity for them is not at all what it is for older children or adults. The young child tends to confuse religious identity with nationality and racial designations. Their religious identification is a name with no clear referent. By eight or nine years of age, however, children have a more concrete conception of their religious identity. They can distinguish religious from nonreligious designations and can attach behavioral description to various religious groups. However, it is not till the age of ten to twelve that an abstract dimension of religious identification is added; only then do youngsters begin to speak of cognitive elements such as beliefs and try to explain why particular religious groups engage in certain activities.[10]

[10]David Elkind, "Age Changes in the Meaning of Religious Identity," *Review of Religious Research* 6, No. 1 (1964); 36–40.

The Role of the Family

As mentioned earlier in this chapter, much religious socialization occurs outside the formal structure of the organization, with a significant portion taking place in family interaction. Religious groups recognize this. Some have programs which focus on trying to help parents perform this task, while others at least point out the importance of the family. However, John L. Thomas, a Jesuit sociologist, found through research that the kind of religious socialization that the Catholic church hopes parents will conduct for their children is not in fact occurring on the scale expected. Thomas states that although persons professionally involved in promoting organized religion agree that an important function of the family is the inculcation of religious beliefs and practices in their children, he finds that the religious training of the Catholic preschool child at home falls far short of traditional expectations.[11] Family influences are nevertheless significant in the sense of reinforcing and filtering religious influences from elsewhere, particularly from formal agencies such as parochial schools, as noted earlier.

In a study of male college students, Gordon Allport and his associates found that family influence was extremely important regarding present "need" for some form of religious orientation or belief system. They found that a firmly declared need continued for 82 percent of those who had what they termed an "outstanding" religious education during their childhood. Religious need was expressed by decreasing proportions of students as the quality of their childhood religious socialization declined. Thus 78 percent of those who received an "ordinary" religious education, 52 percent of those who described their religious socialization as "superficial," and only 32 percent of those who received no religious education described themselves as having a present clear need for religion.[12] Although the measure of religious socialization or "upbringing" used by Allport does not distinguish family socialization from the socialization stemming from the religious institution itself, it seems reasonable to assume, with the authors, that the prime referent is the influence and training of the family.

The family's religious influence can be important in negative ways as well. For example, John Kotre interviewed a number of graduate stu-

[11] John L. Thomas, "Religious Training in the Roman Catholic Family," *American Journal of Sociology* 62, No. 2 (1951); 178–83.
[12] Gordon W. Allport, J. M. Gillespie, and J. Young, "The Religion of the Post-War College Student," *Journal of Psychology* 25, No. 1 (1948); 3–33.

dents who had attended Catholic schools for sixteen years, some of whom at the time of his study defined themselves as still "in" the Catholic church and others of whom considered themselves "out," and found a strong correlation between being "out" and the existence of religious conflict in the home—conflict operationally defined as either an interfaith marriage or one parent a nonpracticing Catholic.[13]

RELIGIOUS CONVERSION

As stated at the outset of the preceding section, the process of internalizing religion and developing the religious self is, so far as can be determined, essentially similar to the process of internalizing other knowledge, beliefs, and skills and merely adds another dimension to one's initial concept of self. A more dramatic form of religious internalization is that of conversion.

We shall not delve deeply into the conversion phenomenon itself, which is of course strongly psychological in nature and for the most part nonempirical. We cannot, for example, determine whether a particular individual's conversion is in fact a personal experience with God himself in which the Holy Spirit enters the person and leads him to certain convictions. We can, however, provide some sociological insight into the context within which conversions occur, pointing out that conversion is not wholly a psychological phenomenon, nor does it occur in a wholly religious context as distinct from a social one.

The Group Context

First we must note the somewhat obvious yet important fact that conversion as a form of behavior or process is affected by the group within which it occurs. That is, what constitutes conversion, what one can expect to experience, and even whether one should expect a conversion experience at all are matters defined by the religious group one belongs to or happens to be under the influence of at the moment (during an evangelistic service, for example).

In a study of young people in the fundamentalist Swedish Mission Covenant Church, Hans Zetterberg found a number of group influences on the conversion phenomenon, which he defined as itself a stage in the social role of membership. For one thing, every member had a clear background of being religiously influenced before entering the group and

13John Kotre, *The View from the Border* (Chicago: Aldine-Atherton, 1971), p. 143.

undergoing the conversion experience; in fact, eight of every ten converts came from families in which at least one parent was already a member of the group. Secondly, conversion does not necessarily imply a change in one's way of life: the convert already has "pious habits and right belief." Conversion is simply a signal of a more conscious acceptance of this life. Third, a clear majority of conversions occur under conditions that are created and manipulated by the group (revival meetings, church camps, and the like). Fourth, although a sudden change in life-style may be the stereotype of conversion, such conversions are relatively unlikely. Zetterberg found that only 16 percent of his sample had conversions of this type. Much more likely are two other, more modest, types of conversion. Most likely is "sudden role identification," in which a person who has been undergoing socialization by the group suddenly feels certain of his salvation (although his behavior does not change noticeably because he had been living the role of the converted for some time). The other type of conversion is "role assimilation," in which the person gradually becomes sure of his saved condition over an extended period of membership.[14]

The Age Factor

A second major point about conversion is that—in its dramatic form, at least—it is primarily an adolescent phenomenon. It is understandably no accident that the Jewish boy has his Bar Mitzvah and the Jewish girl her confirmation in early adolescence. Similarly in liturgical Christian churches, confirmation is in early adolescence, and in nonliturgical churches baptism and/or profession of faith occur at this time. Walter H. Clark cites two early studies in the psychology of religion by E. D. Starbuck and E. T. Clark (1899 and 1929 respectively) that found the most common age for conversion of males to be about sixteen and for females about fourteen or fifteen.[15]

David Elkind makes the point that until adolescence the child "knows much more than he understands about his religious identity."[16] Gordon Allport describes adolescence as the time when the person must transform his religious attitudes from second-hand to first-hand fittings of his personality.[17]

[14]Hans Zetterberg, "The Religious Conversion as a Change of Social Roles," *Sociology and Social Research* 36, No. 1 (1952); 159–66.
[15]Walter H. Clark, *The Psychology of Religion* (New York: Macmillan, 1958), p. 207.
[16]Elkind, "Age Changes," p. 40.
[17]Gordon W. Allport, *The Individual and His Religion* (New York: Macmillan, 1957), p. 32.

That conversion should frequently occur during adolescence is probably not surprising considering the hormonal changes, opportunities for new experiences, and intellectual awakening that occur at this stage in the life cycle. Religion may be something new to embrace. Or it may have developed to a peaking point at this time. Although we shall not discuss them at this point (see Chapter 16), it is no mere coincidence that most "Jesus freaks" and most American devotees of Eastern religions are adolescents, with most of the others just barely out of adolescence and only a few well beyond this stage.

Stages in Conversion

Our third sociological observation about conversion focuses on its socialization aspect. In describing the process of conversion into a small cult called the Divine Precepts, John Lofland distinguishes between predisposing conditions (attributes of persons prior to contact with the group) and situational contingencies—social factors and influences in operation after contact with the group is made.

The first of three predisposing conditions is tension, which those who later became converts perceived themselves to have been enduring at fairly high levels for some time. Second, the potential converts for various reasons did not avail themselves of more conventional mechanisms for solving problems and reducing tension. Third, having found no psychological or political avenue for releasing their tension, they sought a religious solution in conventional religious institutions, but came away unsatisfied.

Four situational factors now developed. The first Lofland calls the "turning point"—that is, when the preconverts first encountered the Divine Precepts cult they had reached or were about to reach a crisis in their lives, for whatever they had done before either had been disrupted, was completed, or had failed. Second, there developed or already existed an "affective bond" between the potential recruit and one or more group members. Third, the preconvert's affective relationships outside the cult were either weak or ineffectual. Fourth, total conversion required a period of intensive interaction, often abetted by residence in the group's communal dwelling.[18]

Lofland's analysis is a clear blend of situational and social environmental prerequisites, psychological needs, receptivity on the part of the individual, and, above all, active socialization activity by group members.

[18]John Lofland, *Doomsday Cult* (Englewood Cliffs, N.J.: Prentice-Hall, 1966), pp. 31–62.

The result is conversion—a blending of the individual, the social environment, and the socializing group.

CONCLUSION

Religious socialization, the process of becoming religious, is not some unique or unusual process. It is simply socialization by a group into a body of norms that provide a set of meanings and interpretations that individuals internalize and relate to the large body of other meanings they possess. Although the ultimate authentication of particular meanings may be different (revering a supernatural being or a sacred book, for example), the process and ultimate outcome is not unlike learning the role and meaning construct of Italian citizen, Venezuelan mother, or offensive center for a professional football team. Certain elements common to all in a social category are learned. Yet a unique pattern emerges, for each individual has a unique combination of interactions and observations that eventuate in his meaning construct. Thus, although we continue to search for significant commonalities, differences, and consequent generalizations so far as religious behavior is concerned (the basic assignment for the remaining chapters in this text), we recognize that religion is at some ultimate point unique to the individual, for socialization, religious and otherwise, is a unique experience for each individual. Moreover, recognizing this helps explain the difficulty in measuring religiosity that we encountered in Chapter 4.

RELIGION
IN
SOCIETY

Part **III**

7

Religion as
Social Organization

In Chapter 1 we made the point that as a social phenomenon religion exhibits patterns of interaction and process that duplicate at many if not all points the patterns that all other social groups exhibit. In Chapter 2 we suggested more explicitly that religion is a group phenomenon. We now pick up on these fundamental sociological observations and expand them as we look more specifically at the social organization of religion. That is, we want to see how religious ideas, regardless of their real or supposed source, become embodied in groups, and how in turn these groups proceed to function, evidence similarities among themselves and with other groups, and distinguish themselves both from one another and from other kinds of groups in society.

RELIGION AS A GROUP PHENOMENON

In Chapter 2 we briefly defined a *group* as two or more interacting people who (1) share common goals or aims that stem from common problems and a desire to resolve them; (2) agree upon a set of norms they hope will help them achieve their common goals; (3) combine certain norms into roles that they expect persons within the group to fill and carry out in the interests of the group; (4) agree (often only implicitly) on certain status dimensions and distinctions on the basis of which they rate one another; and (5) identify with the group and express or exhibit some degree of commitment to the group, what it proposes to do, and how it proposes to do it.

Clearly religious organizations meet all of these criteria. Religious groups are concerned with problems and with expressing aspirations, hopes, and goals. Some interacting people want to know why certain things happen (cognitive understanding of accident, death, thunder, or whatever); or they want to express their dependency relationship with a deity (proper worship and ritual activity); or they want to devise methods of gaining rewards from the deities (techniques of prayer or magic); or they want to achieve a proper existence after this present life (salvation). In each case we are observing goals and the process of establishing goals.

Intimately associated with goal establishment, of course, is agreement on norms. To agree that it is an appropriate goal to appease a jealous god is to establish a norm—namely, that there is such a god, that so and so is his name, etc. Any belief or assertion about the supernatural, any explanation of what it does, any established practice or ritual directed toward it is a norm. Christianity with its elaborate doctrines, dogmas, and theological tomes clearly possesses an extensive normative system. Its historic emphasis on "right belief" becomes partially understandable in this context. Yet "primitive" religions that appear more to emphasize behavior—the ritual that involves proper steps and stages in the rain dance, the puberty rite, or the battle preparation—equally emphasize norms—norms of right behavior perhaps more than norms of right belief.

As immediately as norms follow goals, so do roles follow both. The group agrees on a leader (priest, shaman, rabbi, guru, prophet, pastor) and defines his duties. It specializes ritual functions into dancers, cantors, sorcerers, choirs, treasurers, acolytes, deacons, temple prostitutes, theological professors, executive secretaries of evangelism, directors of research and survey, public relations directors, news release writers, members of the commission on church literature, ushers, chairman of the annual spaghetti supper, and so on.

Partly but not solely as a result of such specialization of roles, status differences appear in religious groups. Quite naturally the leader, the coordinator, the spokesman, and the teacher of religious truths early acquire greater status—greater prestige and respect, if nothing else—than the rank-and-file participant. The status of such persons also involves greater authority and, perhaps as a spinoff, greater power as well. Possibly greater wealth and more leisure may accrue. But there are other status distinctions, too. There are those members who appear to follow the norms of the group more closely than others. Such behavior will likely be recognized by many members, who will characterize those who are most assiduously normative as "very religious," "most sincere," "Zoroastrian of the Decade," "Methodist of the Year," and the like.

Related to such ideas of status differentiation is the factor of group identification. Identification and commitment are variables that range from low (if not zero) to high. Groups tend to tolerate variability here, though most strive for high commitment from all members. Of course, as we'll point out shortly, the larger the group, the more likely that the range of commitment and identification will increase.

The major point we are making is that although the subject matter of religion may be unique and although it may claim a unique (namely, supernatural) source for its norms and roles, yet as the religious group organizes itself and sets about doing what it feels it should be doing, it exhibits all the features of any and all other groups. At the level of organization and structure it is no different from other groups. The focus of the goals may be different, the specific set of norms may be different, the combination of norms into particular roles may be unique, the criteria for status assessment may vary. But the religious group, as any other group, will have all of these ingredients and must constantly work at resolving differences of interpretation and application of its goals, norms, and roles. It must adjust them, expand them, and so on, just as any group must. Just as nations or social clubs or political parties or nuclear families differ among themselves yet also evidence similarities in the problems they need to adjust to and the ultimate resolutions and patterns they exhibit, so do religious groups, though unique in certain ways, evidence similarities among themselves and in fact with all other social groups.

RELIGION AND THE FIVE FUNCTIONAL
PREREQUISITES OF GROUP LIFE

Recruitment/Reproduction

Religious groups, no less than other groups, are involved with meeting the challenges of the five functional prerequisites of group life.[1] First, any group must pay attention to the prerequisite of recruitment or reproduction to replace its members who die, defect, or become inca-

[1]David Aberle, "The Functional Prerequisites of a Society," *Ethics* 60, no. 2 (1950); 100–11.

pacitated. Societies accomplish this through natural reproduction (births), acceptance of immigrants, or annexation of neighboring territories and populations. Other groups rely primarily on natural reproduction and recruitment of new members through voluntary affiliation with the group. Religious groups have historically not been unmindful of meeting this prerequisite for group continuity. In fact, many religious groups have explicitly urged maximum natural reproduction. Prohibitions against birth control, emphasis on conception as the only valid motive for sexual relations, and social ridicule or pity for the barren woman all enter in here. Although the Old Testament injunction to be fruitful and multiply has more recently been interpreted simply as a predictive statement of what would naturally happen as men and women mated, it was histori- cally interpreted as a divine command to reproduce as prolifically as possible. Some groups have explicitly urged their members to bear as many children as possible so as to increase the numbers of God's people. Many religious groups have also worked hard at adding to their numbers through recruitment of members from outside the group—by converting or proselytizing. Jesus' injunction quoted in Matthew, "Go ye therefore, and teach all nations," has been followed to greater and lesser degrees throughout history. Ever since (and even before), Charlemagne "con- verted" the barbarians through mass baptisms in 722, Christian mission- aries have been attempting to expedite conversion of nonbelievers and pagans. Actually, however, it was not until the eighteenth and nineteenth centuries, when the new worlds of the Americas, Asia, Africa, and the Pacific experienced extensive exploration and colonization, that Christian groups began subsidizing significant missionary activity.

Other major religions, such as Islam and Buddhism, have also actively courted nonmembers, not infrequently using force and political means when ordinary persuasion was insufficient. In fact, in Islam the political/military and religious motivations are so mixed as to be im- possible to separate (true throughout the history of Christianity also, of course). Early in the history of Islam the conquering of both surround- ing and distant territories for both booty and land became an absorbing goal and activity. Subjugated peoples were of course also pledged to the religion of Islam. Buddhism used religious missionaries, monks, and teachers to spread their message. In fact, as early as two centuries after Gautama Buddha's death the Indian emperor Asoka, who came to the throne in 273 B.C., conceived of Buddhism as a world religion and sent missionaries as far as Egypt and Greece.[2]

A classic example of a group's failure to meet the requirement of

2John B. Noss, *Man's Religions* (New York: Macmillan, 1949), pp. 175–76.

reproduction and recruitment of new members is that of the American religious group called the Shakers, founded in 1787. One of their primary tenets was strict separation of the sexes and complete sexual continence. Therefore, a prime source of new members (natural reproduction) was deliberately eliminated. Sole reliance was placed on adult conversion to the faith. Perhaps in great part because of the limited number of persons willing to observe sexual continence, the group had trouble gaining enough new members to maintain itself. Not surprisingly, the group no longer exists.

Socialization

A second prerequisite any group must be concerned with is developing a process of training and educating new members—what we have been calling socialization. The norms and practices of the group must be taught to the new member, whether he be a child of current members, a convert, or a conquered subject. Religious groups of course face this challenge continually. The doctrines and the practices of the group must be inculcated in the new member. He must know and believe certain bits and bodies of doctrine and ritual first of all for his own good and also if he is to become and remain a member in good standing. Further, he must know and believe certain things if he is to help in preserving the group's beliefs and practices and in handing them down to succeeding generations of followers.

Accordingly, the teaching or educative function or aspect of religion becomes a major task for religious groups. It is not by chance, for example, that the full-time religious leader in Judaism, both ancient and contemporary, has the title *rabbi,* meaning "teacher." In "primitive" religions, of course, the socialization process was largely informal and accomplished through emulation as the young watched the old and began to participate in the ritual activities and as they listened to the sagas and tales that elaborated the group's beliefs. However, religious systems that also emphasize various systematic cognitive elements of understanding and belief develop formal mechanisms for conveying such knowledge and for training in ritual performance: confirmation classes, Sunday or other church schools, and study groups of all kinds. Religious groups that tend to rely on generalists called ministers or priests may at some point add specialists to their staff called ministers of education. An early development among American Christian denominations, for example, was to establish a publishing house to produce aids to ritual activities (e.g., hymnbooks) and educational material designed to air the religious growth and maturation (socialization) of members.

Producing Satisfactory Levels of Goods and Services

A third prerequisite for the continued existence of all groups is the production and distribution of a level of goods and services that will satisfy at least the minimal requirements or demands of their members. In the case of a total society, this task involves satisfying at least the minimal survival needs of its citizens for such items as food, shelter, and clothing. For voluntary associations such as contemporary religious groups it means giving members what they have come to the group to find, or else run the risk of watching members lose interest or even defect. Presumably, members of religious groups receive certain expected benefits from their affiliation, or they won't stay or wouldn't have joined in the first place. Perhaps they are seeking eternal salvation, or comfort and reassurance, or good fellowship, or a vehicle through which they can help those in need. A religious group therefore must either "deliver the goods," so to speak—or at least convince its members that the goods are being delivered or will be in the hereafter—or see its constituency evaporate.

Religious groups that we'll be defining as "cults" later in this chapter, which tend to be centered around a charismatic leader, are notoriously unstable and likely to disband as quickly as they formed when the leader becomes discredited or dies or the competition promises more. Followers may decide they are not receiving what they were seeking, or believe that they will more fully or more quickly receive what they seek from the competition that has appeared on the scene.

The relationship of most members to their religious group is of course not so tenuous or easily shifted as this. Certainly lifelong adherents to a group must overcome apathy and inertia, if nothing else, if they wish to defect—yet defect they will (and do) if evidence accumulates and the conviction mounts that what was sought has not been found or is no longer being offered fully enough by the group.

Researchers have recently been observing declining memberships in several major denominations in the United States (and increasing memberships in others). Interestingly, those with declining memberships tend to be more theologically and socially liberal; those with increasing memberships tend to be conservative on both counts. We shall not at the moment evaluate the hypothesis that people are increasingly becoming disenchanted with liberal theology and the intrusion of liberal social and political views into the major Christian denominations and as a consequence are leaving such groups to join more traditional groups that emphasize personal comfort and the reassurance of absolute rather than relative truths. But we can certainly agree that most people who leave a religious group, whether or not they affiliate with another one, are expressing a dissatisfaction with the "goods and services" delivered by that group: it no longer provides them what they want, or at least not enough of what they want to maintain their allegiance.

Preserving Order

The fourth primary task that groups must perform is that of preserving order. Essentially this task involves coordinative roles, but above all it means motivating members to pursue group goals while employing and abiding by group norms. Within total societies this centers in the political process and the exercising of governmental controls and sanctions—the range of rewards and punishments meted out for adherence to or deviation from the norms, as the case may be. On the positive side, it involves encouraging members to cooperate with one another and to supplement, rather than interfere with, the performance of others' roles. It involves providing a context for freedom of movement and action of individuals within limits agreed upon by the group. On the negative side, it may involve incarceration, the death penalty, or ostracism.

So far as religious groups are concerned we think here of the various types of church government established to reach their goals. For example, the episcopal type (e.g., Episcopal and Roman Catholic churches), in which authority rests with the congregation's clergyman and with higher-ranking clergy such as popes and bishops. Or the Presbyterian type, in which authority rests with representative committees of clergy and church members. Or the congregational type, in which ultimate organizational authority resides in local church members and with their representatives meeting periodically in regional or national convention or assembly.

We also think of heresy trials and inquisitions, in which those accused of deviating from official doctrine or practice are sought out, tried, and punished. Fundamental here is the conviction that if such controls are not employed, radical changes may be introduced resulting in the alienation and loss of members to the point of ultimate dissolution and destruction of the group.

Maintaining a Sense of Purpose

The fifth primary prerequisite that groups must fulfill if they hope to survive is the maintenance of a sense of purpose among its members. This task is concerned with the sixth feature of groups mentioned in Chapter 2—namely, the identification factor. Groups must develop and maintain among members a feeling of commitment to and identification with the group. Groups that fail continually to reinforce members' commitment run the risk of takeover or collapse in the face of internal opposition or outside threat. A society, for example, needs citizens sufficiently committed to pick up arms and risk death on the battlefield in the face of enemy invasion. A religious group wants to be able to count on sufficient loyalty and commitment among its members so that they are not swayed (or possibly even converted) by every new attractive wind of doctrine that blows by. They want members who take pride in their affiliation and who will resist the wiles of other groups or philosophies that may try to win them away. Most religious groups (Jews an exception) in addition want members who will in fact try to bring others into their fold. "We've got a great group here and would like you to share its benefits with us!" Failing to maintain a sense of purpose can bring a group to the brink of destruction just as does failure in any of the other four primary tasks already discussed.

THE EFFECTS OF INCREASING GROUP SIZE

Having examined one aspect of religion as a group phenomenon—in terms of the tasks that face all groups, not just religious ones—we now turn to a discussion of the pressures for change that religious groups (no less than other groups) experience. Of particular interest and significance is the effect on groups of increasing size. Important changes occur, and new challenges develop. Although a group may in one sense be successful by increasing its membership, serious problems may arise as a consequence. Paul Mott has summarized well the various developments associated with a group's increasing size.[3] We include only some of them— those with particular salience to religious groups.

As groups increase in size, the degree of consensus among members concerning goals and especially norms declines. In great part a basic problem of communication and interaction is involved here. As groups grow, a point is reached when not everyone can interact with everyone else; nor can any one person interact with all others. Levels of understanding and commitment to goals and norms cannot be maintained. Not only can't people share as fully with one another and reach truly common understandings by involving everyone in decision and policy making, but also problems of increasing diversity arise as more members come in. In fact, each new person is a potential disrupter, if not a

---

[3]Paul E. Mott, *The Organization of Society* (Englewood Cliffs, N.J.: Prentice-Hall, 1965), pp. 48–69.

potential revolutionary, inasmuch as the ideas he brings with him or those that he may develop may challenge fundamental tenets of the group. Obviously the tight-knit, integrated, primary-group–like relationship that may have existed at a group's inception and during its early development begins to submit to increasing diversity and more specialized interests as different elements enter.

An almost inevitable outcome of increased diversity and reduced consensus resulting from an increase in size is increasing deviance from group norms. Since norms influence behavior, the introduction of diverse or conflicting norms results in diverse behavior. Some members may assent to many of the group's norms (they probably wouldn't be members otherwise), yet not share others. They are likely to act consonant with their norms, thereby deviating from the group's expectations. For example, a religious group may have explicit norms defining alcoholic beverages as the Devil's instrument. The member who would still like a nip or two is more likely to depart from the group norm as the group grows larger. Perhaps the norm and its importance to the group has not been explained fully to him or is no longer reinforced through discussion and conversation; perhaps he doesn't feel as closely united with the other members as he did when the group was small, and thus doesn't feel so bad about disappointing them should they find out about his deviance. Actually, as the group grows larger it becomes physically and emotionally impossible to feel or express as much concern about other individual members as was possible when the group was smaller and members more intimate.

A third development as groups grow larger is that roles tend to become more specialized and part-time roles to become full-time ones. Such specialization removes the nonspecialist from intimate contact with the tasks of various roles. Greater autonomy for roles develops. Members who originally were involved to some degree in almost everything the group did and decided now know less and less about what others are doing.

As groups increase in size there is greater need for coordination. As the number of roles increases there is greater need for coordinators to interrelate those roles and insure that they are performed in proper sequence. Nothing wrong with that, of course. But in the process, the coordinators gain greater knowledge about the operation of the total organization than ordinary members possess; having by definition greater authority, they become increasingly isolated from the rank and file. Obviously the original intimacy and democracy of the group fade fast in the face of this tendency. There are also, of course, increased opportunities for abusing one's power and perpetuating oneself in office, for example.

And so on.... Mott lists thirteen developments within groups related to increasing group size. The four discussed above, however, are sufficient to make the point that one measure of success that groups often use—namely, membership growth—sets them on an irreversible course involving change along a variety of dimensions. Later in this chapter we shall refer back to these dimensions in our discussion of the church-sect typology. First, however, we want to look more closely at one of the developments in groups related to increasing size—the bureaucratization trend that we identified before as an increase in the coordinative element in groups.

THE BUREAUCRATIZATION OF RELIGION

In a direct way the bureaucratization tendency of growing religious groups is related to the question of authority in religious groups. That is, although bureaucratization appears to be an inevitable trend in groups as they grow large and develop an increasingly complex division of labor requiring careful coordination, it may also have unintended and unwanted consequences. As Hammond and Johnson point out, a key issue in the Protestant Reformation of the fifteenth century concerned how authority was to be exercised within the church. Implicitly this was a question of what to do about the church bureaucracy.[4] Certainly the Roman Catholic church had long been organized along rather classic bureaucratic lines. An elaborate hierarchy of authority passed down through pope, archbishops, bishops, and priests, with other levels in between. Specialized training and experience were required of those who filled various specialized roles. Explicit rules were in effect for nearly every situation and role. An air of impartiality and impersonality pervaded relationships among leaders and between them and members.

The leaders of the Protestant Reformation, however, wanted greater involvement and a stronger voice for the laity. A key theological tenet stressed within early Protestantism was that every person can have direct contact with and access to God. No intermediary such as church, pope, or priest was required. Some groups were convinced that no church authority should exist or exercise control beyond the democratic assembly of each local congregation: no level of authority above the congregation (except God himself) should require the member or the congregation to do anything. Congregationalists, Lutherans, and Baptists are among Protestant denominations that still espouse this principle, though in modified form in each case.

[4]Philip E. Hammond and Benton Johnson, *American Mosaic* (New York: Random House, 1970), p. 149.

How successful have such religious groups been in implementing this philosophy, in avoiding the bureaucratization that sociologists have documented in other types of groups? We gain some insight into the issue when we observe what happens when an individual or a local body of believers strives to maintain its autonomy but also finds it expedient to cooperate with other individuals or congregations in various joint ventures. Perhaps several congregations discover that training future clergymen is a difficult task to accomplish alone, for example, and so they join together in establishing a theological seminary. Or they may want to send missionaries to foreign lands. A single congregation can't afford to support a missionary, but several congregations can. So they establish a missionary society or board or commission to handle the details, such as collecting mission contributions from the several congregations. Or they may want to produce lessons and literature for their Sunday schools, but local ministers don't have the time or perhaps lack the specialized skills. Therefore, several congregations organize a Sunday School Board or a Commission on Church Literature to handle the planning, writing, editing, and publishing tasks.

The outcome of such developments is that, although no one particularly intends it, the local congregations lose some of their autonomy. The boards or agencies or commissions assume some measure of authority and independence and in turn gain influence over the congregations. It is a reciprocal relationship: while local congregations may have established the goals and even some of the policies for such administrative groups, once in existence the latter influence the congregations. They train the ministers, organize and supervise the missionary endeavors, and write the Sunday school material. Thus they become innovators and not simply implementers of policy.

The interaction and relationship between such boards and the local congregation and its members is therefore somewhat uncertain, uneasy, and tenuous. Such a situation is highlighted when one or more local congregations or individuals discover they don't like the theological inclinations and emphases of their seminary's ministerial graduates, or feel that extraneous or heretical ideas are slipping into their Sunday school material. The local congregation of course has the option of severing the relationship, but then it faces the problem of carrying on all these tasks by itself or linking up with another, perhaps similar, organization. The common reaction is to go along with the established pattern, even though the congregation loses some of its cherished autonomy in the process.

A method observed by Paul Harrison in the American Baptist Church that bridges the gap between national boards and local independent congregations is the action of the executive who heads a board or agency. If the executive secretary or other administrator of a national board or commission has charismatic qualities, he can gain broad-based support among local clergy and laymen that grants him greater flexibility and autonomy and ultimately substantial authority and influence over local decisions.[5] Of course, even without charisma the denominational executive will have some measure of autonomous power because much of his day-to-day work goes on unseen and unknown by most of the constituency. As Harrison points out, most lay members have no knowledge of the internal operation of the larger church body, never attend national, state, or even local associational meetings, and most likely do not even know the names of their officials let alone the policies they set.[6]

In other words, a bureaucracy, once formed, tends to take on a life of its own, initiates and implements policy partly of its own making, and may begin to direct the larger organization of which it is a specialized part in new directions.

Robert Michels's classic "iron law of oligarchy" can be seen operating in many religious groups: the tendency, as responsibilities and authority are transferred to leaders (a process seemingly inherent and inevitable in group life), for a number of developments in combination to lead to oligarchy. Delegating responsibility and power to leaders, for example, concentrates both skills and informal prerogatives in their hands. Leaders become more skilled than rank-and-file members in administration, coordination, manipulation, diplomacy, and so on, and they have access to information not available to others. Along with such skills and knowledge goes power. The gratitude and allegience of members to their leaders for doing jobs they would not care to do also strengthens the leaders' position of power and influence. Further, leaders tend to be self-perpetuating in their positions. They like their power and privilege, and they want to keep it. As a result, incumbents are hard to remove.[7]

Religious organizations are not immune to such organizational tendencies. In fact, they join on an equal footing with all other democratic organizations in this tendency. This is true regardless of how jealously a group may strive to remain a pure democracy. Even those religious groups which make a strong theological point that local and individual religious autonomy is sacred are faced with the tendency to oligarchy. Of course, other religious groups, such as the Roman Catholic church, stress a hierarchical authority pattern in the first place and have little problem living with the oligarchy tendency. Although there has been

---

[5]Paul M. Harrison, *Authority and Power in a Free Church Tradition: A Social Case Study of the American Baptist Convention* (Princeton: Princeton University Press, 1959), pp. 74–77.
[6]Ibid., p. 92.
[7]Robert Michels, *Political Parties*, trans. Eden and Cedar Paul (Glencoe, Ill.: Free Press, 1949). First published in England in 1915.

some change recently, with laymen demanding more input into decision and policy making, the issue in such a group has traditionally been less one of laymen wanting to curtail the power of bureaucratic church executives as that of church officials trying to keep the laymen from becoming too independent and free-thinking. It's a struggle for power either way. It's a struggle based on the two characteristics of groups, religious or otherwise: (1) diversity in a number of dimensions within the group, and (2) the oligarchic tendency for leaders to accumulate power. Internal diversity within a group makes effective total control next to impossible, yet oligarchic tendencies serve to override diversity in the interests of bureaucratic efficiency.

THE CHURCH-SECT TYPOLOGY

So far in this chapter we have been exploring both the similarities among religious groups themselves and the similarities they share with all social organizations. We now turn to some important distinctions among religious groups—distinctions that are fundamentally matters of organization—that is, sociological, not theological, differences. We begin with the *church-sect typology*—a way of identifying differences among religious groups that was given its fullest early conceptualization by the theologian Ernst Troeltsch, but which was introduced into sociology by his teacher Max Weber and which has been used and expanded by numerous sociologists since their time.

As we shall soon see, the dichotomy of church and sect actually only identifies two polar types of religious organization that occupy the ends of a social continuum that has several gradation points (other types of organization) in between. We first shall contrast the polar types and then discuss three other types of religious organization that investigations following those of Troeltsch and Weber have shown to be important additions to the typology.

Demerath and Hammond suggest that differences between churches and sects can be observed from either of two perspectives, one concerning the internal characteristics of the organization, the other the external relationships of the group with the features of its social environment.[8] Focusing on internal differences, we can observe the following about sects: (1) A sect sees itself as a fellowship of the elect—i.e., an embodiment of true believers. (2) Sects encourage spontaneity of religious expression involving extensive group participation. (3) Sects deemphasize organiza-

[8]N. J. Demerath III and Philip E. Hammond, *Religion in Social Context* (New York: Random House, 1969), pp. 70–71.

tion and strive to maintain maximum democratic participation of members within an explicitly nonbureaucratic structure. (4) A sect is usually small, and deliberately so. (5) Sects utilize laymen as leaders. Frequently part-time, such leaders likely have little if any formal theological training. Commitment to the principles avowed by the group is seen as more important than "book learning." The element of charisma is a common feature of leaders. (6) A sect emphasizes purity of doctrine and usually demands a return to original religious teaching. This involves a renunciation of the doctrinal perversions and aberrations that it accuses the established denominational religious groups of having allowed to intrude into true religion. (7) A sect emphasizes traditional ethical principles and strives to influence its members along a broad spectrum of behavior. (8) Sects tend to concentrate on otherworldly issues (salvation, deliverance, heaven and hell) and discount or deprecate this world's concerns. Even their emphasis on ethics (point 7, above) is focused more on its relevance to ultimate otherworldly concerns, less on the relationship of man to man. (9) A sect gains new members primarily through conversion. It is initially a fellowship of adults, although eventually they must turn their attention to the religious socialization of children. (10) A sect draws disproportionately from the lower social classes in the society.

Implicit in many of the characteristics outlined above is the prime characteristic of a sect, namely, protest. Usually it is protest against both (1) established traditional religious forms and groups that sect members feel have strayed too far from pristine religion, and (2) the surrounding secular society, which is viewed as embodying all kinds of evil. A sect thus reflects schism—a breaking away from and a rejection of established patterns, both religious and secular.

Although we have summarized ten characteristics of sects, other writers have listed more: for example, Liston Pope makes twenty-one distinctions between the church and the sect,[9] while Benton Johnson lists only one essential distinction: whether a religious group accepts or rejects its larger social environment (the sect rejects, the church or denomination accepts).[10]

It should also be mentioned that many different types of sects exist. Although it is important to recognize the diversity of sects, we shall not explicate them here. Two typologies the reader may wish to explore are those of Elmer T. Clark and Bryan Wilson. Clark distinguishes the pessimistic/adventist sects, the perfectionist/subjectivist sects, the

[9]Liston Pope, *Millhands and Preachers* (New Haven: Yale University Press, 1942), pp. 122–24.
[10]Benton Johnson, "On Church and Sect," *American Sociological Review* 28, no. 4 (1963); 539–49.

charismatic/pentecostal sects, the legalistic/objectivist sects, and the communistic sects.[11] Wilson distinguishes the revolutionist, introversionist, manipulationist, thaumaturgical, reformist, and utopian sects.[12]

The Church

Before presenting the corresponding characteristics of the church type we need to make clear that the church (the sect also) is clearly what in sociology we call an ideal type. That is, the concept of church or sect or any of the other types of religious organization that we shall describe later in the chapter represents a summary or distillation of social characteristics and phenomena that frequently appear together and in combination help to distinguish one set of organizations from another. It is a kind of model that expresses in pure, complete form the central characteristics of a pattern of organization or behavior. Although we do not expect to find all the characteristics of an ideal type in pure form in a particular organization at a given moment in time, we will expect most of them. In a sense an ideal type is used for dramatic purposes to heighten one's awareness of salient characteristics of a social phenomenon. For example, we listed ten characteristics of the sect. Yet a religious group may accurately be identified as a sect and yet lack one or two of the characteristics on the list, or not reproduce all ten characteristics in "pure" form. Similarly the church type represents one "extreme" form of religious organization that may have appeared at some time in history in essentially all its characteristics, but probably never in pure form on all dimensions. That is, an ideal type is more a concept and less an empirical reality, though based on substantial empirical observations. Its value lies in providing a clear-cut base of comparison for what we observe empirically at a given point in time. Although we may be unable to observe an empirical example of a "church" at this point in history, we can understand more clearly what we do observe because of either its similarities to or differences from the ideal type we have as a base of contrast.

But now to the major characteristics of the *church* type of religious organization. The church: (1) claims universality and includes all members of the society within its ranks; there is a strong tendency for "citizen" to be equated with "member"; (2) exercises religious monopoly and tries to eliminate religious competition; (3) is very closely allied with the state and secular powers; frequently there is overlapping of responsibilities and much mutual reinforcement; (4) is extensively organized as

[11]Elmer T. Clark, *The Small Sects in America* (Nashville: Abingdon Press, 1949).
[12]Bryan Wilson, *Religious Sects* (New York: McGraw-Hill, Company, 1970).

a hierarchical bureaucratic institution with a complex division of labor; (5) employs a professional, full-time clergy who possess the appropriate credentials of education and formal ordination; (6) almost by definition gains new members through natural reproduction and the socialization of children into its ranks.

A prime example of a church is the medieval Roman Catholic church. Another close approximation was the Russian Orthodox Church of the nineteenth century. For that matter, contemporary European state churches approximate this model, though they all now at least formally tolerate religious diversity and competition—something the pure church type does not do. Although there is no really good example of a church type of religious organization to be observed today, the concept retains considerable value as a point of reference for understanding the other types of religious organization that are in clear evidence today.

Although we shall not elaborate them here, the reader should be aware that refinements and further specification of the church type have been made. For example, J. Milton Yinger has distinguished the "universal church" from the "ecclesia" (Greek word for church) and has further divided both into institutionalized and diffused forms.[13]

The Denomination

The *denomination* is in a mediating position between the church and the sect, and as such is the most important addition to the original dichotomous church-sect typology. When the church loses its position of religious dominance and monopoly, denominationalism is the result. In fact, the moment the protesting, struggling sects that have been striving to attain autonomy are tolerated, however reluctantly, by the established church the church is by definition dead and is immediately transformed into a denomination—that is, one religion among several. As some of the protesting sects evolve (we'll discuss this evolutionary process later in the chapter), they too become denominations, and this type of religious organization—denominationalism—becomes a distinct, identifiable type.

A denomination can be defined as follows: (1) It is similar to the church, but unlike the sect, in being on relatively good terms with the state and secular powers. The denomination's most extreme stance in this respect would be "loyal opposition." It is at home in the halls of government and occasionally tries to exert some influence in that direction— something few sects try to do. (2) A denomination maintains tolerant and not infrequently friendly relationships with other denominations in

---

13J. Milton Yinger, *The Scientific Study of Religion* (New York: Macmillan, 1970), pp. 256–64.

a context of religious pluralism. (3) It relies primarily on birth for membership increase, though it will also accept converts; some groups even actively pursue evangelistic programs, though directed primarily to the unconverted, unchurched citizens, not persons presently members of other denominations. (4) A denomination accepts the principle of at least modestly changing doctrine and practice, and tolerates some theological diversity and dispute—something a true sect will not do. (5) It follows a fairly routinized ritual and worship service that explicitly discourages spontaneous emotional expression. (6) It trains and employs a professional clergy who must meet certain formal normative requirements before certification. (7) It recognizes competing demands from other affiliations upon its members' commitment and involvement; thus it accepts less extensive involvement from members than a sect does, but often expects more than the church (where by virtue of the citizen–church member equation it is recognized that many persons will be minimally or non-involved members). (8) A denomination draws disproportionately from the middle and upper classes of the society.

Before proceeding to look at two other important types of religious organizations within the framework of the church-sect typology—namely, the cult and the institutionalized sect—we need to analyze a bit further the relationship between sect and denomination. First we want to look at the point of rupture when the sect protests to the point of breaking with the denomination or church. Second, we'll trace the evolutionary pattern that most sects follow which eventually leads them to denominational status.

The Formation of Sects

We stated earlier that the fundamental theme of the religious sect is protest—protest which leads to schism and a breaking away from the parent religious group, be it church or denomination. Such action, however, is not the only method of resolving conflict within a religious group. One method historically employed by church-type religious groups—of which the Roman Catholic church is a paramount example—is by allowing, often in fact encouraging, the formation of specialized groups within the larger body. If some persons feel they cannot worship properly in the established ritual form of ordinary local congregational groups (the reasoning goes), then allow them to form a subgroup or order within the larger body that emphasizes extensive contemplation and private meditation, or one that encourages active participation in social and political activities, or one that engages in spontaneous, emotional, pentecostal-type behaviors. Monastic orders within the Roman Catholic church have served this purpose admirably. Even today the tacit permission if not encouragement of pentecostal subgroups within such standard denominations as the Catholic, Lutheran, Presbyterian, and Episcopalian churches is an excellent example of this tactic of channeling deviant and/or specialized groups within the overarching structure of the denomination.

Probably the most familiar method of resolving dissatisfaction within a denomination is simply for individuals or families to withdraw—either to drift from organized religion altogether or to affiliate with another religious group that seems to satisfy one's wishes and concerns more fully. How many present-day denominational switches are such expressions of religious protest we do not know. Undoubtedly many are relatively simple transfers of convenience when a family moves and cannot find its denomination represented nearby; or when upward mobility (as opposed to ideological conflict) suggests to a person that he should forsake, say, his Baptist background and affiliate with a "higher-status" Presbyterian or Episcopalian congregation; or when an interfaith marriage leads one partner to switch to the mate's religious group as a matter of form.

Another way of resolving religious conflict is for those who are dissatisfied simply to split off and form another denomination. We'll soon emphasize that a prime ingredient in sect formation is the factor of social class. But if social class is not a particularly primary factor in a given controversy and the issue is more strictly political or ideological, then a denomination may simply split into two. The division of both the Baptists and the Presbyterians into northern and southern denominations during the Civil War are good examples of this process. The split within the Presbyterian Church in the 1930s over certain doctrinal issues is another example; not a sect but another denomination formed as a result.

The final method of resolving religious group conflict is the one we keep referring to—the process of sect formation. What happens in this process and why? Ostensibly, on the surface, the issue is almost invariably doctrinal or theological. Potential sect members are likely to talk about the loss of true Christianity in the parent denomination—how doctrine has become liberalized and people aren't living their Christianity the way they should. Some members finally opt out and form their own small group in order to preserve or recapture the basics and the essence of true religion and save themselves from further theological contamination and perversion. Undoubtedly most sectarians are sincere and truly believe that theological or doctrinal issues are the real issues. Yet one suspects there is more to it than that. The social scientist continually looks for latent factors lurking behind manifest behaviors, definitions of the situation, and rationalizations. We are thus particularly intrigued when we observe that sectarians are quite predominantly of lower-class social status. Aware that social status influences all manner of social behavior and attitudes, sociologists thus regard it very likely that social status also relates in some way with the sectarian break from the denomination.

Liston Pope in his classic analysis of the interrelationship of religion and social structure reviews several hypotheses that try to account for the phenomenon of sect formation. Most writers, he notes, pay serious attention to the status dimension, or at least by implication suggest that lower social status is somehow significantly involved in the motivation for sectarian involvement.[14] For example, the "cultural shock" hypothesis of John B. Holt suggests that migrants to cities seek out or form sects as a means of preserving rural religious life-styles and values and as a defense against the anonymity of the city and the urban denominational congregations.[15] Although such factors may be relevant for some persons, Holt's analysis does not account for the formation of sects in rural and small-town settings. Holt does point out, however, that persons attracted to sects, whether migrants experiencing cultural shock or not, are predominantly lower class.

Many theorists, then, see sect formation as some form of compensation for those deficiencies epitomized by inferior social status. Pope notes that sects "substitute religious status for social status."[16] The sectarian is likely to say something like: "I may not be high society, but I'm on God's first string" or, "I may not have a big house, a fancy car, and a college education, but I've got what's really important—I've got true religion." Pope observes: "They transmute poverty into a symptom of Grace."[17] Socially separated from those above them in the stratification system, they then emphasize separation from "the world" as a virtue. Although they feel excluded from fellowship with those of higher education and social and economic position, they in turn exclude from their fellowship those who dance, play cards, smoke, drink, and bet on the races. Unable to afford jewelry, they make wearing of any such adornment a sin. Pope again observes: "Excluded from secular society, they set up a religious society of their own, in which standards of membership are more rigid than those of the general culture that has ignored them."[18] Reaching heaven, which is the supreme, ultimate reward, becomes eminently more important than earthly success and the good life here and now, which is only temporal and not eternal.

[14]Pope, *Millhands and Preachers*, pp. 133–34.
[15]John B. Holt, "Holiness Religion: Cultural Shock and Social Reorganization," *American Sociological Review* 5, no. 5 (1940); 740–47.
[16]Pope, *Millhands and Preachers*, p. 137.
[17]Ibid.
[18]Ibid., p. 138.

The Impact of Deprivation on Sect Development

To this point we have been concentrating on a rather simplistic distinction between high and low socioeconomic status. Charles Y. Glock has added specification to this general hypothesis by introducing the concept of "deprivation" and making distinctions between five types of deprivation.[19] First, there is *economic deprivation,* which consists of limited income and access to the material necessities of life. It may be objectively defined and measured as well as subjectively experienced and perceived. That is, although a person may technically not be categorized as living at the poverty level, he may perceive of himself as poor. Such a perception can influence his behavior and attitude as much as or more than the objective facts of his existence.

Second, *social deprivation* refers to the relative absence of such societal rewards as prestige, power, social status, and opportunity for participation in various activities and organizations. This is frequently a concomitant of economic deprivation in the sense that low economic status likely means low prestige or respect, little power or influence over others, and exclusion from much of the social and organizational life of the community. But social deprivation is not necessarily strictly correlated with economic deprivation. A person may be socially deprived yet be economically solvent, even successful. Social deprivation is one of the main emphases of the women's liberation movement. "Although I can buy all that my heart desires, I'm considered 'just a housewife' because it's my husband's income I'm spending." "I may be receiving a very livable salary, but it's less than that of a man doing comparable work." And so on. Or social deprivation may be along age lines. Consider the very young and the very old who have relatively little power and prestige even though economically they may be facing no difficulty. Further, the minority-group member such as a Chicano or black or American Indian may be economically successful yet a secondclass citizen on other dimensions of status.

A third type of deprivation is *organismic.* This refers to the deprived condition of some in society along the dimension of physical and mental health and biological/physical abilities. Some suffer from neuroses or psychoses; some are deaf or blind; some are paraplegics; some are mentally retarded; others suffer from one or more of an almost infinite variety of other conditions.

[19]Charles Y. Glock, "The Role of Deprivation in the Origin and Evolution of Religious Groups," in *Religion and Social Conflict,* ed. Robert Lee and Martin E. Marty (New York: Oxford University Press, 1964), pp. 24–36.

Another type of deprivation is what Glock calls *ethical*. This exists when an individual comes to feel that the dominant values and norms of the society no longer provide him with a meaningful way of organizing his life. The ethically deprived person has trouble finding meaning in his life and can't decide where to go or how to proceed to find it.

Finally there is *psychic deprivation,* which affects the person who may enjoy the material rewards of society and may subscribe to society's norms but who nevertheless lacks an adequate share of psychic rewards: he doesn't *feel* satisfied or really accepted in society. Such deprivation frequently accompanies social deprivation—for example, in the black professional in American society who has superior specialized skill and education, who may be economically successful, but who still feels looked down upon because of his color, who in many situations is made to feel inferior, second-rate. Whereas social deprivation is more or less an objective measure or dimension, psychic deprivation is a psychological matter and thus highly subjective.

To relate these types of deprivation to the sources of sectarianism, we can first of all observe with Glock that the emergence of any protest movement or group—religious or otherwise—requires some feeling of deprivation on the part of the participants.[20] They face a problem that is either not being met by the groups they are presently affiliated with or is in some way produced by a group or groups with which they are affiliated (or both). Glock suggests, however, that while some felt deprivation is a necessary condition for protest group formation, it is not a sufficient condition: there are additional requirements. The deprivation must be shared with others, and these people need to find one another; a leader must emerge to suggest a solution or at least organize a group around a proposed solution; and no alternative existing institutional arrangements or processes must appear to be available.[21] When such factors combine, a protest group can get underway.

But what form will it take? For example, will it be a secular group or movement, or will it be a religious organization such as a sect breaking away from a denomination? If the deprivation is either economic or social, it is likely that a religious route will be followed (1) when the nature of the deprivation is inaccurately perceived or inadequately understood—that is, when people don't realize that a prime factor in their unhappiness and frustration is their economic or social position relative to others; or (2) when, even though the nature of the deprivation is accurately perceived, people feel powerless to work directly at eliminating its causes.[22] In either case, persons may retreat into an emotionally releas-

[20]Ibid., p. 29.
[21]Ibid.
[22]Ibid.

ing, rationalizing, otherworldly sectarian religious group and activity as a conscious or subconscious means of escaping from the harsh realities of economic or social deprivation. On the other hand, if people accurately perceive the problem and feel capable of attacking and resolving it through social change, then they are more likely to form a secular organization or attempt some other secular resolution. In other words, religious resolutions such as the formation of sects are essentially compensatory mechanisms for alleviating feelings of deprivation, while secular resolutions try to strike directly at the causes of the deprivation.

A striking example of both of these attempts can be seen in the black community in the United States. Historically much black religious behavior and involvement has tended to be of the sect variety, quite clearly responding to economic and social deprivation in a compensatory way. More recently, however, as more blacks have become cognizant of the real nature of their problems, have rejected doctrines of inherent inferiority, and have become convinced that the system could be effectively challenged, the civil rights movement has flowered. Young blacks in particular have increasingly turned to secular organizations such as CORE and the Black Panthers or in some cases to groups like the Black Muslims rather than to traditional black religious organizations. More on this phenomenon and on black religion in general appears in Chapter 14.

When social deprivation is not intimately associated with or reinforced by economic deprivation, another route may be followed that is neither sectarian nor secular: very simply, another religious denomination may result. Again we turn to the American black community for an example: the African Methodist Episcopal Church came into being not as a sect but as a denomination when freed blacks, many of them of essentially middle-class economic status, reacted to unequal participation privileges and unequal voice in the white-dominated Methodist Episcopal Church and broke away in 1796.

Although we have not discussed the cult as a type of religious organization, we should mention at this point that either ethical or psychic deprivation is less likely to result in sectarian development and more likely, for reasons that will become evident later, to cause people to form or be attracted to a religious cult. It is of course also possible that ethical or psychic deprivation may be a prelude to secular solutions and the formation of nonreligious groups.

The Evolution of Sects

So much for the phenomenon of sect formation. We now turn to the issue of sect evolution and an investigation of the factors involved in the nearly universal tendency of sects (if they survive at all) to change and to move away from their original "pure" state—in fact, to move toward eventual denominational status and to begin manifesting the characteristics of an organization from which they originally withdrew and which they earlier repudiated. We refer to the sect in its pure state as a religious group composed of the exclusive "elect" or select few, who practice what they see as "pure," authentic religion and who avoid secular involvement and contamination; and we begin with the empirical observation that a sect cannot remain a sect.

A major causative factor in the evolution of sect to denomination is quite nonreligious and very sociological. We refer here to the laws of increasing group size that we outlined earlier in this chapter. For these laws to apply, we assume, of course, that the originally small sect grows. And even if a sect does not grow enough to call into play the laws of increasing group size, other nonreligious factors apply that we'll discuss later. But assuming a sect adds to its numbers—as most do, since they usually want to spread their gospel and share their discovery of true religion—then some inevitable developments come about. More people automatically means a greater diversity of background. New members will not share precisely the same experiences of the original core group, and some will have significantly different personal objectives and goals that they expect the group to fulfill. Thus problems of unanimity and total consensus arise, even though everyone may sincerely believe that he subscribes to the same goals and norms as everyone else. The foundation is therefore laid for ultimate modification of the sect's central goals and values.

As a group increases in size, subgroups inevitably develop. Although this phenomenon occurs the moment any few people form a group, it intensifies in geometric proportion as the group grows. Subgroups develop their own unique combinations of goals, norms, and roles while still subscribing to the overarching ideology of the larger group and respecting its structure. Subgroups not only provide internal diversity, but represent the distinct possibility that a particular subgroup may become increasingly more deviant, gain more adherents, and ultimately dominate the larger group and assume guiding control. Obviously under such circumstances the group will change.

We just mentioned deviance. As groups increase in size, deviance increases, largely through subgroup action. But not only that. Tolerance of deviance increases either because it is unknown or unrecognized or because it becomes more and more difficult to control and enforce strict normative behavior as the membership increases. Clearly the original conformity and unanimity is breaking down.

A prime need for groups as they grow larger is greater coordination. Strictly democratic decision making in all matters becomes impractical and impossible. Responsibility for coordinating the activities of many persons and roles is centralized in specialists. A side effect will likely be a declining intensity of commitment and sense of involvement among ordinary members. Also, the distance between elite and rank-and-file members will increase. The person who sees original principles changed or lost will find it increasingly difficult to communicate his concern to the elites in the group. Not only will change remain unchecked, but the individual who objects to change will become increasingly dissatisfied and disenchanted (while others, of course, will applaud the change).

A result may well be a legitimacy crisis, with some concluding that they must reject the authority of the leaders and coordinators. But perhaps they are voiceless or powerless. What to do? Go along silently but unhappily, or leave and form a new group—a new sect that can once again restore purity and truth to religion?

But what if a sectarian religious group manages to avoid the problems inherent in organizational growth by simply not growing, or at least by not growing to the extent where a bureaucratic structure develops and members become isolated from one another? Even with no growth or only limited growth, sources of change are present and begin to work. Almost immediately after formation a formalization of norms begins and the group loses some of its spontaneity and flexibility. Then the group must answer two questions: (1) Where does authority lie? In a book? With a leader? In a doctrinal statement? That is, who or what is the ultimate arbiter? (2) What are correct beliefs? What are we going to teach our children and the adults who knock on our door and inquire about coming in?

With each development the group is becoming more stabilized, it is formalizing its norms, structurally it is becoming just a bit more like the group from which it severed itself. There is a little less chance for innovations; it is becoming a little more difficult to substantiate that the Holy Spirit is working through you to bring new insight. It becomes increasingly more necessary to reconcile that which is introduced with what the group has established as normative in answering the two questions above.

Furthermore, the group must provide for leadership succession. If the group begins with a charismatic leader, what happens if he dies or is incapacitated or is discredited as morally or otherwise unfit to continue as leader? Norms must therefore be established that outline the process of leader selection and succession. Perhaps it will involve a training program for potential leaders. Above all, it will require specification of the qualifications and duties of the leader. After all, if we bring in a new leader, he has to know what his duties are. At this point something highly significant has happened: the leader has become an officeholder.

His role has been routinized and formalized. And one observes the beginning of formal structure and ultimately perhaps bureaucracy itself.

Also, any expansion beyond the few initial individuals or families will require attention to financial matters. A hall for meetings must be rented or purchased; some minimal equipment and fixtures must be provided; a checking account must be opened at a local bank. And again we see the spontaneous, flexible group becoming structured and routinized. It's taking an early short but definite step down the road toward the type of organization from which it came. "That organized denomination paid too much attention to mundane matters like meeting budgets, fundraising, and building maintenance. It didn't pay enough attention to spiritual matters—the really important things." So says the sectarian. Yet the sect itself must soon begin to have similar concerns, though at first on a smaller scale, of course.

Another factor contributing to change in the sect is the strong tendency within any group for higher-status persons to assume positions of power and be elected to office. The sect is no exception. Low-status members of a group tend to defer to those with more education, a higher-status job, and greater prestige. The result tends to be a conservative influence on the group—conservative in the sense that such higher-status leaders are likely to want to modify and tone down extremes in the sect's stance and ideology. They have more at stake in the surrounding community and don't want their names associated with too weird a group. Thus the sect begins to change, to accommodate itself, and it becomes more compatible with the surrounding culture.

A final important factor involved in turning the sect around and leading it back toward the denominational form is the upward status mobility of some of its members. Insofar as sect formation is primarily a lower-status phenomenon, what happens when some of these lower-status members improve their social and economic condition? They will either bring the group with them along the lines of modification and accommodation just discussed, or they will leave the group and affiliate with another group (more denominational in character) that is more compatible with their enhanced social status. If they stay, conceivably they could even more or less force those in the group who have not begun to change their status level and conditions to pull out and form a new sect; this could be done consciously or unconsciously. What is involved here is effectively and poignantly stated by John Wesley, himself a founder of a sect—what has become the Methodist Church in its various denominational forms:

> *Wherever riches have increased, the essence of religion has decreased in the same proportion. Therefore, I do not see how it is possible, in the*

nature of things, for any revival of religion to continue long. For religion must necessarily produce both industry and frugality, and these cannot but produce riches. But as riches increase, so will pride, anger, and love of the world in all its branches. . . . Is there no way to prevent this—this continual decay of pure religion? We ought not to prevent people from being diligent and frugal; we must exhort all Christians to gain all they can, and to save all they can; that is in effect to grow rich. What way then can we take, that our money may not sink us into the nethermost hell?[23]

In other words, the sect has an inherent problem—in Marxian phraseology, a seed of self-destruction or change—that leads it out of its "pure" state and into something it rebelled against at an earlier point in time. And out of a sect grows a denomination. This is precisely what happened with Wesley's Methodists; indeed, it is a pattern that has also been followed by most of the other major Christian denominations today. Such groups as the Baptists, the Lutherans, the Presbyterians, and the Seventh-Day Adventists all began at one point as sects, but each has evolved to full-fledged denominational status today. David Harrell, who focuses on this manner of development in tracing the evolution of the Church of Christ sect, mentions that the evolution of some of these sectarian groups is directly related to the changing character of the membership of the group: "The cultured element in the movement . . . simply [begins] the search for a more sophisticated type of religion."[24]

The Institutionalized Sect

Another important type of religious organization is what Yinger calls the *established sect* and what Demerath and Hammond call the *institutionalized sect*. It has been necessary to develop this concept to cover a route that sects occasionally take as an alternate to the predominant sect-to-denomination pattern. There is of course yet a third path that many sects follow—the sect-to-oblivion route. In fact, most sects do not survive long. Internal rivalries and personality clashes, problems with leadership succession, the geographic mobility of members, urban renewal that disperses constituencies and removes facilities—all conspire to make most sects transitory. Those that survive tend to evolve into denominations. However, some become institutionalized sects. Such groups manage to retain elements of their radical protest and a strong commitment to ideology while avoiding the accommodation and modification that results in developing into a denomination. Some denominational char-

---

[23]Quoted in H. Richard Niebuhr, *The Social Sources of Denominationalism* (New York: Meridian Books, 1957), pp. 70–71.
[24]David E. Harrell, Jr., *Emergence of the "Church of Christ" Denomination* (Lufkin, Tex.: Gospel Guardian Company, 1967), p. 28.

acteristics, however, usually become incorporated into the group: the group becomes somewhat bureaucratized; its norms and procedures become formalized; some of its members gain higher social status. Yet it does not become a denomination, even though it is no longer a pure sect either. An institutionalized sect is halfway between the denomination and the sect on the church-sect continuum. What is of crucial significance, however, is that it is in a state of arrested development: the evolutionary process has been brought to a standstill.

Some examples will help clarify this type of religious organization. Religious cooperative and utopian groups such as the Amish, the Hutterites, the Dukhobors, and various Mennonite groups are excellent examples. The Quakers (Society of Friends) are a fairly well-known group that also qualifies quite well as an institutionalized sect. These groups are like the pure sect in the sense of being relatively small in numbers, engaging in protest against both the way religion has been routinized in denominations and the society itself, and emphasizing democratic involvement of members and thereby avoiding extensive bureaucratization. In fact, many such groups do not employ full-time clergymen. These groups are unlike pure sects, however, in that they are somewhat more bureaucratically organized than the latter. The Quakers, for example, have organized two agencies for political influence in Washington and elsewhere as well as the various service and social action functions that are well-organized lobbying groups—the American Friends Service Committee and the Friends' Committee on National Legislation.

Members of institutionalized sects are unlike members of ordinary sects in that their socioeconomic status is often higher. Further, their religious expression in worship is less emotionally charged, and they are more concerned about education than the newly formed sect, which is primarily a fellowship of adults.

How does one account for the arrested development of the institutionalized sect? The cooperative religious groups provide one significant element in suggesting an answer to this question. Groups such as the Amish have avoided unsettling influences from the surrounding society and from other religious groups by the rather dramatic tactic of withdrawing to a considerable degree from the surrounding society. This includes physical or geographic isolation to the degree that such is possible in a modern society by establishing themselves exclusively in rural environments. In the process their members collectively become nearly self-sufficient, depending on the outside world for little except machinery, fuel, and building materials. Thus their members engage in only minimal contact with people outside their group. Such groups further increase their isolation by forbidding television sets and radios and by limiting the education of their children to elementary school. By specifying a very simple life-style and adopting distinctive clothing they deliberately set themselves apart from others and maintain a readily discernable identity, besides avoiding the interaction with the outside world involved in keeping up with new styles. By deliberately minimizing contact with the outside, by making a virtue out of their uniqueness, and by carefully socializing their children they contribute significantly to their protracted period of "suspended animation." Some of these groups have existed for hundreds of years with very little change, and show essentially no signs of accelerating their pace of change today.

The Quakers, on the other hand, have not physically isolated themselves. In fact, among their members are many high-status, highly educated professionals. Quakers, moreover, are politically and socially motivated and involved. Yet the Quaker sect, which originated in the mid-1600s, has not become a full-fledged denomination. The Methodist Church and the Society of Friends today are quite different kinds of organization, although both started out as sectarian movements. Yinger contrasts these two groups in making a very important theoretical suggestion concerning why one group will proceed along the continuum to denominational status while another will stop short at the institutionalized-sect stage. He states that differential status improvement could not be a cause, since members of both groups have moved up the class ladder in fairly equal proportions. There does seem to be some difference, however, in intensity of persecution. Quakers were more vigorously opposed and persecuted than Methodists ever were. Thus conceivably the Quakers could have developed a stronger feeling of cultural isolation and thus greater internal solidarity.

But at best Yinger suggests that such could only be a proximate cause. The really important question is: why were the Quakers more vigorously opposed than the Methodists? Answering this question requires examining the nature of the group's original protest. Yinger's theoretical suggestion is that those sects that emphasize problems of individual anxiety, sin, and salvation tend to evolve into denominations, while sects whose concern is focused on social evils and injustices will become established or institutionalized sects.[25] Radically different kinds of protest distinguished the early Methodists from the early Quakers. The Welsey brothers and other early Methodists were concerned primarily with individual morality and worked primarily to raise its level. Quakers, however, attacked society and called for political reforms, for an end to societal injustice and discrimination, for an end to poverty. Certainly society could more easily tolerate the Methodists' emphasis and

[25]Yinger, *The Scientific Study of Religion*, pp. 266–68.

feel threatened by the Quakers', a fact that goes far in explaining why one sect was persecuted vigorously and the other not nearly so much.

The point here is not so much that as a result of societal persecution and opposition a group (such as the Quakers) may be forced back on its own resources and develop higher group identification and morale. The point is that such a group finds its feeling of estrangement from society intensified; it feels less at home in society and is less likely to evolve to fullblown denominational status, one characteristic of which is a relatively cozy, supportive relationship with the governing structure of the society. The stance the Quakers adopted placed them in a role more like that of an antagonist, and less like that of even "loyal opposition."

In a sense, the physical isolation of the cooperative religious groups is matched by the political and social isolation of the Quakers. Moreover, the established cooperative sects are also in opposition to much that exists in society, which is viewed as basically evil, as a source of contamination. Many of these groups do not even vote in national or local elections. Established sects such as the Quakers, on the other hand, do not express their opposition to society by withdrawing; they become activists and try to change society. In either case, however, such groups are inhibited in moving along the path to standard denominational status.

The Cult

The final type of religious organization to consider is the religious cult. A *cult* is similar to a sect in its rejection of the religious patterns and formulations of denominations—or of whatever the society's dominant form(s) of religion happens to be. Cult members were either not attracted to dominant religious groups in the first place or, like sectarians, became disenchanted with commonly accepted religious forms. The cult differs from the sect, however, in that the former does not call for a return to the original, pure religion, but rather emphasizes the new—a new revelation or insight provided by a supernatural power, say, or the rediscovery of an old revelation that had been lost and unknown these many years (and which is therefore new to this age). Cults thus tend to be out of the mainstream of the dominant religious system in a society. Although there will usually be some overlapping of ideology and terminology, cults deliberately contrast themselves with dominant traditional religious groups. As might be expected, cults frequently employ new terminology and symbols. Discourses of some groups, such as the Great I Am, are almost unintelligible to the uninitiated. The themes of cults tend to be mystical and esoteric. Further, a cult is more likely than any other type of religious group to be centered around a charismatic leader

—that is, a person who is believed to have been given the special revelation or knowledge and can open the door of truth and insight to the uninitiated. Father Divine, Daddy Grace, and Mary Baker Eddy are such types.

Cults also have a strong individualistic emphasis, stressing peace of mind and getting the individual in tune with the supernatural, while exhibiting relatively little concern with social change. Cults tend to be urban-centered, in part because they have traditionally not attracted great hordes of people and therefore need a large population to draw from, but likely also in part because cults tend to attract the disenchanted, those persons looking for meaningful attachments to counterbalance their anonymity—persons more likely to be found in urban settings. Cults seldom develop much of an organizational structure, often tend to remain small and informal, and can be quite casual about membership requirements. They may not even require followers to sever their other religious affiliations.

Cults tend to be rather transitory and short-lived. Being dependent on a charismatic leader, they tend to dissolve when the leader dies, disappears, or is discredited. Occasionally, however, a cult persists, develops a structure and means of leadership succession, grows in size, and actually moves toward denominational status on the church-sect continuum. In a study of cults in Alberta, W. E. Mann found the following characteristics of members: Anglo-Saxon by ethnic background, more female than male, individuals rather than family units, avid readers with above-average educational attainment, highly mobile, and although of comfortable financial means seeming to lack full middle-class acceptance.[26] Although a few writers have placed the cult beyond the extreme end of the church-sect continuum, another way of viewing it is to see it as an alternate to the sect at one end which may move onto the continuum at some point and give evidence of evolution toward denominational or quasidenominational status. Figure 7–1 shows what we are suggesting. The dotted line associated with the cult indicates the possibility that it may change, not die, and get on the evolutionary road toward denominational status. A classic example is Christian Science, which began as a cult (with Mary Baker Eddy as its leader), but which today exhibits most of the characteristics of a standard denomination. Similarly, the Nation of Islam ("Black Muslims"), which originally met all the criteria of a cult—it began as a small group with a charismatic leader (Elijah Muhammed) who preached a new doctrine of black supremacy and Islam (out of the mainstream of Christianity), it emphasized individual self-

---

[26]W. E. Mann, *Sect, Cult, and Church in Alberta* (Toronto: University of Toronto Press, 1955), pp. 5–8, 37–40.

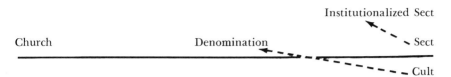

FIGURE 7–1

help rather than societal reform, and it was primarily urban—is now showing definite signs of moving toward a denominational pattern.

It must be noted that cults constitute a most viable phenomenon today. If anything, their numbers and popularity are increasing. Faith-healing cults continue to abound; cults that center around Eastern religious ideas and individual gurus have gained in popularity; interest in the occult and the formation of groups around the practice of the occult have increased; and segments of the drug culture that celebrate the use of mind-expanding drugs as a religious enterprise continue to emerge. All of these constitute groups or movements. The cult phenomenon is very much alive and well, although individual cults themselves may be extremely transitory as they flower today and wither tomorrow.

The Future of the Church-Sect Typology

It should be noted in conclusion that several sociologists have recently leveled searching criticisms against the church-sect typology and have questioned both its accuracy in describing religious reality and its utility for research in the sociology of religion.[27] The reader may well wish to explore this area of critique. In fact, we recommend class discussion on the issue of the utility of the church-sect typology. The position taken here is that while many criticisms of the typology are well taken, and while the typology is admittedly only one way of looking at the social organization of religion, it is still useful so long as the original

[27]See, e.g., Benton Johnson, "A Critical Appraisal of the Church-Sect Typology," *American Sociological Review* 22, no. 1 (1957); 88–92; idem, "On Church and Sect," *American Sociological Review* 28, no. 1 (1967); 64–68; idem, "Church-Sect Revisited," *Journal for the Scientific Study of Religion* 10, no. 2 (1971); 124–37; Erich Goode, "Some Critical Observations on the Church-Sect Dimension," *Journal for the Scientific Study of Religion* 6, no. 1 (1967); 69–77; idem, "Further Reflections on the Church-Sect Dimension," *Journal for the Scientific Study of Religion* 6, no. 2 (1967); 270–75; N. J. Demerath III, "In a Sow's Ear," *Journal for the Scientific Study of Religion* 6, no. 1 (1967); 77–84; Allan W. Eister, "Toward a Radical Critique of Church-Sect Typologizing," *Journal for the Scientific Study of Religion* 6, no. 1 (1967); 85–90; and J. Kenneth Benson and James Dorsett, "Church-Sect Replaced," *Journal for the Scientific Study of Religion* 10, no. 2 (1971); 138–51.

church-sect dichotomy is supplemented by additional types. The typology has been so widely used in analyzing religious phenomena and appears to be such a firm basis for continuing discussion that an introduction to the social organization of religion can well start here. However, even an elaborated version of the typology such as presented in this chapter is incapable of capturing the diversity of religious organization. In fact, typologies inevitably breed elaboration and further specification. In the process, knowledge and insight are advanced. For example, Stephen Steinberg has analyzed the emergence of Reform Judaism from its "parent," Orthodox Judaism, not as formation of a sect but as a "church movement." That is, Reform Judaism did not object to any "perversion of true religion" embodied in Orthodox Judaism but to the continued insistence by Orthodox Judaism on retaining the "old ways": the Reform movement sought to "modernize" Judaism. Building on Benton Johnson's single-variable distinction between church and sect that we earlier described—in which a religious organization accepting the surrounding social environment is defined as a church and one rejecting it as a sect—Steinberg points out that the rebel group (Reform Judaism) did not follow the common route of the sect by rejecting its social environment, but accepted and accommodated to that environment.[28] Although Steinberg notes that conditions giving rise to such a "church movement" are rare, such a development is well worth noting. Furthermore, our understanding of the dynamics of such a development is enhanced by our understanding of what "normally" happens along the church-sect continuum.

But continued elaboration and creation of new types is hardly advisable unless we have arrived at measurable dimensions of religious organizations that groups either possess or don't possess, or exhibit to a greater or lesser degree. What we need is specification of characteristics of religious groups that can be measured with some precision. Groups can then be placed on a continuum for each dimension or variable. In addition, a composite of the individual measures can possibly be constructed to yield a composite continuum. This approach is currently being developed and shows definite promise of adding insight into the form and nature of religious organizations. It has the advantage of retaining much of the terminology of the church-sect typology while permitting more precise location of groups along the continuum.

Before Johnson's single-variable measure (1963), Yinger (1957) had proposed two criteria for differentiating churches from sects: degree of inclusiveness/exclusiveness of the group, and degree of attention paid by the group to the task of social integration as opposed to satisfaction of

---

28Stephen Steinberg, "Reform Judaism: The Origin and Evolution of a 'Church Movement,'" *Journal for the Scientific Study of Religion* 5, no. 1 (1965); 117–29.

personal need.[29] By 1970 Yinger added Johnson's criterion and changed his earlier second criterion to emphasize degree of bureaucratization and success in integrating a variety of subunits into one structure.[30]

Roland Robertson has suggested two criteria: the basis of legitimacy as perceived by the leaders of the religious group, and the principle of membership implemented by the group.[31] The legitimacy measure contrasts views of religious leaders: (1) the view that one's group is only one among other sets of acceptable or valid religious vehicles (religious pluralism), (2) the view that one's group is the only valid religious form (unique, true religion). The membership principle contrasts "relatively demanding standards of admission and/or religious performance" (exclusivism) with low standards of acceptance (inclusivism).[32]

The value of developing and applying such analytic concepts rests in their ability to focus on measurable features that distinguish one religious organization from another and to arrange groups at various points along a continuum. The ultimate set of measures has not yet been devised; nor is it certain that one ever can be. But further development in the direction taken by Johnson, Yinger, and Robertson describes the future so far as the church-sect typology is concerned.

[29]J. Milton Yinger, *Religion, Society, and the Individual* (New York: Macmillan, 1957), pp. 147–48.
[30]Ibid., p. 257.
[31]Roland Robertson, *The Sociological Interpretation of Religion* (New York: Schocken Books, 1970), pp. 123ff.
[32]Ibid., p. 124.

8

Religion
in Society:
The Interdependent
Relationship

In this chapter we propose to elaborate and specify further the dominant theme of this text, mentioned at several points previously—that religion and the other institutions and units in society are in an interdependent, reciprocal relationship. As such, we shall be setting the stage for the next three chapters, which look more specifically at the interrelationship of religion with three major institutions or societal phenomena—namely, the economy, the political system, and the class system. As we discuss the reciprocal relationship we shall among other things summarize the central points and basic perspective of structural-functional theory in sociology, particularly as such theory relates to religion.

In general terms, the *structural-functional approach* (or simply, "functional") to the study of society asserts that all elements in a society are interrelated, that each contributes in some way to the attainment of both individual and collective goals, and that each responds to change in the other elements by adapting and adjusting. Implicit in the terms themselves is the idea that the elements that constitute the *structural* units and arrangements of the society supplement one another in a *functional* manner. When such assumptions and modes of analysis are applied to religion, two emphases predominate: (1) religion is part of the social structure and as such can be expected to "fit" at least reasonably well with the other parts and elements of the social structure, and (2) religion by virtue of its presence in society performs certain functions for the society as a whole—that is, religion is beneficial in various ways to the society generally and to certain of its subparts in particular.

These two emphases provide the basis for the two sections into which most of this chapter is divided. In the first section that is introduced by a brief discussion of functional theory we shall be concerned with the influence that other societal elements exert on religion to get it to mesh reasonably well with the rest of the social system. In the second section (beginning on p. 141) we shall focus on the "functions" of religion—in particular, the integrative functions that religion performs for the society and the impact it has on other elements in the social structure.

Although it is impossible to keep these two emphases or perspectives completely separate or distinct as we discuss one or the other, the attempt is worthwhile if only to emphasize that the relationship between religion and the rest of society is a reciprocal one: the social structure affects religion, and religion affects the social structure.

The Impact of Social Structure on Religion

FUNCTIONAL THEORY

We begin with a discussion of functional theory. Although there is a great deal of controversy concerning the application of functional theory to the role of religion in society, some of its perspectives definitely advance our understanding of the relationship of religion to other elements in the social structure. Actually, not only functional theory, but some concepts of conflict theory will prove handy as well. But first let us summarize those perspectives in functional theory that help explicate the role of religion in society.

Basic Functional Theories

Structural-functionalism as used in the social sciences involves the application to social groups and systems the biological observation that every organism has a structure consisting of a relatively stable interrelationship of parts, each of which performs a specialized task or "function" that in conjunction with the others permits the organism both to survive and to act. Social scientists' early expectations of finding precise interrelationships and functions in social "organisms" have been scaled down to the point where they are content in finding parallels and analogies between the biological organism and the social "organism." Yet the analogy does remain, and it is valid and helpful to a point—that is, any social system consists of parts and subunits that are interrelated, exert influence one upon the other, and function only so long as other subunits are present and functioning. Our earlier discussion of the five functional prerequisites of groups is meaningful within this context of thought. If any of these tasks—personnel replacement, production and distribution of goods and services, preservation of order, socialization of new members, or maintenance of a sense of group purpose—is absent or ineffective for very long, then the group will have difficulty functioning and likely will ultimately cease functioning altogether. The "functional imperatives" of Talcott Parsons represent another statement of similar structural-functional needs or requisites of groups. According to Parsons, if it is to survive and to act, a social system or group must engage in goal-attainment activities, adaptation techniques, integrating mechanisms, and pattern-maintenance and tension-management procedures.[1]

An inherent assumption—actually an important observation—with respect to the above is that societies (as all groups for that matter) consist of elements (subgroups, institutions, individuals) that perform specific functions, often of a highly narrow and specialized nature, that contribute to their overall functioning. This is of course not to say that all elements perform equally well or even adequately at any given point in time. In fact, some may fail and be compensated for by others. Some may begin to wage war against other parts or the whole. Some may raise questions about their own function or the function of other elements and may initiate change.

The Equilibrium Concept

Such qualifications immediately raise serious questions about another concept within the structural-functional perspective that theorists as a result have modified. This is the *equilibrium concept* as enunciated by Vilfredo Pareto—the view that society exists in a state of equilibrium in which interdependent parts continually readjust to any change in other subunits of the system.[2] This concept has value in recognizing the

---

[1]Talcott Parsons, "An Outline of the Social System," in *Theories of Society*, ed. Talcott Parsons, Edward Shils, Kaspar D. Naegle, and Jesse R. Pitts (New York: Free Press, 1961), pp. 38–41.
[2]Vilfredo Pareto, *The Mind and Society* (New York: Harcourt, Brace and World, 1935), vol. 1.

interdependence of the subparts that make up a system, a phenomenon we have noted often so far as the relationship of religion to other units in the society is concerned. The flaw in Pareto's concept, then, is not that it stresses the interdependence of parts, but that it emphasizes the equilibrium aspect; that is, it implies that all is well in society, or—even more debatable—that balance and continuous smooth functioning are even possible. An attempt to salvage the equilibrium concept by referring to a "moving" equilibrium still does not adequately account for discrepancies and conflicts in the group—in a real sense, it does not adequately recognize the time-honored sociological concept of "cultural lag." For instance, although religion tends to adjust and stay "in tune with" society and its actions, religion can also change so slowly in relation to changes in other elements of the social structure that it eventually comes into conflict with the new directions and commitments of a particular group, element, etc. Although there may well be an underlying tendency in social systems toward balance and equilibrium, the latter may not always if ever occur in anything approaching a perfect fashion. Thus, although Newton's third law of motion in physics—that for every action there is an equal and opposite reaction—loosely applies to social systems, we cannot assume, in social contexts, that the reaction will be appropriate to the activity: a unit can also overreact or underreact, and the system may limp along as a result. Of course, it need not collapse—although neither will we expect it to function as well as it might if reactions were actually appropriate to actions.

Functional Alternatives

Without trying to be encyclopedic in our presentation of functional theory, we must still mention the major contribution made by Robert Merton—namely, the possibility of *functional alternatives*. That is, the fact that a given action or role of a particular subunit in a social system is functional, does not mean it is the only action that may be functional in that way in that particular place and time.[3] This concept is extremely relevant to understanding the role of religion in social systems; note also that it casts serious doubt on those theories referred to earlier (in Chapter 3) that relate the orgins of religion to the functions religion performs in society. That is, the fact that religion performs certain functions and satisfies certain needs of society and its individual members does not mean that religion is either inevitable or nonexpendable; other systems or mechanisms could conceivably satisfy these needs as well or

[3]Robert K. Merton, *Social Theory and Social Structure* (Glencoe, Ill.: Free Press, 1957), pp. 33–34.

better. In fact, perhaps this explains why some persons are "religious" (and in a variety of ways), while others are not at all religious. That is, while some people practice major religions, others avail themselves of nonreligious functional alternatives or of religious alternatives outside the mainstream of formalized religion (cf. the earlier discussion of Yinger in footnote 30, Chapter 4).

SOCIAL STRUCTURE AFFECTS RELIGION: FUNCTIONAL THEORY APPLIED

Now, how do these central ideas in structural-functional theory relate to religion? As a start, let us recall our brief consideration of Durkheim and Swanson in Chapter 3. Durkheim's central thesis, we noted, is that religion is a fairly direct outgrowth and reflection of the social structure, even to the degree that when people talk of "God" they are really talking about their society, which they have unconsciously elevated to a position of ultimate authority. Swanson built on Durkheim's very general approach and specified relationships between specific features of society or relationships among people, on the one hand, and certain religious beliefs on the other. The contention in Swanson's modification of Durkheim, then, is that various features of the social structure provide a model for religion, and that specific religious beliefs "fit" or mesh with a particular social structure.

Although a direct cause-and-effect relationship between features of social structure and features of religion are impossible to establish conclusively, the tendency toward consistency between social structure and religion seems quite clear. That is, whether or not social structure "causes" certain religious beliefs, it appears likely that particular beliefs will be accepted and incorporated into a religious system only if they are essentially compatible with the social structure. Thus we might hypothesize that, say, in a society whose contacts with other societies have not involved warfare, religious beliefs that conceive of God seeking vengeance against his enemies and the enemies of his chosen people are unlikely to rise.

Within the context of functionalism we point again to a body of material already presented (in Chapter 7). We refer to our discussion of the differences in religious understanding and perspective related to differences in social class: sect versus denomination and Pope's discussion of the needs of lower-status persons that are served by sectarian religious participation. Briefly, then, in a real sense the entire discussion of the influence of social-status elements on religion begun in Chapter 7 (and elaborated further in Chapter 11) fits in well in our present discussion. The point is that certain needs generated by the social structure find a response in religion. The social structure produces a stratification system, for example, and thereby generates inequities among people. Religion frequently salves, for some, the pain of being victim to such inequity, while for others it justifies or celebrates the joy of being the beneficiary of inequity.

The phenomenon of messianic and millenarian cults throughout the world, a clear example of the impact of social-structural factors on religion, is also strongly linked to stratification factors. Such religious groups look for a way out of present conditions and situations through, respectively, the coming of a messiah, or the dawning of a new age when past and present structures will be wiped out and a new world will arise. Millenialism seems almost always to appear in groups that either are or perceive themselves to be marginal and deprived with respect to other groups with whom they compare themselves.[4] As Burridge notes, they seem to be seeking "a new situation and status which, providing the basis for a new integrity, will enable life to be lived more abundantly."[5] Talmon points out that three conditions are likely to precede the emergence of millennial movements (assuming all the while the condition of marginality): (1) a period of transition from a relatively stable social situation when accepted relationships and norms are disrupted; (2) a cumulative deterioration of life conditions in which means provided to reach personal goals and expectations are inadequate; and (3) a sudden crisis that crystallizes discontent and precipitates action to resolve it.[6]

We shall have occasion later to discuss other examples where the impact of structural and ideological factors in the society on religious structure and ideology expresses a "strain toward consistency." For example, the slavery controversy that resulted in the Civil War divided national religious groups into northern and southern factions, each of which expressed religious sanctions for the prevailing political ideology of its region. Certainly there were exceptions—lonely individual voices who voiced religious support for a point of view opposite to that of the region in which they were located; but the strain toward consistency of religious ideology with social or political ideology was dominant.

Similarly we could observe that throughout most of history—when children were not just mouths to feed and minds to educate, but potential productive resources and economic assets that not only helped increase the productivity of the family's piece of ground but replaced those

[4]Roland Robertson, *The Sociological Interpretation of Religion* (New York: Schocken Books, 1970), p. 166.
[5]Kenelm Burridge, *New Heaven, New Earth* (New York: Schocken Books, 1969), p. 171.
[6]Yonina Talmon, "Millenarian Movements," *European Journal of Sociology* 7 (1966); 159–200. Quoted in Robertson, *Sociological Interpretation*, pp. 166–67.

who quickly perished in these times of high death rates—much of the time the religious injunction to "be fruitful and multiply" meshed well with societal needs. It is certainly more than coincidence that as population growth has exploded and as questions pour in from around the globe about the wisdom of allowing population growth to proceed unchecked, religious groups have begun to reassess their stands. Many religious groups have reversed themselves on this issue. Officially (i.e., at the papal level), the Roman Catholic church still opposes "artificial" means of contraception, though that position, too, will change. Yet even the pope ex-expresses concern over problems of population growth and urges that it not continue unchecked.

In a similar vein, we can observe the trend, developing among major denominations in the United States and elsewhere, that favors ordaining women into the ministry. The ordination of women into the Christian ministry did not originate with the women's liberation movement, but began much earlier when women were granted the franchise and when employment opportunities formerly exclusively or primarily in the male domain were opened to women.

Another set of data concerns the broad area of societal norms, particularly the relative congruence of religious norms with the society's norms and values. One could reasonably raise the issue here of which comes first, the religious norms or the societal norms. If society's norms grew out of religious norms in the distant past, then perhaps we should be insinuating not that religion reflects the society, but the reverse. Actually, we do not wish to suggest that religion has no independent impact on the society; we'll get to that subject later in this chapter. Nor do we have to resolve the chicken-or-the-egg issue of which norms come first—certainly not at this point. We are content simply to observe a consistency between religious norms and societal norms and find reinforcement for the contention that there is a strain toward consistency among the units that make up the society. Although the norms of religious groups may be more strict than those of the society, they rarely conflict.

S. F. Nadel provides some fascinating data from two primitive societies that illustrate well the major proposition of this chapter—that other features of the societal structure have an impact on religion. Nadel observed that while two tribes in the southern Sudan, the Huban and the Otoro, lived in similar physical environments and exhibited many similar cultural elements, their religious practices and beliefs differed considerably. The basic religious orientation of the Huban is pessimistic, coercive, aggressive, and emotionally tense. On the other hand, the Otoro are calm, dispassionate, submissive, and optimistic in their religious orientation and practice. In exploring possible explanations for such differences, Nadel observed that although there were many similarities in the other cultural elements of the society, there are important differences as well—differences that apparently help to produce differences in religion. For one thing, the Huban lack clear norms for handling adolescent transfer to adult roles, while the Otoro have devised procedures and norms that handle the shift quite gracefully. Also, among the Huban a wife is never completely integrated into her husband's family, whereas among the Otoro the integration of a wife into her husband's family is smooth and complete. As consequence, the Huban experience conflicts of loyalty, anxiety over marital relationships, and uncertainty concerning juridical authority. In summary, the Huban tend to intensify anomie and role ambiguity, while the Otoro tend to reduce them. The religious beliefs of each group, then, reflect such features of the social structure.[7]

Within the general context of the relationship between social structure and religious form and expression in a society, J. Milton Yinger suggests some perceptive questions that should be asked in any study. For example: What kind of society are we examining? Is it small and homogeneous, or large and diverse? Is it isolated from or in contact with other societies that have differing value systems? Is it authoritarian in its distribution of power, or democratic? How far has the technical development of the society allowed it to bring hunger and disease under control?[8] To these we would add: Is the society cooperatively or competitively oriented? How successful is the society in regulating and controlling aggression? Is the physical environment stingy or generous in providing food and other resources? Is the society based on a hunting-and-gathering, agrarian, or industrial economy? The implicit assumption in asking such questions is that the type of society under discussion and how it is structured will have an impact on the religious ideas and expressions of the society.

What we are trying to make clear is that there is definitely a relationship between the features of a society, of which religion is one. That is to say, all features of society—whether economic structure, political system, family structure, values with regard to life-and-death problems, technological mechanisms, religion, and so on—are interrelated. Change in one will at some point have an impact on the other elements or units. Also, the units tend to be compatible with one another—at least in the long run. For example, any religion that advocates violent overthrow of the existing political structure will be unable to maintain that position in the long run. Either it will be forced to cease and desist, or it will

[7]S. F. Nadel, "Two Nuba Religions: An Essay in Comparison," *American Anthropologist* 57, no. 4 (1955); 661–79.
[8]J. Milton Yinger, *The Scientific Study of Religion* (New York: Macmillan, 1970), p. 217.

gradually tone down the excesses of its position, unless, of course, it succeeds in its revolutionary program. The point is simply that protracted conflict is nearly impossible. One will expect success, failure, or modification, not continual open conflict.

It should be clear, however, that we are employing the structural-functional approach in only a limited way. We reject, as does Merton, the more extreme positions that so-called functionalists have occasionally taken in the past. Merton summarized three of these positions or postulates as follows: (1) The postulate of the functional unity of a society—that every normative action or belief is functional in the sense of being necessary and useful for the total social system. (2) The postulate that every social form has a positive function—that no parts or forms of culture survive unless they are performing services for the society. (3) The postulate of indispensability—that particular social forms are indispensable in carrying out societal functions.[9]

With reference to postulates (1) and (2), we need to observe that simply because a social form exists and is likely to perform some function for individuals or subunits within the society, this need not imply that the total society benefits thereby. Not that society is necessarily harmed, either. Many social acts appear to be essentially neutral, so far as the overall society is concerned. For example, it appears that neither voluntary attendance nor compulsory attendance at college classes is necessary for the continued existence of the society. In fact, that both forms of attendance regulation survive suggests their very neutrality in this sense. On the other hand, the institution of higher education and the availability of college classes are, we trust, necessary for society as structured today.

Objection to postulate (3) is even easier to see. That a given factor in society performs a function for the society is simply insufficient grounds for concluding that it is indispensable. For one thing, other social factors or units may perform the function as well or better. Although Grandmother O'Conner feels good every day after attending morning mass, and although it may be important to society that Grandmother O'Conner feel good (perhaps she is secretary of state or chairperson of the Federal Reserve Board), she, or another Grandmother O'Conner, may feel just as good, and the society may benefit as much, if she joined a daily coffee klatsch of cronies from the old country.

At this point we are finding it increasingly difficult to keep apart the two emphases we mentioned at the beginning of this chapter. We are beginning inevitably to refer to the "functions" of religion—that is, how religion benefits or provides services to the society as a whole and to

[9]Merton, *Social Theory*, pp. 25–37.

other subunits in particular. As we confront this matter head-on in the second major section of this chapter, it will be important to keep in mind our reservations about the three postulates summarized above. That is, something may be functional and yet not be indispensable. Although certain tasks or functions must be performed, the particular form or mechanism that performs that task today may not be doing the job as well as it might and may not perform it at all tomorrow.

The Impact of Religion on Social Structure

Quite specifically this section extends the one just concluded. That is, we shall flip over the coin and turn from the discussion of social structure influencing religion and now look at what functions religion performs for a society—in particular, how religion performs an *integrative* or cohesive function for society. Note well, however, that to speak of "functions" and "integration" does not necessarily imply a cause-and-effect relationship. It may well be simply happenstance or coincidence that religion does certain things for the society. Moreover, religion may reinforce the integration of society without "causing" such integration. Also, we need to pay attention to Yinger's cautionary observation that our language may mislead and fail us when we use the word *integration*.[10] That is, it is hard to think of integration in anything other than positive terms. Yet integration may involve negative side effects for some people. Think again of Marx's view of religion—it helps "integrate" the masses into the productive mechanism of society, thereby making them vulnerable to manipulation and exploitation. That is, the masses may be "integrated" into society for the benefit of the elites, and thus ultimately to their own personal detriment.

Further, we need to observe that although our starting point in discussing the impact of religion on society is on religion as integrative—that is, simply in some way(s) helpful—we must be alert to a possible opposite consequence—namely, religion as disruptive or segmenting. This simply states the fundamental sociological observation that social phenomena are seldom either functional or dysfunctional in an exclusive sense, but exhibit major or minor effects of both.

Actually, the cautions and qualifications we are mentioning here constitute the outline of this section. We shall begin with a discussion of the theory of religion as an integrative factor in society and the evi-

[10]Yinger, *Scientific Study*, p. 106.

dence supporting it. Next we shall consider whether and to what extent the integrative idea obscures underlying negative effects. That is, we intend to cast at least some doubts on what may be a naïve view of religion as integrating. Finally, we shall become explicit concerning how religion is or may actually be segmenting and disruptive in addition to or instead of integrating.

RELIGION AS AN INTEGRATING INFLUENCE

One of the early proponents in sociology of the view that religion is an integrating factor within a society was Emile Durkheim. His stance is obvious in his assertion that religion came into being in response to the needs of social structure to reinforce itself.[11] His views of the integrative (functional) role of religion are well illustrated in his discussion of the social functions of religious and ceremonial ritual, as summarized by Alpert.[12] Durkheim sees four primary social functions of such ritual: (1) It serves a disciplinary and preparatory function. That is, ritual imposes a self-discipline that is necessary for social life. Members of society need to accommodate constraints, controls, boundaries. Learning to follow religious rituals facilitates development of this ability. (2) Ceremonial ritual provides a cohesive function. That is, it brings people together, reaffirms their common bonds, and reinforces social solidarity. By doing things jointly and repetitively, the members of the group strengthen their bonds of relatedness. "The essential thing is that men are assembled, that sentiments are felt in common, and that they are expressed in common acts."[13] (3) It serves a revitalizing function. That is, it makes members of the society aware of their common social heritage. It links them to the past: What we do has a history; we ourselves have a history. Such awareness can provide motivation and inspiration to carry on. (4) It serves a euphoric function. It aids in establishing a pleasant feeling of social well-being. This function takes on special significance when a group is faced with calamities, disappointments, losses of treasured members, and other threats to its stability. It helps straighten out the sharp curves and adds some rays of light in the dark tunnels of disappointment and despair.

It needs to be observed in any discussion of Durkheim's views of the relationship of religion and social structure that he viewed religion as a product of the society. Religion was an unconscious development

[11]Emile Durkheim, *The Elementary Forms of the Religious Life*, trans. Joseph W. Swain (New York: Collier Books, 1961), p. 464.
[12]Harry Alpert, *Emile Durkheim and His Sociology* (New York: Russell & Russell, 1961), pp. 198–203.
[13]Durkheim, *Elementary Forms*, pp. 431–32.

within society used by the society to reinforce its norms and priorities—not simply in terms of "we say . . .," or "I the king say . . .," but "God says. . . ." It is the ultimate legitimation of the forms and norms that society has already developed. Thus religion is viewed as performing a reinforcement function for the society. In the process it integrates or binds the group together. In expressing common beliefs about the nature of reality and the supernatural, in engaging in joint ritual and worship activities, in retelling the sagas and myths of the past, the group (society) is brought closer together and linked with the ancestral past.

Quite clearly the model for such a view of the integrating functions of religion is the small and probably "primitive" society in which essentially no religious or philosophical diversity is present and in which religion is practically inseparable from the thought systems and world views of the society generally. Much of the discussion of the integrating functions of religion comes from anthropological investigations of such small "primitive" societies. Durkheim himself based his views on investigations of small aboriginal tribes in Australia.

Thus the view that religion helps to integrate the society in which it is found may need to be qualified when we analyze the functions of religion in complex societies, particularly those in which one finds religious diversity, competition among religious groups, and perhaps some individuals professing no religious commitments at all. But more on that in the next section of this chapter. At the moment, although holding some tentative reservations about how extensively religion is able to integrate a society, particularly a complex one, we want to consider some of the ways in which religion has been viewed as exerting an integrating influence in societies.

Normative Reinforcement   Religion serves a reinforcement function in society to the degree that it teaches and emphasizes the same norms and values as the society's. This may be at the very general level of teaching such values as human dignity and freedom, equality before the law, respect for legitimate authority, faithfulness to one's role, and the like. Or it may be more specific, such as: "Thou shalt not kill, steal, or procreate illegitimate children." In a direct sense, religion is here being viewed as a socializing agent in the society. Although allowing for the possibility that religious groups, just as all other kinds of groups, socialize their members into some norms unique unto themselves, we are here speaking of religion as one among several institutions involved in socializing citizens to the core norms of the society. Educational agencies, families, peer groups, mass media, and various voluntary associations are all involved in this process. Religion is but one such agent. But it is one.

Although the issue could be raised, we do not need to try to resolve the chicken-or-the-egg question here. That is, which came first—the religious norms and values, or the societal norms and values? Is the reason religion and society teach a common core of values because religious values were divinely inspired or somehow appeared first and then informed the society? Or has religion adopted societal values and attached divine sanctions to them, along the lines Durkheim suggested? Even if such priorities could be determined with absolute assurance, it is really unnecessary, for our purposes, to seek a resolution. When we look from the overall perspective of the society, religion can today be viewed as reinforcing societal norms, and whether at some distant point in the past some or all of those norms derived from religious sources then becomes irrelevant. Actually, indications from the recent past suggest that norms tend to change or surface in other sectors of the society first, and then are adopted and reinforced by religious groups. For example, although religious voices were in the forefront of the civil rights movement, civil rights legislation had to be passed first before most religious groups began to champion the cause. Neither do most religious groups appear to have initiated the call for changes in society's norms regarding capital punishment, abortion, and attitudes toward homosexuality. Yet as laws change and as the norms of society begin to change, religious groups come along, some quite quickly, with support and theological justification for such change. Without even trying to resolve a controversy we may here be stimulating—what is likely an unsolvable question, unresolvable at least to everyone's satisfaction—we can observe again that religion does reinforce many of the norms of society. To the degree that it does, it performs an integrative function for the society.

Closely related to what we've just been discussing is the possibility that religion not only socializes people in the "thou shalts" and "thou shalt nots" of society in a reinforcing sense, but occasionally pushes those norms even farther. For example, society has norms against murder, but doesn't usually try to control what you think about your neighbor so long as you don't harm him or his property or infringe on his rights. A religious system may go farther: "Whoso hateth his brother is a murderer." "Love your neighbor." "Do good to those who despitefully use you and persecute you." If a religion is successful in inculcating norms more stringent than those the society imposes and thereby creates a "super-Christian" (or "super-Buddhist," or "super-Hindu," or whatever), to that degree one may also see a "supercitizen." That is to say, society would probably be even better off if people not only avoided destroying their neighbors but actually loved them and tried to help them. The key here, of course, is discovering whether and to what degree religion actually produces such "supercitizens." Undoubtedly there are some: they tend to be called "saints," and they may even be societal heroes and models for behavior. But there is no clear evidence that, on the average, religion produces many such "supercitizens." Yet we must again observe: To the degree that it happens, the society would benefit.

Integration into Meaningful Group Relationships An exceptionally important function religion performs is that of bringing individuals into meaningful relationships with others in a group. Religious groups bring immigrants, social isolates, various minorities, and some socially maladjusted persons into a group and put them into contact with others. Not that religion reaches every such person or is successful in integrating all of those with whom it establishes contact. Nor is religion unique in performing this task or function for society—so do labor unions, fraternal lodges, newcomers' clubs, political parties, and innumerable other voluntary associations and groups of all sizes, constituencies, and purposes. However, religious groups, in large part because of their reputation for being concerned about life purposes and adjustment as well as for raising a person's sights beyond current mundane problems, attract relatively large proportions of persons in need of meaningful interpersonal contact. Society needs such groups to do this. Society needs members who can function well in their roles. People function better when they feel some personal worth and have meaningful, satisfying relationships with other people. To the extent that religious groups provide this service to some who feel isolated and are not being relieved of their anxieties and problems elsewhere, to that extent religion is serving the society.

Catalyst for Reaffirming Societal Values Another way in which religion contributes to the integration of society is by serving as a focal point—in a sense, as a catalyst—for the society to reaffirm some of its basic values. Religion everywhere does this through festivals. Think, for example, of what happens in our society in connection with the religious festival called Christmas. Although there's plenty of growling about gifts yet to buy, overdrawn checking accounts, and crass commercialism conspiring to do us all in, there is something else as well. There is a pervasive spirit in the air of good will and joviality. There are increases in gifts to charities. There is more attention given to those less fortunate than the majority. Not that what emerges is particularly enduring. Yet periodically through such rites and festivals that reach out beyond the religious group itself, some of the fundamental values of the society are dramatized for people, and they reaffirm them at least intellectually and momentarily. Certainly not every Scrooge does an about-face—above all, one that lasts beyond the festival itself; yet some do, and most citizens are at least temporarily affected.

In this connection we also think of the religious imagery and terminology as well as the appeals to a religious authority and legitimation that so many politicians employ. "As a religious nation we reaffirm such and so and must do such and so." "In accord with our Judeo-Christian heritage. ...." And so on. Note that we'll discuss this phenomenon at greater length when we consider "civil religion" in Chapter 15.

Aid in Adjusting to Personal Crises   Another integrating function of religion that some feel is actually getting close to the fundamental purpose or essence of religion itself is the help it gives to people facing various crisis situations in their lives. To the degree that religion helps people grapple with emotional crisis, with death and bereavement, with uncertainties and disappointments of all kinds, religion is performing an important service for society. We introduced the idea of relativizing suffering and crisis in Chapter 3; this again is what we're talking about. Religion attempts to relativize human problems by placing them in an eternal perspective, interpreting events as God's will ("All things work for good to those who love God") and providing "answers" for unrational events. Whether the answers and explanations are "true" is for our purposes—and for society's—beside the point. What is important is whether people feel better as a result of what religion does for them in periods of crisis and imbalance. The society needs functioning members who fill their social roles with skill and attention. Society cannot afford to have great numbers of members incapacited for extended periods of time. To the extent that religion helps with this task, society is greatly aided.

We are of course involved here with what many have seen as the major focus or purpose of religion. Recall the cognitive and emotional needs that the early anthropologists described religion as meeting. Think of the explanations for religion that stem from psychology as people are seen as relieving their anxieties through religious rites and activities. Whether or not such understandings or interpretations of religion explain its origin is unimportant at the moment so long as we recognize that people not only turn to religion for help in trouble and for relief from their anxieties, but they feel better off as a consequence. Research by three social psychologists indicates not only that people with problems seek out clergymen, but that many report feeling better as a result of the contact. In fact, clergymen were sought out more often than any other category of professional in the helping fields. The research found that of those seeking help of some kind, 42 percent went to clergymen. Others in order of the frequency with which they were contacted included medical doctors (29 percent), psychiatrists and psychologists (18 percent), lawyers (6 percent), and marriage counselors (3 percent).[14]

With respect to the degree of perceived help gained from the various sources, clergymen ranked high, although no higher than some other

[14]Gerald Gurin, Joseph Veroff, and Sheila Feld, *Americans View Their Mental Health* (New York: Basic Books, 1960), p. 307.

TABLE 8–1

Perception of Helpfulness of Therapy (First-mentioned Responses Only), by Source of Help Used

How Much the Therapy Helped	*Source of Help*						
	Clergy	*Doctor*	*Psychia-trist*	*Marriage counselor*	*Other psycho-logical agencies*	*Non-psycho-logical agencies*	*Lawyer*
Helped, helped a lot	65%	65%	46%	25%	39%	60%	62%
Helped (qualified)	13	11	13	8	33	20	15
Did not help	18	13	24	67	17	20	15
Don't know whether it helped	—	1	6	—	—	—	—
Not ascertained	4	10	11	—	11	—	8
Number of people	130	89	46	12	18	10	13

Source: Gerald Gurin, Joseph Veroff, and Sheila Feld, *Americans View Their Mental Health* (New York: Basic Books, 1960), p. 319.

categories of helpers. The data in Table 8–1 show that medical doctors, lawyers, and various nonpsychological agencies were judged about as helpful as clergymen by those who sought them out. We must realize, of course, that people seek out different sources of help depending on their specific problem. For example, 46 percent of the people who contacted clergymen went for help with a marital problem, while the figure for those who contacted a marriage counselor for marital problems was 92 percent. And whereas 8 percent of the people going to a clergyman had problems concerning children, 20 percent and 39 percent respectively of people who went to psychiatrists and psychological agencies went with child-related problems.[15]

Perhaps nowhere does religion become more clearly significant than with respect to death. Not that all people resort to religious values or practices in adjusting to death, whether that of a friend or loved one or their own impending death. But many do. Beliefs about the meaning of death and what one can expect afterward, although of course incapable of eradicating death, help people face it and adjust to it. As we indicated earlier, society cannot afford to have its members out of commission for very long because of sorrow and bereavement. Religious assertions about death as the beginning of a better life eternal, death as having released the departed one from a vale of tears and world of toil and trouble, or death as a step up the ladder of karma (as in Hinduism and

[15]Ibid., p. 309.

Buddhism) leading to ultimate Nirvana, to the release from the seemingly endless transmigration of souls—all such views tend to make the survivors feel better about the loss. The idea that the dead person is now better off reduces the intensity of grief.

Stimulus to Aesthetic Expression   Another function that religion performs for societies is in the area of aesthetics. Again, this is not exclusively the province of religion. Yet observe how many of the great architectural monuments, musical compositions, and fine works of sculpture and painting use religious themes and subjects. The bejeweled, gold-covered Buddhas, the countless biblical characters and scenes in medieval and Renaissance painting, the architectural marvels that comprise medieval cathedrals, the universally acclaimed music of Bach and Handel—all these provide evidence that religion has been a highly significant source or stimulus for artistic expression.

Source of Social Welfare   A final fairly major function religion performs in society is its service as a welfare institution. Religious groups were in the forefront of the nineteenth-century movement for establishing orphanages, schools for the deaf, blind, and mentally retarded, adoption and family-service agencies, hospitals, and similar welfare and service institutions. Earle E. Cairns has documented the significant impact of numerous Christian religious groups on drives for prison reforms, the abolition of slavery, humane treatment of the mentally ill, and improved working conditions for industrial workers in the wake of the Industrial Revolution.[16] Even today many lists of United Fund agencies include a number of organizations that either retain a religious name or were founded by a religious organization. Today most of these agencies derive the major portion of their monetary support from nonreligious sources through fees, voluntary contributions and solicitations from the general public, and governmental subsidy. But initially they were religiously motivated and funded and represented a direct response of religious groups to human need. Although the majority of funds in social-welfare areas are today collected and distributed by government, much of the original stimulus and efforts in these directions were religious. That religious groups are not so significantly involved in such efforts today is a result of two factors: increasing governmental awareness of its responsibility toward its citizens, and what David Moberg calls the "Great Reversal"—the pulling back from welfare and eleemosynary concern by various Christian groups beginning in the 1920s.[17] We only mention this reversal here, but shall return to a discussion of it in Chapter 12.

[16]Earle E. Cairns, *Saints and Society* (Chicago: Moody Press, 1960).
[17]David O. Moberg, *The Great Reversal* (Philadelphia: Lippincott, 1972).

QUALIFICATIONS OF THE INTEGRATING FUNCTIONS OF RELIGION

Throughout the preceding section we continually qualified our assertions about the integrative functions of religion with the phrase "to the degree that . . . ." That is, we have been at least implicitly suggesting that religion does not automatically integrate in the ways we have been discussing. Further, the effectiveness of such integration will vary from one situation, era, or society to another. That is, one must know the specifics of a given situation, time, and place before one can speak of religion as an integrating force. There are several primary qualifying conditions with respect to the integrative impact of religion upon society.

First, the integrative impact of religion will be reduced in societies in which there is religious diversity. Religious diversity implies competition and possibly opposed ideologies. Religion in general will be less integrative in a society in which, for example, one religious group wholeheartedly supports the policies and actions of the state to the point of killing the enemy while another religious group opposes lifting a weapon or hand against anyone, even an enemy soldier. This is saying that "other things being equal," a society with a church (as defined in Chapter 7) will likely find religion more integrating than a society dotted with various denominations and sects.

Second, the integrative impact of religion will be reduced in societies that are experiencing social change and in which established economic and role patterns and relationships are being supplanted. Thus religion is likely less integrative in the contemporary United States than it was in eighteenth-century Russia, less integrative in a developing nation in Africa than in a "primitive" society in the Upper Amazon. Although the intrusion of science as a challenger or alternative to religion may intensify and accelerate the tendency of religion to be less successful at integrating a society as social change proceeds, science need not be the only "culprit." Any technological innovation, whether of tool or technique, challenges the established ways and can disrupt the influence of religion, particularly if religion (as it often does) opposes the change.

The challenge of social change may not be simply a new thought system or source of knowledge such as science or technological innovation arising from within or diffusing from without. It may involve disprivileged subgroups and categories of citizens rising to challenge existing patterns of the distribution of societal rewards; it may involve political diversity that challenges the hereditary monarchy, or it may be little more than increasing contact with other societies and the resultant recognition of and experimentation with alternative life styles.

A third possible qualification of the integrative, functional characteristic of religion is reflected in data suggesting that religion, or at least certain religious systems, inhibit creativity. Although this has little to do directly with the integrative aspect of religion, potentially it has much to do with the broader view of religion as functional. That is, anything that inhibits the development and application of the creative potential in a society costs the society something, whether in terms of improving the quality of life, enhancing the security and safety of life, or contributing to the length of productive life.

By no means should religion be viewed as automatically or universally inhibiting creativity. Yet those religions that stress fatalistic acceptance of "God's will" or "the nature of things," that operate with a deductive cognitive system that stresses the absoluteness of doctrinal formulations, and that are suspicious of "learning" and science as potential challenges to accepted faith and doctrine—such religions appear to inhibit creativity and exploration of the new and unknown.

Great caution must be exercised here, because not all religious groups are alike in their views on science and "learning." In a well-known essay, Robert Merton has drawn important connections between Puritan theology and the development of modern science along the lines of Max Weber's connection between the Protestant ethic and the spirit of capitalism. Merton sees the Puritan ethic, or as sometimes called, ascetic Protestantism, as at least one important element in the growth of seventeenth-century science in Europe. The Puritan idea that man has an obligation to learn as much as possible about God's creation—ultimately all as a means of glorifying God—encouraged scientific endeavor. According to the Puritan view, reaching a fuller understanding and appreciation of God's works and creation naturally leads the learner or discoverer to a greater appreciation of the greatness and goodness of God.

Merton cites data concerning the British scientific Royal Society, of which a great majority of members (62 percent) were of Puritan affiliation and training, despite the fact that Puritans were a relatively small minority in the English population. During the same period, Protestants registered disproportionately high enrollments in German schools that emphasized scientific and technological training, while Catholic students tended more to concentrate on classical and theological training.[18]

Jews also have long shown a greater-than-average interest in scientific training. This is in part traceable to a traditionally high regard among Jews for learning in general—a regard that has carried forward to

[18]Merton, *Social Theory*, p. 591.

the present. For example, consistent with Merton's observation is Mayer and Sharp's finding, in a study of social correlates with religious preference in Detroit, that the highest average level of educational attainment was among Jews and those Protestants of a Calvinist heritage. Jews were also clearly ahead of all others in high-status occupations.[19]

RELIGION AS A SEGMENTING FACTOR

Segmentation Related to Doctrine

We now turn full circle to view religion as a possible segmenting or divisive influence in society. In an extreme form it is possible that religion may aggressively compete with other social institutions for the allegiance of people and may seriously disrupt the society. This extreme form of divisiveness, in which religion attempts consciously and directly to counter and undermine existing societal and governmental forms, occurs relatively seldom or on only a few relatively minor fronts at one time. It does happen even today in the United States, although on a small scale, when, for example, people refuse for religious reasons to salute the flag or to serve in a military capacity in the armed forces. Such behavior when based on religious principles is an obvious segmenting or divisive influence in society. That is, it sets people apart, brands them as different and possibly disloyal, and inhibits communication among subgroups.

This introduces us to a major way in which religion may segment a society—that is, segmentation which is the net result of doctrinal differences. Whereas in Chapter 5 we asserted that religion makes a difference, we can now specify that further by stating that doctrine makes a difference. Probably the most obvious manifestation of such religious segmentation in the name of religious doctrine or teachings is the division of Christianity, and Protestantism particularly, into so many different denominations and sects, each distinguishing itself on one or more doctrinal issues. There is a popular belief among many people in our society that everybody believes essentially the same thing. Just as while there are many brands of hand soap, they all get your hands clean, so the many denominations and sects are seen as simply different brand names for the same product. Though there may be some truth in this point of view, we shall essentially challenge it in our discussion of denominationalism in Chapter 13. For the moment, suffice it to say that there are at least

---

[19]Albert J. Mayer and Harry Sharp, "Religious Preference and Worldly Success," *American Sociological Review* 27, no. 2 (1962); 218–27.

256 religious groups in the United States today that report membership statistics, plus many more that don't. Besides Catholics, Jews, Presbyterians, Episcopalians, Methodists, Baptists, Lutherans, Unitarians, and other familiar denominations, there are dozens of others that most of us have never heard of. There are such groups as the Church of God, Incorporated; the Mountain Assembly Church of God; the Two-Seed-in-the-Spirit Predestinarian Baptist Church; and the one with the distinction of coming up with the longest name of all—the House of God, the Holy Church of Living God, the Pillar and Grounds of Truth, House of Prayer for All People, Inc. Furthermore, there are twenty-seven brands of Baptists, twenty-one brands of Methodists, twelve brands of Lutherans, ten of Presbyterians, and so on.

The important element we wish to abstract from these observations about the fragmentation of American religion into hundreds of groups is that they all have different religious doctrines, perspectives, and emphases. Many of them, in fact, are convinced they have a corner on truth and have more perfectly than any other group formulated and practiced the message and will of God. Although probably fewer in number than thirty years ago, there are some groups that still maintain that their members alone will go to heaven, that all others are in error and will be doomed. Although definitely deemphasized today, traditional Roman Catholic doctrine states that unless a person is a member of the Roman Catholic church he cannot be saved. One branch of Lutheranism maintained for many years that it was the one pure, true visible church of God on earth. Jehovah's Witnesses yet today insist that unless you join their ranks you will not be among the 144,000 that alone will be saved.

A story illustrative of this point tells of Saint Peter giving a guided tour of heaven to a prospective angel. Down the golden street Peter points out the various groups—the Methodists, the Catholics, the Presbyterians, and so on. As they approach a high brick wall Peter begins walking on tiptoe, and whispers to the prospective angel: "We have to be quiet here because the _____ (insert your own favorite or nonfavorite group) live behind that wall and they think they're the only ones up here. They'd be terribly disappointed if they found out someone else was up here too." In other words, religious groups are understandably partial to themselves. But more than that: such views may lead to exclusivism and an intolerance of others' views. As such, religion segments; it drives wedges between people.

The real significance of our point about doctrinal differences among religious groups, however, concerns not so much their teachings about the correct way to get to heaven, or the relationship between the natural and the supernatural elements in the Lord's Supper, or the doctrine of latitudinarianism. Much of this remains within church walls, between the covers of theological books, and in seminary classrooms. What we are primarily interested in here are those doctrinal or theological differences and issues that have practical, social, and political implications, doctrinal differences that can be clearly seen as segmenting so far as the society is concerned. For example, some religious groups believe that fluoridation of drinking water and immunization against diseases are sinful. An entire community rages in controversy as a result. Or: should birth-control information and related material be distributed through public, tax-supported medical and counseling agencies? Communities with substantial Roman Catholic populations have become embroiled over this issue. Kenneth Underwood has documented well how in Holyoke, Massachusetts (1940), the community polarized between Catholics and Protestants over the issue of Margaret Sanger's scheduled address on birth control.[20] Then there is the case of Alfred E. Smith's presidential candidacy in 1928; significant credit for his defeat in the election is generally given to Protestant opposition to him on the grounds of his Catholicism. The anti-Catholic issue was again raised in the 1960 presidential campaign. And although a majority of Protestants and Catholics alike agreed to downplay this factor, a considerable amount of virulent anti-Kennedy and anti-Catholic literature rolled out of certain small Protestant enclaves. For that matter, on the other side of the coin Catholics were urged by some churchmen to vote *for* Kennedy simply because he *was* Catholic. Or, consider the ongoing controversy over federal aid to parochial schools that tends to pit Catholic and a few Protestant and Jewish groups against most Protestant denominations—or the more recent controversy over abortion reform in state after state, where certain religious groups make clear their opposition.

Much of this sort of controversy and "dissension" admittedly represents an admirable manifestation of some of America's basic societal values—values regarding freedom of choice, democratic decision making, and open discussion of issues. Our only point is that when such discussion and controversy is translated by many into a religious issue, and when that issue then polarizes a community, state, or nation into two religious factions and results in discriminatory and harassing practices against minority religious groups, then religion becomes a segmenting, divisive influence in the society.

We also need to point out that behavior surrounding such religious issues has not always remained at the level of heated discussion, suspicion, name-calling, or even at the level of the courts. It has occasionally erupted in violence. For example, Louisville's "Bloody Monday"—August 5, 1855—in which more than twenty persons were killed and several hun-

---

[20]Kenneth Underwood, *Protestant and Catholic* (Boston: Beacon Press, 1957).

dred wounded, was basically a conflict between Protestants and Catholics
—the former having been aroused by a "no-popery" campaign carried
on by the *Louisville Journal*, all within the context of the notoriously
anti-Catholic Know-Nothing party and philosophy. And the Philadelphia
riots of 1844 represented a clear case of anti-Catholicism that saw Catholic churches destroyed and the homes of Catholics burned, not to mention
considerable bloodshed. Periodically Jews have also become the objects
of harassment. As recently as 1960, during a two-month period 643 incidents of anti-Jewish swastika painting on synagogue walls, vandalism
against Jewish property, and beatings of Jews were recorded in the
United States.[21] German Lutherans during World War I who persisted
in using the German language in their worship services and conversation
were harassed in some communities in similar ways. Certainly one can't
help but think of the continuing civil disturbances in Northern Ireland,
in which Protestant is pitted against Catholic, or of the recurrent Arab-
Israeli conflicts. Although both of these situations represent far more
than religious clashes, particularly in their political or nationalistic expressions, the religious element nevertheless looms large in each.

In short, religion serves as a source of differentiation among people. But more: it can in many ways also be a source of divisiveness among
people, a segmenting factor so far as the fabric of society is concerned.

Segmentation Reinforced by Religion

The segmentation and divisiveness in the name of or caused by religion that we have been discussing is overt and none too subtle. There is
another type of segmentation that is perhaps best described as associated
with religion or intensified by religion—that is, segmentation originating
elsewhere but reinforced by religion. We refer to two examples in particular: (1) segmentation inherent in social-class divisions but enhanced
by religion, and (2) segmentation inherent in racial prejudice and discrimination but reinforced by religion.

We shall consider in much greater detail in Chapter 11 the relationship between religion and social class. We now wish simply to say that
both so far as national denominations and local congregations are concerned, religious groups evidence a class bias. That is, every religious
group tends to draw disproportionately, although rarely in a completely
distinctive manner, from a fairly narrow range on the class scale. This is
not surprising or unusual so far as social groups are concerned. It is indeed the rare group of any sort whose constituency is truly representa-

---

21Charles Y. Glock and Rodney Stark, *Christian Beliefs and Anti-Semitism*
(New York: Harper & Row, 1966), p. xi.

tive of the full range of the class system. Yet this tendency toward disproportionate class representation is a marked characteristic of religious groups. Thus religion appears to have done little—and to be incapable of doing much—to reduce the segmentation that exists within society due to class differences. In fact, religion tends to reinforce the segmentation that already exists.

Similarly with race. Religion has tended to encourage and reinforce existing segmentation due to racial prejudice, discrimination, and segregation. The observation popularized by Martin Luther King, Jr. that "eleven o'clock Sunday morning is the most segregated hour of the week" is all too true. Probably little more than 1 percent of blacks who are members of churches belong to an integrated congregation. Granted, part of this is today a type of self-selection on the part of blacks, not outright, blatant exclusion from white congregations. Nonetheless, divisiveness due to racism in our society has not been overcome by religion. Quite the reverse: racism has historically been reinforced by religion in American society.

9

Religion and the Economy

In the last chapter we presented a general introduction to the reciprocal or interdependent relationship of religion and society. We now proceed to specify this interrelationship by looking at basic institutions within the society—in this chapter the economy, in Chapter 10 politics, in Chapter 11 the class system.

We can initially observe that religion, although often legitimately viewed as a semi-autonomous social system (societal institution) paralleling others, it is itself in various ways a part of the inclusive economic system of a society: it is an employer; it buys and it sells; it owns property; it contributes to the gross national product (the amount spent annually on all goods and services). A brief look at religion as an active participant in the economy constitutes the first section of this chapter. The major section following looks at religion's influence on economic relationships in a society. We shall then, in a third section, conclude with an assessment of how and to what degree religion has an impact on the economy and vice versa.

RELIGION AS AN ECONOMIC INSTITUTION

Two obvious ways in which organized religion plays an economic role in most societies is as an employer (providing the economic livelihood for religious professionals and their families) and as an owner of property and a builder of facilities. Although there are no precise figures available concerning the number of persons employed by religious organizations, we do know (from figures published by the National Council of Churches) that as of 1973 there were at least 463,987 clergymen in the United States.[1] But even this figure is not comprehensive, inasmuch as not all religious groups report statistics to the National Council of Churches—or to any one source, for that matter. Conservatively we would therefore estimate that there are at least 400,000 clergymen in the United States alone. Add to this the members of monastic and other religious orders in the Catholic church, the tens of thousands of church secretaries, janitors and sextons, employees of religious publishing companies, parochial-school personnel, clerical and secretarial staff for area, state, regional, and national denominations and ecumenical organizations, social workers employed by religious welfare agencies, and the like—and a total of 800,000 or more families deriving part or, for many, all of their family income from religious organizations would probably not be too high an estimate.

In 1957 church property and endowments in the United States were valued at $13.7 billion.[2] Although there has been a steady decline in new construction by religious groups since 1965, the total new construction in 1970 alone totaled $921 million.[3] In 1958 churches accounted for one dollar in every forty spent on privately financed construction.[4]

Even more impressive are the figures for contributions to religious groups. In 1971 the American Association of Fund-Raising Councils reported contributions to religious groups in the amount of $8.2 billion.[5] Of the total U.S. gross national product of $1.04 trillion in 1971, 1.4 percent consisted of contributions to religious, welfare, and charitable institutions. While not the biggest business in this country or the world, religion is a significant element in the economy as an owner of great amounts of property and as an agent for the collection and distribution of billions of dollars annually.

Religious organizations also engage in a great number of activities and enterprises that are not intrinsically religious: they own and derive income from apartment and office buildings, parking lots, factories, and of course stocks and bonds held as endowments by local congregations, national denominations, and church workers' pension funds. Although

[1]National Council of Churches, of Christ in the U.S.A., Office of Planning and Program, *Yearbook of American Churches, 1972*, ed. Constant H. Jacquet, Jr. (Nashville: Abingdon Press, 1972), p. 229.
[2]David O. Moberg, *The Church as a Social Institution* (Englewood Cliffs, N.J.: Prentice-Hall, 1962), p. 169.
[3]National Council of Churches, *Yearbook*, p. 260.
[4]Moberg, *The Church*, pp. 169–170.
[5]National Council of Churches, *Yearbook*, p. 238.

the controversial tax-exempt status of such income is a topic dealt with in the next chapter, we can't resist mentioning here that one religious organization—the Cathedral of Tomorrow, in Ohio—at one time owned a shopping center, an apartment building, an electronics firm, a wire and plastics company—and the Real Form Girdle Company.[6] Regarding this last holding, *Women's Wear Daily* once quipped in a headline: "Rock of Ages on Firm Foundation."[7]

RELIGION AS A SHAPER OF ECONOMIC ATTITUDES AND BEHAVIOR

Throughout history religious groups have faced a dilemma with regard to attempting to influence economic attitudes and behavior. On the one hand, there has been a tendency to treat poverty as a virtue and to discourage the faithful from becoming encumbered by material goods and concerns. Certainly the Bible extols poverty in these terms in such statements as "Blessed are the poor for they shall inherit the earth," or, "How hard it is for a rich man to enter the kingdom of heaven." Buddhism extols the mendicant monk who travels light and remains free from economic concerns in order to engage in a life of contemplation.

Yet any religious group, particularly as its organization begins to get the least bit complex, requires funds to operate. The group then begins to get involved in economic affairs, want to or not. It finds itself appreciating substantial contributions from wealthy members. It may exact a tithe from its adherents. As at least some members rise out of poverty it doesn't kick them out, but perhaps even extols them for their industry and frugality. It is this tendency of religious groups to become fairly actively engaged in economic activities that is one of several stimuli to the formation of sects. We observed in Chapter 7 that sects tend to turn poverty into a virtue. This is what Max Weber calls a "theodicy of disprivilege" or "theodicy of escape."[8]—that is, a rationalization and justification of one's disprivileged economic and social status as an advantage so far as salvation is concerned. True riches and enhanced status will accrue in the hereafter, when it really counts—when it's for eternity, not just sixty years or so of toil and trouble on this earth.

As the child says of the toy he grabs from another child but has to return to its rightful owner after a stern parental reprimand, "That's the dumbest toy I ever saw—I didn't want that crummy old thing anyway,"

[6]Alfred Balk, *The Religion Business* (Richmond, Va.: John Knox Press, 1968), p. 11.
[7]Quoted in Balk, *The Religion Business*, p. 11.
[8]Max Weber, *The Sociology of Religion*, trans. Ephriam Fischoff (Boston: Beacon Press, 1963), p. 113.

so the sectarians of low socioeconomic status are likely to define what is denied them as evil, or at least as unimportant and undesirable. Wealth, fancy clothes, "highfalutin" manners and language?—Who needs them! Actually Weber identifies three different forms release from earthly disprivilege might take: the expectation of a better life in the hereafter (paradise or heaven); hope for oneself, or at least for one's progeny, in a new world to be created by God for the faithful called the Messianic Age or the millenium; hope for another life or rebirth in this world that will be better or higher than the present one (the concept of transmigration of souls in Hinduism, for example).[9]

There is also the "theodicy of good fortune" identified by Weber. Here there is theological justification for superior economic and social status. Weber says that "the fortunate is seldom satisfied with the fact of being fortunate. Beyond this he needs to know that he has the *right* to his good fortune, ... that he 'deserves' it."[10] Good fortune wants to be "legitimate" fortune. Religion legitimates the favored conditions of "religious men, the propertied, the victorious, and the healthy. In short, religion provides the theodicy of good fortune for those who are fortunate."[11]

Here we find ourselves drifting into the perspective where religion is seen as being influenced by forces outside itself—in this case, economic factors, which are seen as influencing religious doctrine. There is of course much evidence supporting this point of view, and we'll look at the matter more closely in the third section of this chapter. But first let us examine how and to what extent religion affects economic attitudes and behavior.

David Moberg mentions several ways in which religion to varying degrees of intensity and significance affects economic attitudes and behavior. First, insofar as such personal and business virtues as honesty, fair play, and honoring one's commitments are essential in economic life, and to the extent that religion is successful in inculcating such virtues in its members it has an impact on the economy. Second, religion also on occasion stimulates consumption. Religious holidays implicitly encourage material consumption by followers, even if it's only special candles to light and special foods to eat. Third, in emphasizing one's work as a "calling," religion (Protestant Christianity in particular) has glorified and elevated work at one's job, however menial it may be. To the extent that people internalize this view it is likely to increase produc-

[9]Max Weber, "The Social Psychology of the World Religions," *From Max Weber: Essays in Sociology*, ed. and trans. H. H. Gerth and C. Wright Mills (New York: Oxford University Press, 1958), p. 275.
[10]Ibid., p. 271.
[11]Ibid.

tivity: "I'm working for God, not just for my employer or for myself. Therefore, I'd better put out a little more and do the best job possible."[12]

Vogt and O'Dea[13] provide interesting evidence related to this point. Although located in the same natural environment, the communities of Homestead and Rimrock (fictitious names) evidence quite different social systems. Rimrock, which stresses cooperative community effort and achieves great productivity as a consequence, appears to be strongly influenced by the Mormon ideology held by a majority of its citizens. Homestead, with its individualistic orientation and less successful farming endeavors, evidences the influence of competitive and divisive Protestant denominationalism that inhibits community-oriented cooperative efforts.

A fourth way in which religion may influence the economy is by explicitly endorsing certain economic systems or certain types of economic or business activities. For example, Liston Pope notes that religious leaders were influential in helping establish the cotton mill industry in Gaston County, North Carolina around the turn of the twentieth century. This was accomplished directly through supportive sermonizing and pronouncements that helped create public approval of the textile enterprise. Religion also indirectly influenced economic endeavor in Gaston County by supporting Prohibition. With the advent of Prohibition, economic capital which had been invested in distilleries was released for investment in the textile mills. Also, mill workers were slightly more likely to appear for work Monday mornings in better condition now that weekend "benders" were more unlikely. Above all, religion helped the mills (and thus influenced the economy) by exerting moral influence over the workers, encouraging them to do a good day's work and do what the boss told them.[14]

Weber's Protestant Ethic and the Spirit of Capitalism

Probably the greatest single contribution to the discussion of the impact of religion on the economy is Max Weber's seminal study *The Protestant Ethic and the Spirit of Capitalism* (1905), which has stimulated massive amounts of research and discussion over the past half-century. Weber's thesis is that Calvinistic Protestantism as a theological belief system exerted an important influence on the emergence and growth of capitalism as a mode of economic organization. Quite explicitly

[12]Moberg, *The Church*, pp. 170–74.
[13]Evon Z. Vogt and Thomas F. O'Dea, "A Comparative Study of the Role of Values in Social Action in Two Southwestern Communities," *American Sociological Review* 18, no. 6 (1953); 645–54.
[14]Liston Pope, *Millhands and Preachers* (New Haven: Yale University Press, 1942), chapter 2.

Weber was trying to answer Karl Marx's assertion that society's normative system, including such phenomena as religious values and principles, in fact consists of epiphenomena produced, or at least conditioned in a primary way, by factors in the economy. Weber was essentially saying that at the very least the influential relationship between religion and the economy is a two-way street. Accordingly he set out to show how religion, as embodied in Calvinism, affected the economy, as represented by capitalism.

The Prime Elements in Calvinistic Theology

In order to see the relationship hypothesized by Weber we first need to understand a bit of Calvinistic theology. At the center of Calvinistic theology is the concept and goal of the *glory of God:* everything man does should somehow add to God's glory. Since God does not exist for man, but man for God,[15] it is not too surprising that an early Calvinist theologian has been quoted as saying that he would eagerly and joyfully be damned in hell if that would somehow glorify God.

A second central doctrine of Calvinism is that of *predestination.* This teaching speaks of the foreknowledge and above all the foreordaining by God of all people either to eternal salvation or eternal damnation. In Lutheran theology the attempt had been to use this doctrine as a source of comfort and encouragement to the believer. The emphasis was on God's foreknowledge. God knows in advance who will become a true and faithful follower and believer and who will not. Those whom he foresees as believing he then predestines to heaven: God does not, however explicitly predestine to hell those whom he foresees as rejecting him of their own free will; rather, they seal their own fate themselves, so to speak.

In Calvinism, however, God appears a bit more arbitrary. With less emphasis on God's foreknowledge, Calvinism sees God as assigning some to one fate, some to the other. An important implication of Calvinism's version of predestination was that a person has to proceed all alone down the path of life to meet the destiny decreed for him from eternity.[16] No priest, no church, no sacrament, nothing human can avail to the contrary. This is because what God has decided beforehand cannot be changed. Of course, someone who is damned will still belong to a church and observe the sacraments, because in such activities God is glorified. But it won't do him any good so far as his eternal destiny is concerned.

---

[15]Max Weber, *The Protestant Ethic and the Spirit of Capitalism,* trans. Talcott Parsons (New York: Scribner's, 1958), pp. 102–3.
[16]Ibid., p. 104.

Such activities won't change God's mind. This is so because Christ died only for the "elect" (those predestined to salvation).[17] Obviously this view is a radical departure from Catholicism, which emphasized the church, the sacraments, and the priesthood as channels of God's gifts of hope and salvation to men.

A social consequence of this combination of predestination and obligation to glorify God was the encouragement of a rather extreme kind of individualism. Not only are you on your own in the sense that no other individual or group can help you change the direction of your predestined end, but you must be careful lest your relationships with people become too strong and important. Watch out lest you get carried away in involvement with and commitment to husband, wife, children, or friends. Remember, your primary task is to glorify God.

We now add one more element to complete the basic theological ingredients, as Weber saw them, that provided the foundation for the Protestant (Calvinist) ethic: the concept of the *"calling."* This is a concept, elaborated by Luther, which emphasized using one's secular occupation, whether farmer, artisan, soldier, king, or housewife, to glorify God and to help your neighbor by doing a good job and faithfully carrying out your tasks. Don't despise or belittle your job or role in life. See it as a "calling" by God. Calvinism picked up this concept and placed even greater emphasis on hard work; whatever your calling, you must carry out its duties to the best of your ability and with your last ounce of energy.

Implications for the Individual

We have to realize that the Calvinist was placed in a rather uneasy position with the combining of these three theological elements. He was to glorify God by working to the fullest in his calling, all the while aware that he had been predestined—yet not knowing whether to heaven or to hell. Hence a highly important question in his mind was: Is there any way I can know or at least infer that I'm one of the elect? Catholics had little problem with this question. If they were members of the church and performed at least the minimal ritual and confessional requirements, they had nothing to worry about. Lutherans also were little worried about predestination. Since predestination was viewed as being based on God's foreknowledge, if they believed the Gospel and did not reject God's offer of salvation then they had every reason to believe that they were numbered among the elect. Furthermore, they were promised the inner working of the Holy Spirit, who would develop in them a consciousness and conviction that they were specially chosen by God. True, they could

[17]Ibid.

"fall from grace"—but only if they lost their faith and rejected God's offered hand of deliverance. So as long as one believed and didn't reject, one needn't worry.

The Calvinist, however, didn't have such assurance. He couldn't truly know or be convinced. But he could make inferences—inferences from essentially empirical evidence, evidence of an ability consistently to perform well, of success in his calling, of the feeling that God seemed to be providing him with opportunities and was working through him. Would God be likely to choose to work through someone who was not one of his elect? The upshot was that the three theological elements, in combination with a desire to know whether one was predestined to salvation, produced a tremendous drive toward action. This resulted in what Weber calls "ascetic Protestantism"—a life of strict discipline. Hard work in one's calling is the best discipline. Work is not only the best prophylactic against a sensual, immoral, life, but also the best means for glorifying God. Time, then, becomes infinitely valuable. Thus one must avoid idle conversation, unproductive recreation, or more sleep than absolutely necessary, in order to have maximum time for work.

Now, if you work harder than people around you, if you put in more hours at your job, if you live frugally and ascetically, you will likely be economically more successful than those around you. This is not bad. In fact, it's good—in two ways. First, this might be inferential evidence that you are one of God's elect. Second, God is being glorified. In the meantime, however, you may become rich. Now what? Such wealth dare not be used for personal sensual pleasure, to buy wine, women, and frolic. It shouldn't be used to buy early retirement from one's calling. What alternative is there, then? The answer is *investment*—investment of capital to produce more goods, which create more profits, which in turn represent more capital for investment, ad infinitum—which is the heart of entrepreneurial capitalism. The option of giving away the surplus in philanthropic activity was seldom recommended inasmuch as the poor might then be distracted from doing their duty in their calling to menial but important tasks.

Implications for Economics

This returns us to Weber's thesis regarding the effect of religious norms and patterns on economic relationships and institutions. Attempting "to ascertain whether and to what extent religious forces have taken part in the qualitative formation and the quantitative expansion of [the] spirit of capitalism over the world," Weber concludes that Calvinism was indeed just such a force. However, Weber is quick to warn that no one should be so foolish as to maintain that capitalism or the spirit of capitalism could therefore only have developed as a result of the

Reformation or that it is a direct product of Calvinism.[18] Rather, he essentially maintains that Calvinism served an important stimulating and reinforcing function for capitalism. Calvinism did not create capitalism, nor was it even absolutely necessary for the triumph of capitalism. Rather, Calvinism encouraged capitalism and, if nothing else, hastened its development in those societies where Calvinism wielded an influence.

Weber was much more careful than some of his followers in hypothesizing about the relationship between Calvinistic Protestantism and capitalism, a point not always appreciated by those critics who represent him as arguing that the former "caused" the latter.

Alternatives to Weber's Hypothesis

At this point we shall briefly consider some of the alternatives to and modified versions of Weber's thesis that have been suggested. Kurt Samuelsson cites four early objections to Weber's position raised by Felix Rachfahl four years after Weber first made it public in a series of articles in 1905. Rachfahl first questions the validity of representing ethical-religious motivation as a crucial factor in economic activity. More reasonable factors, he suggests, are such things as the desire to enjoy life, solicitude for the family, and the urge to work for one's fellow man, for the common good, or for the nation and its welfare. Second, Rachfahl points to several limiting conditions imposed by Calvin on economic activity that taken together do not at all condone a free-for-all capitalism. Third, the differences between Catholicism and Calvinism with regard to economic activity should not be exaggerated. Catholic monastic orders such as the Benedictines, Franciscans, and Jesuits were not too different from Calvinism in this respect. Fourth, Weber's distinction between Catholic and Protestant countries and cities with regard to economic activity are not so neatly associated with one religion or the other as Weber seems to suggest. Some supposedly Protestant capitalistic cities, for example, had strong Catholic influence.[19]

R. H. Tawney also emphasizes this fourth point, observing that capitalism had clearly existed in medieval Italy and Flanders (both Catholic areas) and that the capitalistic spirit was "only too familiar to the saints and sages of the Middle Ages." He goes on to point out that Catholic cities were the chief commercial capitals of medieval Europe, and Catholic bankers its leading financiers.[20]

[18]Ibid., p. 91.
[19]Kurt Samuelsson, *Religion and Economic Action: A Critique of Max Weber,* trans. E. Geoffrey French (New York: Harper & Row, 1961), pp. 8–9.
[20]R. H. Tawney, *Religion and the Rise of Capitalism* (Gloucester, Mass.: Peter Smith, 1962), pp. 84, 316.

Another hypothesis is that the social situation of Calvinists rather than their theology encouraged their entrance into capitalistic ventures. Calvinists constituted a religious minority almost everywhere except Geneva, and in some countries and communities they were barred from governmental positions and professions such as medicine and law. Where else to turn but to business enterprises? Thus we observe a process similar to that affecting Jews during the Middle Ages, who undertook money-lending and money-handling positions partly by default—because Christians didn't want to "dirty their hands" with such activities or break the church's laws against usury.

One could also argue that the simultaneous rise of capitalism and Calvinism was a mere historical coincidence. Hudson speaks along these lines in suggesting that Calvinists were a typical persecuted group and that such groups naturally tend to become industrious and frugal.[21]

Personality factors might also be suggested. Perhaps the very persons who were most energetic and independent, who were most willing to take business risks, were those most attracted by Calvinism as a theological system because of its stress on individualism and effort. That is, perhaps at least some people choose a religion because it meshes with their own value system and commitments.

Tawney, questioning Weber's concept of capitalism itself, does not see Calvinism fitting into the free-for-all capitalism of the eighteenth and nineteenth centuries. Rather, Tawney credits Calvinism with providing a business ethic to a "world of small traders and handicrafts.[22] The huge fortunes required and created by capitalism were not produced merely by thrift, Tawney notes, but by exploitation and by deliberately creating "opportunities."

As one scans four centuries of Calvinist theological writing one is impressed with the dilemma mentioned earlier in this chapter—the dilemma of a fundamental distrust in wealth and a belief in its likely insidious undermining of fundamental Christian principles such as "keeping oneself unstained by the world" as opposed to the religious group's need for money in order to survive and the need to justify its members' accumulation of wealth. In this connection, some have stressed the distinction between early and later Calvinism—the theology of Calvin himself contrasted with that of later followers and interpreters. John McNeill points out that Calvin had a profound mistrust of economic success, and he suggests that to argue that Calvin characterized the prosperity of believers as inferential proof of their election to heaven is to completely

[21]Winthrop S. Hudson, "Puritanism and the Spirit of Capitalism," *Church History* 15, no. 1 (1949); 89.
[22]Tawney, *Religion*, p. 31.

misinterpret the evidence we have of Calvin's thought, as reflected in
such statements as: "Wherever prosperity flows uninterruptedly its de-
light corrupts even the best of us. . . . The faithful are more miserable
than despisers of God. . . . Prosperity like wine inebriates men. . . . Property is like rust or mildew"[23]

Indeed, only later did Calvinists rationalize economic success and
interpret economic gain as a sign of virtue. It is interesting that Weber
quotes extensively from Richard Baxter, a late seventeenth-century Puri-
tan-Calvinist theologian writing approximately 150 years after Calvin.
Weber also quotes Benjamin Franklin, who was not only considerably
removed in time from Calvin, but not a Calvinist theologian at all. Thus
it was Baxter, not Calvin, who made such statements as: "Be wholly
taken up in diligent business of your lawful calling. . . . It is for action
that God maintaineth us. . . . Keep up a high esteem of time and be
every day more careful that you lose none of your time. . . . [and] if vain
recreation, dressings, feastings, idle talk, unprofitable company, or sleep
be any of them temptations to rob you of any of your time, accordingly
heighten your watchfulness."[24]

Toward a Resolution of the Issue

While still other critiques of Weber's hypothesis could be introduced, enough have been summarized to make the point that the link
between Calvinism and capitalism, if one exists at all, is far from a unitary causal one. Of course, Weber himself spoke not of cause but of strong
encouragement and support—what we today tend to call *reinforcement*.
Actually, most of Weber's critics grant some such supportive role for Calvinism. This is the position taken by Tawney, who says that the "capitalistic spirit, though "as old as history, found in certain aspects of
Puritanism a tonic which braced its energies and fortified its already
vigorous temper."[25] And Rachfahl, the first to criticize the Weberian
hypothesis, points out several indirect ways in which the doctrinal positions of Protestant theologians influenced economic matters and concludes that despite important weaknesses in Weber's interpretation of
evidence, the basic contention that Calvinism had an important influence
upon economic activity is valid—though not in the specific way suggested
by Weber.[26] Rachfahl's observations are the following:

23John T. McNeill, *The History and Character of Calvinism* (New York: Oxford
University Press, 1954), p. 222.
24See Weber, *The Protestant Ethic*, pp. 262, 260, 261.
25Tawney, *Religion*, pp. 226–27.
26Quoted in Samuelsson, *Religion and Economic Action*, p. 10.

1. Protestantism permitted the intellect to be devoted to worldly pursuits, whereas in Catholic countries many of the best minds went into the priesthood.
2. Protestantism introduced education to the masses.
3. Protestantism reversed the tendency toward indolence and distaste for work associated with Catholic renunciation of the world.
4. Protestantism encouraged independence and personal responsibility for one's fate—something down-played in Catholicism.
5. Protestantism created a "higher type of morality" than did Catholicism.
6. Protestantism distinguished politics from religion more clearly than did Catholicism. This freed persons to engage in more diverse economic activities and, by tolerating a greater diversity of views, ultimately resulted in economic change.[27]

Although some of these points tend to make false or at least strained comparisons, in combination they constitute the essence of the observation made recently by Hammond and Demerath. These writers suggest a way of salvaging Weber's thesis without having to accept all that he says by noting that the advent of Protestantism—i.e., the fact that it appeared at all—implies a weakening and ultimate breakdown of medieval Catholic control, resulting in greater freedom to experiment with new political and economic forms, one of which was capitalism.[28]

In a very real sense, then, the success of Protestantism represented the destruction of the church type of religious organization (discussed in Chapter 7), and the introduction of religious pluralism, which is intimately associated with political and ultimately with economic pluralism as well. That is, people were beginning to face options and make choices—political and economic choices, and religious ones as well. The positive influence of Protestantism on capitalism is of course only an indirect one, and must take second place to primary developments: the discovery and colonization of the New World, the expansion of trade, the second agrarian revolution that increased food production and thus resulted in a labor surplus available for commercial and manufacturing occupations, the Enlightenment, political revolutions, and ultimately the Industrial Revolution itself.

Guy Swanson analyzes the relationship of Protestantism and capitalism along somewhat the same lines as Rachfahl and Hammond/Demerath by seeing the general "loosening" of the social structure as the important ingredient. But for Swanson religion is essentially the middle variable in a three-variable chain that begins with political structure and ends with social structure, of which capitalism is only one aspect. Com-

[27]Ibid.
[28]N. J. Demerath III and Phillip E. Hammond, *Religion in Social Context* (New York: Random House, 1969), p. 150.

paring the social structures of various European states in late medieval Europe, he notes that important differences in political structure preceded and served as a base for different religious commitments (Protestantism or Catholicism). Thus societies that remained Catholic had one primary source or center of decision making. By contrast, Protestantism was more likely to appear in those societies in which there were a variety of decision-making sources. Thus political diversity encouraged Protestantism, and together they encouraged capitalism.[29]

Whether one agrees with Samuelson that there is "no support for Weber's theories," that "almost all the evidence contradicts them,"[30] or with others who hold out for at least an indirect relationship of some kind between Calvinistic Protestantism and the growth of capitalism, one conclusion seems clear: although religion has some impact on the economy, it is likely to be indirect and to be effective only as a supportive, reinforcing ingredient in concert with others in a complex causal chain.

Evidence from the Present

There have been several attempts to test the validity of the Weberian hypothesis by determining, on the basis of contemporary data, whether there exist now any differences between Protestants and Catholics that conceivably resulted from the different religious bases postulated by Weber in his discussion of the Protestant ethic. The logic has been that if differences in economic attitudes and behavior exist between present-day Protestants and Catholics, similar and perhaps greater differences may have existed in the past. Of course, data demonstrating contemporary differences cannot be used to validate a causal hypothesis regarding the historical relationship of Calvinism to capitalism; they would only increase our confidence that such a relationship might have existed.

Gerhard Lenski concludes in *The Religious Factor* that although the differences in economic attitudes and behavior that he found between white Protestants and white Catholics were not always consistent or of great magnitude, the Protestants tended to identify more clearly than the Catholics with the individualistic and competitive pattern of thought and behavior associated historically with the Protestant ethic and capitalistic activity.[31] Some have challenged Lenski's interpretation of his own data and find little support in them for positing significant residual differ-

---

[29]Guy E. Swanson, *Religion and Regime* (Ann Arbor: University of Michigan Press, 1967).

[30]Samuelsson, *Religion and Economic Action*, p. 154.

[31]Gerhard E. Lenski, *The Religious Factor* (Garden City, N.Y.: Doubleday, 1961), pp. 75–102.

ences between Catholics and Protestants in the economic sphere.[32] Others, using data from their own studies, have found little or no support at all for such conclusions. And still other researchers have found evidence for differences in the opposite direction: such are the findings of Glenn and Hyland based on their analysis of eighteen national surveys conducted by the Gallup organization and by the National Opinion Research Center between 1943 and 1965. Focusing on income, occupation, and educational attainment, the authors discovered that although Protestants ranked significantly higher than Catholics in these three areas prior to the end of World War II, Catholics have since gained appreciably, even to the point of surpassing Protestants in most measures of these status measures. Catholics, they found, have had the advantage of being more highly concentrated outside the South in metropolitan areas that present greater opportunities for high-status jobs, high incomes, and education. Such propitious location appears to have overcome Catholics' disadvantage or limitation in being, on the average, more recent immigrants than Protestants.[33]

It thus appears quite clearly that contemporary differences between Catholics and Protestants in terms of success in economic endeavors do not lend latter-day support to the Protestant-ethic thesis. Of course, an absence of differences in the predicted direction today does not necessarily invalidate the hypothesis of an historical difference. It is possible that Catholics have gained in economic status *in spite of* ideological and attitudinal differences implicit in Weber's hypothesized difference between Protestants and Catholics. Yet it is important to reemphasize that whatever the historical relationship might have been, no direct or even clear inferential contemporary evidence supports the hypothesis related to differential economic success of Protestant and Catholic Americans.

AN ASSESSMENT OF THE RELATIONSHIP BETWEEN RELIGION AND ECONOMICS

It is clear that religion is, among other things, an economic institution—in the sense that it participates in the economy and is an economic "force" as a buyer and seller of goods and services, in the sense that it is an employer, and in the sense that it influences the buying habits of be-

[32]Andrew Greeley, "The Protestant Ethic: Time for a Moratorium," *Sociological Analysis* 25, no. 1 (1964); 20–33.
[33]Norval D. Glenn and Ruth Hyland, "Religious Preference and Worldly Success: Some Evidence from National Surveys," *American Sociological Review* 32, no. 1 (1967); 73–85.

lievers. Even in such relatively simple, small ways as creating a market for devotional and "peace of mind" literature published even by so-called secular or commercial publishing houses, and in supporting industries that produce religious artifacts such as religious vestments, statues, medallions, church pews, and baptismal fonts, religion has an impact on the economy of the society.

Religion's Influence on the Economy

It is important to realize, however, that the economic influence or impact of religion is seldom radical or revolutionary. It is unlikely to send the economy in new directions. The buying-and-selling and economic-stimulating role of religion in the society is both stable and predictable. It creates few new markets, and demands few innovative products. Religion is a relatively stable employer that neither stimulates nor retards economic swings of recession, depression, or inflation. It does, however, tend to respond to economic change. During the Great Depression of the 1930s in the United States thousands of seminary graduates of all denominations went without calls to religious vocations because congregations could not afford to hire and pay them and denominations could not afford the cost of establishing new congregations that would need clergy leaders. During the period of economic expansion beginning in the late 1940s and continuing into the 1950s, when new congregations proliferated and established congregations expanded their membership and their programs, seminaries could not launch enough graduates into the religious sea. Demand was greater than supply.

Of course, some religious leaders occasionally attempt to exert a significant influence on the economy of the society. A prime example, though not consciously directed toward economic change, consists of the attempts by religious groups to reinforce traditional moral values. Sometimes religious groups or persons attempt to ban the sale of certain "immoral" books or curtail the distribution of pornographic films. When this happens, an obvious indirect influence on the economy is being attempted. The most dramatic and economically influential instance of this in recent times is the movement leading to enactment of the Prohibition amendment in 1919. Conservative religious forces are generally credited with pushing this amendment through the states. The economic impact upon specific segments of the economy (liquor producers, wholesalers, retailers, bootleggers, and the like) was significant, though the impact on the overall economy was not that great. Eventually minor readjustments by subunits in the economy were required, not major changes in its direction or form.

A contemporary example involves the use of moral suasion by religious leaders in an attempt to influence the corporate policy of large organizations in favor of the objectives of the civil rights movement. Some attempts have been made by religious leaders to encourage, even force, organizations to divest themselves of stock in companies that blatantly discriminate against blacks and other minorities. Primary attention has been focused on corporations that do business with the Union of South Africa and thus implicitly support the apartheid policies of that country's government. Some leaders, for example, have tried to force the National Council of Churches and various denominations to sell the stock they hold in corporations that do business with South Africa and to withdraw savings deposits and cancel checking accounts with banks that have investments in or do business with that nation. We must observe that these attempts have not been particularly successful. And even if they were successful, the overall impact on the economy of the United States—or for that matter, of the Union of South Africa—would not be great.

A success story in this area occurred in Detroit (and in a few other cities) in the early 1960s, and involved action by black ministers designed to reduce employment discrimination in specified manufacturing and service industries. In Detroit, a group calling itself the Negro Preachers of Detroit and Vicinity followed a set procedure. First they attempted to negotiate with executives of target companies that were observed to employ only small proportions of blacks (and those few only in low-status, low-paying jobs). Failing in negotiation attempts, the next step was to contact the black ministers of the more than three hundred black churches in the Detroit area and urge them to suggest strongly to their members on a given Sunday morning to stop buying a given firm's products. Target firms included bread companies, oil companies, and milk distributors. Usually within two weeks the sales of target companies would be down by as much as 25 percent. Once the black ministers made their point, they usually secured concessions from the companies in question. It also appeared that other companies began paying attention and acted to eliminate discriminatory practices before they were faced with similar boycotts.

The Economy's Influence on Religion

Although we have been concentrating in this chapter on ways in which religion impinges on the economy, we do not mean to imply that there is no relationship between religion and the economy that proceeds in the opposite direction. In fact, many have suggested that the primary or most frequently observed relationship between religion and the economy is that of the economy influencing religion. Probably the most extreme view along these lines is the familiar perspective of Karl Marx, who saw religion—and all normative features of society, for that matter—as growing out of and reflecting economic factors and relationships. For Marx, religion was little more than a tool in the hands of the society's elites for pacifying the masses and maintaining prevailing economic patterns and the respective relationships of owners and nonowners to the means of production. First there is the economy and a stratification system that reflects the relationship of various people to the means of production within that economy; then comes religion, both reflecting these economic relationships and reinforcing them. Although we do not subscribe to the whole of Marx's point of view, some of this perspective is implicit in Chapter 7's discussion of the importance of lower socioeconomic status in sect formation. Certainly differential economic status is associated with different needs of all kinds, religious included. We need only recall Weber's distinction between the theodicy of escape and the theodicy of good fortune to see a relationship between economic status and religious perspective and expression.

It can hardly be accidental that most religious groups in a society implicitly, and often explicitly, support prevailing economic norms and institutional patterns. For example, one would hear few if any sermons on any given Sunday in the United States of America decrying capitalism. Social norms—in this case, economic norms—get absorbed into all institutions and most groups in a society, religious institutions and groups included. Although one could find as many precedents, examples, and specific injunctions in the New Testament for communal ownership, sharing of wealth, and giving to the needy till it truly hurts as one could find for a capitalistic economic structure and private accumulation of wealth, it is not by chance that Christian churches in nonsocialistic lands usually support a capitalistic ideology. Very simply, the dominant economic norms of a society tend to be reflected by religion in that society.

We have referred before to Liston Pope's *Millhands and Preachers*. Pope provides some fascinating documentation of the impact of economic factors on religion. For one thing, he discovered, religion prospers as the economy prospers and expands: new churches are founded, old ones add members, and all groups tend to prosper as the economic base of the community expands, attracts workers, and provides salaries and wages for those people. Pope observes that in the mill towns in Gaston County the mills provided land and built churches for the workers and often subsidized ministers' salaries. But at a price. Mill management expected and usually received religious support and reinforcement of their policies and ideology. At the very least, the mill churches and clergy kept silent on economic issues, sticking to "religious" concerns, thereby of course implicitly supporting company economic policy and practice.[34]

By way of a final summary comment we must repeat that although religion is definitely involved in and a part of the economy of the society in which it exists, its overall impact is relatively slight. Primarily it reinforces economic norms and patterns through participation as one among many buyers and sellers of goods and services and as a reinforcer or socializing agent for individuals in the prevailing economic norms. Although occasionally religion challenges specific aspects of economic relationships or the activities of specific economic units, its challenges tend to be of slight impact in the long run.

[34]Pope, *Millhands*, ch. 8 and 9.

10

Religion
and Politics

Although politics is nearly as variously defined as religion, there is consensus about at least two characteristics. First of all, politics (like its corollary, government) consists fundamentally of norms—that is, ways of reaching decisions, procedures for carrying out certain tasks, expectations about rights and privileges. Second, politics is more concerned with the societal norms that stipulate how and by whom coercive power shall be used in the pursuit of societal goals.[1] The employment of coercive power by government appears necessary primarily because the available supply of rewards that people strive for, both individually and collectively, is limited. Such rewards include money (or other means of obtaining goods and services), prestige, honor, respect, power, love, affection, and the like. Although such rewards are not necessarily in scarce supply, their supply is finite. That is to say, it is a relatively rare person who feels satiated so far as his share of such rewards is concerned. Most people want at least a few more dollars, a few more things, than they presently possess. And universally people could use a little more love and affection and a little more respect, even if they are not specifically seeking fame or power over others.

[1]J. Milton Yinger, *The Scientific Study of Religion* (New York: Macmillan, 1970), p. 408.

The resulting discrepancy between supply and demand places people inevitably into a competitive position with respect to garnering their desired share of available rewards. At this point we encounter politics and government as the system or social institution in a society that develops to regulate the process of reward seeking and to reduce the disruptive tendency inherent in the competition for rewards which could result in a war of all against all. Thus we understand the concept of politics to be the norms that designate the ultimate coercive power and the process by which the norms that regulate the exercise of power and authority get implemented. This accords well with Harold Lasswell's classic definition of politics as who gets what, when, and how—that is, the process of determining the distribution of society's rewards and balancing power relationships and claims.[2]

THE RELATIONSHIP OF RELIGION AND POLITICS

What, then, is the relationship of religion to politics? We should expect, considering the broad scope of our definition of politics, which implies a great diversity of processes, norms, and behavior, that there will be a variety of ways in which religion relates to the institution of politics.

J. Milton Yinger has suggested three possible general relationships. The first is the reinforcing relationship that religion has with other societal institutions, a phenomenon we have mentioned previously. To the extent that religious norms coincide with political norms, religion performs an integrating function in the society and helps to reduce tensions resulting from the pursuit of the limited and perhaps scarce rewards. Religion may justify unequal success in gaining rewards and encourage submission to the ultimate coercive power (i.e., the state or government). It may require believers to submit to governmental authorities as representatives placed by God to rule. Although religion may work to influence or limit the use of coercive power by those who possess it, the relationship here identified is basically one of partnership and mutual reinforcement or supplementation. The less complex the society, the more likely this relationship will be observed in pure form. This is so in large part because in less complex societies religion is so intimately involved in all other institutions as to be nearly indistinguishable as a distinctive institution.

A second possible relationship noted by Yinger is that in which the political institutions assume control over religion to the extent that for

---

[2]Harold Lasswell, *Politics: Who Gets What, When, and How* (New York: Meridian Books, 1958).

all practical purposes religion becomes another instrument of coercion, one of the appendages of an organism called the state. In such circumstances religion, whether willingly or not, has been stripped of any independent status or voice it may have had and becomes a tool in the hands of political elites. Marx's view of religion as the opium of the masses is a perfect summary of this possible relationship between religion and politics, though, as Yinger asserts, nowhere has this relationship been observed in its extreme, pure form.

Third, by way of direct contrast with the second possibility, there may develop a sharp tension between religion and the political system. The requirements and norms of religion may contradict and challenge those of the political system. Primary allegiance to an overarching religious system that transcends political boundaries may undermine political demands for jurisdictional allegiances. Political revolution as the ultimate expression of disenchantment with prevailing political structures and norms could even be fomented by religious factions. Here we have religion at odds with the state and in competition with it for the allegiance of its citizens.[3]

TYPES OF RELATIONSHIP BETWEEN CHURCH AND STATE

So much for an extremely general account of possible relationships between religion and politics. It is useful at this point to suggest several somewhat specific types of relationship between religion and politics—or church and state, to use a more common phrase that we shall employ repeatedly as this chapter progresses.

Pure Theocracy   This occurs when political authority is held and exercised by the heads of the religious organization in a society. The term *theocracy* literally means "rule by God." Thus religious leaders are seen as ruling all of society in God's name and stead and ostensibly according to his wishes. Actually, the state as a distinct entity doesn't exist, though of course an observer from outside a society so governed might be able to distinguish when rulers were acting as strictly political leaders and when they were acting as religious leaders. The rule of Israel by prophets in the Old Testament is an example of the pure theocracy. A prophet such as Samuel was seen as God's spokesman regarding not only religious matters but political and governmental matters as well. Interestingly, the people chafed under this arrangement, pleaded embarrassment in the face of surrounding societies who were under the rule of

[3]Yinger, *Scientific Study*, p. 409.

kings, and appealed for a similar "separation" of church and state. The papal states in Italy during medieval times are further examples of pure theocracies.

Modified Theocracy   In this case, while the state is subordinate to the religious institution and its leaders, even in temporal affairs, the state nevertheless exists as a separate entity. The state is seen here as the enforcement agency of religion, an agency necessary because of the tendency of people to deviate from societal norms but dependent on religion for its authority. Most medieval European societies dominated by Roman Catholicism were of this type. Similarly, John Calvin's Geneva, as well as the early Massachusetts Bay Colony (in which governmental officials were required to be Congregationalists), are good examples.

Erastianism   Though not the exact opposite of the theocratic types mentioned above, Erastianism is in clear contrast to them. Here the state exerts control over religion rather than vice versa. While state control is not absolute or total, the state still makes the major decisions and establishes a state church. It is important to note that the state does not create an official state religion de novo but selects one (or conceivably even several) already existing in the society and officially sanctions it (or them). All citizens must then be members of and subscribe to the dogma and ritual of the official religion. The concept is essentially identical with Caesaropapism, in which the political ruler controlled the church and its hierarchy. Actually, the tension between theocracy and Erastianism or Caesaropapism constituted a continuous running battle between ecclesiastical and political powers throughout the Roman Catholic and Eastern Orthodox European countries during the Middle Ages.

Totalitarianism   Whereas Erastianism assumes that religion is allowed some autonomy and some areas of life over which it has ultimate authority or influence, totalitarianism allows religion no such freedom but instead tells it exactly what to teach. Religion is thus used as a tool or enforcement arm of the state. Totalitarianism may actually outlaw religion if the latter threatens to compete for people's allegiance. But not necessarily: it may simply attempt to control and use religion for its own ends.

Total Separation   In this arrangement the arenas in which religion and politics operate are entirely distinct with no overlap. There one must assume that religion serves the soul and the state the body— or that religion is entirely an individualized, subjective, internalized phenomenon, while politics and the state serve the group, deal with externals relative to survival, and are entirely secular. Such total separation has never been achieved, and thus remains a purely theoretical possibility.

A variant on the total-separation theme is total conflict. Instead of a happy coincidence at all points between religion and politics, or mutual tolerance of a stalemate type, this situation is characterized by point-for-point fundamental conflict and disagreement. Religion says one thing and pulls in one direction; the state and political forces say the opposite and pull in the opposite direction. Pure examples of such total conflict are impossible to find, in large part because the idea is sociologically unsound. Probably the closest one could come to an empirical example would be early Communist Russia after the 1917 revolution, as religious authorities opposed the irreligious and antireligious philosophy of the revolutionaries and the latter just as vehemently opposed religion. Something had to give. It was religion. Essentially a totalitarian relationship resulted.

Partial Separation   What we have left is the most common relationship between church and state, at least in our contemporary world. Most societies today exhibit some variation on this pattern—that is, some independence for both the political and religious institutions, but some overlapping and mutual influence as well. We shall spend most of the rest of this chapter in an explication of the American experience with the partial-separation approach to the relationship of church and state.

Implicit in this brief overview of various possible relationships between religion and political institutions is an underlying potential if not real conflict. Because the state has specialized functions of governing and coordinating the body politic, while religion relates to the supernatural and to coming to grips with various "ultimate problems," there is almost automatically competition between the two for people's loyalty, attention, commitment, and time. Such does not generally occur of course in small, less complex societies, but only as societies begin to grow in population, expand in territory to include diverse cultural groups, and differentiate and specialize in terms of role, so that some persons fill part-time or even full-time governing roles, others fill roles of religious leadership and function, while still others fill a variety of productive and service roles.

Consistent with our earlier reference to the oligarchic tendencies in growing groups,[4] we can here note that whenever religious specialists appear, even if they are seen as little more than political functionaries, they and their organization begin to assume some semblance of independence. This will be so because they are experts in their field and have primary, first-hand control over ritual and teaching. To the degree that people follow their lead and give primary allegiance to "spiritual" teachings and leaders, and to the degree that religious leaders gain power, to that degree the stage is set for conflict, or at least competition, between

[4]See Chapter 7.

religious and governmental powers. The various ways this competition or conflict gets worked out are summarized in the six possible relationships between church and state outlined above.

As already indicated, the most common resolution of such real or potential conflict at least today is some pattern of partial separation. We turn now to a closer look at this pattern as it has developed in the United States.

CHURCH AND STATE IN THE UNITED STATES

Early Patterns

It is interesting to note that while American society today upholds the concept of separation of church and state, such has not always been the case. What amounted to state churches or government-sanctioned religions were common in the early settlements and colonies. It is doubly interesting to note that although a familiar theme among settlers and immigrants to this country has been religious freedom from various European tyrannies and established religions, many of these same people did not allow religious freedom for minority religious groups in their settlements or colonies. Two prime examples are the Massachusetts Bay Colony and Virginia. Massachusetts' Puritan settlers established what for all intents and purposes was a state church. The colonial government was expected, as part of its service to its citizens, to support public worship and suppress heresy. Taxes were used to support the Congregational Church and its clergy. The Congregationalist meeting house was used for both governmental and religious activities. Colonial law compelled all people to attend church services regardless of their personal beliefs and denied equal rights to the "unorthodox." Citizens were subject to trial by the colonial government for what the church called sins but the government called crimes—heresy, blasphemy, and idolatry. People like Roger Williams, Anne Hutchinson, and various Presbyterians, Quakers, and Catholics quickly found out what the laws meant as they were fined, imprisoned, and even banished.

In Virginia, Anglicanism was established as the official church, but in a somewhat different form than in Massachusetts.[5] Whereas in Massachusetts the church tended to control the government, in Virginia the government tended to control the church. In Virginia all citizens were required to attend Anglican services and were taxed to support the

[5]Anson Phelps Stokes and Leo Pfeffer, *Church and State in the United States* (New York: Harper & Row, 1964), p. 7.

Anglican church, no non-Anglican clergymen were allowed to perform the clergy role, no non-Anglican religious group could hold services, specifically no Catholic or Quaker could hold public office, and no one who didn't believe in infant baptism could even become a citizen of the colony.

With the founding of the new nation and the adoption of the Constitution, however, the United States officially repudiated the concept of such church-government ties: the First Amendment, part of the Bill of Rights added to the Constitution in 1791, states that "Congress shall make no law respecting an establishment of religion, or prohibiting the free exercise thereof." However, it was not until the passage of the Fourteenth Amendment in 1868 that the above limitation was applied at the state level. Theoretically, any state could have had an official state religion up to that time; but none did after 1833, when Massachusetts rescinded its state-church commitments, the last state to do so.

The establishment of an official state church has thus been explicitly forbidden in this society. But interpreting where to draw the line between church and state and what "separation of church and state" means in the context of this society has not been easy. In fact, it has been variously interpreted throughout our history, and in every generation the relationship between church and state has been a lively issue. Undoubtedly it shall ever remain so. To expect final resolution of the issue and some kind of perfect distinction and separation of church and state is to fly in the face of sociological reality and to try to reject fundamental sociological principles. So long as we assume and can demonstrate the interdependence of all societal elements we must expect a recurrent problem with the separation of church and state. In fact, to try seriously to separate church and state is to attempt the impossible so long as church and state exist side by side in society. They interact; they overlap; they touch the same people; they seek commitment and involvement from the same people. Thus partial separation describes the reality, even though something approaching total separation may be the goal of many.

The Constitutional Provision

Part of the problem in American society is the brevity and vagueness of the constitutional provision in the First Amendment. Joseph Tussman states the problem well:

> *The First Amendment in its attractive brevity leaves much unstated and seems to take much for granted. Even its spirit is elusive. Is it a practical expression of "a religious people"? Or is it a tolerant statement of commitment to a secular experiment? Does it indeed put us "under God"?*

> *What is "establishment" and what is an "exercise" of religion? The Amendment does not explain itself.*[6]

Although it would be of great help, it is impossible to "get into the mind," so to speak, of the framers of the Constitution and discover their intentions. Were they flaunting sociological realities? Or were they acknowledging them? That is, were they trying to do something that can't be done—namely, separate religion from politics and government in society? Or, recognizing that interaction and overlap between the two is inevitable, were they simply trying to avoid excesses from arising therefrom?

Although throughout our history people have pointed to the First Amendment as evidence of an "official endorsement" of religion and have suggested that we are therefore fundamentally a religious people, it is not all that clear that the Founding Fathers were so much encouraging religion as they were trying to place some limitations on its power and influence. Clearly they did not want a repetition of early Massachusetts Bay Colony or Virginia at the national level. We need to remember that many of the Founding Fathers and framers of the Constitution were freethinkers, deists, and sons of the Enlightenment who doubted if not rejected much of traditional Christian orthodoxy. Further, at the official birth of the new nation relatively few of its citizens were formal members of churches.[7] Quite clearly the early emphasis seems to be one of limitation of religious power and influence rather than support and encouragement of such influence. If this is so, it represents quite a shift from the strong religious (Christian) influence in the early days of the colonies. Yet note the action of the Supreme Court fifty years later (1844) as it interprets the First Amendment. In 1831, Stephen Girard, a wealthy Philadelphian, provided in his will for the establishment of a college for orphans—on condition that although the orphans were to be taught the "purest principles of morality," no clergymen representing any religion whatsoever was to teach at, hold office in, or even visit the proposed institution. Daniel Webster, in challenging the will, stated: "No fault can be found with Girard for wishing a marble college to bear his name forever, but it is not valuable unless it has a fragrance of Christianity about it. . . . A cruel experiment is to be made upon these orphans to ascertain whether they cannot be brought up without religion."[8]

The Supreme Court upheld Girard's will interpreting it as bearing no animosity to Christianity, but only to clergymen, since nonclergymen

---

[6]Joseph Tussman, *The Supreme Court on Church and State* (New York: Oxford University Press, 1962), p. xiii.

[7]According to the first U.S. Census in 1907, only 5 percent of U.S. citizens reported being members of churches.

[8]Quoted in Tussman, *The Supreme Court*, pp. 5–6.

were left free to teach Christian principles. In fact, regarding the requirement that teachers in the school "instill into the minds of the scholars
the purest principles of morality" the Court commented: "Where can the
purest principles of morality be learned so clearly or so perfectly as from
the New Testament?"[9] In other words, Christianity should be taught—
by lay Christians instead of clergymen if necessary. Quite clearly there
was a Christian bias abroad in the land, and it was certainly encouraged
by the Supreme Court's interpretation of the Constitution.

Two summary observations at this point: First, despite the constitutional prohibitions against the establishment of a state church, the history
of our society evidences strong favor toward religion—Christianity in particular. Second, opinion regarding how and to what extent the state is
to be allowed to exercise its support for religion has fluctuated. Although
we lack the space to document this point in detail, some semblance of
a pendulum motion has been in operation throughout our history in
terms of degree of involvement in and support for religion on the part
of the state and political elements.

The United States' original Protestant Christian bias was challenged
and broadened by waves of Roman Catholic and Jewish immigrants in
the nineteenth and early twentieth centuries and later by agnostics and
secularists. Mormons demanded the right to practice polygamy as a free
exercise of their religion, but ultimately were denied it. John T. Scopes
taught evolution in a Tennessee high school in contradiction to fundamentalist Christianity and although a loser in court was granted by many
a "moral" victory because of the national publicity and lampooning of
the prosecution by the press. Prohibition came and went. Oregon required that every child be educated in its public schools, but the Supreme
Court declared religious (parochial) schools a valid alternative (1925).
And so the pendulum has swung. To a great extent the problem
centers around balancing the requirement of nonestablishment of religion and its inherent neutrality stance, on the one hand, with providing
opportunity for free exercise of religion on the other. When the state
emphasizes neutrality, its action is interpreted by some as antagonism.
When the state encourages free exercise, it is accused of establishment.
For example, if the state says it can't allow observance of Christmas in
public schools lest it thereby favor Christianity, objectors claim that their
freedom to act out their religious convictions wherever they may be is
infringed upon. If Christmas observances are allowed, members of non-
Christian religions or those with no religious affiliation or commitment
cry "foul" and "establishment of religion." Quite obviously, the First
Amendment provides the political system with a built-in dilemma that

9Quoted in ibid., p. 6.

shall never be fully resolved. And so the problem of separating religion from other social phenomena, which we earlier branded as sociologically impossible in the first place, is now merely compounded.

The Parochial School Issue

The Oregon case mentioned above in a sense introduced the current period of controversy over church-state relations in our society that has had a major focus on the issue of religion and public schools. The Oregon decision (*Pierce* v. *Society of Sisters*), which affirmed the right of parents to send their children to nonpublic schools, has become the parochial schools' Magna Carta. Since then a number of Supreme Court decisions have centered around two issues: (1) How much (if any) state support can be given to parochial schools? (2) How much (if any) religion is allowable in public schools? Again we see the two horns of the dilemma —(1) the free-exercise issue, (2) the establishment-of-religion issue.

Regarding the first issue of state support for parochial schools there have been several Supreme Court decisions. In *Cochrane* v. *State of Louisiana Board of Education* (1930), a basis was established for providing free textbooks for all children whether they attended a public or private school. The logic of this decision centered around the "child-benefit" view, which recurs in subsequent cases, holding that it is the child who first of all must be benefited and that the state must provide stipulated services to its citizens without discrimination based on the type of school the child attends. Although a private school benefits indirectly from such a provision—for example, insofar as it now doesn't have to buy certain textbooks for its pupils—denying this free service, the Court held, interferes with the free-exercise clause of the First Amendment.[10]

In *Everson* v. *State of New Jersey Board of Education* (1947), free tax-supported bus transportation for children attending parochial schools was established. The following quotation from the Court's opinion presents the logic and rationale of the decision:

> *The establishment of religion clause of the First Amendment means at least this: Neither a state nor the federal government can set up a church. Neither can pass laws which aid one religion, aid all religions, or prefer one religion over another. Neither can force nor influence a person to go to or to remain away from church against his will or force him to profess a belief or disbelief in any religion. No person can be punished for entertaining or professing religious beliefs or disbeliefs, for church attendance or non-attendance. No tax in any amount, large or small, can be levied to support any religious activity or institution, whatever they may be called, or whatever form they may adopt to teach or practice religion. Neither a*

[10]Ibid., p. 49.

> *state nor the federal government can, openly or secretly, participate in the affairs of any religious organizations or groups and vice versa.*
>
> *Measured by these standards, we cannot say that the First Amendment prohibits New Jersey from spending tax raised funds to pay the bus fares of parochial school pupils as a part of a general program under which it pays the fares of pupils attending public and other schools. It is undoubtedly true that children are helped to get to church schools. There is even a possibility that some of the children might not be sent to the church schools if the parents were compelled to pay their children's bus fares out of their own pockets. Cutting off church schools from these services would make it far more difficult for the schools to operate. But such is obviously not the purpose of the First Amendment. That amendment requires the state to be a neutral in its relations with groups of religious believers and non-believers; it does not require the state to be their adversary. State power is no more to be used so as to handicap religions, than it is to favor them. . . . The First Amendment has erected a wall between church and state. That wall must be kept high and impregnable. We could not approve the slightest breach. New Jersey has not breached it here.[11]*

The most recent case in which the Supreme Court has upheld the constitutionality of providing textbooks for children in nonpublic schools was *Allen* v. *State of New York Board of Education* (1968). Justice Byron White, writing for the majority of the Court (six of nine), asserted that previous Court decisions involving government assistance to nonpublic education constitute "a recognition that private education has played and is playing a significant and valuable role in raising national levels of knowledge, competence, and experience."[12] White went on to say:

> *Continued willingness to rely on private school systems, including parochial systems, strongly suggests that a wide segment of informed opinion, legislative and otherwise, has found that those schools do an acceptable job of providing secular education to their students. This judgment is further evidence that parochial schools are performing, in addition to their sectarian function, the task of secular education.[13]*

The issue remains controversial, however, as states and private groups inquire what other services should be provided under the "child-benefit" theory. For example, what about paying the costs of instruction in "secular" subjects in church-related schools—the so-called parochaid issue? Several states have experimented with a purchase-of-services plan in which the state pays part of the salary of teachers in parochial schools. The range of such state support is from 15 percent in Rhode Island to 100 percent in Pennsylvania. The Pennsylvania statute has been upheld

---

[11]Everson v. Board of Education, 330 U.S. 1 (1947).
[12]Allen v. Board of Education, 392 U.S. 236 (1968).
[13]Ibid.

by the U.S. Court of Appeals in Philadelphia, which ruled that the child benefits whether state funds go to him, his parents, or his school.[14]

A Michigan statute allowing up to 50 percent payment of salaries for nonpublic school teachers was passed by the legislature on July 4, 1970, but was rescinded by popular vote in the November election of that same year. Although the Supreme Court has promised to consider this issue and to hear appeals on the Pennsylvania case, it has done neither as of this writing.

Several states, including California, New Jersey, New York, Texas, and Wisconsin, are considering a voucher plan whereby the state would issue vouchers to parents in amounts equal to the average cost of education in the local public schools. Parents would then decide to which schools to send their children and apply the vouchers to tuition costs at these schools.[15] Such procedures will, however, undoubtedly be called into question in the light of the action of the Supreme Court on October 10, 1972, when it upheld, by an eight-to-one decision, a lower-court ruling which declared unconstitutional a state plan for paying direct subsidies to parents of nonpublic schoolchildren. This decision spoke to an Ohio case in which the legislature voted to pay six hundred dollars a year to parents of pupils in public school and ninety dollars to those with children in parochial and other private schools.

The attitudes of religious groups, their members, and other religiously interested persons with regard to the issue of state support for religious schools varies greatly. The Catholic position has traditionally been one of trying to secure as much state financial support as possible. In fact, in those states where parochaid has been an issue it has almost developed into a Catholic-versus-Protestant issue. The Protestant group that has the largest number of parochial schools is The Lutheran Church —Missouri Synod. From its founding in the United States in 1839 until the 1960s this group vigorously opposed state aid for religious schools, whether its own or others. But by the 1960s it had reversed its position, and today it generally joins Catholics in seeking and encouraging legislation that grants certain kinds of state aid to parochial schools. There is no consensus among Protestant denominations, however. Some favor state support, others oppose it, and still others take no official stand at all.

Although there is diversity among American Jews over this issue, a majority oppose use of public tax monies for support of parochial education not only because they feel such support clearly violates the

[14]Lemon v. Kurtzman, 403 U.S. 602 (1971).
[15]*Religion and the Schools: From Prayer to Public Aid* (Washington, D.C.: National School Public Relations Association, n.d.), p. 16.

separation-of-church-and-state principle enunciated in the First Amendment, but because such support would tend to undermine the public
school system. The feeling is that each of the more than two hundred
religious groups would be encouraged to establish such schools and in the
process impede racial integration and intensify religious and ethnic
animosities and divisiveness. However, the Aquadath Israel of America,
an Orthodox Jewish educational movement with approximately eighty
thousand students in four hundred schools, favors public aid and has
requested a hundred-dollar-per-pupil federal subsidy for children in
nonpublic schools.[16]

A group calling itself Protestants and Other Americans United for
the Separation of Church and State (POAU) has vigorously opposed state
aid to parochial schools since the 1940s. The charter membership of this
organization included the presidents of two Protestant seminaries, a
prominent Methodist bishop, the president of the Southern Baptist Convention, the secretary of the National Association of Evangelicals, a
former editor of the *Christian Century*, an associate editor of a Scottish
Rite journal, and an official of the National Education Association—
certainly a mixed group, though decidedly Protestant.[17] This group
seems particularly concerned with Catholic attempts to secure state aid
and has been critical of the Supreme Court decisions permitting state
aid for textbooks and bus transportation for parochial school pupils.

Religion in Public Schools

The second issue mentioned earlier was: How much religion is to
be allowed in public schools?—that is, how to balance the nonestablishment and free-exercise provisions in permitting or excluding religion in
public schools? Some of the specific points at issue are Bible readings,
prayers, and religious festival observance (Christmas, for example) in
public schools. The present controversy began with the case *McCollum*
v. *State of Illinois Board of Education* (1948). At issue was whether public
schoolchildren released from regular classes for an hour or so of weekly
religious instruction (taught by representatives of the child's religious
group) should be allowed to use public school facilities for this purpose.
The Supreme Court ruled that such a use of public school buildings
violated the separation-of-church-and-state provision of the First Amendment. Speaking for the majority, Justice Black stated:

16*Detroit Free Press*, October 11, 1973.
17Robert Michaelsen, *Piety in the Public School* (New York: Macmillan, 1970),
p. 228.

*Here not only are the state's tax-supported public school buildings used
for the dissemination of religious doctrines. The State also affords sectarian
groups an invaluable aid in that it helps to provide pupils for their religious classes through use of the state's compulsory public school machinery.
This is not separation of Church and State.*[18]

In concurring with the majority decision Justice Frankfurter wrote:
"Separation means separation, not something less. Jefferson's metaphor in
describing the relationship between Church and State speaks of a 'wall
of separation,' not a fine line easily overstepped."[19] It is worth noting
that in dissenting from the majority decision Justice Reed expressed the
view of not a few citizens: "A rule of law should not be drawn from a
figure of speech. . . . Devotion to the great principle of religious liberty
should not lead us into a rigid interpretation of the constitutional guarantee that conflicts with the accepted habits of our people."[20]

In 1952, in *Zorach* v. *Clauson*, the Court dealt with the issue again.
In attempting to implement the *McCollum* decision, New York City developed a program which permitted its public schools to release students
during the school day so that they might leave the school grounds and
go to religious centers for religious instruction or worship exercises.
Under this plan, a student would be released upon the written request
of his parents, and the religious group would submit weekly attendance
reports to his school. Such a program was challenged as violating the First
Amendment as interpreted by the *McCollum* decision. The majority
opinion of the Court written by Justice Douglas affirmed that New York's
program involved neither religious instruction in public schools nor the
expenditure of public funds, and therefore it neither violated the Constitution nor disregarded the earlier *McCollum* decision. Douglas wrote:

*We follow the McCollum case. But we cannot expand it to cover the
present released time program unless separation of Church and State means
that public institutions can make no adjustment of their schedules to accommodate the religious needs of the people. We cannot read into the Bill
of Rights such a philosophy of hostility to religion.*[21]

The issues of Bible reading and prayer in public schools have been
dealt with in two fairly recent Supreme Court decisions. In *Abington
School District* v. *Schempp* (1963) the Court declared unconstitutional
the Pennsylvania law that required daily Bible reading in public schools.
The original Pennsylvania law read as follows:

[18]Illinois ex rel. McCollum v. Board of Education, 333 U.S. 203 (1948).
[19]Ibid.
[20]Ibid.
[21]Zorach v. Clauson, 343 U.S. 306 (1952).

> *At least 10 verses from the Holy Bible shall be read, or caused to be read, without comment, at the opening of each public school on each school day, by the teacher in charge. . . . If any teacher, whose duty it shall be to read the Holy Bible, or cause it to be read, shall fail or omit so to do, said teacher shall (upon charges and proof before the school board) be discharged.*[22]

This law had been amended in response to the Schempp family's suit that they had won before the District Court for the Eastern District of Pennsylvania in 1959. The compulsory feature had been eliminated by the addition of the following sentence: "Any child shall be excused from such Bible reading, or attending such Bible reading, upon written request of his parents or his guardian."

The practice at Abington Senior High School was that at the beginning of the school day, while students were in their homerooms, the following exercises were broadcast into each room through an intercom system: a reading by a student of ten verses of the Bible; a recitation of the Lord's Prayer, for which students in the classrooms were asked to stand and join in; a flag salute and recitation of the Pledge of Allegiance; and announcements of interest to the students.

The Schempp family contended that such a practice amounted to an establishment of religion (Christianity or at least the Judeo-Christian heritage) and violated the free-exercise clause of the First Amendment inasmuch as the law required the Schempps and their children to take a public action of belief or disbelief. Mr. Schempp contended that the noncompulsory provision in the revised law was not a satisfactory resolution in that his children, should they be excused, would be labeled as "oddballs" by fellow students and teachers alike, that they would likely be branded atheists, with the "un-American–atheistic–Communist" connotation that atheism implies for many people. Further, missing the exercises would cause his children to miss announcements important to all students. It was also contended that the Pennsylvania law clearly intended the exercises as a religious or devotional act and thus disregarded the 1947 *Everson* decision (see the preceding section, "The Parochial School Issue"), which among other things stated that neither a state nor the federal government can force a person "to profess a belief or disbelief in any religion."

The district court supported the Schempps, and its decision was upheld by the Supreme Court in 1963. The opinion of the district court stated:

> *The reading of the verses, even without comment, possesses a devotional and religious character and constitutes, in effect, a religious observance.*

[22]Pennsylvania Public Law 1928 (Supp. 1960), Oct. 17, 1959.

> The devotional and religious nature of the morning exercises is made all the more apparent by the fact that the Bible reading is followed immediately by a recital in unison by the pupils of the Lord's Prayer.
>
> The fact that some pupils, or theoretically all pupils, might be excused from attendance at the exercises does not mitigate the obligatory nature of the ceremony because the state law unequivocally requires that the school exercises be held every school day in every school in the Commonwealth.
>
> The exercises are held in the school buildings and perforce are conducted by and under the authority of the local school authorities and during school sessions.
>
> Since the statute requires the reading of the Holy Bible, a Christian document, the practice prefers the Christian religion. The record demonstrates that it was the intention of the Commonwealth to introduce a religious ceremony into the public schools of the Commonwealth.[23]

In 1962 the Supreme Court, in *Engel* v. *Vitale*, had declared unconstitutional the following prayer required to be recited each school day in New York State Public schools: "Almighty God, we acknowledge our dependence upon Thee, and we beg Thy blessings upon us, our parents, our teachers, and our country." Many people had been unhappy with this prayer in the first place. Some felt it was too Christian; others thought it wasn't Christian enough; and still others thought it much too self-centered and parochial in the sense that it didn't pray for the billions of others who are also in need for "blessings" but who are not U.S. citizens. More crucial, of course, was the issue of whether the state should be in the business of writing and requiring prayers in its public schools in the first place. The Supreme Court said clearly, "No." No unit of government may prescribe or sanction by law any official prayer or act of worship. Actually, this decision had a fairly narrow focus. It did not eliminate the possibility of praying in public schools; it simply denied the state the right to compose them or require their recitation in school.

The same year, 1962, a potentially more explosive case was heard before the Florida Supreme Court (*Chamberlin* v. *Dade County Board of Public Instruction*). The original complaint attempted to have the following public school practices declared unconstitutional:

1. Regular reading of the Bible
2. Comments on the Bible passages that are read
3. Distribution of sectarian literature to schoolchildren
4. After-school Bible instruction in school buildings
5. Regular recitation of the Lord's Prayer and prayer before lunch
6. Religious observances of Christmas, Hanukkah, and Easter, including instruction in the dogma of the Nativity and the Resurrection

[23]U.S. District Court for the Eastern District of Pennsylvania, 201 F. Supp. 819; reported in Abington School District v. Schempp, 374 U.S. 211 (1963).

7. Display of religious symbols
8. Baccalaureate (sermon) programs
9. Conducting a religious census of pupils
10. Use of religious tests in hiring or promoting school employees[24]

Three of these practices were stopped by a lower trial court and thus, because they were not appealed by the school board, did not come before the Florida Supreme Court: sectarian comments on the Bible, use of school buildings for religious instruction after school hours, and religious observance of religious holidays. However, the Florida Supreme Court on appeal held that Bible reading, recitation of the Lord's Prayer, the conducting of baccalaureate services, a religious census, and asking prospective employees, "Do you believe in God," plus other practices such as singing religious hymns and displaying students' religious art work were all constitutionally unobjectionable. (Duker mentions that somewhere the issue of the distribution of sectarian literature got lost in the shuffle and was never discussed.[25] The case was appealed to the U.S. Supreme Court, which finally, after a series of delays, ruled that Florida's prayer and Bible-reading provisions were unconstitutional; it did not rule on the remaining four issues.

That four similar decisions—*Schempp, Engle, Chamberlin,* and one similar to *Schempp* arising in Baltimore, *Murry* v. *Curlett*—came so close together in the early 1960s caused a flurry of excitement and controversy. Many religiously committed people feared that their society was coming loose from its religious moorings, was becoming atheistic and secularistic, was losing its moral fiber. Grass-roots as well as nationally organized movements were launched in favor of a new constitutional amendment, or at least a revision of the First Amendment, that would explicitly permit Bible reading and prayer in public schools. These activities were highlighted by Senator Everett Dirksen's (R.-Ill.) "prayer amendment," which twice failed to pass the Senate. Dirksen's proposal would have altered the First Amendment by specifying that nothing in the Constitution could prohibit public schools from "providing for or permitting the voluntary participation by students or others in prayer." Quite clearly, such a constitutional provision would contribute to orienting the federal Government and the Supreme Court to an official position that was friendly with respect to religion—not simply neutral, and certainly not antagonistic.

On the other hand, some of those who agreed with the Supreme

---

[24]Sam Duker, *The Public Schools and Religion* (New York: Harper & Row, 1966), pp. 177–78.
[25]Duker, *Public Schools*, p. 178.

Court's rulings were emboldened to press for further action, particularly on those issues listed but not acted on in the *Chamberlin* case. Still others, such as Madelyn Murray O'Hair (whose activities have been much publicized), have tried to go beyond the issue of religion in public schools and remove religion from other areas of public life—including such things as the phrase "under God" in the Pledge of Allegiance, religious chaplains in Congress, the broadcasting of readings from the Bible by astronauts in space, and property tax exemption for religious groups. Although numerous attempts have been made to bring such issues before the Supreme Court, the Court has so far refused to hear them.

Robert Michaelsen mentions two major results from the modern period of Supreme Court decisions regarding religion and the public schools and the controversy and discussion that have followed such decisions: (1) the "wall-of-separation" concept the Court has been trying to implement has tended to polarize religious opinion and religious groups; and (2) these decisions have nonetheless contributed to increasing dialogue across religious lines.[26] Although there has been fairly solid Roman Catholic opposition to the wall-of-separation concept, particularly in the form of its most recent interpretation by the Supreme Court, Jewish opinion has been just about as solid in support of the concept and the Court's recent interpretations of it. Liberal Protestants—and, interestingly, some very conservative Protestants in the POAU—have joined the Jews in backing the wall-of-separation idea. Other Protestants, however, have registered deep regret at the course the Supreme Court has been taking. Thus there has been considerable polarization. Yet, as litigation surrounding the issue of religion in public schools has progressed, the examination of constitutional principles by both laymen and experts has increased and religious groups have begun to get together to discuss the issue.

Proposed Solutions

Various proposals have been suggested and discussed for resolving the issue of religion in the public schools. An old suggestion that has received considerable recent support is that schools teach *about* religion —the historical and cultural relationships of religion and society. Although there is absolutely no constitutional problem here, this practice appears to be less than satisfactory to many religious persons who feel that religion's "higher authority" would be jeopardized if religion were placed alongside other social forces, philosophies, and ideologies.

Another suggestion is that the schools teach and inculcate common

[26]Michaelsen, *Piety*, p. 235.

"moral and spiritual values." Implicit here is the recognition that public schools are by their nature quite deeply involved in the task of value formation. In fact partly as a result of discussion following the *McCollum* case, the Educational Policies Commission of the National Educational Association in 1951 published a list of ten values common to the American people that the NEA felt can and should be taught in the public schools:

1. Human personality as the basic value
2. Moral responsibility
3. Institutions as the servants of men
4. Common consent
5. Devotion to truth
6. Respect for excellence
7. Moral equality
8. Brotherhood
9. The pursuit of happiness
10. Spiritual enrichment[27]

Michaelsen notes how this particular choice of values served several purposes quite well:

> Stress on spiritual values countered those critics who accused the school of giving over to secularism. It also fitted well with the prevailing mood of public piety. At the same time "spiritual" did not stir up either sectarian or constitutional hackles like "religious" might have done. It was acceptable to the Court, to most religionists, and even to many secularists.[28]

One can't help but observe, however, that accepting a list of vaguely defined values is an easy task compared with operationalizing such values and achieving consensus concerning how to include them in classroom teaching.

Two other proposals that are being experimented with in numerous places are, first, some form of released-time program which does not entail use of public school buildings and, second, what has been variously called "shared time" or "dual enrollment," in which public and parochial school resources supplement one another.

The issue of religion in the schools is of course far from being resolved, and it probably never will be. Part of the difficulty stems from the Constitution's lack of specificity. Precedents established in Supreme

27Ibid., p. 242.
28Ibid.

Court decisions become extremely important as a result. Hence, if events are to move in one or another direction, both religious instruction and devotional activities will probably be increasingly eliminated from public schools.

Another extremely important aspect of this issue is the question of balancing minority rights with majority rule. In the past, when it came to religion in public schools, the concept of "majority rule" held sway—the view that ours is a religious nation—specifically, a Christian nation—in which secular and religious education, particularly as they touch on moral issues, are ideally intertwined. This approach is still taken in countless communities where particular religious groups that constitute the majority utilize local public schools in various ways to reinforce the dominant religious values—the Supreme Court notwithstanding. All the while the Court has of course been trying in recent decisions to protect the rights of minorities—those of the Unitarian Schempp family, for example.

Unresolved Issues

Many unresolved questions surrounding the relationship of church and state remain. The following paragraphs outline several of these.[29]

First, although our society has successfully avoided the establishment of a state church or granting official support for a particular denomination, it needs to be observed that the First Amendment says: "Congress shall make no law respecting an establishment of religion." Do we today have an established Christianity, just as earlier it was an established Protestantism? Or if not Christianity today, then something we might call Judeo-Christianity? By acknowledging in the Pledge of Allegiance that we are a nation "under God," are we "establishing religion"—that is, officially affirming that God exists and that religion is valid?

Second, the current position of the Supreme Court is exemplified in the majority opinion in the *Everson* case (discussed in the section "The Parochial School Issue"): "Neither a state nor the federal government . . . can pass laws which aid one religion, aid all religions, or prefer one religion over another." What about governmental policy and law that renders tax-exempt not only any property used for religious purposes but also income accruing to religious organizations, whether it comes from voluntary contributions, from rents from office buildings and apartment houses owned by churches, from dividends and interest from corporate

[29]Some of these issues have been suggested by Tussman, *The Supreme Court,* pp. xiv–xxiv.

stocks and bonds—or from the profits of the Real Form Girdle Company mentioned in the previous chapter? Isn't this "aiding all religions"? Certainly the society is saying that it values religion and wants to encourage it by giving it a tax break. But in asserting the value of religion, is society also saying that religion as expressed in this society is valid and is thereby "established"?

Third, regarding the "free-exercise" provision of the First Amendment, an important question is whether the government as it regulates the action of the citizenry interferes with free exercise of religion by individuals. What about the pacifist who refuses to serve in a military capacity in the armed forces, or the person who refuses to take an oath, or parents who refuse to allow a blood transfusion for their child, or the person who refuses to take out automobile liability insurance—all from religious conviction? Significantly, in real cases of the sort cited the free-exercise provision has in fact been upheld—but not without having to challenge the law and not without hardship, harassment, and in some cases imprisonment. Undoubtedly new situations will arise requiring interpretation and application (or misapplication) of this constitutional provision.

Fourth, while trying to provide opportunities for free exercise and freedom of belief, do we grant equal latitude for freedom of unbelief? What happens when Congress inserts "under God" into the Pledge of Allegiance or when it passes legislation (as it came close to doing) that would permit if not require prayer to God in public schools? What about those who do not believe in God, or at least not in the kind of God most Americans conceive to exist? Are they thereby excluded from the circle of allegiance? Or is the nonbeliever expected to lie? Or is he to do what a stalwart church member once related to the author: "You know I can't buy everything that's in the Apostles' Creed. So when we come to those parts I don't agree with I just keep my mouth shut and nobody knows the difference."

Fifth, does separating religion from politics require religious groups totally to refrain from acting in the political arena or from attempting to influence political decisions and policy? What about the politically oriented and socially concerned religious group that feels obliged to try to improve the society by influencing the political process? Are there differences between the rights of religious groups and groups such as the American Medical Association, the American Dairy Farmers Association, or the National Association of Manufacturers? While it is true that the federal government distinguishes between profit and nonprofit organizations for lobbying purposes, there is no consensus either outside or inside religious groups on the issue just raised. Inside the churches there are, on the one hand, the "new breed" of younger clergymen who feel that involvement in the civil rights movement and welfare/poverty struggles is part of their obligation as clergymen and part of the responsibility of the church in society. On the other hand, there are numerous clergymen and laymen who just as adamantly maintain that the church has no business whatsoever "meddling" in political matters. An already-classic summary of such a separationist view is that of J. Howard Pew, wealthy industrialist and prominent Presbyterian layman, who says, "I go to church to hear heralded the mind of Christ, not the mind of man. I want to hear expounded the timeless truth contained in the Scriptures, the kind of preaching that gets its power from 'Thus with the Lord.' "[30] Pew feels strongly that for clergymen or the church as an organization to become involved in secular social issues—i.e., to become political—is to subvert the purpose and function of religion.

An objection somewhat different from Pew's that some have is that when religious organizations become politically involved they begin to look like most any other self-interested lobbying group. Such an image is seen as likely to subvert the image many religious groups would like to maintain—namely, that of dealing with ultimate problems and concerns and being able to provide ultimate answers. Involvement in the political arena increases the risk of making mistakes and of hooking up with groups that may later be discredited. The issue is thus a concern about credibility.

THE INFLUENCE OF RELIGION ON POLITICS

We turn now from the general issue of the relationship between religion and politics—between church and state—to look at specific ways in which religion is an influential factor, an independent variable, so far as politics is concerned.

Legislating Morality

One significant area in which religion influences politics is that of the legislation of morality. American state and local governments have been riddled with so-called blue laws, many of which are still on the books—and most of which reflect strong religious influence. Laws restricting Sunday business activity, laws specifying how close to schools and churches bars and taverns may operate, laws restricting the sale of in-

[30]J. Howard Pew, "Should the Church 'Meddle' in Civil Affairs?" *Reader's Digest*, May 1966, p. 51.

toxicating beverages, laws regarding the sale and distribution of birth-control devices—all evidence strong influences by religious groups. Some are carryovers from Puritan colonization; some are related to concentrations of Catholic immigrants; some are traceable to conservative Protestantism, which has been influential throughout our history.

The struggle against "demon rum" that eventually resulted in ratification of the Eighteenth Amendment (1919) prohibiting the sale of most intoxicating beverages in the United States is a clear example of the influence of religious groups in the political arena. The Prohibition amendment was very largely the work of a well-organized church lobby, the Anti-Saloon League. The league was organized in the Calvary Baptist Church in Washington, D.C., in 1895, and although similar temperance societies cooperated with it, churches were the primary source of its membership, support, and leadership. Leo Pfeffer reports that between 1911 and 1925 an annual average of thirty thousand local churches, predominantly Baptist, Methodist, Presbyterian, and Congregational, were affiliated with the league.[31]

Pfeffer notes that the Anti-Saloon League did not deny that it was a political organization. When confronted with that charge, a league representative replied: "The Church is a machine and the League is a machine within a machine."[32] Pfeffer goes on to say:

> *Its effectiveness as a machine, as of any political machine, is measured by the fruits thereof; and the fruit of the league was the adoption of the Eighteenth Amendment within six years after the League formally launched its campaign for national prohibition. Though the League was less successful in retaining the victory it had won, its influence was respected and feared by many.*[33]

The adoption of prohibition is a prime example of Protestant influences on the political system, while Catholics have an analogous influence with reference to birth-control legislation. Since Catholic doctrine maintains that any "artificial" interference with conception is inherently evil and sinful, the Catholic church has worked long and hard to resist attempts to repeal or modify existing laws that prohibit the sale of birth-control devices or dissemination of information regarding their use. Earlier in American history Catholics were not alone in this stance: the "Comstock law," actually a set of laws passed by Congress in 1873 prohibiting mailing, transporting, or importing "obscene, lewd, or lascivious" materials, had support that also included Protestants and some groups

[31]Leo Pfeffer, *Church, State, and Freedom* (Boston: Beacon Press, 1953), p. 200.
[32]Quoted in ibid., p. 200.
[33]Ibid.

that were at least ostensibly secular. Birth-control information and devices were interpreted as being included among the prohibitions detailed by these laws. Soon thereafter twenty-two states passed "little Comstock laws" that imposed strictures ranging from New York's restriction on physicians' freedom to prescribe lawful contraceptives (and then only "for the cure or prevention of disease"), to Massachusetts' ban on the publication of information and the distribution of material dealing with contraception, to Connecticut's absolute ban on birth control extending even to the private use of contraceptive devices.[34]

Religion and Voting Behavior

Another area in which we see the influence of religion on politics is voting behavior. Although religion is certainly not the only significant factor influencing how a person votes, both religious affiliation and indices of religiosity have repeatedly shown fairly strong correlations with certain voting patterns.

Nearly everyone is aware of the historical tendency for American Catholics to vote Democratic and for Protestants to be more likely to favor the Republican party. For example, Lenski's Detroit data, though also showing the particularly strong influence of social class and that of race as well, document clearly fairly substantial differences between Catholics and Protestants with regard to political party affiliation. Note in Table 10–1 the fairly large differences between Catholics and Protestants at both class levels with respect to party preference. Note also the almost total disaffection of Jews with the Republican Party.

From national survey data gathered in 1970, we find the following political party identifications by religious preference. Among Protestants, 44 percent identify with the Democratic party, while 55 percent of Catholics and 67 percent of Jews so identified. Such differences are as one might expect, closely matched by differences in Republican party identification: Protestants (27 percent) are more likely than either Catholics (14 percent) or Jews (8 percent) to identify with the Republican party. Approximately equal proportions in each religious group identify themselves as Independents (22 percent of Protestants and 25 percent of both Catholics and Jews).[35] The data with respect to the 1968 presidential election in Table 10–2 are consistent with the 1970 findings and support the casual observation made repeatedly that Protestants are more likely to vote Republican, Catholics and Jews more likely to vote Democratic.

[34]David M. Kennedy, *Birth Control in America* (New Haven: Yale University Press, 1970), p. 218.
[35]Ronald L. Johnstone (director), National Opinion Research Center survey conducted for the Lutheran Council in the U.S.A., 1970.

TABLE 10–1

Party Preference of Selected Socioreligious Groups in Detroit, Combined 1957 and 1958 Data

Social Class and Socioreligious Group	Republican	Democrat	No preference or Independent	Number of Cases
Middle Class				
White Protestant	54%	23%	23%	259
White Catholic	30	40	30	172
Black Protestant	13	45	42	31
Jewish	3	64	33	36
Working Class				
White Protestant	30	48	23	365
White Catholic	13	67	20	307
Black Protestant	16	72	12	193
Jewish	0	75	25	12

Source: Adapted from Gerhard E. Lenski, *The Religious Factor* (Garden City, N.Y.: Doubleday, 1961), p. 125.

As we have noted in earlier chapters, data on Protestant denominations also reflect characteristic differences. Table 10–3 shows these differences with respect to voting behavior (as reflected by respondents' self-report of voting behavior). Note that only the Baptists were more likely to vote for the Democratic candidate than for the Republican. In fact, Baptists were also more likely than other Protestant groups to vote for Wallace. The remaining denominations preferred Nixon over Humphrey by margins of more than two to one, with the margin for Episcopalians reaching nearly six to one (68.8 percent vs. 12.5 percent).

TABLE 10–2

Presidential Candidate Preference of Selected Religious Groups, 1968

Religious Affiliation	Humphrey (Democratic)	Nixon (Republican)	Wallace (American Independent)	No Answer	Didn't Vote
Protestant (N=975)	21.7%	36.5%	7.3%	3.4%	31.0%
Catholic (N=355)	37.7	25.9	4.5	3.4	28.5
Jewish (N=24)	83.3	8.3	0.0	4.2	4.2
Other (N=42)	28.6	23.8	2.4	0.0	45.2
None (N=66)	24.5	33.0	1.1	9.6	31.9

Source: Ronald L. Johnstone (director), National Opinion Research Center survey conducted for the Lutheran Council in the U.S.A., 1970.

TABLE 10–3

Presidential Candidate Preference of Selected Protestant Denominations, 1968

Denomination	Humphrey (Democratic)	Nixon (Republican)	Wallace (American Independent)	No Answer	Didn't Vote
Baptist (N=333)	28.2%	20.1%	9.9%	2.1%	39.6%
Episcopalian (N=32)	12.5	68.8	3.1	2.1	12.5
Lutheran (N=120)	22.5	47.5	4.2	4.2	21.7
Methodist (N=187)	20.9	44.4	5.3	2.1	27.3
Presbyterian (N=67)	13.4	58.2	6.0	4.5	17.9
United Church of Christ (N=51)	23.5	49.0	0.0	7.8	19.6
Others and no preference (N=185)	14.6	34.1	9.7	4.9	36.8

Source: Ronald L. Johnstone (director), National Opinion Research Center survey conducted for the Lutheran Council in the U.S.A., 1970.

Although a detailed discussion of the relationship of social class to religion is reserved for the next chapter, we must point out here that an extremely important social-class factor accompanies these observed relationships between denominational affiliation and voting behavior: Episcopalians and Presbyterians, who were so extremely likely to choose Nixon over Humphrey in 1968, are also more likely than members of other Protestant groups to be of high socioeconomic status. Since higher-status persons tend to favor Republican over Democratic candidates, we find that status and religious affiliation reinforce one another and in combination yield dramatic differences in support for particular political parties and their candidates.

We suggested earlier that differences in political party affiliation and political behavior are not only related to religious affiliation but also to indices of religiosity, including persons' perceptions of their own religious commitments and orientation. For example, Hadden reports dramatic differences among a sample of more than seven thousand Protestant clergymen in terms of party affiliation related to their self-designation of theological inclination. The data in Table 10–4 show clearly that the more theologically liberal a clergyman is, the less likely he is to prefer the Republican party and the more likely he is to prefer the Democrats or be an uncommitted independent.

Using religiosity indices similar to those of Glock and Stark discussed in Chapter 5, Kersten found differences among Lutherans that on some measures were quite substantial. In Table 10–5 we see that the higher a Lutheran scores on any given index—in terms of belief, or

TABLE 10–4
Party Preference of Protestant Clergymen, by Theological Position

Theological Position	Republican	Independent	Democrat
Fundamentalist	68%	18%	13%
Conservative	62	22	15
Neo-Orthodox	39	26	35
Liberal	36	28	36

Source: Jeffrey Hadden, *The Gathering Storm in the Churches* (Garden City, N.Y.: Doubleday, 1969), p. 74.

degree of involvement in the activities of one's religious organization (associational-involvement index), or frequency of engaging in religious practices such as prayer (religious-practices index), or religious knowledge (religious-knowledge index), or involvement in the religious subcommunity (communal-involvement index)—the more likely he is to identify with the Republican party.

Radical Right Politics and Religion

A fascinating subject when discussing the relationship of religion and politics is the relationship and intermingling of radical right political philosophies and activities with fundamentalist Protestant religion. Although the strident anticommunism of the numerous radical right political groups that flowered in the 1950s and 1960s had lost some of

TABLE 10–5
Proportion of Lutherans Identifying with the Republican Party, by Type and Degree of Religious Commitment

	Index Rating		
	Low	Moderate	High
Belief Index (n.s.)	50%	53%	56%
Associational-Involvement Index (sig. at .01 level)	47	52	60
Religious-Practices Index (sig. at .05 level)	49	54	57
Religious-Knowledge Index (sig. at .01 level)	46	51	60
Communal-Involvement Index (sig. at .001 level)	44	56	63

Source: Lawrence K. Kersten, *The Lutheran Ethic* (Detroit: Wayne State University Press, 1970), p. 57. Reprinted by permission of Wayne State University Press.

its resonance and support by the 1970s, the radical right still exists, and certainly its place in history and its relationship to religion should at least be noted. Particularly intriguing is the intimate association of fundamentalist Protestant theology with right-wing politics among many of the anti-Communist crusaders. As Janson and Eismann state:

> *Ultraconservative leaders have had considerable success, simply by preaching anticommunism, in rallying not only religious fundamentalists concerned about heresy but also political, economic, and social fundamentalists concerned about the liberal trends that are threatening their values.*[36]

Some of the radical right groups have tried to remain aloof from religion—Robert Welch's John Birch Society, for one. Welch has never revealed his personal religious convictions, if any, and has said that he doesn't care what religion a person is. His ultimate appeal is not to religious beliefs but to what he views as fundamental American values. Other prominent right-wing political groups, however, make an intimate connection between the two. Fred C. Schwarz's Christian Anti-Communist Crusade, Billy James Hargis's Christian Crusade, and Carl McIntire's "20th Century Reformation Hour" are major groups that have deep, explicit roots in Protestant fundamentalism. As Hargis has said: "I fight Communism . . . because it is part of my ordination vows, of my creed."[37] In his publication *Christian Crusade*, he states:

> *Christian Crusade's fight against Communism is Christ's fight. Christ is using this Movement. The very fact that Christian Crusade has existed through fourteen years of opposition from powerful forces in high and low circles, is proof that it is of God. . . . I know we are on the right track, getting the job done for Jesus.*[38]

The union of religious and political goals is clearly stated by Hargis: "We feel our mission to be God-given; to awaken our fellow citizens to the twin dangers of Communism and/or socialism and religious apostacy."[39] In fact, it becomes essentially impossible to separate religious from political and economic elements in these groups' positions. Such a merger is clearly seen in the following list of institutions for which the

---

[36]Donald Janson and Bernard Eismann, *The Far Right* (New York: McGraw-Hill Book Company, 1963), p. 239.
[37]Billy James Hargis, television address, KAIL-TV, Fresno, California, October 25, 1964. Quoted in John H. Redekop, *The American Far Right* (Grand Rapids, Mich.: William B. Eerdmans, 1968), p. 17.
[38]Billy James Hargis, *Christian Crusade*, January-February 1962, p. 3. Quoted in Redekop, *The American Far Right*, p. 18.
[39]Hargis, *Christian Crusade*, December 1962, p. 1. Quoted in Redekop, *The American Far Right*, p. 18.

American Nazi party is fighting: "(1) the White Race, which must be preserved above all; (2) the American Constitutional Republic; (3) the Christian traditions and culture of the West; (4) free enterprise and private property without the evil of criminal speculators."[40]

In discussing the connection between religion and politics that tends to exist among radical right groups, Murray Havens states that most of these groups "would substitute for religious tolerance an insistence on uniform acceptance not only for Christianity but of their particular highly dogmatic version of Christianity."[41] Their urging of Protestant fundamentalism merges smoothly with appeals for maximum cultural conformity based on small-town and rural America, an explicit antiintellectualism, and a defense of the status quo so far as economic and racial disparities are concerned.

It is interesting that while most authors who have analyzed radical right groups note the congruence and close association between right-wing political views and fundamentalist Protestant religion, seldom do they carry out much analysis of the relationship. One important exception is John Redekop, who discusses several intimate connections. One is a simplistic dualism. The fundamentalist sees only two categories, good and evil, with nothing in between. The radical right-winger sees his fellow citizens as either Americans or Communists, one or the other. Tolerance is only for those who don't believe strongly in anything. Hatred of evil is therefore perfectly logical and heresy hunting perfectly legitimate. Another characteristic of both fundamentalism and radical right philosophy is a conspiratorial view of the world. Satan conspires to detour people from the path of righteousness; communism does the same. Communism actually becomes the Devil personified—or better, politicized. As a result, all political discussion takes on a strong moral fervor. Politics thus becomes a crusade and one's patriotism proof of a mature Christianity.

A third connection is the individualistic emphasis in fundamentalism (individual salvation) and a corresponding disapproval of social action and public welfare programs, which matches the radical right's laissez-faire economic and political ideology. The individual is more important than society and is capable of satisfying his wants and needs in the free-enterprise marketplace. Governmental intervention here is morally wrong. Communism is therefore readily viewed as the epitome of evil.[42]

[40]American Nazi Party, form letter mailed in response to routine inquiry signed by Lincoln Rockwell, commander, 1961, p. 2.
[41]Murray C. Havens, *The Challenges to Democracy* (Austin: University of Texas Press, 1965), pp. 82–83.
[42]Redekop, *The American Far Right*, chapter 10.

Although Murray Stedman is likely correct when he contends that "there is no apparent dictate in the inner logic of fundamentalism that would necessarily predispose its followers to political authoritarianism"[43] —that is, not all fundamentalists are or will become radical right-wingers— there is nevertheless a ready alliance between the two. When they coincide, as they frequently do, the connection is easy to understand, for the religious and the political views reinforce one another.

Religion and Politics in the Third World

Although religious issues periodically surface as political issues in every society of the world, a politico-religious phenomenon virtually unknown in the United States but fairly common in the Third World (the underdeveloped nations of Asia, Africa, and Latin America) is the emergence of religious political parties—that is, political parties whose constituency is a particular religious group and which pursue religious as well as political ends. Donald Smith distinguishes three kinds of Third World politico-religious parties.[44] There are first of all the *communal parties*, such as the Hindu Mahasabha or the Jana Sangh in India, which form within a national context of religious pluralism. Their self-styled function is to "protect and promote the largely secular economic and political interests of their respective communal groups."[45] Such political parties are better-organized manifestations of communal conflict and violence of the sort that might erupt between Hindus and Muslims were the latter alleged to have killed sacred cows or if a Hindu procession were accused of disturbing Muslims in their mosques at prayer—violence of the sort paralleled in the West by the protracted Protestant-Catholic conflict in Northen Ireland. An excellent example of a Third World communal party is the Freedom party led by S. W. R. D. Bandaranaike that pledged itself to restore Buddhism to its rightful place in the national life of Sri Lanka (formerly Ceylon). The focus of its attack was Christianity, particularly the Roman Catholic church, which was felt to be favored by governing authorities. Bandaranaike succeeded in becoming prime minister in the election of 1956, but was assassinated three years later. The subsequent administration under his wife found its power considerably weakened through expedient compromises with Marxists.

The second type of religious political party is the *sect-based party.* Smith cites the Ummah in the northern Sudan as a prime example.

---

[43]Murray Stedman, *Religion and Politics in America* (New York: Harcourt, Brace, and World, 1964), p. 129.
[44]Donald E. Smith, *Religion, Politics, and Social Change in the Third World* (New York: Free Press, 1971), pp. 140–69.
[45]Ibid., p. 140.

Although the northern portion of the Sudan is solidly Muslim, the Ummah is a minority political party that derives its constituency from the Ansar sect within that branch of Islam. In other words, unlike the interreligious conflict inherent in the communal parties, here there is intrareligious conflict of sect with parent religious group finding expression in political action and party formation.

The third type is the *ideological religious party* which, Smith notes, functions in societies in which religious minorities are politically unimportant. Such parties are not oriented to conflict with other religious groups, but desire to speak to the ideological assumptions that undergird and shape the society. They may be conservative and attempt to preserve traditional patterns, such as many Latin American conservative parties, particularly of thirty and more years ago. Or they may be modernizing or reforming as they challenge aspects of the fundamental societal ideology. Examples of the latter are the Christian Democrats in Chile and the Masjumi in Indonesia.

The point to appreciate in this extremely brief look at religion and politics in the Third World is the widespread tendency of citizens in Third World societies to refuse to relegate religion solely to the private sphere of individual faith and practice. The politico-religious conflict that ensues is abetted by the onrush of social change and the inevitable challenges to traditional ideologies that social change involves. Such developments may upset traditional delicate compromises and stalemates among religions leading to intergroup conflict, or religious groups may organize themselves politically to uphold traditional values in some cases or promote other ones in other instances. The point, then, is that in many Third World societies religion and politics are less clearly separated than in, say, the United States.

A prime reason for this, as Smith points out, is that Third World societies began much more recently to question the view of government as ordained by God and of governmental leaders as gods or direct agents of God.[46] These societies have not become as secularized as most societies of the West, though this process seems to be accelerating. It is thus unlikely that religion will remain the political force that it has represented in the recent past. An important reason for this is that in many Third World countries religion has become intimately associated with nationalistic sentiments and activities. With political independence already a fact in many of these societies, a major purpose of the politico-religious parties has been all but eliminated. Further, as Smith points out, participation in the political process itself has an important secularizing

[46]Ibid., pp. 1–2.

effect.[47] The political party with an Islamic ideology, for example, may work within a pluralistic ideological milieu and find itself making deals that are politically expedient but that implicitly deny the absolutist, inviolable precepts of orthodox Islam. They compromise their ideology to capture minority votes. Smith notes that in the long run, "particularistic ideologies such as Islam give ground before universalistic ideologies such as socialism."[48]

[47]Ibid., p. 4.
[48]Ibid.

11

Religion and
the Class System

In Chapter 7 we introduced the topic of the relationship between religion and social class (social stratification) in outlining differences between denominations and sects. In fact, we observed that one of the dominant features of sectarian religion is its close association with lower- or working-class problems and life situations, together with the responses of persons of low social status to those problems and situations.

In generalizing from investigations into the relationships between religion and social class, sociologists have made the primary observation that there are important differences in religious meaning related to social class. That is, religion tends to perform at least somewhat different functions for people in different classes. Or put another way, people tend to seek or construct different things in religion depending on their social-class position.

Such assertions stressing the importance of social class with regard to religion should not really surprise us, inasmuch as nearly every beginning student of sociology becomes aware that one of the most significant variables in social life is social class. Although not strictly determinitive, one's social-class position dramatically influences one's behavior, attitudes, and aspirations—that is, both what one thinks and what one does throughout life. Depending upon one's social-class origins and lifetime position in the stratification system, a person finds his life affected in a multitude of ways—voting propensities, likelihood of psychosis, amount of travel, attitudes toward social issues, age of marriage, size of family, sexual behavior, even life expectancy. Small wonder, then, that important relationships between social class and religion have also been found. Differences by social-class levels can be seen in differential affiliation with various religious groups, type and degree of involvement in the activities of religious groups, perceptions of the purposes and functions of religion for people, motivation for joining and belonging to religious groups, religious knowledgeability, and the like.

DIFFERENCES IN RELIGIOUS MEANING AND EXPRESSION AMONG SOCIAL CLASSES

A classic distinction regarding differences in the functions of religion by social class is that made by Karl Marx. In defining religion as the "opium of the people," he was actually drawing an implicit distinction between the religion of the bourgeoisie (property-owning capitalist) and that of the proletariat (working class). For the proletariat, in Marx's view, religion is a sedative, a narcotic that dulls people's sensitivity to and understanding of the plight of their life situation; it provides an escape from the harshness of reality. But more. As Marx wrote: "Religion is the sigh of the oppressed creature, the mind of a heartless world, as it is the spirit of unspiritual conditions. . . . the removal of religion as the illusory happiness of the people is the requirement for their real happiness."[1]

By way of contrast, for the bourgeoisie and elites in society, Marx contended, religion serves both as a tool of oppression—a means of placating and keeping the proletariat in line—and as a rationalization and justification for the elite's own position of power and privilege. Inasmuch as Marx viewed the normative aspects of social life as deriving from the most fundamental fact and relationship in society—namely, the economy —religion becomes really nothing more than an expression of prevailing economic relationships and thus, in the capitalistic economy, a means of preserving and reinforcing endemic class distinctions. The intertwining of capitalism and prevailing religions is so complete, and the alienation of man from his true destiny so truly reflected in religion, that Marx's associate Engels could predict that religion would disappear when the prevailing capitalistic economies disappeared.[2]

[1]Karl Marx and Friedrich Engels, *Toward the Criticism of Hegel's Philosophy of Right* (Paris, 1843), trans. Glenn Waas, quoted in Robert Freedman, *Marxist Social Thought* (New York: Harcourt, Brace & World, 1968), p. 230.
[2]Friedrich Engels, *Anti-Dühring* (Moscow: Foreign Language Publishing House, 1954), pp. 438–40; quoted in Freedman, *Marxist Social Thought*, p. 228.

Although Max Weber objected to the unidirectional nature of the relationship that Marx portrayed between the economy and social norms and values (including religion), and although he wrote *The Protestant Ethic and the Spirit of Capitalism* in large part to refute or at least modify or offer an alternative to Marx's theory, Weber actually held much the same view of differential functions of religion for the various social classes. We have already spoken of Weber's distinction, between the religion of the disprivileged and that of the privileged, underlying the concepts "theodicy of despair or escape" and "theodicy of good fortune."[3] In the first case one thinks of the proletariat for whom religion promises release and some kind of eventual "salvation" if they can only endure, and remain eternally faithful. Interestingly, according to Weber, the need for compensation and hope in the face of an adverse existence is relatively seldom colored by resentment or rebellion. In other words, some of the disprivileged appear to be satisfied that hell is reserved for wealthy sinners. (Recall our earlier discussion of the sect in Chapter 7.) The privileged classes, however, learn and express religious justification of their good fortune and emphasize their "blessings" as evidence of the favor with which God looks upon them. Wealth and privilege for them are not a detriment to salvation, but an indication not only that all is going well for them now but that it will likely continue to do so in any future life.[4]

Liston Pope discovered similar differences by social class in his study of Gaston County, North Carolina. This county became an important textile mill center in the 1920s and 1930s and attracted thousands of unskilled and semiskilled laborers for the mills. Quite early, during this period, a division of residents between "uptown" people and mill workers was made—a distinction corresponding roughly to Marx's bourgeoisie and proletariat and to Weber's privileged and disprivileged. Religious behavior and ideology differed rather markedly among these two major segments of the population. Pope describes the religion of the mill worker as follows:

> In the theology of the mill worker, the world is a great battlefield on which the Lord and the Devil struggle for each individual soul. The "blood of Jesus" and the reading of the Bible turn the tide of victory toward the Lord. As one mill minister summarized it, "You have to carry a bucket of blood into the pulpit to satisfy these people." The principal sins, in the eyes of mill villagers, are such uptown "worldly amusements" as playing cards, dancing, gambling, drinking, and swimming with members of the opposite sex.

[3]See Chapter 9.
[4]Max Weber, "The Social Psychology of the World Religions," in *From Max Weber*, trans. and ed. Hans Gerth and C. Wright Mills (New York: Oxford University Press, 1958), p. 276.

. . . But the worker also looks to his church to find transvaluation of life, which may take the form of reassurance or of escape, or both. By affirmation of values denied in the economic world, the church provides comfort and ultimate assurance; in its religious services it often affords escape temporarily from the economic and social situation in which workaday life must be spent. The difficulties of life for the mill worker in this world help to explain the noteworthy emphasis on otherworldliness in his churches. Most of the hymns and sermons in village churches point toward a more placid state and have little concern with mundane economic or social relations. . . . A well-loved stanza, typical in ideas of many others, says:

> *While some live in splendid mansions,*
> *And have wealth at their command,*
> *I'm a stranger and a pilgrim*
> *Passing through this barren land.*[5]

In short, religion for the mill worker provides a relief or escape from the harshness of his life. For an hour or two once or twice a week he can transcend the mundane and focus on a future that promises to be far better than the present.

Pope points out, by way of contrast, that "if religion in the mill churches is largely an escape from economic conditions, religion in the uptown churches is to considerable degree a sanction of prevailing economic arrangements."[6] Pope reports that major sins for the uptown church members include sexual immorality, breaking one's word, not paying one's debts, engaging in "shady business," and failing to carry out one's civic and social obligations.[7] Although religion attempts to invade the personal life of the mill worker, religion is not to meddle in the private lives of the middle- and upper-class town residents. Pope suggests that "greater economic security breeds personal independence."[8] Such independence and individualism are also major features of the religion of the bourgeoisie according to Emile Pin. Pin states that individualism characterizes essentially every aspect of the life of the bourgeois, "who has reached, through his own efforts, a worldly 'salvation,' does not depend on religion to regulate his existence, but rather appeals to it only to assure the continuation of this salvation in the other world."[9]

Pope points out that for the privileged classes in Gaston County,

[5]Liston Pope, *Millhands and Preachers* (New Haven: Yale University Press, 1942), pp. 88–90.
[6]Ibid., p. 92.
[7]Ibid.
[8]Ibid.
[9]Emile Pin, "Social Classes and Their Religious Approaches," in *Religion, Culture, and Society,* ed. Louis Schneider (New York: Wiley, 1964), p. 411.

religion is for the most part a specialized sphere of life. Their religious attitudes, as he observes them, are

> *That a man ought to belong to a church, and should attend as often as convenient, and should bear his part of the financial burden,*
>
> *that churches are essential to the welfare of the community,*
>
> *that there is no use in getting all wrought up or emotional about religion,*
>
> *that if a person lives as decently as he can, that's all that God can expect of him,*
>
> *that a minister ought to be a good fellow in his private life, joining civic clubs, attending baseball games, and the like,*
>
> *that a minister ought to be a leader in all community enterprises, such as projects sponsored by the Chamber of Commerce,*
>
> *that religion ought not to meddle in politics, except where moral issues, such as prohibition, are involved,*
>
> *that Holy Rollers are ignorant, and are to be pitied,*
>
> *that mill churches meet the needs of mill workers very satisfactorily.*[10]

Pope summarizes by saying, "The role of the uptown minister, and of his church, is not to transcend immediate cultural boundaries but to symbolize and sanction the rightness of things as they are."[11]

DIFFERENTIAL DENOMINATIONAL AFFILIATION BY SOCIAL CLASS

As would be expected, differences in the meaning and expression of religion by social class is reflected in denominational affiliation—that is, denominations differ in their social-class composition. The data in Table 11–1, though obtained in the early 1950s, do not appear to be much different today. Clearly some denominations are composed predominantly of middle- and upper-class members while others are primarily lower- or working-class in constituency. Although we have already noted in Chapter 7 the class differences between denominations as a whole and sects as a whole, Table 11–1 indicates the existence of clear class distinctions among denominations themselves. Note, for example, that there are proportionately twice as many lower-class Baptists or Roman Catholics as there are lower-class Congregationalists.

The factors underlying such class differences among denominations are many. In part it is a self-selection process of like seeking like—of people affiliating with a church whose current members are reasonably like themselves. There is the theological dimension also—the theological cele-

10Pope, *Millhands and Preachers*, pp. 93–94.
11Ibid., p. 95.

TABLE 11–1

Social-Class Profiles of American Religious Groups

Denomination	Class		
	Upper	Middle	Lower
Christian Scientist	24.8%	36.5%	38.7%
Episcopal	24.1	33.7	42.2
Congregational	23.9	42.6	33.5
Presbyterian	21.9	40.0	38.1
Jewish	21.8	32.0	46.2
Reformed (Christian)	19.1	31.3	49.6
Methodist	12.7	35.6	51.7
Lutheran	10.9	36.1	53.0
Christian	10.0	35.4	54.6
Protestant (small bodies)	10.0	27.3	62.7
Roman Catholic	8.7	24.7	66.6
Baptist	8.0	24.0	68.0
Mormon	5.1	28.6	66.3
No preference	13.3	26.0	60.7
Protestant (undesignated)	12.4	24.1	63.5
Atheist, Agnostic	33.3	46.7	20.0
No Answer or Don't Know	11.0	29.5	59.5

Source: Herbert Schneider, *Religion in 20th Century America* (Cambridge: Harvard University Press, 1952), p. 228.

bration of success in this world in some religious groups versus the emphasis on otherworldly salvation in others. In large part the class differences by denomination are a product of history. The highest-status denominations in Table 11–1 (those with the lowest proportion of lower-class members), with the exception of the Christian Scientist, have been well-established in this country for the longest periods. Thus their members have had greater opportunities to accumulate family wealth—another factor. On the other hand, Lutherans and particularly Roman Catholics are composed of more recent arrivals in this country who have had less opportunity for upward mobility. The Lutherans also are predominantly rural in their constituency and hence likely to rank lower on such dimensions of status as education, cash income, and occupational prestige.

Of course no religious group is completely class-exclusive—that is, there is a range of classes represented in every religious group. Class exclusiveness, however, is often more pronounced at the local congregational level. Thus the fact that one-third of all Congregationalists are lower-class, for example, does not mean that a third of the members of every local Congregational church, or even of a majority of them, are from the lower class. What it does mean is that there are some congregations with a majority of lower-class members, others with a majority of middle- and/

or upper-class members. This should not be surprising inasmuch as congregations tend to attract a majority of their members from the neighborhoods in which they are located, and neighborhoods tend to be fairly class-exclusive.

This phenomenon is clearly in evidence in Pope's study of Gaston County. In 1939 Pope tallied thirty-four rural churches, only five of which had a significant minority (a minimum of 20 percent) of mill workers and none of which had a significant minority of uptown members. Similarly, of seventy-six mill churches only one had a significant minority of rural members and only eight a significant minority of uptown members. Uptown churches were less likely to be so predominantly of one class. Yet in only seventeen of thirty-five were even 20 percent of the members mill workers, and in only three were there significant minorities of rural members. In total, only 23 percent of the churches in Gaston County had significant minority membership, and only 6 percent lacked a majority group of at least 66.6 percent.[12] Clearly, then, a religious group is very likely to represent the class constituency of the geographic area in which it is located.

Demerath has pointed out that although there may be a mixture of social classes in a national denomination and even in its local congregations, the members of these classes may not be looking for or receiving the same things out of their affiliation and participation.[13] Demerath first reports Fukuyama's 1961 study demonstrating differences in religiosity among Congregationalists by social class. Fukuyama's data, reported in Table 11–2, show that the higher social classes are more likely than the lowest social class to express their religion in cultic and cognitive ways, whereas the lowest social class is more likely than the others to express religion devotionally (the differences along the creedal dimension are not significant). Demerath dichotomizes the possible relationship to one's religious group for his sample (Lutherans) into "churchlike" and "sectlike" religiosity. Some of his findings are included in Table 11–3, which indicates quite clearly that the lower a Lutheran's social-class position, the less likely he is to exhibit a churchlike attachment to religion. As would be expected, a corresponding opposite relationship is observed with respect to sectlike commitment. The progression for high sectlike commitment from the upper through the middle, working, and lower classes is 10 percent, 15 percent, 25 percent, and 35 percent, respectively.[14]

All these data indicate that social status appears to have an effect upon the meaning and expression of religion for people. This is not only

---

[12]Ibid., pp. 70–71.
[13]N. J. Demerath III, *Social Class in American Protestantism* (Chicago: Rand McNally, 1965).
[14]Ibid., p. 88.

TABLE 11–2

Proportion of Congregationalists Scoring High on Selected Measures of Religiosity, by Social Class

Measure	Socioeconomic Status		
	High	*Medium*	*Low*
Cultic	53%	43%	35%
Cognitive	28	24	15
Creedal	27	28	31
Devotional	16	23	32

Source: Adapted from Yoshio Fukuyama, "The Major Dimensions of Church Membership," *Review of Religious Research* 2, no. 4 (1960); 159.

Note: Cultic = measure of church attendance and organizational participation
  Cognitive = measure of knowledge of religious doctrine and congregational affairs
  Creedal = measure of personal allegiance to traditional doctrine
  Devotional = measure of personal prayer and expression of reliance on religion beyond the church itself

evidenced by the fact that people of one status level tend to be members of particular denominations or sects, but people within a particular denomination and even within a local congregation are both looking for and finding different things.

Referring back to our discussion in Chapter 4 of the problem of measuring religiosity, Demerath's data highlight the need for multidimensional measures of religiosity. That low-status people attach less significance to regular and frequent attendance at worship services, particularly if they hold membership in an essentially middle-class church, does not

TABLE 11–3

Churchlike Religiosity Among Lutherans, by Social Class

*Degree of Churchlike Commitment**	Socioeconomic Status			
	Upper	*Middle*	*Working*	*Lower*
High	51%	45%	32%	24%
Moderate	20	20	19	19
Low	29	35	48	57

Source: N. J. Demerath III, *Social Class in American Protestantism* (Chicago: Rand McNally, 1965), p. 87.

*Based on frequency of church attendance, participation in parish organizations, and membership in outside organizations.

necessarily mean that they are less religious than some of their middle-class counterparts who are there in their accustomed pews every Sunday. The former's manner of expressing their religion and what they see as religiously important are simply somewhat different from middle-class expressions and definitions.

That the meaning of religion and participation in religious activities varies among social classes is of course not unique to Western Christianity. Such differences are noted particularly in Hinduism. The division into social classes of Brahmins, Kshatriyas, Vaisyas, Shudras, and "outcasts" or "untouchables" correlate quite closely with differences in the historical meaning and expression of Hinduism as a religion. The fact that originally only the two upper classes were literate and could read and become familiar with the holy books predetermined important differences. For example, even today the upper classes tend to be monistic, believe in one Absolute with all other gods a part of expression of the One. The common people tend to be polytheists and believe in many local gods and spirits, tend to identify the image or statue itself with the divine living reality, and believe in a heaven and hell which the higher classes do not. The upper classes believe more firmly in the doctrines of samsara (the transmigration of souls), karma (the principle of cause and effect—what you sow you reap), and dharma (the standard of determining whether you move socially upward or downward in the next life). The upper classes are more firmly committed to the belief that if you follow the rules of your caste you can move upward, from one life to another, all the way to an ultimate goal of being released from the nearly endless cycle of transmigration of souls and realize unity with the Brahman or Absolute (attain Nirvana). Noss notes that the masses have never had a clear conception of the finer points of Hinduism such as the various "ways" of salvation and release from the miseries and responsibilities of life (Way of Works, Way of Knowledge, Way of Devotion). He says that the masses go about being religious in the traditional manner of their local area. They practice and reflect animism, fetishism, shamanism, demonolatry, animal worship, and devotion to local spirits and godlings, often without the "higher" worship of the supreme deities in the Hindu pantheon.[15] Noss goes on to say that in some areas Hinduism can hardly be recognized as such; a primitive animism takes its place. This sub-Hinduism is common among the millions of "untouchables."[16]

Along a similar vein, Buddhism in its original form found little or no response among the masses. But the masses gradually become interested, as Noss observes, not in the theologian Gautama Buddha but in

---

[15]John B. Noss, *Man's Religions* (New York: Macmillan, 1949), p. 243.
[16]Ibid., p. 244.

the man.[17] Worship of the person and the idea of salvation through various saviors became popular with the lower classes.[18]

Class differences are of course evident in traditional Confucianism and Taoism in China inasmuch as religion centers in the family. Lacking a congregation or even a parish system of group instruction and community, as in Christianity, there is little possibility of controlling the nature of the family religion or overcoming the local or neighborhood coloring of religious ideology and expression. The social-class perspective of a given family and neighborhood or locality is reflected in the religion of that family or geographic unit.

SOCIAL STRATIFICATION WITHIN RELIGIOUS GROUPS

If we define social stratification as a hierarchical arrangement or ordering of people in a group according to criteria or standards determined and accepted by that group—a definition implicit in this chapter so far—then it is easy to see that such stratification is an integral part of religion. Although many religious groups preach the equality of everyone before God, this often implies only equality among the specially favored people in their own group. Religious groups are historically notorious for their clear distinction between the "ins" and the "outs," the believers and the nonbelievers, the saved and the unsaved or damned. Moreover, stratification appears even within the group itself. Stratification is endemic in two senses. First, there is the distinction between prophet and people, or leader and followers. Those who are considered to have special insights or are credited with special revelation are accorded elevated positions relative to those who listen and follow. The person with deeper knowledge of sacred things (rituals and writings)—the teacher or priest—is ranked higher than those who are his pupils and followers. Second, there is the recognition that even among the followers, some follow the norms of the group more closely than others and are more holy, more knowledgeable, more dedicated than the "average" or "majority" of followers or members. Even though the majority of rank-and-file members may not personally aspire to such status, they tend to acknowledge its validity and pay at least lip service to those who embody most perfectly the virtues and knowledge that the group has defined as praiseworthy. Such distinctions are readily observed in the panoply of saints in the Roman Catholic church—persons have gone an extra mile or two in perfecting the expression and application of the Catholic faith.

17Ibid., p. 171.
18Ibid., p. 188.

The great majority of Buddhists also recognize the elevated status of the numerous monks and "holy men" who have proceeded farther along the path in search of the ultimate goal—the elimination of desire—than has the ordinary follower of the Buddha.

Jehovah's Witnesses speak of the 144,000 higher-caste believers who will be rewarded with "heaven," while others will simply be inhabitants of "paradise." Although the sacred number of 144,000 appears to be taken more figuratively than literally today, particularly as the membership in the group has surpassed that number, the idea of a greater reward for the few who are most holy remains.

As Vernon suggests, probably the best known "celestial caste system" is that of the Roman Catholic church, with its four levels of heaven, hell, purgatory, and limbo for persons after death: heaven for the purest believers, hell for the nonbelievers, purgatory for the believers who still need some "cleansing" before entering heaven, limbo a place to which people went before Christ's work of redemption was completed and from which he thereafter liberated them.[19]

Other groups talk of the visible church on earth—the voluntary association including not only sincere believers but also some nonbelievers and hypocrites who are professed but insincere members—as contrasted with the invisible church, which is composed only of true believers whom only God can know by looking within one's heart and assessing his sincerity.

We have already mentioned the religious stratification in Hinduism that is so intimately associated with the societal stratification system. Lower-caste persons are not just lower-status socially but religiously as well. To move upward in successive lives through the process of samsara (transmigration of the soul) into higher castes in the social sense is to move upward religiously as well. One would thereby not only enjoy more and more of the amenities of life, but would also come ever closer to the ultimate goal of union with or absorbtion into the timeless or eternal Brahaman, thus finding release from the cycle of transmigration. In this connection Charles Eliot makes the point that it is the caste structure of Indian society that influences Hinduism, not vice versa. He states that many Hindu religious leaders have declared unequivocally that there ought to be no social distinctions among believers. But caste continually reasserts itself. Social structure and precedents, Eliot concludes, are stronger than theology.[20]

[19]Glenn M. Vernon, *Sociology of Religion* (New York: McGraw-Hill, 1962), p. 380.
[20]Charles Eliot, *Hinduism and Buddhism* (London: Routledge & Kegan Paul, 1921), 2: 176–78.

STRATIFICATION, RELIGION, AND RACE

We now turn to a somewhat extended example of how stratification and religion interrelate when a third variable, race or ethnic background, is introduced. Here again we shall see the reciprocal-interaction relationship between religion and other features of the society.

Although each of the major religions of the world has tended officially to welcome all comers into its fellowship of faith, in practice most have at some time or other discriminated against racial or ethnic groups living in the same society. Of course, we need to emphasize that the religious element in such discrimination is usually inextricably bound up with political and economic factors as well. This point will be amply demonstrated as we proceed.

One quick example before proceeding with our primary one. The interaction of political and religious factors is dramatically seen in India and Pakistan, where the centuries-old conflict between Hinduism and Islam culminated in the 1971 war over Bangladesh (formerly East Pakistan). When East Pakistan was still part of the larger nation, the government located in the western portion, which has a Muslim majority, systematically discriminated against Hindus within both West Pakistan and East Pakistan, which has a Hindu majority. Thus a basic ingredient of the military and political conflict was the religious antagonism between Muslims and Hindus.

Similar examples of prejudice and discrimination appear throughout the history of Western Christianity. One thinks of the Inquisition in medieval Europe, the execution of various Protestant reformers by Roman Catholic state and ecclesiastical powers, the Thirty Years' War in seventeenth-century Europe between Protestant and Roman Catholic forces, the present Protestant-Catholic civil conflict in Northern Ireland, and, along a somewhat different line, the prejudice and discrimination in the name of religion that has been directed against blacks throughout American history. We shall focus just a bit on this last phenomenon particularly because it so well portrays the intimate connection of the three variables mentioned above: religion, race, and social class.

By definition, slaves in any society are at the very bottom of the stratification system. This is no problem in itself in a society that tolerates slavery and includes it in its normative system—if we assume a society has the right to determine its own structure in the absence of universal human rights.[21] But the phenomenon of slavery presented a problem for

---

[21]This is not the place to discuss whether norms that condone slavery run counter to the "nature" of man or violate fundamental human rights to such

the Christian religion. In fact, it became a dilemma in the sense that Christian theology had developed the principle that although slavery itself was not forbidden by God, a Christian should not hold another Christian in bondage. The dilemma arose when that principle came in contact with the conversion principle—that is, the mandate to "make disciples of all nations" and convert everyone possible.

The Early American Experience

Early in colonial American history the question arose concerning what to do about the religion of black slaves. One mandate said: Convert them to Christianity. But the other said: You shouldn't hold a fellow Christian as a slave. Therefore, what to do? Some slaveowners quite expectedly opposed the conversion of slaves. Unconverted they presented no problem, since the slaveowner would not be holding a fellow Christian as a slave. But theologians and clergymen said it was the Christian's obligation to teach the slaves Christianity and convert them. Some Southerners resolved the issue by defining blacks as less than human. We don't convert dogs, kudus, or zebras; therefore, we don't need to convert blacks: as a lower animal form, they lack a soul to be saved.

And so the controversy went on. Ultimately a compromise was reached. Religious leaders abandoned their original position and said that the church would no longer maintain the position that conversion required emancipation. This meant that the church could save souls and the slaveowners their investment. This compromise led to substantial missionary activity among slaves, who were rapidly converted to Christianity, since of course they had little choice in the matter.

The process of this religious about-face is well documented for the Methodist Church and merits a somewhat extended examination as an example of social-class and economic influences on religious ideology and practice. In its beginning American Methodism quite naturally looked to its English founder John Wesley for guidance on the issue of slavery. They did not look in vain. Among Wesley's *General Rules*, prepared in 1739, was a rule forbidding "the buying or selling of the bodies and souls of men, women, or children, with an intention to enslave them."[22] And in 1772 he denounced the slave trade as "the sum of all villainies."[23]

---

things as life, liberty, and the pursuit of happiness. Although we happen to agree that involuntary servitude is in direct violation of universal human rights, we need not debate the issue to understand the sociological points that this chapter is making.

[22]Quoted in W. W. Sweet, *The Methodist Episcopal Church and the Civil War* (Cincinnati: Methodist Book Concern Press, 1912), p. 15.

[23]Quoted in Charles Swaney, *Episcopal Methodism and Slavery* (Boston: R. G. Badger, 1926), p. 1.

Accordingly, the Methodist Episcopal Church, organized in Baltimore in 1784, proposed and adopted the following six special rules designed to destroy slavery among its members:

1. Every slave-holding member, within 12 months was required to execute a deed of manumission.
2. All infants who were born after these rules went into effect were to have immediate freedom.
3. Members who chose not to comply were allowed to withdraw within 12 months.
4. The sacrament of the Lord's Supper was to be denied to all such thenceforward.
5. No Slave-holders were to be admitted thereafter into church membership.
6. Any members who bought, sold, or gave slaves away, except on purpose to free them, were immediately to be expelled.[24]

This, then, was the official stand of the Methodist Church on the question of slavery.

Thus during these early days of Methodism in the United States there appeared to be no great problem with slavery. Apparently no members were slaveholders, and, moreover, Wesley's principles were in force. Slavery, however, seems to have found its way into the Methodist Church during the Revolutionary War, probably without the knowledge of John Wesley or his American assistant Francis Asbury.[25] It seems to have entered gradually and unobtrusively. In this connection it is important to note that rather lax church administration prevailed at this time. By 1778 every English missionary preacher had returned to the mother country except Asbury, and the latter restricted himself primarily to the small state of Delaware. The job of expanding the church was thus committed to young, inexperienced, poorly educated men. Almost all of these young ministers had been born and reared in a slave culture and appeared to have no clear understanding that slavery was wrong. DeVinne states that the forty-eight preachers who had been received into the ministry during the Revolutionary War belonged almost exclusively to this class.[26] Further, the early work of these Methodist preachers was primarily in the slaveholding states. Out of a national membership of about fourteen thousand, only about two thousand resided in nonsouthern states.[27]

It is not surprising, then, that the formal resolutions of Methodist conferences and conventions during the last decade of the eighteenth

---

[24]Sweet, *The Methodist Episcopal Church*, p. 16.
[25]Daniel DeVinne, *The Methodist Episcopal Church and Slavery* (New York: F. Hart, 1857), p. 12.
[26]Ibid.
[27]Ibid.

century, although disapproving slavery, became ever more modified in tone.[28] Mattison reports that by 1808 "all that related to slaveholding among private members [i.e., laymen] was stricken out of the Methodist body of rules and regulations and the following put in its place: 'The General Conference authorizes each Annual Conference to form their own regulations, relative to buying and selling slaves.' "[29] It is important to note that it was the buying and selling of slaves that each conference was to regulate, not the holding of slaves. Apparently, the possession of slaves, at least by laymen, now had the church's tacit approval. By 1840, the ownership of slave property was extended to ministers.[30]

A crisis developed in 1844 when a bishop of the Methodist Church, the Reverend James Andrew, was found to be a slaveholder. This necessitated a clear decision. Either do something with Bishop Andrew, or openly tolerate slaveholding in the highest positions of the church. Was the Methodist Episcopal Church a slaveholding church, or was it not? The issue was essentially resolved that same year when the Methodist Episcopal Church split into what amounted to northern and southern branches—the former condemning slavery, the latter citing Scripture to support it.

What we observe quite clearly in this piece of historical development is the influence of social and situational factors upon the institution of religion. To summarize briefly: Early American Methodist successes were in the South. As the plantation system grew and as it became economically profitable to own slaves, Methodist laymen, preachers, and finally bishops acceded to the practice. Bishop Asbury, residing in Baltimore, had little knowledge or control over his fellow Methodists scattered throughout the South. Also, the Methodist ministers during this period were little educated, poorly informed, and Southerners by background, orientation, and ways of thinking.

And so, quite apart from official theological statements or the moral convictions and commitments of church leaders, social factors exerted their influence on the religious group. Economic pressures, organizational features, and characteristics both of the members and lower-level leadership combined to override theological and moral mandates. Because religion exists in society and in the subcommunities and regions of that society, it finds itself influenced by the norms and structure of that society and by those of its subunits.

American Presbyterians followed a similar route. Murray states that

---

[28]Lucius Matlack, *History of American Slavery and Methodism from 1780 to 1849* (New York: Lucius Matlack, 1849), pp. 33 ff.

[29]Hiram Mattison, *The Impending Crisis of 1860* (New York: Mason Brothers, 1859), p. 30.

[30]Ibid., p. 34.

most colonial Presbyterians viewed slavery as permitted by God and tended to accept the customs of the areas in which they settled.[31] As slaveholding became more economically significant, the battlelines between North and South were more clearly drawn. This was true of religious groups no less than other groups and institutions in the society. Actually, although some southern Presbyterians vigorously opposed slavery, it was not only the issue of theological liberalism but also the controversy over slavery that resulted in the "schism of 1837" between "old-school" and "new-school" Presbyterians.[32] This schism was sealed by the advent of the Civil War, as the northern and southern Presbyterians went their separate ways.

With the outbreak of the Civil War in 1861, all the major Protestant denominations either officially split into northern and southern branches or allowed local political policy to dictate the church's position. For example, C. F. W. Walther, leader of what is now known as The Lutheran Church—Missouri Synod, saw the slavery issue as a matter for government, not churches, to decide. In doing so he relied on a strict interpretation of the principle of separation of church and state: church members are to respect and abide by the laws established by the political process in the governmental units of which they are citizens.

Into the Present

Slight variations of this principle appear to have guided much religious thinking on the slavery issue and thus set the stage for the relative noninvolvement of religious groups in civil rights struggles following the Civil War until very recently. Most religious groups at both the national and local levels remained on balance silent on the issue of black civil rights for nearly ten decades. It was a stand of aloofness which relegated first the issue of slavery, then equal rights for blacks, to the political and social realm and asserted that it was "not the business of the church" to interfere in such social and political (i.e., nonreligious) matters.[33] It is in fact this very silence which prompts our excursion into the question of the relationship of white Christianity in the United States to black Americans. White churches have tended to reinforce the class and caste gap between whites and blacks, sometimes by lending active support to claims of blacks' inherent inferiority and to justifications for their second-class citizenship, most often by remaining silent and thereby giving tacit ap-

---

[31]Andrew E. Murray, *Presbyterians and the Negro—A History* (Philadelphia: Presbyterian Historical Society, 1966), p. 12.
[32]Ibid., pp. 103 ff.
[33]Ralph Moellering, *Christian Conscience and Negro Emancipation* (Philadelphia: Fortress Press, 1965), p. 76.

proval to racial segregation, discrimination, and prejudice. Furthermore, racial or ethnic differences which became closely associated with class differences were reflected in religious differences. In other words, white churches were for whites, black churches for blacks. Kyle Haselden asserts that "long before the little signs—'White Only' and 'Colored'—appeared in the public utilities they had appeared in the Church."[34]

In the 1950s and 1960s nearly every major religious group issued official statements and passed resolutions at their national convention favoring equality for blacks and calling for an end to discrimination and segregation, although not always issuing clear calls for integration as such. Also during this period white faces in clerical collars became highly visible in sit-ins, marches, and demonstrations, as numerous white clergymen and some laymen as well provided leadership and helped fill the ranks of participants in the civil rights struggle. They sincerely wanted to tell the nation and the world that the white Christian churches were concerned and committed, and they wanted by example and exhortation to bring their fellow white church members along. Yet their voices and presence do not seem to have been representative or typical.

A strong antiblack animus remained within the white Christian denominations. In a nationwide survey as recently as 1967, nearly half (44 percent) of the white respondents registered basic disapproval of the black civil rights movement in this country.[35] Of significant interest, this proportion compares with from only 4 to 8 percent of clergymen (some slight differences by denomination) who disapprove of the movement.[36]

Actually, it is generally believed that the 44 percent of laymen expressed disapproval of the civil rights movement represented a decline from earlier periods. Paul Sheatsley of the National Opinion Research Center believes that various polls conducted since the 1940s indicate a steady, unambiguous increase in positive sentiment toward civil rights issues.[37] Hadden suggests, however, that the growing positive attitudes toward civil rights are at the level of general values and do not represent an increasing acceptance of the specific implications of the movement.[38] The white American church member, although more likely than not to to accept the principle of improved rights and conditions for blacks is less and less likely to support specific developments along that line the closer to home they are. Hadden reports a Brink and Harris survey which

34Kyle Haselden, *The Racial Problem in Christian Perspective* (New York: Harper & Row, 1959), p. 29.
35Jeffery K. Hadden, *The Gathering Storm in the Churches* (Garden City, N.Y.: Doubleday, 1969), p. 127.
36Ibid., p. 104.
37Paul B. Sheatsley, "White Attitudes Toward the Negro," *Daedalus* 95, no. 1 (1966); 217–38; quoted in Hadden, *The Gathering Storm*, p. 130.
38Hadden, *The Gathering Storm*, p. 130.

found that 52 percent of white Americans would be upset if blacks moved into their neighborhood (as compared to the 44 percent he found who disapprove of the movement generally). But 76 percent of whites who live in neighborhoods into which blacks would like to move would be upset at such a development.[39]

Hadden's own data reveal that nearly three-fourths (72 percent) of white laymen in the mid-1960s would have been upset if their own clergyman were to participate in a civil rights picket line or demonstration.[40] Further, most did not regard Martin Luther King as an outstanding example of making Christianity relevant and meaningful for the present (only 29 percent agreed that King was an "outstanding example").[41] Clearly white members of religious organizations no less than whites generally had not lost a pervading uneasiness and feeling of threat concerning black civil rights activities and their implications.

Religion, Social Class, and Racial Attitudes

Quite obviously religion in the United States has not reversed, even to the degree it has tried, its long history of maintaining major class distinctions between whites and blacks. There are, however, important differences in this regard among major religious groups. Jews, for example, express far less suspicion of and animosity toward Blacks than do Protestants and Catholics, with Catholics actually slightly less likely than Protestants to express such suspicion and hostility. For example, on the two issues mentioned before, the proportion of Jews, Catholics, and Protestants were as follows: 43, 68, and 77 percent respectively who would be upset at their clergymen participating in civil rights activities; 59, 30, and 27 percent respectively who agree that Martin Luther King was an outstanding example of making Christianity relevant and meaningful.[42]

The social class of respondents also appears to be extremely relevant here. It is very likely that the lower the social class of an individual, the more likely he is to express suspicion of and resentment toward blacks. Using level of educational achievement as the independent measure of social class, we observe some dramatic contrasts in Hadden's sample, as shown in Table 11–4.

One must note, of course, that not all religious persons of low educational attainment or low social status are opposed to black progress or express measurable prejudice against blacks. In fact, David Harrell has noted that some southern whites of working- or lower-class social status

[39]Ibid.
[40]Ibid., p. 136.
[41]Ibid., p. 137.
[42]Ibid., pp. 136–37.

TABLE 11–4

Proportion Expressing Selected Attitudes on Civil Rights Issues, by Level of Educational Attainment

	Education			
Attitude	*Some high school*	*High school graduate*	*Some college*	*College graduate*
"Clergy should stick to religion and not concern themselves with social, economic, and political questions."	63%	47%	38%	23%
"I would be upset if my (minister/priest/rabbi) were to participate in a picket line or demonstration."	77	72	69	59
"I basically disapprove of the Negro civil rights movement in America."	53	43	33	28
"Martin Luther King, Jr., is an outstanding example of making Christianity relevant and meaningful for our day."	27	27	32	40

Source: Adapted from Jeffrey K. Hadden, *The Gathering Storm in the Churches* (Garden City, N.Y.: Doubleday, 1969), p. 145.

and some religious sects whose members are primarily of working-class status, have related well to blacks at the same class level, express little or no racial prejudice, and engage in integrated religious activities.[43]

It has frequently been suggested that part of the reason for prejudice against blacks, particularly by whites of at least moderately low socioeconomic status, is the latter's fear of economic threat and of a potential undermining of their only "claim to fame," so to speak—namely, having higher status than at least one other "category" of people (the blacks around them). Christian antagonism toward Jews has some of this same flavor—not strictly a class phenomenon, but an uneasiness and resentment in the face of Jewish economic, educational, and political success and influence which is frequently seen as disproportionate to their numbers in the population. More on this in Chapter 13.

[43]David E. Harrell, Jr., *White Sects and Black Men in the Recent South* (Nashville: Vanderbilt University Press, 1971).

RELIGION
IN
AMERICA

Part **IV**

12

Dominant
Historical
Patterns

In this chapter we shall discuss seven specific themes or developments in the history of American religion, proceeding roughly chronologically. Moreover, this discussion can be viewed within the context of two more general themes that the reader will find helpful to keep in mind as we proceed: first, that the outward manifestation or pattern of religion has constantly changed during the nearly four centuries since the initial European settlement of this country; and second, that the relationships between religion and other features of the social structure have also changed.

Because any attempt to summarize the history of religion in America is next to impossible, the great selectivity of topics covered in this chapter is inevitable. Yet our two general themes indicate that we shall be doing here more of what we have been doing throughout this book. That is, amid great diversity in the phenomenon we call religion, we shall try to draw generalizations and to point to those phenomena that seem to have greatest salience to later developments. This latter feature will be of prime importance inasmuch as the developments we cover in this chapter have been included for their relevance to concepts and developments that we have either discussed earlier or will present in subsequent chapters.

INTOLERANT BEGINNINGS

The first theme or stage in the history of religion in America we call the period of intolerant beginnings. Although many of the early colonists were themselves religious dissenters and minorities extolled by our history books for their courage and principles in struggling for religious freedom and liberty to the extent of making perilous voyages in search of a place where they could practice their religious convictions unhampered, many of these same seekers and champions of religious freedom were inclined to deny to others what they demanded for themselves. Those who asked that others be tolerant of their views were themselves intolerant of the divergent religious views of still others.

During the colonial period the settlers, though speaking of a new world and a new age, had reproduced an ancient pattern of officially established religion that was supported by law and governmental authority. The state-church pattern predominated. Nine of the thirteen original colonies recognized officially established religious systems. Persons who dissented were frequently expelled from these colonies, or at best accorded only second-class citizenship if allowed to remain.

The situation is well summarized in the following excerpt from the U.S. Supreme Court's opinion in the historic 1947 *Everson* decision (see Chapter 10):

> *Catholics found themselves hounded and proscribed because of their faith; Quakers who followed their conscience went to jail; Baptists were peculiarly obnoxious to certain dominant Protestant sects; men and women of varied faiths who happened to be in a minority in a particular locality were persecuted because they steadfastly persisted in worshipping God only as their own consciences dictated. And all of these dissenters were compelled to pay tithes and taxes to support government-sponsored churches whose ministers preached inflammatory sermons designed to strengthen and consolidate the established faith by generating a burning hatred against dissenters.*[1]

Anne Hutchinson, whose history is one of the better-known examples of such victimization, was interestingly enough not a representative of a dissenting or deviant religious group in the Massachusetts Bay Colony where she resided. Although what she taught was defined as deviant, heretical doctrine, she was technically a Congregationalist, like all the other (acceptable) residents of Boston. Her heresy lay in her stress on a

[1]Everson v. Board of Education, 333 U.S. 1.

"convenant of grace"—a religion in which a person could have direct access to God's love and grace—in opposition to the "covenant of works" that stressed obedience to the laws of church and state. In 1638 both she and her doctrines were tried and condemned—her teaching as heresy and she as a blasphemer of God and seducer of the faithful.

Earlier, in 1636, Roger Williams and four companions, having been banished from the same colony, settled in "Rogues' Island" (i.e., Rhode Island) and established a community there as a haven for Quakers, Baptists, and other deviant and dissenting religious groups. Even in this tolerant colony, however, approximately a century later a law was passed restricting both citizenship and eligibility to public office to Protestants.[2]

Quakers were particularly obnoxious to the colonists in Massachusetts, as reflected by laws there specifying that any of that "cursed sect of heretics" who entered the colony were to be jailed, whipped with twenty stripes, and then expelled from the colony. Four Quakers were even executed.

Early Virginia laws, later reduced in severity, specified that anyone convicted a third time for failure to attend religious services was to spend six months in the galleys and that a third offense of working on the Sabbath was punishable by death.

THE CONSTITUTIONAL COMPROMISE

With the Revolution and the adoption of the Constitution, the colonial pattern became subject to forces resulting in drastic change. In significant part this change was to occur because no single religious group could claim anything near the majority of supporters throughout the thirteen states necessary to establish it as the officially sanctioned religion of the new nation. Not that particular groups (Congregationalists, for example, who probably had the greatest number of members of any group), wouldn't have wanted such status; it was simply that none had sufficient numbers. Every state had a goodly number of dissenters and minority-religious-group members; there were even substantial numbers of "free-thinkers" who professed no formal religious affiliation. Therefore, only one practical solution appeared feasible, and that was to cut off churches both legally and financially from government support. Hence the clause in the First Amendment specifying that "Congress shall make no law respecting an establishment of religion."

Looking at the situation from a slightly different angle, at the birth

[2]Evarts B. Greene, *Religion and the State* (New York: New York University Press, 1941), p. 51.

of the new nation every religious group, whether dissenting or firmly established, now found itself occupying a minority status; each group, even those constituting a majority in one or more states, was now a minority in the context of all thirteen states. Thus each was now quite naturally concerned with keeping government from interfering with what it wanted to do and teach religiously: What if another religious group should later gain a majority—what would happen to us? Hence the second clause dealing with religion in the First Amendment stating that Congress shall make no law "prohibiting the free exercise thereof."

With disestablishment came voluntarism and the rise of denominationalism as described in Chapter 7. People could join any religious group of their choice, or they could choose to join none at all. They could even form antireligious groups. Thus religious groups now had to find ways of becoming self-supporting. Competition for members and for scarce resources developed, and religious innovation was implicitly encouraged as a consequence.

It is difficult to overstate the significance and the dramatic impact of this serverance of religion from state auspices. Sanford H. Cobb, an expert on the history of religious liberty, maintains that the American pattern of religious freedom was "the most striking contribution of America to the science of Government."[3]

As dramatic and innovative as the Constitution was with respect to the social organization of both religion and government, it appears that these arrangements provoked relatively little struggle. Martin Marty notes that in only three of the thirteen original states was there much resistance to these First Amendment provisions.[4] Marty adds: "In most other colonies the change was made as if with a sigh of relief, in a spirit of tidying up, and with only whimpers of reactions."[5]

As we recounted in some detail in Chapter 10, while the First Amendment stand on religion may have obviated certain undesirable historical possibilities, it could not avoid a host of new problems. Our society in fact still struggles mightily in interpreting and applying those few words.

THE FRONTIER CHALLENGE

We mentioned in the preceding section that the Constitution's disestablishment of religion demanded innovation on the part of religious groups if they were to thrive—or perhaps just to survive. This need to inno-

---

[3] Quoted in Martin E. Marty, *Righteous Empire* (New York: Dial Press, 1970), p. 36.
[4] Ibid., p. 37.
[5] Ibid.

vate was significantly compounded by the opening of the frontier and increased westward migration. In a sense, the frontier almost immediately presented opportunities for religious groups to "test their mettle," so to speak. Here was territory. Here were people. And no one religious group had a monopoly on either.

Frontier Conditions

A number of characteristics of the frontier and the people who ventured there are of direct relevance both to the response and to the success or failure of religious groups in the frontier environment. One obvious feature was a sparse population located in small, widely separated settlements. This situation fostered among frontier settlers loneliness and the need for emotional outlets. These factors gave rise to an essential requirement of frontier life—a spirit of independence and self-sufficiency. If frontiersmen were going to make it, they had to do it on their own. Further, in the absence of external restraints, of social-control mechanisms for monitoring people's behavior, the task of checking antisocial behavior fell to control mechanisms internal to the individual. Overarching all this was another factor—namely, the constant threat of physical danger and insecurity, whether from disease, accident, inadequate food supply, Indian raids, or fellow citizens turned brigand. A final feature of the frontier worth mentioning is the fact that the frontier effected selective migration. Those who traveled westward were not a representative cross section of the inhabitants of the eastern seaboard. Rather, the roads west tended to fill up with those who had less at stake on the east coast—specifically, those of lower socioeconomic status and with little education. Not all of the latter traveled west of course, but primarily those with an adventuresome spirit, a willingness to work, and long-range aspirations.

Responses by Organized Religion

The established social institutions on the east coast, particularly the churches, were generally ill equipped to meet the combination of challenges described above. The established eastern churches, which were of the denominational type, tended to require a trained, professional full-time clergyman to head a self-supporting congregation. They were used to meeting in a specially dedicated, permanent facility containing the standard accouterments—pews, hymnbooks, a pulpit, and perhaps a keyboard instrument. Transplanting this pattern to the frontier was infeasible, if for no other reason than a sparse population with little ready cash cannot support such a standard religious organization.

Recognizing this problem, some eastern ecclesiastical leaders and organizations turned to sponsoring revivals and camp meetings (occasional gatherings of large groups of people at a central location for several days of spiritual exhortation and instruction)—techniques that were actually better suited to such emerging sectarian groups as the Methodists and the Baptists. Nevertheless, as a result for a brief period after the Revolution there occurred what came to be known as the Second Great Awakening. (The First Great Awakening began in 1734 in New England with the evangelistic preaching of Jonathan Edwards, George Whitfield, and others, and spread through the colonies in the 1730s to 1750s.) This general religious revival was epitomized in the Cane Ridge, Kentucky, camp meeting of 1801, which twenty thousand persons are estimated to have attended. Considering the sparse population of "the West" at that time, this is an impressive number that says a great deal about the eagerness of people for human contact, for an emotional outlet, and, probably for many if not most, for religious participation and expression as well. The Second Great Awakening was relatively short-lived, however, and produced no durable institutional forms.

The Baptist and Methodist Solutions

So far as religion was concerned, the Methodists and the Baptists became the inheritors of the frontier, for they were better able than the established churches to meet the challenges and brave the conditions of the frontier by application of the necessary innovation. Thus the Methodists, who had numbered approximately nine thousand in 1776, grew to become the largest religious group in the country by 1850. Baptist growth was nearly as great. No doubt, then, about their rapid success. But why? What exactly did they do? The answer is basically twofold: (1) Both groups developed innovative organizational structures for reaching widely scattered people. (2) As sects that had rejected many traditional denominational patterns and that seemed capable of adapting to and growing up with the frontier, they enjoyed a response among frontier settlers that the established denominations could not duplicate.

First, regarding strategy, the Methodists employed the technique of the *circuit-riding preacher.* Initially these were men with some theological training who were commissioned as missionaries to the frontier by John Wesley in England or by Bishop Asbury, his representative in the colonies and then in the states. Their strategy was simply to go from house to house preaching the Gospel within the family setting, delivering sermons from a tree stump or wagon bed when a larger group could be gathered, creating "Methodists" as they went. They asked little more than food and shelter from those who received them. Periodically they would return on their circuit to rally the faithful, solemnize marriages, and conduct baptisms. They traveled thousands of miles a year along circuits that took a minimum of three to four weeks, often a month or two, to complete.

The Baptists settled on a different, though equally successful, approach: the *lay preacher*, a farmer for six days, a preacher for one. The success of this technique required only a concentration of families on adjoining farms. The genius of the Baptist plan was that it required no recruitment from the outside. Anyone with a "call" from God to preach and with some oratorical and pedagogical ability could do it. The people whom such lay preachers gathered together began to think of themselves as Baptists.

And so the Baptist and Methodist sects grew. But these groups had more going for them than their strategies for overcoming the problem of sparse populations. The preachers themselves were as uneducated as their flocks, or at least nearly so. In other words, they could effectively communicate. They encouraged emotional response and involvement in everyone. Religion for them was not a spectator sport. Revival services were frequent and they were popular, for they met people's need for emotional release. The democratic slant of these sects—which included the concepts that anyone could interpret Scripture as God directed him and that parents were responsible for the spiritual welfare of their own children between visits by the circuit rider or Sunday gatherings for worship—agreed with the individualism and self-sufficiency of the frontiersman. The typical emphasis of these sects on internal controls in the face of all manner of temptations to sin meshed well with the need for such internal controls in the absence of external ones.

Later Religious Responses

As the harshness of the frontier waned, as towns developed, and as social structures became more stabilized, further developments arose in the religious life of the frontier. For one thing, the Methodists and the Baptists consolidated their gains, for as people improved their lot and their communities became more firmly established they did not suddenly forsake the religious group that had been serving them well. In great part such continuity was maintained because the Methodist and the Baptist religious groups evolved and developed along with the frontier. Originally sects, they became full-fledged denominations. More attention was paid to theological training, colleges and seminaries were established throughout the Midwest, circuit riders became resident clergymen, part-time Sunday preachers became full-time ministers.

As more middle-class business and professional people came west, the established eastern denominations followed, establishing their churches in the growing towns. Some of the upwardly mobile early settlers also affiliated with these "higher-status" Episcopalian, Presbyterian, and Congregational churches, though not in sufficient numbers to seriously erode the membership gains the Baptists and Methodists had already made.

As the nineteenth century neared and passed midpoint, groups of Lutherans from Germany and the Scandinavian countries came to settle and tame the farmland of the Midwest and the north-central United States. They brought their churches with them and by virtue of different language and religion remained relatively isolated from those Protestants who had preceded them. Catholics came also and established their ethnically oriented churches in both urban and rural areas. Thus the frontier was becoming religiously diverse primarily through the immigration of groups from outside the United States.

A pair of unique frontier phenomena need yet to be mentioned. One was the emergence of two new denominations that were born essentially as denominations and did not follow the sect-to-denomination evolutionary route. These were the Disciples of Christ and the Churches of Christ. Both groups downplayed denominational differences and stepped into the developing towns and cities as the frontier moved ever westward, picking up some of the people left behind as many of the Methodist and Baptist preachers moved on to follow the scattering pioneers. These groups formed what today are often called "community" churches or "nondenominational" churches that preach an "average" Protestantism and express little interest in the denominational "brand name" a member may have had before. Many of these preachers were dissident Methodists, Baptists, and Presbyterians who did not wish to be regarded as comprising yet another denomination but did so nonetheless.

The other unique frontier religious phenomenon is the Church of Jesus Christ of the Latter-Day Saints (Mormons), founded by Joseph Smith in western New York State in the early 1840s. This group, regarded by some outsiders as neither Protestant nor even Christian, experienced serious opposition from an alliance of established Protestant denominations and growing Protestant sects who otherwise only competed among themselves. To escape harassment that often reached violent proportions, the Mormons moved from New York to Ohio to Missouri to Illinois and finally to Utah. But even the Mormons, which were probably best viewed as a religious cult in the beginning, evolved. Today the Mormon church is generally acknowledged to belong among the ranks of standard religious denominations, even though it is more aggressive in proselytizing than many of the latter.

THE ORDEAL OF PLURALISM

Anti-Catholicism

Although there had really never been much doubt, by the beginning of the nineteenth century the new American nation saw itself as definitely a Protestant domain. Probably this is one important reason why citizens generally accepted so graciously the radically new concept of separation of church and state enunciated in the First Amendment. Of the approximately 4½ million citizens at the birth of the nation, estimates suggest there were only about twenty thousand Roman Catholics—a small minority indeed. Not that they were ignored. In fact, they were almost universally mistrusted. Small wonder, then, at the chagrin, uneasiness, and outright fear many citizens experienced and expressed as substantial migrations of Roman Catholics from Ireland, Germany, and Eastern Europe began in the 1830s.

The First Amendment's protection of the free exercise of religion was now to be put to its first serious test. The concept of *religious pluralism*, of freedom of religious expression and conviction and of tolerance of religious diversity to which Protestants had paid lip service, now became a bitter pill for the many spokesmen for and supporters of the view that the United States was God's Protestant kingdom on earth. Not only were substantial efforts expended in trying to amend immigration laws to keep Catholics out of this country or, failing that, to convert them to Protestantism and thereby dilute their "poison," but the society witnessed several decades of physical abuse directed against Catholics in the middle of the nineteenth century.

Martin Marty points out that the anti-Catholic agitators had deep reservoirs of suspicion from which to draw. He summarizes the historical setting as follows:

The original colonists had felt themselves beleaguered, with French Catholics to the north and Spanish-Portuguese Catholics to the south. They had emotionally protected themselves against Catholic intrusions into the thirteen colonies. Where possible they isolated the Catholics, mostly in Maryland. Where necessary they began to accept them, as in the case of prestigious families like the Carrolls. But with few Catholics on the scene, it had been easy for colonial parsons to exaggerate stories of Catholic superstition and horror; no one was around to refute them. People could thus constantly reaffirm the prejudices their fathers had brought with them from England and elsewhere across the Atlantic.

*As the 20,000 or 25,000 colonial Roman Catholics grew to a body of
40,000 at the beginning of the [nineteenth] century and multiplied forty
times by 1850 to 1,606,000, there were ever-increasing levels of animus and
threat in the Protestant rhetoric.[6]*

Reacting to this dramatic upsurge in Catholic immigration, a few
outspoken propagandists—such as Samuel F. B. Morse, who painted visions of a foreign conspiracy based in the Vatican to take over America—
were able to render Protestant Americans ready to believe almost anything. By mid-century the nativist Know-Nothing political party was
formed with anti-Catholicism as one of its unifying themes. At this point
we observe the blooming of what R. A. Billington terms the "Protestant
Crusade."[7] The reader may wish to refer to our reference at the end of
Chapter 8 to two of the more violent incidents associated with this anti-
Catholic Protestant Crusade to appreciate the intensity of feeling and
extremity of action that characterized Protestant-Catholic relations during this period. Protestants, feeling threatened by the waves of Catholic
immigration, were willing to believe most any accusation or innuendo
about Catholics and to react both impetuously and violently.

It appears that Roman Catholics in this country may have unwit-
tingly and quite coincidentally provided some fuel for the Protestant fires
that were smoldering. Consider, for example, the Philadelphia trustee
conflict of the 1820s within the Roman Catholic church, which revolved
around the question of whether church property should be controlled by
trustees representing laymen or by the bishop of the diocese. The issue
dated back to 1808, when St. Mary's Cathedral had been erected by the
congregation and control of the property had been vested in a board of
lay trustees instead of the bishop, as was usual. The long battle, during
which the priest of the congregation was excommunicated, ended in
1830. The church was placed under an interdict which caused members
to abandon it for other churches and thus forced the trustees, left without
financial support, to submit to the bishop.

This Philadelphia controversy did American Catholicism much
harm. It attracted the hostile attention of the entire nation, inspired a
great deal of "bad press" and negative literature, and left the impression
in the minds of many Protestants that Catholicism was the sworn enemy
of democratic institutions and thus a dangerous influence in the United
States.[8] Ironically, the Philadelphia episode in fact marked an attempt by
Catholic laymen to pattern their church after typically American Protes-

---

[6]Ibid., pp. 127–28.
[7]Ray Allen Billington, *The Protestant Crusade, 1800–1860* (Gloucester, Mass.:
Peter Smith, 1963).
[8]Ibid., pp. 38–40.

tant autonomous churches and to establish an independent Catholic church in America.[9]

Opposition by Catholics to the reading of the "Protestant" King James Version of the Bible in New York public schools, Protestant resentment and suspicion of the Catholic parochial schools as "un-American" and subversive, Catholic bloc voting as evidence of considerable political strength, "native American" resentment of "cheap" Irish Catholic labor— all are factors that have contributed to anti-Catholicism in this country.

By the Civil War anti-Catholic sentiment had lost much of its intensity. And the war itself certainly diverted energy and attention away from the issue. After the war, Catholic immigration proceeded steadily and then soared in the late 1800s with the arrival of waves of southern and eastern European Catholics. By now, lacking evidence of any "papal plot," American Protestants established a somewhat uneasy but workable peace with their Catholic countrymen. The flames of conflict have been kindled sporadically ever since, however, over such issues as public aid to parochial schools, birth control and abortion, and official government or presidential representation to the Vatican. But as we'll observe in the next chapter, the animosities have been greatly reduced.

Anti-Semitism

The issue of religious pluralism and the challenge to Protestant domination was not limited to Catholic-Protestant relations. Significant numbers of Jews also emigrated to the United States between 1880 and the First World War. Until that time there had been relatively so few Jews in this country—in 1815, for example there were only about three thousand—that they were not regarded as a threat to established Protestantism. Although Jews had been excluded from full political participation in some of the colonies (e.g., Virginia) by Trinitarian belief requirements, and although the depiction of Jews in the denominational literature of that period would today properly be termed anti-Semitic, the small number of Jews elicited little explicit reaction from their fellow citizens. Anti-Semitism in this country began in earnest with the substantial immigration of Russian Jews in the 1880s when the Ku Klux Klan made anti-Semitism one of its major stances. Many of the Jews who emigrated to the United States after 1880, although often quite secularized (and sometimes politically radical), retained their ethnic identity, settling almost exclusively in urban areas and engaging in mutual assistance in

---

[9] Will Herberg, *Protestant, Catholic, Jew* (Garden City, N.Y.: Doubleday, 1956), p. 140.

establishing business enterprises. Other ethnic groups and Protestant "native Americans" began to resent their presence, and anti-Semitism began to surface. Jews thus found it necessary to establish various defense organizations, of which the Anti-Defamation League of the B'nai B'rith is the best known.

Anti-Semitism came to be a significant feature of American life—one which though significantly diminished is still alive today. Anti-Semitism probably reached its zenith in this country in the 1920s and 1930s, when anti-Semitic newspapers and radio columnists proliferated and reached out into many American homes. Such blatant anti-Semitism has been relegated to the fringes of our society today, and many of the most blatant forms of anti-Semitic discrimination in housing, education, employment, and voluntary-association membership have been eliminated.

Recent studies by Bernard Olson and by Glock and Stark have shown a connection between conservative Protestant theology and anti-Semitism, though the nature of this connection and its intensity is not clear.[10] A serious difficulty arises in trying to separate what we might call *social anti-Semitism*—hatred of Jews as social beings, as persons—from *religious anti-Semitism,* which from the conservative Christian viewpoint is the concept that Jews need salvation and that it will be denied them until they accept Jesus as the Savior. Unfortunately, these two "types" of anti-Semitism, although undoubtedly intermingled in many cases, are not adequately distinguished in existing measures and indices of anti-Semitism.

Other groups, of course, come in for their share of aspersion and harassment. We have already mentioned the Mormons, who were forced literally to flee for their lives to new territory, ultimately standing their ground in Utah Territory. Similar though not so violent harassment has been directed against Jehovah's Witnesses in many communities. It is interesting from the sociological perspective to note that both these groups traditionally engage in vigorous conversion and missionary activities. That is, they implicitly reject the pluralism concept that includes respect for every other group's autonomy and right to be and do as it chooses. Whereas adherence to the spirit of pluralism demands that one accept diversity—in fact, that one champion it—these groups actively seek to bring everyone into their ranks—an aggressive stance that undoubtedly encourages resentment.

The outcome of the religious pluralism controversy in this country has, however, been the triumph of pluralism and the peaceful acceptance of religious diversity by nearly all. This of course has not stopped many

---

10See Bernard Olson, *Faith and Prejudice* (New Haven: Yale University Press, 1963), and Charles Y. Glock and Rodney Stark, *Christian Beliefs and Anti-Semitism* (New York: Harper & Row, 1966).

religious groups from actively proselytizing and openly criticizing the theology of other religious groups. But the practice of taking the process a step further by associating what appears theologically inadequate or incorrect from one's religious perspective with "un-Americanism," inferior citizenship, subversion, and the like has almost totally disappeared.

RELIGIOUS SOCIAL CONCERN

The second half of the nineteenth century marked the beginning of a highly significant controversy within American Protestantism that continues today—a fundamental argument over the proper focus of Christianity. In simplest terms, is it the salvation of souls or the improvement of society? Although few if any proponents of either alternative then would have asserted that Christianity should be exclusively devoted to one or the other goal, the controversy tended to place most Christians, theologian and layman alike, into one camp or the other.

This period is known for the emergence of the so-called *social gospel* and the rise of such proponents of socially concerned Christianity as Horace Bushnell, Walter Rauschenbush, and Washington Gladden. These were men who argued that Christianity is not fulfilled and not true to its origins and history unless and until it immerses itself in alleviating the world's miseries and social pathologies—social problems that emerged with advancing industrialization, increasing urbanization, and the appearance, already then, of decay in portions of the mushrooming cities. These spokesmen contended that their emphasis on social responsibility was the old, authentic emphasis of the Bible. They pointed to the prophets in the Old Testament Scriptures and to the Jesus of the New Testament Gospels, who evidenced great concern for the physical and social needs and problems of people. On the other side, those who stressed the more individualistic, salvation-centered focus for Christianity tended to stress the emphasis of the New Testament Epistles of Paul on the atonement of Jesus and his rescue of men from the wrath of a just and judging God.

Although we shall more thoroughly look into this controversy in its present-day form in Chapter 15, we shall simply highlight the emergence of the "new" emphasis in Christianity (or, as many contended, the resurgence of the original one) that loomed so significant during the last century. It is of interest sociologically in part because it happened to develop concomitantly with the development of sociology as a field of study and of social concern as an emphasis in the social sciences. But the development of a social-concern emphasis in American religion is of interest sociologically primarily because of the change in American religion this

represented. Although it did not turn American religion completely
around, for some individuals and groups it did radically change the focus
and purpose of religion; at the very least, it added a new dimension.

As we noted briefly in the previous chapter, some significant developments in the area of general social concern originated with religion.
The establishment of hospitals, orphanages, and settlement houses and
the formation of groups such as the Salvation Army occurred after the
Industrial Revolution was solidly under way and many of the latter's
excesses and abuses were clearly seen adversely affecting great numbers of
people. It is important to note, however, that the emphasis of religious
people during the period of western industrialization was primarily an
individualized one. That is, the primary concern of religious leaders was
with helping individuals. First of all, they wanted to save the individual's
soul. But then, out of compassion for those persons living a materially
disadvantaged existence, they began establishing institutions and mechanisms for the purpose of helping the body. But again, just as the concern
was for the souls of individual people, so the concern was for individual
bodies. The social service activities of salvation-oriented religious groups,
already begun in the 1820s, continued into the early part of the twentieth
century. The emphasis was, as noted, essentially that of John Wesley in
the eighteenth century—namely, concern for individuals: replacing individual vices with individual virtues, changing the direction of individuals
from hell to heaven, making physically healthy bodies out of ill and
broken ones.

Later, other religious leaders, such as the aforementioned Bushnell,
Rauschenbush, and Gladden, began to direct primary attention away
from salvation and toward physical and social well-being; above all, they
began to shift the focus from individual vices to societal ones. That is,
they saw the locus of social problems not in individuals but in society
and in institutional structures and patterns beyond the immediate control of individuals. To these social reformers the goal was one of "Chris-
tianizing" the social order, of applying the teachings of Jesus to the social
and economic institutions of the society, of reforming the social environment in which people lived and worked: they expounded what came to
be known as the social gospel.

Those who followed in the footsteps of the earlier, individual-
oriented religious leaders became increasingly uneasy with the social
gospel, which they felt operated at the expense of individual salvation—
the preeminent responsibility of Christianity, in their view. Influential
evangelistic preachers who emphasized individual salvation such as Dwight
L. Moody and Billy Sunday thus began challenging the social gospel and
in fact essentially carried the day so far as rank-and-file preachers and
church members were concerned. Marty reports how the flamboyant

evangelist Sunday took on the most noted advocate of the social gospel still at work in the parish ministry, Washington Gladden:[11]

> The setting of their encounter was Columbus, Ohio, where Gladden had piled up a record of achievement in a socially oriented ministry over three decades. But when Sunday came to town to carry on one of his pro-evangelistic and apparently "anti-social" revivals, Gladden quietly opposed him, and after the revival, Gladden was more outspoken over the meager returns he saw garnered from Sunday's raucous efforts. But Gladden was attacked by the vast majority of Columbus's ministers of all Protestant denominations. They rose to the defense of Sunday's approach and clearly identified with the conversionism of the revivalist.[12]

In their attempts to discredit the social gospel, the individual-oriented evangelists began what we referred to in Chapter 8 as the "great reversal," a strong reaction against social service and welfare activities and a concurrent dedication to efforts to win souls and raise individual morality by means of such tactics as emphasizing the evil of "demon rum" and supporting the Prohibition movement. The social-gospel wing of American Christianity did not disappear, however. It continued with minority support in the major denominations and through the various agencies of the Federal Council of Churches (now the National Council of Churches) that had been founded in 1908 primarily by social-gospel forces.

Thus the social-gospel movement did not wither away; in fact, it has continued to exert significant influence in American religion up to the present. It enjoyed a resurgence with its involvement in the civil rights movement in the 1950s and 1960s and in the war on poverty of the 1960s and 1970s, although with what still appears to have been a minority of church member support. More on this issue in Chapter 15.

Reconciling the great diversity of opinion and practice regarding social versus individual emphases is of course not uniquely a problem of religious institutions. Religious groups have in fact always reflected the historical ambivalence in American society at large regarding rugged individualism and self-sufficiency and responsibility versus social concerns, welfarism, and mutual responsibility for one's fellow man.

GROWTH OF FUNDAMENTALISM

Another important development within American religion that is important not only in its own right but particularly with regard to understand-

---

[11]Most of the social-gospel advocates were seminary professors, editors, authors, and the like, who remained largely unknown to the rank-and-file church member.
[12]Marty, *Righteous Empire*, p. 183.

ing the contemporary religious scene is that of the emergence of what we today call *fundamentalism*. Its development is in significant part a direct outgrowth of the social-gospel–individual-salvation controversy just discussed. Those leaders we have variously designated evangelists, revivalists, individual-soul-saving churchmen, and traditionalists were becoming increasingly disturbed with two developments during the last quarter of the nineteenth-century. The first was what they viewed as increasing secularism in the society. This is tied up with the advancement of science and the increasing confidence in the inductive scientific method of attaining truth—at the expense of deduction from a standard repository of truth such as the Bible. Of concern to them also were such developments as the dissemination of the Marxist social philosophy, the spread of the accounts of Darwin and others concerning the evolution of man and his world, and the increasing independence of society's institutions from religious influence. In short, the traditionalists or Evangelicals as they are commonly called were disturbed by the erosion of religious influence throughout the rest of the society and its institutions. Second, they felt that the Christian religion was being betrayed from within. The increasing emphasis on social service and the social gospel by individuals and groups within the broad Christian community was a significant part of their concern. For one thing, they felt that when social service was emphasized, the traditional salvation emphasis was of necessity neglected, or at best put in a secondary position. For another, they felt some were rejecting the traditional message of Christianity altogether and substituting the social gospel in all particulars. This was liberal ideology as opposed to their conservative religion—liberal Christianity that attempted to incorporate secular values into the Christian structure. What further alarmed the Evangelicals was the development of a form of biblical scholarship known as *higher criticism*, an approach to the Bible asserting that it is a collection of human documents subject to the same principles of textual criticism as any other group of documents—a perspective that originated in German theological schools and universities in the mid-1800s and was subsequently adopted at many leading seminaries in the United States.

In an effort to combat this "creeping liberalism" and restore Christianity to what they regarded as its original nature and message, many of the Evangelicals coalesced around the publication, beginning in 1910, of their orthodox manifesto in twelve volumes titled *The Fundamentals*. As Stewart Cole says: "In this action the historian finds the clear emergence of fundamentalism."[13] This publication was the capstone to a series

---

[13]Stewart G. Cole, *The History of Fundamentalism* (Hamden, Conn.: Archon Books, 1963), p. 53.

of Bible conferences held by conservatives throughout the country between 1876 and 1900, which Gasper views as "embryonic stirrings" of the fundamentalist movement.[14] At the most significant of these conferences, held in 1895 at Niagara, New York, a declaration was formulated that anticipated the famous "five points" of fundamentalist doctrine as expounded in the twelve volumes of *The Fundamentals*. The five independent points of traditional Protestant Christianity agreed upon at the Niagara Conference were: (1) the inerrancy of the Scriptures, (2) the virgin birth of Jesus Christ, (3) the deity of Jesus Christ, (4) the substitutionary atonement (Jesus taking the punishment for sin in man's place), and (5) the physical resurrection of Jesus Christ and his anticipated bodily return.[15]

The five points of fundamentalist doctrine enunciated in the first volume of *The Fundamentals* were as follows: (1) the verbal and inerrant inspiration of the Bible, (2) the virgin birth of Jesus Christ, (3) the substitutionary atonement of Jesus Christ, (4) the bodily resurrection of Jesus Christ from the tomb, and (5) the imminent second coming of Jesus Christ. Four closely related doctrines that could more or less be inferred from these basic five were: (1) the deity of Jesus Christ, (2) the sinful nature of man, (3) salvation by faith through the free grace of God, and (4) the expectation of the bodily resurrection of true believers on the Last Day.[16] Much attention was also paid to refutation of errors, such as the theory of organic evolution and higher criticism of the Bible, and to such heretical religious groups and movements as Roman Catholics, Mormons, Jehovah's Witnesses, Christian Science, and Spiritualism.

During this period the fundamentalists were organizing schools to combat the increasingly secular nature of both public and private colleges and universities. Gasper reports that over 160 Bible schools enrolling over twenty-five thousand students were organized to promote the centrality of Bible study and prepare leaders for the movement.[17]

The year 1925 probably marks the peak of fundamentalism, at least as an organized phenomenon. This is the date of the Scopes "monkey trial" in which the fundamentalists hoped that their political spokesman and three-time candidate for the presidency William Jennings Bryan would break the back of religious modernism, or at least one vertebra—namely, the teaching of evolution in a public school. Even though Scopes was found guilty, the farcical nature of the trial and the "bad press" the

---

[14]Louis Gasper, *The Fundamentalist Movement* (The Hague: Mouton, 1963), p. 11.

[15]Ibid.

[16]*The Fundamentals: A Testimony to the Truth*, vols. 1–12 (Chicago: Testimony Publishing Company, n.d. [c. 1910]).

[17]Gasper, *The Fundamentalist Movement*, p. 12.

prosecution received turned the trial victory of the fundamentalists into a public relations defeat, and the cohesiveness of the movement began to dissipate. Already by the following year attendance at their annual meeting had fallen off. By their 1930 convention "none of the scheduled speeches contained any reference to modernism or evolution."[18] They began to fight among themselves and a host of sub-groups formed.

Furniss suggests six reasons for the declining influence of fundamentalism: (1) The death of William Jennings Bryan immediately after the Scopes trial left the fundamentalists with no national leader of significant stature and appeal. (2) They had paid too little attention to creating and maintaining a cohesive national organization. (3) The prohibition issue and the fight against repeal of the 1919 Prohibition Amendment diverted the energies of many fundamentalists to this specific and in a sense peripheral issue. (4) The economic crash of 1929 induced many churches to begin working to alleviate human misery and to forget some of their theological quarrels. (5) People who were becoming more sophisticated in their knowledge, scientific and otherwise, recognized that the fundamentalists' representation of science and its theories were often distorted. (6) After losing some battles, the fundamentalists tended to pull back. They became less aggressive, more withdrawn, even petulant. That is, they appeared to lose some of their concern for reforming the theologies of their neighbors and concentrated more on attaining purity for themselves.[19] Gasper suggests that yet another possible factor was the somewhat general reaction against theological liberalism in American theological circles that came to be known as neoorthodoxy—a moderately conservative theological movement led by the Swiss theologian Karl Barth.[20] Thus some of what fundamentalism had been opposing was in fact modified, whether through the efforts of fundamentalists or of others. Certainly their "enemy" became less easy to identify and to caricature.

All of this does not mean, however, that fundamentalism died out in the 1930s. Although fundamentalists were less in public view, they were very hard at work solidifying their gains and exploring possibilities for a viable national organization. They published mightily and began extensively to utilize the new communication medium of radio. It appears that in the 1930s and 1940s religious radio broadcasts, particularly those of the fundamentalists, had a much broader hearing than they do today. Today religious radio broadcasting tends by and large to reach those who are already ideologically or theologically attuned. In other words, those who listen to conservative or fundamentalist religious radio

18Norman F. Furniss, *The Fundamentalist Controversy, 1918–1931* (New Haven: Yale University Press, 1954), p. 56.
19Ibid., pp. 178–81.
20Gasper, *The Fundamentalist Movement*, p. 19.

broadcasts tend to be fundamentalists in the first place, while only few people who have either another religious preference or none at all are likely to tune in.[21]

In the early 1940s two distinct formal associations of fundamentalists were organized, and to this day they preserve a dual focus within fundamentalism. The first to organize called itself the American Council of Christian Churches and set out to perpetuate the early aggressive thrust of fundamentalists in promoting the "historic Gospel." In addition, it identified itself as an exclusivist organization explicitly barring particular individual churches and denominations from its membership. The second organization, the National Association of Evangelicals, intended to "break with apostasy" but also wanted to avoid becoming a "reactionary, negative, or destructive type of organization."[22] It explicitly set out to become an inclusivist organization acting as a "leaven" or influence throughout Protestantism wherever possible, without demanding rigid conformity to a set of absolute standards. The National Association of Evangelicals, apparently the more successful of the two organizations, includes such somewhat familiar groups as the Assemblies of God, the Free Methodist Church of North America, the Free Will Baptists, and several Mennonite and Pentecostal groups.

Following World War II there emerged a host of targets for the fundamentalists, particularly for the American Council of Christian Churches led by Carl McIntire. There was the "liberal" ecumenical movement, particularly as embodied in the National Council of Churches in the U.S.A. and the World Council of Churches, defined by the American Council as compromisers and betrayers of the true Christian Gospel. There was the United Nations, viewed as an enemy of democracy and capitalistic freedom and as a tool of the forces of communism. The supreme spectre of communism was seen lurking not only within the United Nations and its numerous agencies, but even within the Christian churches. Numerous charges of sellouts to and compromises with communism were hurled against such prominent Protestant clergymen as John C. Bennett, Harry Emerson Fosdick, E. Stanley Jones, Reinhold Niebuhr, and Henry VanDusen. New translations of the Bible were judged by fundamentalists as distorting the divinely inspired Hebrew and Greek texts of the Bible and as disagreeing with the all-but-inspired King James Version of 1611. (Consider, for example, the controversy that arose over the Hebrew word *amah* in Isaiah 7:14—translated as "virgin" in the King James Version and as "young woman" or similar, more

---

[21]Ronald L. Johnstone, "Who Listens to Religious Radio Broadcasts Anymore?" *Journal of Broadcasting* 16 no. 1 (1971–72); 91–102.
[22]Gasper, *The Fundamentalist Movement*, p. 25.

general designations in such newer translations as the Revised Standard Version.)

Although some official support for these "causes" and campaigns was forthcoming from fundamentalist associations, particularly the American Council of Christian Churches, most of the agitation was led by individual self-styled leaders of the fundamentalist movement. Not that these persons' activities did not reflect the sentiments of many fundamentalists, but it's only fair to mention that seldom did the associations themselves take specific positions on these issues, particularly those involving opposition of particular individuals.

Throughout all this the basic thrust of fundamentalism has been evangelism, which it constantly promotes through the extensive publication of books, tracts, and magazines, through continuing wide use of radio broadcasts and, on a more limited scale, television, and through such efforts as the Youth for Christ movement with its evangelism rallies for young people throughout the United States.

Fundamentalism today remains alive and well on the American religious scene. In fact, there is even evidence of a current resurgence—an issue we'll consider in some detail in Chapter 15. Certainly an important stimulus for over two decades has been the evangelistic "crusades" of Billy Graham, whose message basically consists of the five fundamentalist points mentioned earlier—but without the exclusivist, separatist emphasis of the American Council of Christian Churches. In fact, representatives of the latter branch of fundamentalists have tended to disavow Graham and to criticize him for his association with persons of questionable loyalty to fundamentalist doctrine. Yet aside from fomenting some internal controversy within fundamentalism, Graham's "crusades" have focused national attention on the fundamentalist message and have helped what we might call legitimate fundamentalism to an extent unparalleled since the 1920s.

THE POST–WORLD WAR II REVIVAL

Following the Second World War the United States experienced what came to be known as a religious "revival." Beginning in the late 1940s and extending into the 1950s, church membership and attendance soared, contributions to religious organizations poured in, literally thousands of new congregations were established and quickly became self-supporting, the value of new construction by religious groups increased dramatically year after year. Some data will document this growth. Between 1940 and 1950 membership in churches rose from 49 to 57 percent of the population, and by 1959 had reached 63.6 percent.[23] Gallup poll data show a comparable increase in church attendance: whereas only 36 percent of the sample in 1942 reported having attended a church service during the week preceding the interview, by 1957 the figure had risen to 51 percent.[24] The value of new construction of religious facilities totaled $28 million in 1935, during the depth of the Depression, and had increased to $59 million by 1940. But the really big increase was still to come: in 1950 the value of new construction was $409 million, and by 1965 the figure reached $1.2 billion. The religion business was indeed a booming one.

Further, there developed what William Lee Miller has called our national "piety along the Potomac," which included Bible breakfasts, congressional prayer groups, and a president named Eisenhower who made numerous religious allusions in his speeches and was himself baptized in the White House following his inauguration.[25] Postage stamps and folding money suddenly began to include "In God We Trust" on their faces. We inserted the phrase "under God" in the Pledge of Allegiance. Popular music and movie extravaganzas followed religious themes. Books of a religious, devotional, or inspirational nature proliferated, and many even made the best-seller list.

The opening passage of this section referred to a religious "revival." At least this is what many called it. Many churchmen who saw their churches filling up, who saw massive building programs quickly underwritten in full with cash and pledges, who noted their denominations annually opening new mission congregations numbering in the dozens and even hundreds can hardly be blamed for speaking in such terms. Finally their preaching and various other efforts in a life of dedication to religion was bearing some tangible fruit. Religion was really "catching on" and getting through to people. Observing these phenomena sociologically, however, we should be more cautious in assessing what was going on. As A. Roy Eckardt observes, there was "a manifest upsurge of *interest* in religion."[23] Whether this reflected a true revivial in the sense of increasing dedication and commitment is difficult if not impossible to determine.

What we do know is that the period following World War II found many more people within our national boundaries, as millions of servicemen and women returned home and as the baby boom of the 1940s got

[23]Benson Y. Landis, ed., *Yearbook of American Churches 1964* (New York: National Council of Churches in the U.S.A., 1964), p. 290.

[24]Ibid., p. 283.

[25]William Lee Miller, "Piety Along the Potomac," *The Reporter*, August 17, 1954, p. 25.

[26]A. Roy Eckardt, *The Surge of Piety in America* (New York: Association Press, 1958), p. 17.

under way. A fantastic building boom accompanied the population growth as many new and some older families moved to the suburbs in search of a place to start a new life. Church facilities that had barely sufficed during a Depression and a world war, when there was relatively little new construction clearly came up short in the face of population and residential expansion. New church facilities were built where the new people now were. In some cases this meant a net gain, as the old facilities in the city remained and new facilities were built near the edges of the spreading suburban frontier. In other instances it was a trade: the downtown and inner-city churches were abandoned for the new, as a majority of the people moved out, or the former were sold for a few cents on the dollar to the sects that emerged to serve the migrants (primarily blacks) who replaced the mobile, more affluent whites who left—an excellent example of human ecological succession.

We do know that the United States was trying to piece itself together again after a long, harsh Depression and an expensive, grief-filled war. No doubt countless people were seeking moorings, eternal verities with which they could start building something new. Paul Hutchinson wrote in 1955 about the "cult of reassurance," which he described as:

> a flocking to religion, especially in middle-class circles, for a renewal of confidence and optimism at a time when these are in short supply. It is a turning to the priest for encouragement to believe that, despite everything that has happened in this dismaying century, the world is good, life is good, and the human story makes sense and comes out where we want it to come out.[27]

Further, there was in the postwar years the unsettled state of mind caused by the spectre of the atomic bomb and the uneasiness of what was termed the "menace" of communism. Many people were undoubtedly seeking a firm base on which to stand and a clear perspective from which to evaluate what was happening.

Yet we can't help but return to our prior comments about the growing population, and above all the suburban migration trends. Without a doubt something quite sociological and not particularly religious was going on as people got involved in building churches and attending them once they were built. These people were in a new place; they had left their neighborhoods of many years, perhaps even of their childhood. They were temporarily without friends or voluntary-association outlets and involvements; they were looking for human contact. A ready place which developed early in the suburban development to resolve some of these needs and problems was the church. In a real sense, our earlier discussion

[27]Quoted in ibid., p. 28.

of religion as an integrating mechanism in society has definite meaning and relevance here: religion provided social contacts, outlets, and activities for people that were quite apart from strictly religious functions or concerns.

At the height of the religious "revival" Will Herberg suggested another partial explanation for the rise of religious interest. His suggestion revolves around the third-generation hypothesis which says that while the sons of immigrants strive to deny their heritage in their struggle to "match up" to what they perceive to be true American standards and characteristics, the grandsons (the third generation), quite secure in their Americanism, look for further identity, for a heritage and a link with the past. This, Herberg feels, is available for nearly all Americans in religion, specifically the three equally alternative religions of our contemporary society—Protestantism, Catholicism, and Judaism. Since in the mid-twentieth-century United States we are essentially a nation of third- or later-generation Americans, it is therefore not surprising to see a renewal of interest in religion—a heightened interest not strictly for "religious" reasons, but for social and psychological ones as well, as people try to identify what they are besides "just an American."[28]

Certainly some reservations are in order concerning how paramount religious identity is for the majority of people. If asked, "What are you?" would not more people respond in terms of their occupation rather than their religion? It is nevertheless likely that, for some people at least, religious identity has come to serve as an important link with the past and as a source of present identity.

At this point recall our earlier discussion, in Chapter 4, of the problem inherent in the measurement of religiosity. Most of the discussion of religious revival has centered around rather low-powered measures, such as church attendance and membership. There has been little assessment of changes in intensity of religious feeling or meaning, or changes in what people believed in and are committed to (ideological dimension), or changes in behavior as a result of religious influences (consequential dimension). Thus even if we could agree that a religious revival occurred in the United States from approximately 1945 to 1965, we may be referring to little more than what Eckhardt noted—an increased *interest* in religion. And this may be somewhat of an overstatement. For example, what does an increase in church membership mean? In part it reflects the fact that requirements for church membership have in many groups become progressively less demanding and restrictive. That is, it appears to be easier to become a church member. Further, the high degree of geographic mobility of people during this period in our history, coupled

[28]Herberg, *Protestant, Catholic, Jew*, pp. 272–75.

with the tardiness of most local congregations to clear their membership lists of dropouts and people who have moved away, have undoubtedly resulted in some—in certain cases perhaps considerable—duplication hidden in comprehensive church membership figures. That is, it is likely that some people were counted two or three times within a given years' totals.

There is no point here in going further in expressing our uneasiness with unqualified assertions of a postwar religious revival, for we have made our basic point.[29] That is, although there appears to have been a definite upswing in religious interest in the post–World War II period, the upswing may not have been so great or significant as some have supposed. In a sense, religion became more highly visible. It was no longer contained solely within the walls of religious organizations. It hit the jukeboxes, the movie theaters, and the drugstore paperback bookracks. Religion was popularized, and it impinged on everyone's consciousness—much as any fad does. Just as any fad, however, some of the glitter and popularity began to fade. Glock and Stark even suggest that, solely in response to wide publicity given church membership growth in the late 1940s, there was "generated a commercial interest in producing and promoting religious literature, songs and plays with a religious motif, and commodities having religious connotations."[30] That is, commercial interests saw a new market, and the resultant visibility of religion through commercial exploitation tended to exaggerate the level of religious interest actually felt and expressed by people.

Although we could now proceed to examine developments in American religion following the postwar religious "revival" and thus bring our discussion up to date, we shall delay such an examination until Chapter 15. In that chapter we shall go into greater detail concerning the contemporary religious scene and what developed out of the postwar religious "revival" period. We now proceed in the next chapter to discuss an important theme in American religion—namely, denominationalism.

[29]Additional questions are raised by Charles Y. Glock, "The Religious Revival in America?" in *Religion and the Face in America*, ed. Jane Zahn (Berkeley: University Extension, University of California, 1959); Seymour Martin Lipset, "Religion in America: What Religious Revival?" *Columbia University Forum* 11, no. 2 (1959); and W. H. Hudson, "Are Churches Really Booming?" *Christian Century* 72, no. 51 (1955): 1494–96.

[30]Charles Y. Glock and Rodney Stark, *Religion and Society in Tension* (Chicago: Rand McNally, 1965), p. 78.

13

Denominationalism

The necessity of devoting a full chapter to a discussion of the denominational phenomenon in American religion is highlighted by a recent comment by the American sociologist Andrew Greeley to the effect that the
United States is nearly unique among world societies as a denominational
society.[1] By "denominational society" Greeley means one characterized
by neither an established church nor a protesting sect, but in which religion and the rest of the society interrelate through a considerable
number of essentially equal religious organizations. These constitute a
social organizational adjustment to the fact of religious pluralism, and
not a halfway house between sect and church.[2] Greeley's emphasis, which
is also this chapter's, is on the social organizational aspect of denominationalism. That is, we are observing here an important social phenomenon, not simply a religious one—a type of social organization that has significant impact on social structure and social interaction in American
society.

[1]Andrew Greeley, *The Denominational Society* (Glenview, Ill.: Scott, Foresman,
1972), p. 1.
[2]Ibid.

THE MULTIPLICITY OF GROUPS

The denominational character of American society is of course rooted in the fact that ours is among other things a pluralistic society, particularly insofar as religion is concerned. As we pointed out in Chapters 10 and 12, the denominational society arose not because everyone desired it, but because at the founding of our nation no one religion was sufficiently powerful to gain predominance and also because of the various philosophical perspectives and commitments of those who framed the Constitution. The result has been one of the most obvious features of denominationalism within American society—that is, the subdivision of religion in American society into a host of independent religious groups. A society could be designated as a denominational society with only a few different religious groups. But American society leaves no doubt as to its diverse denominational character, for it includes literally hundreds of religious groups. Note well that we are not referring here to the thousands of local congregations, but to larger groupings of individual congregations into more or less cohesive associations. That is, several, perhaps thousands of local congregational units identify sufficiently with one another to stand under one umbrella, so to speak, to carry out some activities and functions jointly, to perhaps share a summary statement of belief, and to think of themselves as united together and distinct from other associations of congregations who raise different umbrellas and fly different theological flags. Thus we are talking about Baptists, Methodists, Episcopalians, Presbyterians, Lutherans, Roman Catholics, Mormons, Unitarians, Reform, Conservative, and Orthodox Jews, Jehovah's Witnesses, and other fairly familiar religious groups or denominations as well as a plethora of lesser-known groups such as the Pilgrim Holiness Church, the Plymouth Brethren, the Duck River Baptists, the Free Magyar Reformed Church in America, the Bulgarian Orthodox Church in America, and so on.

There are approximately 230 such groups that maintain membership statistics and report them to the National Council of Churches. There are of course others that either simply fail to report or are opposed on principle to divulging such information. In addition, there are literally thousands of individual local congregations that we might call entrepreneurial churches that are autonomous and begin and end with the entrepreneurial religious leader who founded them. These are particularly numerous in the sect-prone inner-city ghettos, where they remain small, though one sees such entrepreneurial groups elsewhere as well. A fairly common pattern is for an evangelist to attract a following and give up traveling the tent-meeting circuit as he settles down to building a local cathedral and constituency and then broadcasts to a larger radio audience.

THE DIVERSITY OF GROUPS

Recognizing the multiplicity of religious groups in the United States is only an introduction to the great diversity among religious groups that is a second prominent feature of denominationalism in this country. The differences among denominations can be seen along a variety of dimensions, some of which we have alluded to earlier in this text.

At the level of structure and organization there is the basic distinction among episcopal, presbyterian, and congregational forms that we referred to in passing in Chapter 7. These terms refer to the structure of authority within the denomination and the relationship of the local congregation to the larger denomination with which it is affiliated. In the *episcopal* form authority proceeds from the top down—from the head of the denomination (pope, archbishops, bishops, etc.) down to his local representatives. In the *presbyterian* form authority rests more in the middle range, with elected representatives, both clergy and lay, at various levels, from that of the local congregation to the nation itself, holding regulatory and disciplinary authority over the levels below them. In the *congregational* type, authority lies, as the term implies, with the local group, with the national denomination having little authority, at least of a formal nature.

The Familial/Democratic/Dominical Typology

Richard Sommerfeld has described denominational organization from another perspective. He divides American Christian denominations into three types based on the concept of God held by various groups, which in turn he feels affects the social organization of the group and the interaction among its members. Sommerfeld's first type is the *"familial,"* which perceives of the relationship of the three figures of the Godhead as a familylike one. His examples are Roman Catholicism and Eastern Orthodoxy, in which there is a father, a son, and another member (the Holy Spirit), plus a rather prominent mother figure (the Virgin Mary). What Sommerfeld finds emphasized in these groups is the relationship of these persons even to the extent of one interceding with another. Second, he identifies the *"democratic"* type, in which specification and identification of the three figures is downplayed and the unitary character of the Deity is emphasized. Further, there is direct assess to that Deity by the human suppliant. Denominational examples are the Baptists, Methodists, United Church of Christ, and such groups as Pentecostals and Quakers. Third is the *"dominical"* type,[3] which "conceives of the Ultimate in strict Trinitarian terms, with the individual persons of the Godhead characterized by specific functions in a total division of divine labor."[4] The stress here is on the functions and tasks of each member of the Godhead—the specification of each in the division of labor. Prime contemporary examples are Lutherans and Episcopalians.

Following such differentiation in the perception of the Godhead itself, Sommerfeld cites various differences of a sociological nature. With respect to authority, in the familial type it rests with God's designates—the clergy and the clerical hierarchy (consider, for example, the reference in Roman Catholicism to the priest as "father"). In the democratic type, religious authority rests primarily with the individual and his own experience, and secondarily with the democratic vote of the members. In the dominical type, authority lies in the official doctrines of the religious organization—Scriptures and the confessional (doctrinal) statements adopted in times past by the group.

The role of the layman in these three types is consistent with the authority pattern. In the familial type the layman is to be subservient; in the democratic he is limited in influence only by the number of votes he can garner; and in the dominical he is subject to what the documents specify—if he can cite documentary support for his behavior, he is free to act.

With respect to social organization, in the familial type relationships are "vertically structured around allegiance to ranking members of the 'family.' "[5] The church itself acts as a "mother," with the lay members filling the role of "children" in the family. The resulting social organization is strongly characterized by a sense of community as the family adopts an individual both spiritually and temporally. Salvation itself is closely identified with membership in the family. This is succinctly expressed in the classic doctrine *extra ecclesiam non salus est* ("Outside the church there is no salvation").

In the democratic type the organizational emphasis is on "direct, democratic access of the individual to the Ultimate through direct divine

[3]*Dominical* is derived from the Latin word *dominicus*, meaning "belonging to a lord or the Lord"; in Christian usage it means specifically, "pertaining to or derived from Jesus Christ as Lord."
[4]Richard Sommerfeld, "Conceptions of the Ultimate and the Social Organization of Religious Bodies," *Journal for the Scientific Study of Religion* 7, no. 2 (1968); 183.
[5]Ibid., p. 186.

illumination and guidance."[6] The church is seen as a social organization designed to provide a context within which the individual can find his own relationship with the Ultimate. It is in essence a humanly contrived means or mechanism.

In the dominical type, however, the church is believed to have been created by God as the body of Christ, and its organization is strongly rooted in the authoritative documents of Bible, creeds, confessions, and doctrinal statements. Thus social organization is less subject to change than in the democratic type. The minister is God's representative and spokesman and is not simply "first among equals," as in the democratic type.

If the reader is having a bit of trouble keeping these three types completely distinct in his mind he should not be terribly surprised. There is definite overlap among these types in both their theology and their social organization. Further, changes are constantly occurring in all three types. In the familial type greater democratic participation can be observed: the "children" are not so likely simply to "be seen and not heard" as in centuries past, or even a generation ago. From the democratic and dominical ranks there is increasing emphasis on "community" and "family" relationships among the brothers and sisters in the congregation. Also, it must be noted that denominations and congregations of the democratic type also have their traditions and are not so flexible and individualized as the term might imply. In the dominical type the absolute nature of the authority of the documents is being increasingly questioned, and democratic procedures are definitely in evidence.

These categories are obviously far from airtight. We have spent some time with them, however, for two reasons. The first is to reinforce a point we made at some length in Chapter 5—that religion, or more specifically in this case, theology, has an impact on ("makes a difference" with respect to) behavior and (as in this example) on the social organization or structure of religious groups. Differing theological emphases and perceptions of God as the Ultimate contribute to differing social structures designed to worship that God and convey a message about him.

Secondly, and of prime relevance for our discussion here of denominationalism, we note that denominations are different: they have different emphases, and they organize or structure their social relationships differently. Therefore, we cannot expect them all to act the same or respond to given stimuli from the surrounding society in the same way. For example, certain kinds of social change may occur most rapidly in the familial type, with its emphasis on a father's authority along the

[6]Ibid.

lines of an authoritarian family type. If, for example, a bishop orders the integration of black and white churchgoers within his diocese, it must be done. Such integration may well take longer to achieve in the other two types. The majority vote of the church members may prohibit it. Or, in the dominical type, if the documents are unclear as to appropriate action, then a lengthy period of interpretation and conferral must take place before a decision can be reached. On the other hand, change that appears in some way advantageous to the majority can take place virtually overnight in the democratic type of religious organization.

Two important sociological principles are thus highlighted by the above discussion: (1) the theology or religious beliefs of a religious group have an impact on its social organization and patterns of social interaction; and (2) the social structure and organization of a religious group set limits on and in various other ways influence the social actions of that group and its members.

The Apollonian/Dionysian Typology

Another typology contrasts Apollonian with Dionysian religious orientation and worship style of liturgy.[7] The *Apollonian* style assumes that since the human being is basically rational and capable of controlling his biological and emotional urges, his communication with God should reflect such rationality and be characterized by moderation and gentility. The *Dionysian* emphasis rests on the observation that man is more than a strictly rational being. He has emotions and he needs to express himself individualistically. In fact, this orientation contends that an important if not primary feature of religion is the emotional dimension, including ecstatic, mystical experiences of the human with the divine. In religion one must and one does transcend the mundane rationality of life.

These descriptions of the Dionysian and Apollonian styles and orientations are likely to remind one of the religious sect and the denominational type of religious organization, respectively. Appropriately so. Yet neither should be considered an exclusive association. Some groups most properly classified as denominations nevertheless exhibit Dionysian elements, either because they have only recently evolved to denominational status and retain vestiges of their old pattern or because religious leaders, particularly at the local level, are convinced of the importance of the Dionysian element in religion and encourage it. Note, for example, the recent increase in the phenomenon of "speaking in tongues" and related pentecostal elements in such highly Apollonian denomina-

[7]See Greeley, *The Denominational Society*, p. 23.

tions as the Roman Catholic, Episcopal, Presbyterian, and Lutheran churches.

The Salvation/Social Service Typology

Another dichotomy, one alluded to in Chapter 12, is the salvation versus the social-service orientation. Although this is a less useful distinction today than it was thirty or more years ago, we'll introduce evidence later in this chapter to the effect that some differences in emphasis along these lines still exist. That is, it is more common in some denominations than in others to find the contention that the primary if not sole function of religion is to save souls for eternity, that the social problems of this world are only temporary inconveniences and discomforts when rated against the scale of eternity. Other denominations assert that there ought to be a fairly even balance between the salvation and social-service emphases. (This is of course reminiscent of the fundamentalist-modernist controversy that raged earlier in this century and that has to some extent survived in American denominational religion today.) Still other denominations, such as Reform Jews and Unitarians, essentially reverse the fundamentalist position and assert that in assessing the primary purpose of religion social service takes precedence over salvation; in fact, these two groups either deny the validity of the latter altogether or define it quite differently from the traditional Christian understanding.

Another distinction that can be made among denominations—a distinction introduced from a different perspective earlier (in Chapter 4)— is in terms of what we might call religious families or traditions. Of considerable relevance for American society are the different traditions and patterns, both theological and social, among Calvinist, Lutheran, Catholic, Jewish, and other non-Christian religions. We'll not spend time at the moment on these distinctions, inasmuch as much of the discussion would of necessity be concerned with strictly theological matters. Yet note that Sommerfeld's trichotomy presented earlier in this chapter parallels quite closely the Catholic, Calvinist, and Lutheran traditions. Also, in previous chapters we suggested some differences among these major groupings along other lines, such as political views and participation, economic perspectives, and concern for social problems. We shall expand a bit on these contrasts of a social nature in the next section of this chapter.

THE UNANIMITY MYTH

As we mentioned in Chapter 8, there is a widespread impression within American society that although there may well be some differences among at least the major religious groups in this country, especially among those within Protestantism, when you get right down to it, all these religions, particularly in terms of what they believe and profess about the nature of God and man and their interrelationship, are very similar. Stated very simply, the conviction is that all these religions teach essentially the same things—different brand names for the same product, as we described it before. In this section we wish to call this popular belief, we may designate the *"unanimity myth,"* into serious question. Clear evidence from numerous sociological studies during the past decade or so has contradicted this opinion that we call a myth quite conclusively.

The clearest evidence comes from research conducted by Glock and Stark in 1964. Their data on Roman Catholics and several Protestant groups reveal sharp cleavages among them on both doctrinal or theological questions and on social issues. For example, it is clear from Table 13–1 that there exist extreme differences even among American Protestant denominations. It is important to note that the theological issues included in the table are all fundamental, traditional beliefs of historic Christianity, most of them included in the fundamentalist creed formulated early in this century. We'll return to a discussion of the possible implications of this development in Chapter 15. At the moment, our point is simply that great differences exist and that the unanimity thesis, so far as the beliefs of Christian denominations are concerned, is quite definitely a myth.

When two non-Christian groups are compared with the data in Table 13–1 on Protestants and Catholics, the unanimity myth is shattered beyond recognition. We introduce Unitarians and Jews for comparative purposes. For example, no Unitarians in the Glock and Stark sample reported believing in a life beyond death or believing that the Devil actually exists, and only 22 percent had absolutely no doubts about God's existence.[8] Similarly, in this author's national sample, no Jews expressed belief in original sin or expected Jesus to return someday, and only 4 percent believed that the Devil actually exists.[9]

Introducing two measures from this author's national survey, we can amplify our point about the diversity of beliefs among American denominations (See Table 13–2.) Although the differences among Protestant denominations are not quite so marked in this table as in Glock and Stark's data (in part because in Table 13–2 Southern Baptists are not distinguished from other Baptists), the differences are dramatic nonethe-

[8]Charles Y. Glock and Rodney Stark, *Christian Beliefs and Anti-Semitism* (New York: Harper & Row, 1966), pp. 190, 192, 193.
[9]Ronald L. Johnstone (project director), National Opinion Research Center survey conducted for the Lutheran Council in the U.S.A., 1970.

TABLE 13-1

Proportion of Denominational Members Agreeing with Various Doctrinal Statements

Statement	Congrega-tionalist	Methodist	Episco-palian	Disciples of Christ	Presby-terian	American Lutheran	American Baptist	Missouri Lutheran	Southern Baptist	Sects	Roman Catholic
"I know God really exists and I have no doubts about it."	41%	60%	63%	76%	75%	73%	78%	81%	99%	96%	81%
"Jesus is the Divine Son of God and I have no doubts about it."	40	54	59	74	72	74	76	93	99	97	86
"Jesus was born of a virgin." (% saying: "Completely true.")	21	34	39	62	57	66	69	92	99	96	81
"Jesus walked on water." (% saying: "Completely true.")	19	26	30	62	51	58	62	83	99	94	71
"Will Jesus actually return to the earth someday?" (% answering, "Definitely.")	13	21	24	36	43	54	57	75	94	89	47
"Miracles actually happened just as the Bible says they did."	28	37	41	62	58	69	62	89	92	92	74
"There is a life beyond death." (% saying:)	36	49	53	64	69	70	72	84	97	94	75
"A child is born into the world already guilty of sin." (% saying: "Completely true.")	2	7	18	6	21	49	23	86	43	47	68

Source: Rodney Stark and Charles Y. Glock, *American Piety* (Berkeley: University of California Press, 1968), pp. 28, 33, 34, 36, 37, and 40.

TABLE 13-2

Proportion of Denominational Members Expressing Specified Attitudes Toward Selected Theological and Religious Issues

Attitude	United Church of Christ	Methodist	Episcopalian	Presby-terian	Missouri Lutheran	Other Lutheran	Baptist	Sects	Roman Catholic	Jewish
"The story in the Bible of Adam and Eve falling into sin is really only a story and did not actually take place."										
% definitely disagreeing	32%	44%	25%	39%	71%	46%	61%	67%	38%	13%
"The real purpose of religion should be to help people with their problems and needs rather than help them get to heaven."										
% definitely agreeing	39	45	31	49	24	40	27	21	37	71

Source: Ronald L. Johnstone (project director), National Opinion Research Center survey conducted for the Lutheran Council in the U.S.A., 1970.

less. Note that 71 percent of the Missouri Synod Lutherans and 67 percent of the sects disagree with the assertion about the story of Adam and
Eve being fictional and implicitly affirm that the account in Genesis is
factual. On the other hand, far fewer than half of those in the mainline
Protestant denominations (such as Methodists, Episcopalians, and Presbyterians) as well as fewer than half the Catholics disagree that the story
is fictional and appear to accept it as a factual account. Jews are least
likely (only 13 percent) to accept the story as a factual account. Similarly,
less than a quarter of Missouri Synod Lutherans and sectarians affirm
that the purpose of religion is helping with problems rather than salvation, whereas close to half the members of major Protestant denominations so affirm. Fully 71 percent of Jews definitely take the "helping
people with their problems" approach, with the remaining 29 percent
tending to favor this perspective, though not with the certainty of the
rest. No Jews felt that the purpose of religion was to help people get to
heaven.

Despite such theological diversity, American denominations have
shown considerable facility at coexisting peacefully. This is true historically of Protestants with Protestants primarily, of course. We have
already documented examples of considerable suspicion and harassment
of Roman Catholics and Jews, as well as such a religious group as the
Mormons. It has been suggested that, for Protestants at least, different
denominations are regarded by most citizens as equally valid ways of being
a religious American. In fact, the principal occasion for Protestant religious
groups to become suspicious of other Protestant groups has been when
the actions or beliefs of those others suggested less than wholehearted
commitment to the American Republic. German Lutherans, for example,
were prodded and occasionally harassed during World War I, as many
of them continued to use the German language in their churches and
schools and as some openly supported the German "fatherland." A group
such as the Jehovah's Witnesses have repeatedly felt legal and social pres-
sure because of their stands against saluting the flag and serving in the
armed forces. Amish fathers who refused to allow their children to attend
school beyond the eighth grade were periodically jailed for their convictions until 1972, when the Supreme Court ruled in their favor. Choosing
not to use the English language, refusing to salute the flag, and questioning the value of formal education raises questions in many citizens' minds
about a group's loyalty and commitment to basic American principles.
It hardly needs mentioning that both the Jehovah's Witnesses and the
Amish are sectarian groups that protest not simply against what they view
as religious error but against prevailing social structures as well.

Despite certain exceptions, such as those referred to above, we can
say that for most of the United States' history most religious groups have

felt relatively secure and have been able to pursue their business unhampered by government, other religious groups, or fellow citizens. In
short, the constitutional provision for free exercise of religion has been in
fairly effective operation.

There is, of course, a fairly certain way for a religious group to
bring down the wrath of other groups upon itself. That is active proselytizing and seeking converts from other religious groups. Actually, except for a few groups such as the Mormons and Jehovah's Witnesses and
a few small conversionist sects, this has been no serious problem. Not
that most groups have not been willing to make converts to their faith.
But they have tended to concentrate on those who were not affiliated with
any religious group, those who voluntarily knocked on the door, and
those with whom the group has been put in contact because of marriage
with a group member. In fact, most major Protestant groups, concerned
lest they inadvertently overstep the bounds of others and be accused of
proselytizing, commonly established comity arrangements with one another: particularly in expanding communities, denominations typically
divide the territory among themselves so that each has designated areas
in which to work and establish new congregations without competing
with other denominations.

ECUMENISM

The context of cooperation and peaceful coexistence described in the
preceding section is an important background factor in the rise of *ecumenism*—not simply greater cooperation but joint efforts that might lead
ultimately to the organic merger of two or more denominations. The
ecumenical movement is essentially a phenomenon of the twentieth
century and has involved much discussion and commentary. Yet despite
the great volume of literature and discussion, relatively few actual
mergers have taken place. There have been mergers among Lutheran
denominations from various Scandinavian countries once the groups had
become "Americanized," began conversing in English, and realized they
all subscribed to the same confessional and creedal statements. Specifically, there have been three of these: formation of the United Lutheran
Church in America in 1917, of the Lutheran Church in America in 1962,
and of the American Lutheran Church in 1960. All told, these three
mergers brought together ten Lutheran groups. In 1961 the Congregational Christian Churches merged with the Evangelical and Reformed
Church to form the United Church of Christ. And in 1968 a merger
was effected between the Evangelical United Brethren Church and the
United Methodist Church. Stimulated by Eugene Carson Blake's dra-

matic suggestion in 1960 for a merger of most of the major Protestant denominations in the United States, discussions have been going on for a decade within the Consultation on Church Union (COCU), which was formed to facilitate discussion and the possible ultimate merger itself. Twelve denominations originally entered the discussions of COCU. By 1972 four had withdrawn, the latest being the United Presbyterian Church, which, however, voted in 1973 to rescind its action of the previous year and rejoin the discussion.

Those involved in ecumenical discussions have been discovering the extreme difficulty of blending religious groups with unique histories, distinct theologies, and different social constituencies. Here, in a real sense, the theological differences reflected by the data in Table 13-1 become evident and important. Issues involving forms of church government (episcopal, presbyterian, or congregational), differing views of the ministry, the nature and function of the two most common Christian sacraments of baptism and holy communion (Lord's Supper), and a host of other issues make agreement and compromise extremely difficult to achieve.

Nor has ecumenical discussion been limited to Protestantism. Increasingly after 1950, Catholics, Eastern Orthodox, and Jews were brought into the ecumenical discussions, and dialogues and "conversations" began taking place between all manner of combinations of denominations—various Protestant denominations individually, and occasionally jointly with Catholics, Eastern Orthodox, and Jews. Mostly the result has been greater mutual understanding, with occasional official recognition of agreement on certain issues. But to date there is no sign of significant progress toward actual organic unification of these diverse traditions. In fact, these broader ecumenical discussions appear to have reached their zenith in the late 1960s and early 1970s.

Certainly ecumenism has been an absorbing subject for religious leaders and groups. But sociologists have also been interested, for ecumenism is a sociological phenomenon, not simply a religious one. Sociological interest has focused less on what is going on than on why ecumenical interest has developed at all. What, if any, are the social sources of this phenomenon? Peter Berger has suggested that one primary reason is economic—that is, rising costs, particularly for buildings and staff, suggest joint effort and cost sharing.[10] It appears that denominations have become increasingly aware that duplication of effort is not only wasteful, but ultimately impossible to continue forever. Pooling resources, using one missionary governing board to supervise forty missionaries rather than two boards each supervising twenty missionaries, building one church edifice instead of two in a new subdivision—ideas such as these

[10]Peter Berger, "A Market Model for the Analysis of Ecumenity," *Social Research* 30, no. 1 (1963), 77–93.

have begun to make economic sense to denominations. Such recognition would probably not have come so quickly had religious membership expansion continued past the early 1960s at its post–World War II pace. But as we'll discuss in Chapter 15, by the 1970s membership growth in the major denominations had either essentially ceased or in fact begun to decline. In the face of declining membership and a concomitant decline in contributions, denominations have been forced to become cost-conscious and to look for ways to economize and increase efficiency. At this point groups begin regarding the theological justification for ecumenism as more convincing than ever before.

A possible factor underlying the problem of stable or declining membership is that while church membership in this country has shown a fairly steady increase for nearly two centuries, the growth appears to have "topped out" and stabilized, if not begun to slide backward. It is very possible that denominations have "converted" and brought into their folds proportionately nearly all the people they can ever expect to. Few of those not yet convinced to join are likely to be convinced in the future. Thus one of the activities that before the mid-1960s absorbed much of the energy of local churches and of denominations—namely, home missionary activities—(the establishment of new congregations to meet the demands of population shifts)—has declined and no longer commands the attention it once did. What, then, are church leaders at all levels within the structure as well as laymen in the congregations to do by way of church work? What kind of religious frontier is left to explore and conquer? One option that excites the imagination of many is to try to break down ancient barriers that have kept denominations apart. A divided Christendom is defined as a "scandal." What with the recent emphasis in American society on overcoming prejudices, tolerating differences among people, and compromising old absolutes regarding what is good and what is evil, it is only natural that religious groups should begin to work at cleaning up their houses, so to speak, with respect to relating to other religious groups. Ecumenical discussion and activity has become popular as a consequence. The challenge for the churches during the remaining third of the twentieth century has become for many the ecumenical goal of a united Christendom. Yet at this point we need to point out again that enthusiasm and commitment in theory to ecumenism have not been enough to effect much notable success since 1968.

Robert Lee has suggested that increased interest and activity in ecumenism is a fairly natural outgrowth of a growing cultural unity within American society. Writing in 1960, Lee saw signs of growing cultural unity in such phenomena and developments as the pervasiveness of mass culture, the instantaneous dissemination of similar information throughout the land through the mass media, the replacement of sectionalism by the regional concept, and a long list of other signs. Lee of course wrote before the youth counterculture got under way, before the issue of American participation in the Vietnam War exerted its divisive influence, before the development of the black power ideology, before the loss of faith and trust associated with the Watergate revelations. Perhaps these latter developments help explain why there is less talk of ecumenism today than there was ten or fifteen years ago.[11]

Another factor that undoubtedly fostered ecumenism in the two decades following the close of World War II is the long-term trend toward autonomous bureaucracies in the major denominations. As numerous sociological studies have shown, those persons in high-level positions in organizations are the most tolerant and accepting and understanding of competing organizations. High-level labor union officials, for example, often interact more harmoniously with their counterparts in management, from whom they will ultimately be trying to extract concessions to union demands, than they do with the rank-and-file union members they represent. It has been suggested that such leaders may even have difficulty "demanding" certain things that they have come to believe, through their contacts with management, the employer cannot afford. Similarly, officials of church bureaucracies tend to interact with comparable officials of other denominations, whom they find to be much like themselves. They find it easy to get along with them and therefore counsel that the denominations themselves ought to be able to get along as well. These church bureaucrats tend to be more liberal than the rank-and-file clergymen in the denominations in the first place—a fact that may by itself go far in explaining why there is so much discussion of ecumenism by religious leaders but why little of a concrete nature in terms of denominational merger and extensive cooperative endeavors seems to occur. The local churches are likely not so interested or convinced as their representatives in the denominational bureaucracies.

We shall refer to ecumenism again in Chapter 15. Suffice it to say in summarizing our discussion to this point that ecumenism, at least during this century, has paralleled denominationalism. That is to say, both have thrived, even though this would seem to involve an inherent contradiction: denominationalism appears to be as viable as ever, ecumenism is also alive and at least fairly well. Part of the answer to this seeming contradiction is that in ecumenical conversations and activities denominations have found themselves looking more closely not only at others but at themselves, their heritage, and their uniqueness. This analysis may

---

[11]Robert Lee, *The Social Sources of Church Unity* (Nashville, Tenn.: Abingdon Press, 1960).

have led them to a new and strong appreciation of themselves in their uniqueness. In fact, ours is a pluralistic society which today encourages its subgroups to celebrate and preserve their uniqueness so long as they support the fundamental values of the society. The upshot is that denominations may not be particularly ready to give up their identities. Yet they see much value in cooperation and certainly no value in cutthroat competition. Hence ecumenism remains viable also. While not going the whole ecumenical route and effecting outright organizational mergers, denominations feel free to cooperate and engage in joint tasks while each retains its identity. Even if such activities should turn out to be but a single stage or way station on the track leading to ultimate organizational union of several or even all denominations, the train will probably be able to stand at this station for a long time—energized, but with little forward movement down the track.

THE CONTINUED VIABILITY OF DENOMINATIONALISM

We now return more explicitly to the denominational phenomenon with which this chapter is concerned and discuss additional sociological reasons why the denominational phenomenon has remained so dominant a feature of American religion—of American society, for that matter. In the face of such strong pressures, both theological and sociological, toward ecumenism, and given yet another unifying tendency (which we shall discuss in Chapter 16)—the phenomenon of civil religion, which at least implicitly would replace traditional religion with a religion focusing on the society itself—why is American society still divided into so many distinctive religious groups? It is not enough to point out, as we have already, that important doctrinal differences divide denominations, or that another factor keeping denominations distinct is the type of organizational tradition or liturgical emphasis, or the salvation/social-concern issue, or the differences between Apollonian and Dionysian orientations. All of these are significant, and all represent a combination of theological and sociological factors and pressures. But there are two other factors, which are primarily sociological, that reinforce the denominational heritage which American society continually updates.

The Ethnic Factor

The first factor reinforcing denominationalism that we want to discuss—one strongly emphasized by Andrew Greeley—is the important ethnic function that religion in American society continues to serve. That is, one's religious affiliation represents for a great many people much more than commitment to a set of religious beliefs, symbols, and rituals. Religious affiliation may also become a means people use to define their identity—"who they are and where they stand in a large and complex society."[12] Greeley mentions that this definition and location of self may be the most important function religion performs for some people. For others it is intermixed with the belief system and ethical code that the religious group stands for.

The origin of religion as an American ethnic phenomenon rests with the fact that most of the nationality groups that immigrated into the United States brought their churches with them and transplanted them on American soil. The Norwegians, Swedes, Finns, and Danes brought their Lutheran churches. Some Germans brought their Lutheran church; other Germans brought their Catholic church; still others brought their Reformed church. The Irish brought their Catholic church; the Italians and Poles did likewise. And so on. But there's more to it than that. The religious organization for these immigrants was immediately an important source of identification. In many cases it was a safe place for people to use their native tongue, and it linked them in their present insecurity in a new environment to a secure tradition or heritage. As the immigrant left the old cohesive communal relationship of the peasant village, with its primary relationships and awareness of who one was in relation to others, and entered a strange land of secondary relationships, he clung to his ethnic group in order to preserve some semblance of identity and a linkage with people who could provide empathy. Some of these people may not have been particularly "religious" before and perhaps wouldn't have scored high on certain measures of religiosity in the new land, yet many found in the religious group an opportunity to meet those with whom they shared a heritage, people who spoke their language in both a literal and a figurative sense. Andrew Greeley says that denominational membership makes available to Americans "a fellowship which is highly important in compensating for those intimate relationships of life which seem to have been lost when the peasant village was left behind."[13] Clearly, we see religion performing the "belonging" function emphasized by Max Weber and discussed both in the chapter on religious origins (Chapter 3) and the chapter on the societal functions of religion (Chapter 8).

It should be noted that the opportunity for religion to serve an ethnic function, particularly for immigrant groups, was in part made possible by the religious pluralism that had existed in the United States

---

[12]Greeley, *The Denominational Society*, p. 108.
[13]Ibid., p. 114.

from colonial times. Religious diversity (pluralism) was valued and encouraged. Therefore, the immigrant could turn to his religious group as a source of belonging without undue fear of reprisal. Not that the established Americans were always happy with the religious-ethnic enclaves. But they could do little about them and still be true to the American religious heritage and precedent. That resentment and suspicion did erupt in harassment and violence is attested to in the discussion of the "Protestant Crusade" in Chapter 12; the point to be made here is that not only was anti-Catholicism being expressed, but also anti-Irish and anti-cheap urban labor sentiments as well.

Acknowledging the ethnic nature and function of religion in the United States raises some serious questions about the "melting-pot" hypothesis—the idea that the United States has accommodated and homogenized peoples from a diversity of cultures and backgrounds. It is hardly even the triple melting pot of Protestants, Catholics, and Jews that some have suggested. Actually, historically it was Dutch Reformed, German Lutheran, Scottish Presbyterian, and so on, for the Protestant immigrant groups, and the Polish Catholic, Serbian Catholic, Irish Catholic, and so on—not simply Catholic. It was even to some extent Russian Jew, German Jew, and so on—not simply Jewish for the third major religious family in America. That is, Americans were not only ethnically "hyphenated" as citizens (Irish-Americans, German-Americans, Polish-Americans, etc.), but they were ethnically "hyphenated" as members of religious groups as well. The ethnic factor has thus been more important in patterning American religion than has often been recognized.

One final comment in connection with our discussion of the ethnic feature of religion in America is that the numerical strength of American religion is in significant degree related to the ethnic factor. Because the religious group was able to serve as an ethnic rallying point and to provide an identity for people and a sense of belonging to something more intimate and meaningful than the diffuse, cold, and distant society, people gained a religious commitment that, though perhaps less intense for many as the importance of ethnic identity fades for them, they are still reluctant to cut themselves off from completely. Religion has served and does serve an important social function as an ethnic community, which exists quite in addition to any strictly "religious" function it may serve. In many cases people have even been able to live out their entire lives while only rarely leaving the religious-ethnic community. Scattered throughout the land are ethnic-religious communities where nearly 100 percent of the citizens are of a single national origin and a single religious persuasion and where the public schools become almost parochial ones. But one need not be a farmer or a shopkeeper in such a community to live out one's life in an ethnic subcommunity. One may be a city dweller and a medical doctor, or an accountant, or an attorney, or an academician—and still serve only or almost exclusively members of the ethnic community into which he was born.

The Social-Class Factor

The second additional factor which reinforces denominationalism in American society is social class. We spent considerable time in Chapter 11 discussing the relationship between religion and social class and will therefore do little more than mention it again here. But it is of considerable relevance to our present interest in denominationalism. Religion does reflect the class structure. Denominations are disproportionately constituted of different social classes, sects are almost universally a lower-social-status phenomenon, and social mobility frequently results in change in religious group affiliation that corresponds more appropriately in the eyes of the community with one's newly achieved social status.

The fact that religion reflects the class structure of the society is of course not unique to American society. Differences in religious orientation and practice have been observed in less complex societies that have religious systems at an earlier stage on Bellah's continuum of religious evolution.[14] A distinctive feature of the "archaic" stage of religious evolution, according to Bellah, is a clearly stratified society and fairly distinctive religious expressions according to class level. The upper-status people who control the political and military power usually claim superior religious status as well. Bellah states that noble families are proud of their divine descent and often have special priestly functions.[15] We can point, for example, to ancient Greece where there appears to have been a fairly clear distinction between the religion of the plebians and that of the patricians. The plebians related to gods associated with agriculture, localized gods, and gods related to magical animal symbols. The patricians were absorbed with the Olympian gods, such as Zeus, Apollo, Aphrodite, Athena, and Hermes, who oversaw broader areas of life, universal principles and emotions, and broader societal concerns. Similarly in the Hindu religion. The major beliefs and practices associated with the Vedas and Upanishads and the concepts of Brahama and Brahaman are largely unknown to the lower castes, who in fact have traditionally

---

[14]Robert Bellah outlines five states of religious evolution: the primitive, the archaic, the historical, the early modern, and the modern. Robert N. Bellah, "Religious Evolution," *American Sociological Review* 29, no. 3 (1964): 358–74; reprinted in idem, *Beyond Belief* (New York: Harper & Row, 1970), chapter 2.
[15]Bellah, *Beyond Belief*, pp. 30–31.

been deemed unworthy of being given the sacred truths. Instead, the lower castes learn the elemental Hindu ideas of samsara, karma, and dharma and relate to a variety of local gods and spirits.

In American society we have fairly clear evidence of Weber's "theodicy of escape" and of Marx's and Freud's compensation-for-deprivation function of religion for the lower classes, on the one hand, and the "theodicy of good fortune" for the economically and socially successful members of the society on the other hand. The upshot is that various denominations and religious groups appeal disproportionately to different social classes. The fact that the United States has been and continues to be a highly stratified if somewhat mobile society has tended to reinforce and preserve denominational and religious diversity as different religious groups provide different things to different people.

14

The Black Church

In Chapter 11 we introduced the subject of religion and the black American. We focused both on the historical issue once facing American Christians of whether to convert black slaves to Christianity and on the recent issue of the relationship of white churches to the black civil rights movement. In the present chapter we wish to pick up at the historical point when the issue of the conversion of slaves had been resolved, and trace the development of the black church as a social institution. In doing so we shall work within three major sections: an overview of the historical development of the institution; an examination of the role of militancy versus social pacifism so far as the black church is concerned; and a discussion of contemporary religious issues and developments within the black church and the black community, together with an assessment of the continuing role of religion in the black community.

THE HISTORICAL DEVELOPMENT OF THE BLACK CHURCH AS A SOCIAL INSTITUTION

Following the consensus in the United States around the turn of the nineteenth century that slaves should be converted to Christianity and still remain slaves, the early pattern of worship services found black slaves and whites in the same congregations—the blacks usually occupying the balcony, the whites the main floor. Such joint worship was deemed advisable because white masters could then keep an eye on their "possessions" and be reassured that their slaves weren't listening to a different message—such as a call to insurrection.

The Deculturation Process

Whether slaveowners were always conscious of it or not, for blacks conversion to Christianity and joint worship served as part of the deculturation process. At the very least, religious conversion served as a useful follow-up and capstone to the deliberate efforts by slave traders and owners to deculturate the slave, to strip him of his African culture and heritage. This was accomplished by such tactics as breaking up families and prohibiting any two slaves from the same African village or tribe to be sold to work on the same plantation. One highly significant concomitant of this tactic was that the slaves usually shared no common language and thus could only converse in the English language that they had to learn. In short, much of the original culture of these people was stripped from them in less than a generation.

Obviously slaves couldn't very successfully preserve and practice many shared religious patterns either. Christianity, which was substituted for the ancient religions, itself became an agent for subduing and pacifying the slaves. What slaves heard preached was submission to authority, obedience, obligation to perform one's duty, commitment to nonviolence, and promise of splendid eternal rewards in heaven for all who led proper lives and made appropriate commitments during one's earthly sojourn. "Some God has made to be masters, some to be slaves. But we'll all receive a grand reward in the hereafter": this is what has been waggishly referred to as "pie-in-the-sky by and by."

Kenneth Stampp has well summarized the use to which religion was put with regard to controlling the behavior of slaves:

> Through religious instruction the bondsmen learned that slavery had divine sanction, that insolence was as much an offense against God as against the temporal master. They received the Biblical command that servants should obey their masters, and they heard of the punishments awaiting the disobedient slave in the hereafter. They heard, too, that eternal salvation would be their reward for faithful service, and that on the day of judgment God would deal impartially with the poor and the rich, the black man and the white.[1]

Stampp also mentions a book titled *Suggestions on the Religious Instruction of the Negroes in the Southern States* written by Charles C. Jones and published by the national Presbyterian Board of Publication.

[1] Kenneth M. Stampp, *The Peculiar Institution* (New York: Knopf, 1956), p. 158.

Stampp cites Jones as advising missionaries to ignore the "civil condi-tion" of slaves and to pay no attention to complaints against their mas-ters. In preaching to slaves ministers should condemn "every vice and evil custom," urge the "discharge of every duty," and support the "peace and order of society." They should, in sum, teach the slaves to give "re-spect and obedience [to] all those whom God in his providence has placed in authority over them."[2]

Emerging Independence of the Black Church

The early pattern of joint worship of masters and slaves in the same church did not remain the common one, probably in large part because the white masters wanted one message for their slaves, another for them-selves. Therefore, another early pattern on the larger plantations was for the owner to provide special religious leaders and preachers for the slaves. These were not always white preachers, but occasionally trusted slaves who had a "gift" for preaching. Also fairly early the Baptists and Meth-odists began missionary activities among the slaves, and they enjoyed con-siderable success—for many of the same reasons that they succeeded with white settlers on the frontier (see Chapter 12). Thus the early pattern of joint worship in the same congregations was gradually replaced by segre-gated worship in white and black "congregations." Strictly speaking, except in the North and in a few border cities, slaves did not form their own independent congregations, largely because of laws forbidding slave assemblies. Informally, however, on many plantations essentially autono-mous slave churches developed under "trusted" slave ministers. Of course, their services and activities were usually carefully monitored by the mas-ter or his overseer. Nevertheless, such congregations of slaves set the stage for the eventual emergence of the black church as the major, if not the only, formal group or organization over which blacks, after Emancipa-tion, had essential control. Thus we can begin to understand the impor-tance and centrality that black religious organizations have assumed in the black community to this day.

Although for various reasons whites began to tolerate separate reli-gious organizations and activities for blacks, it was not without some apprehension. Richard Wade points out that as late as 1847 "many citi-zens" in Charleston expressed their discomfort over permitting religious institutions for blacks, particularly as it resulted in separate congrega-tions. They feared the independence, the absence of the control and au-thority of the master, the taste of freedom it provided, and the opportu-nity for black leaders to emerge and learn skills.[3]

[2]Quoted in ibid., p. 160.
[3]Richard C. Wade, *Slavery in the Cities: The South, 1820–1860* (New York: Oxford University Press, 1964), p. 83.

In the North, after some initial integrated worship, free blacks began to pull out and form their own congregations and, soon, their own denominations. In fact, the earliest all-black denominations, the African Methodist Episcopal Zion Church and the African Methodist Episcopal Church, organized in 1796 and 1816, respectively, were founded by free blacks who had experienced harassment and "balcony segregation" in white congregations.

The Functions of the Black Church

After the Civil War and Emancipation, with most legal restrictions against black assemblies lifted, there occurred a mass withdrawal of blacks from racially mixed congregations and even denominations. What had begun as an outlet or escape and a focal institution for their lives under slavery continued to serve the same functions after Emancipation. Although the following evaluation by Richard Wade concerns the functions of religion for blacks under slavery, the pattern then established continued after Emancipation.

> Slavery had stripped [blacks] of any meaningful pattern of life beyond that of the master and their bondage. The family could furnish none. No tradition could provide roots into a history without servitude. Neither today nor tomorrow offered any expectation of a life without the present stigma. Deprived of nostalgia for the past and unable to discover any real meaning in the present, the blacks sought relief and consolation in a distant time. In the church, with their own kind, amid songs of redemption and the promises of Paradise, a lifeline could be thrown into the future.[4]

The prominent black leader and sociologist W. E. B. DuBois states that once blacks assumed complete control over their church following Emancipation, the local black church became the center of its members' social life, the primary medium of communication and information exchange and dissemination, and even the organizer of entertainment and amusement. With regard to the last function he lists such activities and functions as concerts, suppers, socials, fairs, literary exercises and debates, cantatas, plays, excursions, picnics, surprise parties, and celebrations.[5]

Gunnar Myrdal describes the black church as a "community center par excellence."[6] In most black communities the church was the only institution where blacks not only enjoyed autonomy and were free from the prying eyes of whites but also had access to physical facilities in which to conduct social activities.

[4]Ibid., pp. 162–63.
[5]W. E. B. DuBois, *The Philadelphia Negro* (Philadelphia: University of Pennsylvania, 1899), p. 201.
[6]Gunnar Myrdal, *An American Dilemma* (New York: Harper & Brothers, 1944), p. 938.

But to note such a function as the above is only to begin to list the important roles of the religious group or institution in the life of black Americans. First there is the economic function: "A study of economic co-operation among Negroes," DuBois has stated, "must begin with the church group."[7] Many black churches early formed mutual-aid or "beneficial" societies designed to help members survive financial crises associated with illness or death of family members. These were actually incipient insurance companies. In rural communities the emphasis seemed to be particularly on burial "insurance" to provide the members with a "decent Christian burial."

The black churches have also played a significant role in education over the years. Frequently black ministers established a school along with a church. Just as the original purpose of slave education had been to communicate the Christian Gospel and enable slaves to read the Bible, these minister-educators sought to raise the spiritual understanding of their people. When the Julius Rosenwald Fund aided in building over five thousand schools for blacks in the South during the first third of the twentieth century, black churches played an important role in supplementing those funds: E. Franklin Frazier notes that southern blacks contributed 17 percent of the total cost of $28 million (Rosenwald Fund, 15 percent; white friends, 4 percent; taxes, 64 percent), and that they raised much of their share through church suppers and various other church-sponsored programs.[8]

There was also impetus among the black denominations following the Civil War to erect educational institutions independent of white philanthropy. This plan was primarily motivated by the desire to provide a better-educated ministry—a project Frazier feels was not eminently successful, since the black denominational schools "never attained a high level as educational institutions . . . [and] have generally nurtured a narrow religious outlook and have restricted the intellectual development of Negroes."[9] Frazier also notes that the authoritarian demeanor and antiintellectualism exhibited by many black ministers have tended to inhibit the black churches from making a strong, positive contribution to education.[10] In other words, although certainly contributing to educational advancement for blacks, the black church has not been as significant an influence in this sphere as it might have been.

Supporting the significance of the black church's role in educating blacks, however, Wade mentions that some of the protracted pre-Emanci-

---

[7]W. E. B. DuBois, *Economic Cooperation Among Negroes* (Atlanta: Atlanta University Press, 1907), p. 54.
[8]E. Franklin Frazier, *The Negro Church in America* (New York: Schocken, 1963), p. 40.
[9]Ibid., p. 41.
[10]Ibid., p. 42.

pation opposition to autonomous black churches—or, for that matter, to Christianity for blacks at all—centered around the observation that some blacks were becoming literate in the process of their religious instruction. For many whites feared black literacy as much as black independence in their religious activities.[11]

A third area of influence and involvement on the part of the black religious institution has been politics. During the Reconstruction period several black ministers and bishops in the South became federal and state officials, state legislators, and U.S. congressmen; one was even elected a U.S. senator. With the end of Reconstruction and the resumption of white supremacy, however, blacks were virtually eliminated from public political life, and the black church then became, as Frazier observes, "the arena of . . . political activities" for black citizens.[12] As the sole major institution over which they had complete control, the church became the major context within which ambitious individuals could aspire to leadership and achieve distinction and status. In particular, the black church turned out to be the most likely source of power, upward mobility, and economic success for black males. Black churches thus soon overflowed with aspiring ministers, apprentice ministers, and "jackleg preachers" who literally waited in the wings for a chance to preach, prove their ability, and gather a following or congregation for themselves.

In the South the church also represented the only outlet of political expression for the black rank and file denied the franchise in local, state, and national elections. The only place they could vote and make significant choices was in their church—as they elected local officers and denominational representatives.

We must note also that as the franchise was granted or returned to blacks, particularly in the North, black churches became more politically involved than most of their white counterparts. Candidates for political office were frequently invited to speak in black churches during or after Sunday services, ministers urged their followers to vote for particular candidates, and partisan campaign literature was made available in church buildings—all to a greater extent than in white churches, most of which counseled keeping politics and religion separate.

Although no hard data on the frequency with which black churches were involved in politics are available from the distant past, 1963 data on black clergymen in Detroit reveals that 45.5 percent allowed political candidates access to their churches, 62.7 percent permitted distribution of campaign literature from their churches, 67.8 percent explicitly encouraged their members to work with the political parties in their neighborhoods, and 30.5 percent even told their members for whom they

11Wade, *Slavery*, pp. 173–77.
12Frazier, *The Negro Church*, p. 43.

should vote. Further, 24.4 percent of black clergymen in Detroit had at some time actively worked for a political party at the local level.[13]

It is important to note that the more militantly committed a black clergyman is to the civil rights movement and its goals, the more likely he is to engage in the political behaviors cited above. We shall focus on important differences among contemporary black clergymen later in this chapter. At this point we simply wish to document that the black church has been and continues to be a fairly active political organization. Although no comparable hard data for white churches are available, every indication is that on the average white churches are not so politically involved. Political officeholders and aspirants have long known that the black clergyman is an important link in their relationship with the black community. In Floyd Hunter's study of the power structure of Atlanta, he found that leaders in the dominant white community believed that if anything was to be done through leadership channels in the black community, the black clergymen needed to be contacted first.[14] In his study of the reform movement in Philadelphia politics, James Reichly designated black clergymen as prime political leaders in the black community[15] And T. R. Solomon found that black clergymen exerted considerable leadership and influence in Detroit so far as the black vote was concerned.[16]

At a more general level than politics per se, it is important to observe that historically the black minister was not only an important leader of black citizens in rural and small-town communities, but often virtually the only one. Even in a city such as New Orleans as recently as 1960, Daniel Thompson concluded that "Negro ministers constitute the largest segment of the leadership class."[17]

Finally, we must say that permeating all of the above functions of the black church is the fundamental function that the black church performs for its members of representing what Frazier calls "a refuge in a hostile white world."[18] The black church has provided a structural context for interaction in which blacks could not only express their deepest feelings and longings but also attain some measure of status (in God's eyes, if in no one else's). Earlier, religion provided black slaves some ca-

[13]Ronald L. Johnstone, "Militant and Conservative Community Leadership Among Negro Clergymen" (Ph.D. dissertation, University of Michigan, 1963), pp. 126–27.
[14]Floyd Hunter, *Community Power Structure* (Chapel Hill: University of North Carolina Press, 1953), pp. 117–118.
[15]James Reichly, *The Art of Government* (Philadelphia: Greater Philadelphia Magazine, 1958), p. 21.
[16]T. R. Solomon, "Participation of Negroes in Detroit Elections" (Ph.D. dissertation, University of Michigan, 1939), p. 65.
[17]Daniel C. Thompson, *The Negro Leadership Class* (Englewood Cliffs, N.J.: Prentice-Hall, 1963), p. 34.
[18]Frazier, *The Negro Church*, p. 44.

tharsis as well as hope for eventual freedom even though they were now in temporal bondage. Later, in a similar way, the "emancipated" blacks, after a brief opportunity to participate somewhat freely in the wider society during Reconstruction, were soon again excluded from participation in the white man's world except as inferiors. They were disfranchised, given a skimpy and inferior education, and accorded far less than justice by a court system that operated with a double standard of justice. These "emancipated" blacks needed escape and hope as much as their enslaved fathers and grandfathers. Where could a black find refuge amid such hostility and discrimination? The place was predominantly the church, which whites left alone.

Most of what we have been describing in the foregoing paragraphs applies most appropriately to the black church since the days of Reconstruction. During slavery, when the black church had to be the "invisible institution," many were the sounds of freedom in black religion. Although it is difficult to distinguish whether calls for freedom in black slaves' religion were for ultimate spiritual freedom in heaven, or for temporal freedom from bondage, or perhaps a subtle and even unconscious combination of both ideas, there is evidence that black religion did somewhat fan slaves' hopes of physical freedom. The leader of the better-known slave uprisings, for example, used ample Biblical imagery and justification for their actions. Consider, for example, the rebellion led by Nat Turner, himself a black minister. Moreover, some of the northern black churches composed of freed blacks stood squarely for slaves' freedom as they served as important links in the "Underground Railway."

But following the Civil War, when the issue was no longer slavery but the pervasive racism that securely kept blacks "in their place," whatever small amount of protest and call for freedom there had been receded in the face of escapist and otherworldly emphases. It is this post–Civil War pattern of black religion that nurtured the stereotype of the black church that so many whites cling to: the revivalist or sectarian emotionalism and escapism that an accommodating "Uncle Tom," albeit a fiery and eloquent preacher, supervised and promoted. Here one sees the subservient, peacemaking, don't-rock-the-boat style of black minister who knew only too well that his job was to keep his place, encourage submission and fatalistic acquiescence on the part of his congregation, and preach an otherworldly gospel. If he did his job well, his choir would receive an invitation to sing in a white church or two during the year, and he could look forward to a little free coal for the church and parsonage in the winter.[19]

[19]See Ronald L. Johnstone, "Negro Preachers Take Sides," *Review of Religious Research* 11, no. 1 (1969); 81.

The black church became overwhelmingly a haven, away from the prying eyes of whites, where blacks could exercise autonomy but where there appeared to be little challenge to the status quo. In fact, the observation by an anonymous black preacher probably conveys even more truth than humor: "Come weal or woe, my status is quo." Rare was the black minister who took up the banner of change or social revolution at the risk of losing a fairly comfortable position whose advantages included high personal status and power and income as great if not usually greater than the majority of his fellow blacks. Black ministers were also occasionally accused of being "bought off" by elements in the white power structure as they were accorded the courtesy of speaking for or representing the black community and serving as the funnel for the table crumbs of white philanthropy.

With little impetus for challenge and change coming from black ministers, who did reasonably well for themselves under a system of racism, and with the rank-and-file black church members finding solace, escape, recreation, and temporal autonomy in the black church, it is not surprising that the black church proceeded through the decades of segregation and discrimination tacitly approving, or at least certainly not openly challenging, prevailing social structures and patterns. Not that there were no voices of protest coming from the black church and its clergy. Not that black religion was totally acquiescent in the face of a dominant racism. On the contrary, there were definite protests and other forms of aggressive reaction in the name of religion. In fact, although we have been stressing the accommodating, otherworldly, withdrawal response of black religion—essentially the sect approach—in the face of white racism and exclusion from the society's mainstream, there has always been a mildly aggressive though persistent reaction stemming from within the ranks of black religion.

MILITANCY IN THE BLACK CHURCH

The Father Divine Style

Four types of black religious "aggression" in the face of racism can be distinguished.[20] One is typified by the Father Divine Peace Mission that flourished in the 1930s and early 1940s. Here was a religious group that provided blacks with food and occasional job opportunities during the Great Depression as many blacks migrated to northern cities in

[20]*Aggression* is understood here and in the discussion that follows in a very general sense of direct action of some kind that is perceived as likely to improve the condition of oneself or one's group.

search of employment. Although the Father Divine Peace Mission presents a fascinating study in theology (Father Divine was viewed as God himself), our interest here is in the group's commitment to a social service type of action that fed and housed thousands of needy persons over a period of years. Although this approach of course did not strike significantly at the root causes of problems facing black Americans and worked only at the remedial level of treating symptoms, there was here and in similar groups a clear manifestation of aggressiveness in the name of black religion. We are forced to conclude, however, that the overall net impact of such food and lodging efforts benefited only a small minority of needy blacks.

The Black Nationalism Style

Another example of aggression in the name of religion in the black community is similar to the foregoing, but more far-reaching and enduring. That is the self-help philosophy and activities of black nationalist religious organizations, best represented (most recently, at least) by the Nation of Islam ("Black Muslims"). Here is a group dating back to the early 1930s that stresses black supremacy, advocates racial separation, and maintains rigid membership requirements (religious dietary laws and moral discipline). Major emphases are to pool economic resources, "buy black," secure an education, learn skills, work hard, cultivate self-discipline, and in general engage in cooperative self-help—all in the name of religion (in this instance a version of Islam whose validity other branches of Islam tend not to recognize). Considerable credit has been given the Black Muslims for their success in rehabilitating ex-convicts and improving the economic welfare of their adherents. While the movement has not attracted hordes of blacks into its ranks, its success with the few it has attracted is worthy of attention. Again, our point here is simply that in the name of religion some American blacks have been aggressive with respect to improving their life situation.

The Individual Aggressive Style

A third example of black aggression in the name of or from the ranks of religion would be the numerous examples of individual black ministers from the more standard black denominations who either took it upon themselves to extract philanthropy from the white community or became involved as individuals in political activities that concerned blacks. An excellent example of the latter activity is seen in Detroit in the late 1930s and early 1940s during the bitter labor struggle to unionize the Ford Motor Company. Using various ingenious techniques, Henry Ford and his aides had long kept a substantial contingent of blacks out of the labor movement. Although Ford as early as 1910 established the policy that at least 10 percent of his employees would be blacks, every prospective black employee needed a letter of recommendation from a black minister attesting to his moral fiber and (at least implicitly) his antiunion commitment. Black ministers were expected to emphasize not only what a benefactor Henry Ford was to blacks, but what a disaster unionization would be for black workers. By a system of judiciously placed contributions and periodic visits, Henry Ford kept a majority of black clergymen "in line." Three "maverick" black ministers, however, became outspoken leaders of the unionization movement and acted on the conviction that unionization would benefit their fellow blacks. The Reverends Horace White, Charles Hill, and Malcom Dade were convinced that accommodation and an otherworldly gospel should be replaced or at least supplemented by challenges to existing structures and concern with the problems and opportunities of this world. Such religious leaders in the black community appear to have been rare, yet their presence merits noting in our summary of aggressive social action emanating from black religious sources.

Organized Militancy

A fourth example of aggression from the black church is more recent. As with the example just cited, the action centers in the clergy, but is more organized and represents a greater proportion of black clergymen. The emergence of black clergymen organized for social protest action directed against institutionalized racism occurred at the height of the civil rights movement in the early 1960s. In various urban communities, such as Baltimore, Detroit, and St. Louis, black clergymen organized what amounted to economic boycotts, called "selective-buying" campaigns, against firms that were guilty of blatant employment and promotion discrimination against blacks and whose representatives refused to discuss the issue.

For example, the usual procedure in Detroit was for a committee of the larger clergy group that called itself The Negro Preachers of Detroit and Vicinity to request an audience with executives of the company suspected of discrimination in order to discuss their policies and to check into the proportion of blacks employed at various levels in the organization. Following this initial contact, the committee would return with specific requests. The hope was that the company would cooperate by agreeing to hire a number of qualified black workers at various levels within the organization as requested by the black preachers. The company was then given a few weeks to implement this proposal, after which time (they would be informed) an economic boycott of their product(s) would commence if compliance with the request was not forthcoming. If, after a three-to-four-week period, the company still delayed and resisted, the committee would contact every black preacher in the community and ask that they cooperate and help their black brothers and sisters in the community by reading a letter to their congregations the following Sunday morning urging their members not to buy the products of a specified company. A typical letter announcing one of their successes is reproduced below.

"The Negro Preachers of Detroit and Vicinity," a core group of some twenty to twenty-five black ministers who organized the selective-buying program and who comprised the negotiating committees, studiously avoided formalizing their organization, had no "official" name, no regular place of meeting, no formal officers, no permanent committees, and no printed constitution. The name they used to sign letters was thus deliberately chosen to present an image of solidarity among all black ministers in the area.

The cases of several other companies were handled similarly to the one referred to in the Detroit letter, and the issues effectively resolved. In fact, estimates at the time indicated that sales of the boycotted companies declined up to 30 percent within a two-to-three-week period following beginning of the boycott. Some companies that were contacted agreed to the clergymen's demands before a boycott was called. Black clergymen who talked to the author at the time reported that still other companies revised their hiring policies favorably with regard to blacks on their own initiative, before being contacted by the clergy group.

Types of Black Religious Leaders

Not every black clergyman in the Detroit area participated in the boycott campaigns described above, of course, although a crucial element in the organizers' strategy was to create just that impression. And not everyone who participated did so to the same degree or in the same manner. In fact, Detroit's black clergymen can be divided into three fairly distinct categories or types: militants, moderates, and traditionalists. The *militants*, who constituted approximately 20 percent of the black clergy, are men deeply committed to civil rights goals who demonstrated, marched, and picketed during the civil rights movement of the 1960s. They comprised the central planning unit of the boycott organization.

TO ALL PASTORS COOPERATING WITH THE SELECTIVE PATRONAGE PROGRAM:

November 22, 1961

Dear Pastor:

Selective Patronage is a program aimed at opening doors of employment for our people that were formerly closed. As you know, our position is a simple one. We wish merely to see Equal Job opportunities for our people. The Taystee Bread Company was not completely providing such opportunities for our people in the past, and they were our first target in the Selective Patronage Program.

While we were aware that there were Negroes in the Taystee Bread Co., we believed that they should employ more than a token number of Negroes. When we began negotiations, there was not a single Negro driving a single Taystee Bread truck on the streets of Detroit.

HERE IS WHAT THEY HAVE DONE:

1. They have hired two Negro Driver salesman;
2. One Negro Swingman(men who relieve the regular drivers on their day off;
3. One Clerk-Typist;
4. Four more persons in the Production Department, and they have agreed that in the future there will be equal job opportunities for all with possible up-grading for those who presently qualify.

We have promised the Taystee Bread Co., that we will call on them within thirty (30) days to see if they are making further progress; in particular, hiring two more driver-salesmen and two more swingmen.

On Sunday, November 26, please announce to your congregation that we have had a successful negotiation with the Taystee Bread Co., and have begun work on another Bread Company. Committees have also been organized to negotiate with the Bottling Industries and the Oil Companies. LOOK TO YOUR PULPITS FOR FURTHER INFORMATION!

Our eyes are open! never again will we stand by and see doors closed in the faces of our people. We cannot, therefore, in good conscience, remain silent while members of our congregations support a companies prejudice with our dollars.

Remember, Sunday, November 26 -- PLEASE MAKE THIS ANNOUNCEMENT, in your own words. After all, WE did it together.

Sincerely,

The Negro Preachers of Detroit and Vicinity

FIGURE 14-1
Letter Sent to Black Ministers in the Detroit Area by the Negro Preachers of Detroit and Vicinity

These ministers tend to be young and highly educated, come from higher-than-average social-status backgrounds, tend toward theological liberalism, serve larger-than-average black congregations, assume an independent stance in their voting behavior, and emphasize social as opposed to other-worldly concerns. It should be noted in passing that the designation "militant" as used throughout this chapter refers to aggressive action to secure constitutionally guaranteed civil rights in an integrated society, not the more separatistic militancy espoused by some black leaders after 1964.

Second, there is the *moderate* black clergyman. Though committed ideologically to improving the lot of blacks in American society, he is a gradualist and more concilatory and accommodating than the militant black clergyman. On the average he is likely to be older than the militant and not so highly educated (a third of the moderates have no formal education beyond high school). Moderates lent support to the Detroit boycott activities by reading the letters from the boycott committee to their congregations, but by and large they refrained from helping plan strategy. In Detroit, 27 percent of black religious leaders fit into this category.

The third category, the *traditionalists*, are passive with regard to challenging the prevailing social order and are spiritually rather than socially oriented: "My job is to preach the Gospel and do spiritual work." They tend to be older men who have had very little formal education (approximately three-fifths have not gone beyond high school), come from low-social-status backgrounds, and serve small congregations, often as only a part-time minister. These men, who constitute slightly over half of all black religious leaders, actually serve fewer total people in their combined congregations in Detroit than do their militant counterparts; thus although they were not directly supportive of the boycott actions, neither could they prevent a clear majority of black church members from hearing about them.

An obvious conclusion we can make on the basis of these observations about the three distinctive types of religious leader in the contemporary black church (based on our Detroit data but likely generalizable to at least the urban north if not the urban south as well) is that the traditional otherworldly pattern of black religion is being effectively challenged. Militant social-action– and civil-rights–oriented religious leaders and perspectives have emerged and have gained substantial followings among members of black churches. Clearly it would be both misleading and blatantly inaccurate to speak of *the* black church today. The range of internal diversity is great. Clearly the militant civil rights perspective has made significant progress within black religious institutions. Yet it is equally important to note that the traditional black religious emphasis on otherworldliness and accommodation persists.

The Dilemma Posed by Black Militancy

The black church has thus only recently begun to face what white Protestant churches have been grappling with for nearly a century—

the social-gospel controversy and the struggle between theological fundamentalism and theological liberalism already discussed in Chapter 12 and
to be discussed at greater length in Chapter 15.

Because of the rapid developments in the civil rights struggle and
the emergence of countless "secular" local and national organizations
combatting racism and discrimination in various ways, the centrality and
dominance of the black church have of course been challenged. It has
been noted that young blacks particularly are becoming increasingly
disenchanted with the churches and are less and less likely to find satisfaction there. Increasingly they are turning to other types of organizations that appear to deal more directly with their life situations and
with the social problems they face. We are reminded of Glock's theory,
introduced in Chapter 7, concerning relative deprivation and various
possible responses to it. Recall that in the cases of economic and social
deprivation, according to Glock's theory, responses are more likely to be
secular than religious if the causes of the deprivation are not only accurately perceived but deemed capable of relief and change. Such seems
increasingly to be the case with blacks, with young blacks in particular
perceiving greater potential in secular organizations than in the traditional religious ones.

Such observations do not of course sound the death knell for the
black church. For one thing, many people in a religious organization—
whether black, white, or whatever—will remain there if for no other reason than simple habit—inertia. Also, for many, disaffiliating requires
a more dramatic stand than they are willing to make. Further, many people over time come to regard their associations and relationships with
others in an organization (such as a church)—as well as with the organization itself—as so meaningful and important that these considerations alone
prevent them from being readily convinced to substitute a new organization and commitment. Thus the historic centrality and importance of the
black church in the life of the black population and community alone
makes it seem particularly unlikely that black church members will easily
or quickly forsake this organization. Also, there still is a large proportion
of the black population for whom the social environment has changed
little despite the progress achieved by the civil rights movement and related activities and developments. If the sectarian nature of much black
religion has served in the past to provide release and escape for low-status
blacks, it might be expected to continue to do so today.

Note, however, that such comments about continuity of function
within organized religion do not necessarily apply to those young blacks
who find escape in any of the three "strategies for survival" described by
Lee Rainwater: (1) the expressive life-style of living "cool" and "working

the game" on the people around you; (2) the violent strategy of more or less blindly striking back at the social structure that holds you down; or (3) the depressive strategy of withdrawal, perhaps into drugs: "I don't bother nobody; don't nobody bother me."[21] Nor do such functions seem to apply well to those blacks who in increasing numbers are escaping the ghetto, securing advanced education, and entering previously closed or severely restricted occupations.

Observing young blacks' relative lack of enthusiasm for traditional black churches prompted black writer Joseph R. Washington essentially to predict, at the height of the civil rights movement in the early 1960s, the eventual demise of the black church—although in 1967 he strongly urged the black church to become involved with the black revolution because it had the potential to be of significant help, since it still had contact with many blacks.[22]

We have already shown a connection between at least a minority of black clergymen and militant civil rights activities. What connection is there between black religion generally, particularly for laymen, and involvement in civil rights activities? In other words, so far as black Americans are concerned, does religion in any way stimulate reform, or does it inhibit social change? Gary Marx has phrased this question well in his book *Protest and Prejudice*, which includes a chapter headed: "Religion: Opiate or Inspiration of Civil Rights Militancy?"[23] Generally, Marx finds traditional otherworldly religion as expressed and practiced by blacks to be inconsistent with militant protest. For example, militants constitute a significantly lower proportion of black sects and cults than they do of black members of the more liberal Protestant denominations (15 percent among sects and cults, 43 and 36 percent among black Episcopalians and Presbyterians, respectively.)[24] Of course, there is an important class bias affecting these data which eliminates virtually any possibility of making a valid inference regarding a cause-and-effect relationship between sectarianism and nonmilitancy; there is an association only. But at least it is interesting to observe that one finds relatively few militants in black sectarian religious groups as compared with the more liberal and predominantly white Protestant denominations.

Other measures of religion add support to the observation that traditional black religion of the otherworldly variety is at best not conducive

21Lee Rainwater, "A World of Trouble: The Pruitt-Igoe Housing Project," *The Public Interest* 8 (Summer 1967); 116–26.
22Joseph R. Washington, Jr., *Black Religion* (Boston: Beacon Press, 1964); *The Politics of God* (Boston: Beacon Press, 1967), pp. 207–27.
23Gary T. Marx, *Protest and Prejudice* (New York: Harper & Row, 1967), chapter 4.
24Ibid., p. 99.

to militancy and that the two approaches are "mutually corrosive kinds of commitments,"[25] if not actually mutually exclusive points of view. Marx found, for example, that the lower in importance black respondents regarded religion, the more likely they would be classed as militant in terms of civil rights philosophy: whereas only 22 percent of those to whom religion was "extremely important" fell into the militant category, 62 percent of those who felt religion was "not at all important" were so classified.[26] Similarly, of those scoring high in orthodoxy only 20 percent were militant, while of those scoring lowest on the orthodoxy scale, 57 percent were militant.[27]

Although our point of emphasis above is that there is an inverse relationship between religious orthodoxy and civil rights militancy, yet it is intriguing that there are a few civil rights militants even among the religiously traditional and orthodox. In this connection we should mention that many of the traditionalist ministers appear to harbor a secret respect for at least some aspects of the militant stance. In our Detroit sample they selected militants over fellow traditionalists as their opinion leaders by a ratio of six to one, even though they may not have known them personally.[28] It is also probable that the message of freedom and release in traditional black sectarian religion, which many have interpreted as salvation- or heaven-oriented, has been generalized by at least some to signify social and political freedom and release as well. There is consensus that the Jordan River referred to in the black spirituals was not solely a symbolic hurdle to cross before entering the bliss of heaven but also was the Ohio River that separated the slave from his freedom in the North.

NEW THEMES IN BLACK RELIGION

Although militant black clergymen have issued calls for change and have had some successes in the attainment of civil rights goals among blacks, the black church as a whole appears to have had only limited influence in the civil rights area. There has been almost no challenge from the black community to the contention, expressed more than once in this chapter, that black religion has concentrated on "religious" matters and salvation concerns to the neglect of social action and reform. Thus it is

[25]Rodney Stark, "Class, Radicalism, and Religious Involvement," *American Sociological Review* 29, no. 5 (1964); 703. Quoted in Marx, *Protest and Prejudice*, p. 105.
[26]Marx, *Protest and Prejudice*, p. 100.
[27]Ibid.
[28]Johnstone, "Community Leadership," pp. 169–70.

of more than passing interest that one black theologian, James Cone, has recently published a proposal for a "Black theology of liberation" in which he contends that Christianity is in essence a religion of liberation and that the struggle of the oppressed for political, social, and economic justice is integral to Jesus Christ's message.[29] Cone condemns the black and the white Protestant churches in the same breath: "Both have marked out their places as havens of retreat, the one to cover the guilt of the oppressors, the other to daub the wounds of the oppressed."[30] Cone is calling for the reform of black theology and of the black church. The view that such reform is crucial in the face of social change is shared by Joseph Washington, who states in a review of Cone's first book that "the future of the black church is in its critical participation in the future of black power—which is, the future of black people."[31] Undoubtedly there is less room today in the black church than in the white church for dual religious tracks—the one proclaiming traditional salvation goals, the other championing social reforms.

Cone chides the black church for emulating the white church and for feeling good when praised by whites. In reality, he asserts, the black church, just because it is black, is automatically among the rejected. He suggests that the black church must accept its true role as sufferer and follow the natural course of being black.[32] One thing this requires is excising the "most corrupting influence among the Black churches"—namely, "their adoption of the 'white lie' that Christianity is primarily concerned with an otherworldly reality. . . . The idea of heaven is irrelevant for Black Theology. The Christian cannot waste time contemplating the next world,"[33] for that reward is not a legitimate motive for action. In fact, it is a denial of the Christian faith, in addition to being a gigantic "put-on" devised by whites to keep blacks in their place.

The Reverend Albert Cleage, another black theologian, also expresses this view when he describes the gift of Christianity to the black slave by the white master:

> The religion which the master gave to his slave was designed for pacification and to support the authority of white supremacy. He said, "This is a picture of God. This is a picture of Jesus. They are both white as you can plainly see. Here are Biblical characters. They are all white. But they love you in spite of your evil Blackness, and they offer you salvation in the

[29] James H. Cone, Liberation (Philadelphia: Lippincott, 1970).
[30] James H. Cone, Black Theology and Black Power (New York: Seabury Press, 1969), p. 115.
[31] Joseph R. Washington, Jr., review of Black Theology and Black Power by James H. Cone, Journal for the Scientific Study of Religion 11, no. 3 (1972); 311.
[32] Cone, Black Theology, p. 113.
[33] Ibid., pp. 121, 125.

*great beyond! You have to live such a life here on earth, that after death,
when you cross over Jordan, there will be a reward for you. Sometimes you
think that all the suffering that you are doing down here is passing un-
noticed by God, but it is not! God is watching everything, every minute
of every day. And every bit of suffering you have down here is written
down in God's big book, and eventually on the other side of Jordan there
will be a reward, milk and honey and golden streets." So Black people
had only to accept the authority of the white world to inherit a glorious
reward in heaven.*[34]

The point emphasized again and again by Cone and Cleage is that
the black church must purge itself of such otherworldly-reward perspectives and join the black power movement. Black pride and social justice
must become the dominant guiding concepts both in the ideology or
theology and in the activities of the black church. Integral to this process,
at least for Cleage, is acceptance of the fact that the Jesus of Christianity
was in reality black. Cleage defines Jesus as a revolutionary black leader
seeking to lead a black nation to freedom.[35] But more than that, Cleage
reflects the ideas of Marcus Garvey, who in the late 1920s organized the
African Orthodox Church and developed an entire black hierarchy of
black God, black Jesus, black Madonna, and black angels.[36] The Reverend Cleage is minister of the Shrine of the Black Madonna, formerly
the Central Congregational Church, in Detroit.

Cone, too, speaks of God as black, but more in a figurative sense
(though he would not wish to use that adjective). God must be known as
he reveals himself in his blackness, by which Cone means that "either
God is identified with the oppressed to the point that their experience
becomes his or he is a God of racism."[37] Cone is referring, in other words,
to total identification of God with black people and their plight. "Because God has made the goal of Black people his own goal, Black Theology believes that it is not only appropriate but necessary to begin the
doctrine of God with an insistence on his blackness."[38]

An intriguing observation applicable to even the "radical" black
theology of Cone and Cleage, as noted earlier with Washington, is the
reality of the conviction that the black church not only must reorient
itself, but that it is capable of doing so. In one sense, such a belief or
assumption appears sound inasmuch as the black church is still by far the
largest social institution in the black community and is in contact with

[34]Albert B. Cleage, Jr., *Black Christian Nationalism* (New York: William Mor-
row, 1972), p. xxviii.
[35]Albert B. Cleage, Jr., *Black Messiah* (New York: Sheed & Ward, 1968), p. 4.
[36]Ibid., p. 8.
[37]Cone, *Liberation*, pp. 120–21
[38]Ibid., p. 121.

the greatest number of people. On the other hand, whether it can turn itself around and make a radical change in direction and focus is problematic. It is undoubtedly true that significant numbers of influential black preachers have at least begun the switch. It is also true, as Cone points out, that the black church and its clergy have retained some of the theme of freedom and injustice from their slave religion heritage.[39] Nonetheless, the black church will, on the whole, likely play little more than a supportive role in the struggle of black citizens for equality and dignity. Our discussion in the next chapter of secularization as either a replacement of religion by secular institutions or as a process by which religion gets differentiated or relegated to specialized functions in the society will implicitly speak to this issue.

[39]Cone, *Black Theology*, chapter 4.

15

Recent
Sociological Trends

Anyone who at any time in the past predicted that religion would by now be a defunct institution would have to be quite surprised at what he would see in the United States today. Not only are many traditional signs of religion in abundance, but new manifestations seem to emerge almost daily. Not only does one continue to observe bumper stickers proclaiming "Jesus Saves," political candidates mouthing religious clichés, evangelists like Billy Graham "packing them in," and freshly painted church spires dotting both countryside and town, but amazing new religious sights and sounds daily bombard our consciousness: smooth-headed young men in flowing saffron robes roaming the streets chanting "Hare Krishna...," jazz and rock liturgies in traditional churches, a proliferation of Eastern mystical cults, sober academic discussions in mainline Protestant churches on the "death of God." Not long ago there was discussion of a "revival" of traditional religion (i.e., Christianity) in the United States.[1] Now there is talk of a revival of religion in the general sense, recognizing that many of the expressions and forms are

[1]For discussions of the 1950s "revival" see, in addition to Chapter 12, A. Roy Eckardt, *The Surge of Piety in America* (New York: Association Press, 1958), and Martin E. Marty, *The New Shape of American Religion* (New York: Harper & Brothers, 1958).

new to American culture, if not totally novel elsewhere. Religion in the United States in a complex variety of forms, not all traditional, not all new, is definitely alive.

Our intention in this chapter is to present an overview of recent developments and trends in American religion that appear to be of significance sociologically. In the process we shall be building upon many of the concepts and typologies discussed in earlier chapters and shall try to extrapolate, from present phenomena, future developments and trends.

A DECLINE IN AMERICAN RELIGION?

A basic observation-prediction that we can make regarding religion in the United States is that there seems to be a decline of interest in and commitment to formalized religion and the institutional church and that this decline is likely to continue. Not that the decline is dramatic or will proceed precipitously, but the peak has apparently been passed so far as affiliation with organized religion is concerned.

Several kinds of evidence support this observation. First, Table 15–1 indicates a recent decline in formal church membership. Although the decline has been slight and did not begin until after 1964, we can see in it the beginning of a trend—continuing slowly, likely with occasional year-to-year fluctuations, but in general steadily downward.

A second piece of evidence for postulating a declining commitment to institutionalized religion in the United States is the steady decline in weekly church attendance since 1959, as indicated in Table 15–2.

A third bit of evidence, which is ostensibly a corollary of the two just mentioned, concerns the amount of new construction of religious facilities. Given a leveling-off and then a decline in both church membership and attendance (Table 15–1 and 15–2), one would expect a corresponding reduction of construction of buildings used for religious purposes. Table 15–3 indicates just such a decline starting in 1966, shortly after the onset of the declines noted in membership and attendance.

TABLE 15–1
Church Membership in the United States as a Proportion of Population

1930	47%	1964	64.4%
1940	49	1968	63.2
1950	57	1970	62.4
1960	63.6	1972	62.4

Source: Yearbook of American Churches (New York: National Council Press, 1959–1973).

TABLE 15–2

Weekly Church Attendance in the United States as a Proportion of Population

1958	49%
1960	47
1962	46
1964	45
1966	44
1969	42
1971	40

Source: Gallup Poll data reported in Lauris B. Whitman, ed., *Yearbook of American Churches*, 1969 (New York: National Council Press, 1969), p. 205, and in Constant H. Jacquet, Jr., ed., *Yearbook of American Churches, 1973* (Nashville: Abingdon Press, 1973), p. 266.

Additional evidence of an inferential nature comes from Gallup Poll data, gathered annually since 1957, on responses to the question, "At the present time, do you think religion as a whole is increasing its influence on American life, or losing its influence?" Figure 15–1 reveals a dramatic increase in the proportion of people who perceive that religion is losing influence and a corresponding decrease in those who see religion as gaining in influence. Of course, these data reflect only what people *think* is happening and do not establish, at least by themselves that the influence of religion in American life has in fact decreased. Nor do the changing proportions tell us the magnitude of either the perceived decline or increase. That is, some may see religion's influence changing dramatically in one direction or the other, others may perceive the change as slight. Yet, as Jeffrey Hadden has perceptively suggested, the time-honored sociological concepts of the "self-fulfilling prophecy" and the

TABLE 15–3

Value of New Construction of Religious Facilities in the United States

1950	$ 409	million	1967	$1,093	million
1955	736	"	1968	1,038	"
1960	1,016	"	1969	949	"
1965	1,207	"	1970	921	"
1966	1,164	"	1971	813	"

Sources: Constant H. Jacquet, Jr., ed., *Yearbook of American Churches, 1972* (Nashville: Abingdon Press, 1972), p. 260, and idem, ed., *Yearbook of American Churches, 1973* (Nashville: Abingdon Press, 1973), p. 266.

Note: Takes into account the Department of Commerce composit cost index (1967 = 100; 1968 = 106; 1969 = 114; 1970 = 122; 1971 = 131).

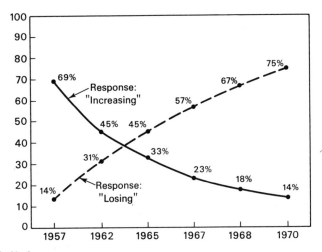

FIGURE 15–1
Proportion of Adult Americans Who Perceive Religion as Increasing or Losing
Its Influence on American Life

Source: George H. Gallup, *The Gallup Poll* (New York: Random House, 1972), 2:1482;
3: 1763, 1934, 2058–59, 2198, 2240.

"definition of the situation" may well be applicable here. That is, people
tend to behave in a manner that contributes to the actualization of what
they expect and have predicted to happen. He who predicts he'll fail
at a new job likely will. She who says nobody wants to be her friend
will likely make few new friends. Similarly with the "definition of the
situation" idea: a person's definition or understanding of reality tends to
have consequences consistent with that definition or understanding.[2]
Thus if enough people feel that religion is declining in influence, its
influence is in fact likely to decline—if only because many of those who
make such an assessment are probably evidencing thereby some personal
disenchantment with the institution themselves. At least it is possible
that they will exert less effort on behalf of an organization that they
feel is dying on the vine. As we pointed out in Chapter 2, a sine qua non
of any social group's survival is the commitment of its members and their
conviction that the group is worthwhile, that it deserves the exertion of
their energies on its behalf, and that it merits their verbal promotion
and support. To the degree that members have lost such convictions,
group members are likely to begin fulfilling their own negative prophe-

2Jeffrey K. Hadden, *The Gathering Storm in the Churches* (Garden City, N.Y.:
Doubleday, 1969), pp. 25–26.

cies. Half-heartedness will evidence itself more dramatically in declining attendance and membership. Something of a falling-domino effect will be observed as unenthusiastic parents themselves who are reluctant to cut their ties with formal religion nevertheless socialize their children, unconsciously perhaps, to view affiliation with institutionalized religion as a "take-it-or-leave-it" matter. The consequence is likely to be an erosion of the prime source of recruitment of new members—namely, the children of present members.

The Influence of Secularization

A concept that relates closely to what we've been considering so far is that of *secularization*—basically, the displacement of religious interpretations of reality and religious orientations toward life by an orientation that seeks explanations for and justifications of human behavior and other phenomena in scientific and rational terms. One has undergone a secularization process if, for example, instead of asserting that marriages are made in heaven and for eternity, he were to say that marriages are made by human beings, in time, on the basis of propinquity, and in response to biological and psychological needs. The results of secularization are that, instead of more or less automatically "explaining" much that happens—death, floods, plane crashes, drought, war, peace, or whatever—as "God's will," more and more people are seeking explanations in the laws of physical science and in the social scientific "laws" of human interaction. In other words, secularization is as much a state of mind as it is a specific, measurable development.

Andrew Greeley is very much on target when he says that secularization as discussed in the United States today means essentially that religion is less important today than it was in the past.[3] If this is in fact what people mean when they refer to the secularization process at work in American society, then the decline of religion in general, and not just in its institutional manifestations, is an empirical question that clamors for sociological investigation and documentation. We have already gone out on a limb in this chapter by suggesting that a recent decline of interest in the institutional form of religion is the beginning of a trend. But such an observation does not necessarily imply that *religion*—i.e., the phenomenon itself—is fast becoming a relic. In fact, we shall make some suggestions to the contrary later in this chapter. Thus, as we have already emphasized, it is important to at least try to make a distinction between religion and the institutional forms of religion, a distinction that is par-

[3]Andrew M. Greeley, *The Denominational Society* (Glenview, Ill.: Scott, Foresman, 1972), p. 127.

ticularly important when trying to assess the secularization question. For much rests on how *religion* is defined—whether in terms of its "essence," or as a particular traditional package of beliefs and principles (such as "our Judeo-Christian heritage"), or in terms of the vitality of its institutional forms (membership, attendance, new construction, etc.).

This problem of achieving a consensus so far as a definition of religion is concerned surfaces in many discussions of the issue of secularization where it happens that one person's understanding of religion does not coincide with those of others. Larry Shriner implies as much when he shows how *secularization* has been defined in a half a dozen ways in recent discussions.[4] Although each of these definitions has its own nuances, two basic connotations of *secularization* can be distilled from them all. First, many see secularization as a process of *replacement* of religious faith with faith in scientific principles. This concept goes back to the beginnings of modern Western science, when scientists first dared to set aside religion's view of reality, at least temporarily, in order to consider and evaluate data objectively. Thus Copernicus and Galileo were secularists in that they repudiated the belief—then a religious doctrine—that the earth is the center of the universe.

The logical extreme of secularism, in this view, is refusing to grant credence to any assertion about man, the world, or the universe that cannot be empirically verified. While some view with alarm and others with joy such a displacement of religious faith with faith in the scientific method, many on both sides see such secularization as a trend in which people evidence less and less interest in sacred and supernatural phenomena, as religious doctrines and institutions lose prestige and influence, with the possible ultimate result of a religionless society emerging.

Note, however, that no simple dichotomy exists of secular scientists hailing the replacement of religious faith with scientific faith versus religionists decrying such replacement. The popular Protestant theologian Harvey Cox, for example, welcomes secularization and sees it as a fulfillment of biblical themes and sources. He defines *secularization* in terms of "emancipation"—as the "liberation of man from religious and metaphysical tutelage, the turning of his attention away from other worlds and toward this one."[5] Cox's view may thus be regarded as a distinct variation on the "secularization-as-replacement" theme, one in which fulfillment is emphasized as a form of replacement.

The second general understanding of *secularization* is that it is a process of increasing differentiation between the religious and the secu-

---

[4]Larry Shriner, "The Concept of Secularization in Empirical Research," *Journal for the Scientific Study of Religion* 6, no. 2 (1967); 207–20.

[5]Harvey Cox, *The Secular City* (New York: Macmillan, 1965), p. 17.

lar (nonreligious) spheres of life—a process, moreover, coinciding with and perhaps in part resulting from increasing specialization within society as it grows and becomes more urbanized and industrialized.[6] Some who hold to the differentiation definition of *secularization* cite the increasing "privatization" of faith—the process of compartmentalizing the religious and the secular, of regarding religion as a mystical, personal, experiential phenomenon that one does not share with others.

Others subscribing to the differentiation view note that public manifestations of religion are becoming more scarce. Some evidence supporting this view appeared in Chapter 10's discussion of recent Supreme Court decisions that have tended to eliminate religious elements from public life, particularly from the public schools.

The haunting question that pervades the above discussion and a myriad of other allegations of spreading secularization is whether such signs reflect gains by "secular" forces and points of view at the expense of religion, or whether religion in its basic sense has remained essentially unaffected. Conceivably the essence of religion may be enjoying greater strength and influence today than during the heyday of the church-type of religious organization in Europe or the early days of the state church in the United States. Further, "privatization" of religion need not mean that religion is not in evidence in people's actions, attitudes, and decisions. Recall Wilfred Smith's distinction, cited in Chapter 2, between the cumulative tradition and individual faith, which although strongly related are nevertheless distinct. Also, many former public manifestations of religion that are no longer in evidence may have been ritualistic, pro forma actions that signified little and influenced people even less.

The point we are making is that before undertaking any analysis of secularization, one must specify his operational definitions of the variables under discussion, for the conclusions one reaches about secularization are inevitably influenced by what one regards as the valuable features of religion and by their current status—that is, whether those features are threatened or disappearing—as well as by what one understands religion to be in the first place: is the institution and its preservation of primary concern, or some understanding of what religion is in its "essence," apart from its institutional manifestations? All we wish to do at this point is raise the issue of secularization, not resolve it. For one thing, we need the information and discussion that follows in this chapter to "flesh out" the issue before trying to answer the question. Secondly, establishing operational definitions of *religion* and *secularization* will be

[6]Talcott Parsons, "Christianity and Modern Industrial Society," in *Sociological Theory, Values, and Socio-Cultural Change*, ed. Edward A. Tiryakin (New York: Free Press, 1963), pp. 33–70.

more helpful in understanding the current status of religion in the United States than will premature conclusions about secularization.

One reason that definitive conclusions about secularization are so difficult to reach is that contemporary American religion evidences numerous seeming paradoxes. While total church membership has been declining and many mainline denominations have been experiencing membership losses, some religious groups have been advancing with firm strides if not leaps and bounds so far as membership is concerned. There is evidence of growing disenchantment with traditional religious forms among young people, yet a broad-based attempt to recapture the "real Jesus" and "authentic Christianity" is the Jesus movement—a movement primarily of young people. In 1966 many Protestant theologians were busy proclaiming the "death of God," yet only seven years later over a hundred denominations and religious associations and alliances from the United States and twenty from Canada banded together to "evangelize the nations in 1973" ("Key '73"). There is much emphasis within denominations on employing modern techniques of management, cost accounting, and computer technology, yet one observes little progress in eliminating duplication of effort by putting ecumenical ideology into practice. Such paradoxes (or seeming paradoxes) simply highlight the importance of one's decisions regarding which phenomena to consider in reaching conclusions about secularization or "religionization." What operational definitions of these concepts, then, do we adopt?

One of the best descriptions of secularization from the differentiation perspective is Robert Bellah's in his account of the evolution of religion through its five stages (see Chapter 13). A dominant theme within this evolutionary process, according to Bellah, is the process of making increasingly more sophisticated distinctions and differentiations between the sacred or supernatural and the secular, a process which has culminated, in the fifth stage (the modern period), in a breakdown of this dualism and its replacement by a multidimensional view of life and reality.[7] At this final stage, everything, including religion, is seen as revisable (though not all people see it this way, of course). Removed, or in the process of being removed, are such "either/or" dualistic descriptions of reality as *this world–other world, sacred-profane, good-evil, salvation-damnation*. Absolutism is replaced with relativity. Man's search for meaning is no longer confined within religious institutions or limited to traditional religious formulations. Such concepts as *situation ethics* and *process theology* typify the modern period. Certain traditional concepts and approaches from the past (*orthodoxy, sin,* and *moral* law, for exam-

[7]Robert N. Bellah, "Religious Evolution," *American Sociological Review* 29, no. 3 (1954); 358–74.

ple) are nevertheless retained by some and appear not about to disappear completely in the near future. This latter observation, of course, only reinforces Bellah's point, for a diversity of approaches and expressions and a broad range of views and interpretations are characteristic of religion in the modern period.

It should be obvious by now that we personally favor the differentiation view or definition of secularization. But differentiation as supplemented by an expansion of the dualistic view of religion versus the secular to a multidimensional range of choices for finding meaning and orientation in life. More on this in Chapter 16 as we discuss the theories of Peter Berger and Thomas Luckmann.

THE CONFLICT OVER THE PURPOSE OF RELIGION

A second feature of contemporary American religion, which although not new, appears to be more pronounced today than formerly, is the controversy over the purpose of religion. Is it for the personal benefit of its practitioners—that is, for the sake of their possible ultimate eternal salvation, in addition to their feelings of well-being, comfort, and reinforcement of life-style? Or is religion primarily a vehicle for helping those with a diversity of human needs and problems? This debate over religion's functions and purposes, pitting social service versus self-service, represents a dilemma in American society at least as old as the social-gospel movement that emerged in the last half of the nineteenth century and the counterchallenge by fundamentalism that followed. Yet the issue has been updated. Not that either perspective or emphasis ever disappeared. Both have remained viable, and in fact have in many instances coexisted within the same denomination. But the original social-gospel or social service emphasis became institutionalized, in the sense that denominations established specialized commissions and boards and subsidiary institutions to handle that aspect of their work. It may have been a part of the annual budget of both the local congregation and the national denomination and called "benevolences." It supported orphanages, hospitals, schools for the physically or mentally handicapped, and the like. Or it may have been supported through annual fundraising drives as peoples' hearts were touched by an emotional appeal and a contribution extracted. In any case, once a religious group's social service and welfare concerns became primarily the responsibility of specialized personnel and agencies operating in the group's name, these same concerns were easily relegated to a peripheral dimension of most churchmembers' lives.

However, with the emergence of the civil rights movement in the late 1950s and early 1960s, the intensified American involvement in the war in Southeast Asia, and growing publicity and concern over such domestic social issues as poverty, capital punishment, abortion, and environmental pollution, individual churchmen and ad hoc religious groups began involving themselves in the issues. They urged their religious groups to become similarly involved and in a real sense forced an issue that had long lain dormant. Protestant, Catholic, and Jewish clergymen began participating in civil rights marches, sit-ins, and demonstrations; administrators of denominational social service programs began to urge more substantial support for existing and additional programs; Martin Luther King, Jr., challenged church people of all colors to support the struggle of black citizens for freedom and dignity. Seminaries intensified their efforts by offering new courses in social ethics and concerns and by implementing social action field-work programs. Denominations began issuing position statements supporting, at least in general terms, the rights of minority and disprivileged groups. Young seminary graduates assuming the leadership of congregations began preaching a gospel that included more than personal comfort and salvation.

The outcome of all this was a crisis of direction or purpose so far as organized religion was concerned. That is, organized religion was caught in the middle of the agonizing confrontation of individual versus social concerns, personal comfort and salvation versus social welfare and help for the disprivileged.

Not that those who championed the social concern emphasis always saw these as polar alternatives. Certainly most people who emphasized social service in the name of religion spoke of it as a concomitant of traditional individual salvation and comfort emphases, though some at least implicitly urged social service emphases at the expense of individual ones. It all became an issue when the ideas left the seminaries and the resolution-forming conferences and conventions and began confronting the local congregations. Then the allegations and accusations implied by such book titles as *The Suburban Captivity of the Churches* and *The Comfortable Pew* became meaningful.[8] The message of these and similar analyses of organized religion in the 1960s was that churches not only were self-serving but would probably not change. The direct implication was that large numbers of both laymen and clergymen sought to retain the individual emphasis of the church at all costs—perhaps out of ideological commitment to the idea that salvation is the only true concern

---

[8]Gibson Winter, *The Suburban Capitivity of the Churches* (Garden City, N.Y.: Doubleday, 1961); Pierre Berton, *The Comfortable Pew* (Philadelphia: Lippincott, 1965).

of churches, or perhaps because of inertia related to the comfort and security and meaningful interpersonal relationships the church provided many people.

In *The Gathering Storm in the Churches* (1969), Jeffrey Hadden provides data from various studies to support his contention that a wide gap exists between many laymen and growing numbers of clergymen on the salvation–versus–social service issue. Centering his discussion on support for the civil rights issue, Hadden points out that although a great majority of Americans interviewed in one study (86 percent) agreed that "the best mark of a person's religiousness is the degree of his concern for others," nearly half (49 percent) of the same sample felt that "clergy should stick to religion and not concern themselves with social, economic, and political questions." Further, nearly three-fourths (72 percent) admitted they would be upset if their minister, priest, or rabbi were to participate in a picket line or demonstration. Only slightly more than a third (37 percent) professed being "basically sympathetic with Northern ministers and students who have gone to the South to work for civil rights." By way of contrast, on this last issue 64 percent of the clergymen interviewed expressed sympathy for such active civil rights involvement.[9]

Such data reflect not only the conflict over the purpose of religion and the proper aims of the church, in which denominations have tended to lean strongly in one direction or the other, but also the conflict between clergy and laymen within a given denomination, particularly those that have tended to emphasize salvation. As a result of the latter conflict, Hadden feels, the traditional authority of clergy is gradually eroding and laymen are beginning to "think for themselves" when their personal views of the purpose of religion are challenged. Such intradenominational conflicts are not new in themselves. Because the number of people involved may be greater, however, the traditional techniques religious groups use for handling internal diversity may no longer be adequate. Agencies, "special ministries," and monastic orders with a social service emphasis no longer seem to provide enough openings to accommodate the number of clergy and serious laymen committed in this direction. Thus religious groups' "segmentation of radicalism" technique that Phillip Hammond and Robert Mitchell discuss can no longer contain the challenge to tradition as it has in the past.[10] While radicals at one time could be "kicked upstairs" into administrative positions or directed into campus ministries where contact with rank-and-file laity in standard con-

[9]Hadden, *The Gathering Storm*, pp. 132, 134, 136.
[10]Phillip E. Hammond and Robert E. Mitchell, "Segmentation of Radicalism: The Case of the Protestant Campus Minister," *American Journal of Sociology* 71, no. 2 (1965); 133–143.

gregations was minimal, such tactics are less effective today. It is interesting that falling back on such options assumes the group is not particularly interested in facing very directly the problems that the challengers are raising.

In general, however, the "crisis" of the salvation–versus–social concern issue seems to have abated somewhat. Many of the major objectives of the civil rights movement have been achieved, at least regarding legislation; the Vietnam War has officially ended; social problems and solutions that appeared simple have been recognized as complex; considerable backlash against social welfare programs has set in; and new issues continue to surface that make a dichotomy of salvation versus social concern not so simple to maintain. Concentrating on a single, specialized issue such as women's rights, gay rights, or abortion reform need not place a protagonist at total odds with a congregation that pursues its own comfort, especially if he does not expect much participation or commitment from the congregation.

The whole issue of why there has been a reduction of such pressures is exceedingly complex, however, and thus the following observations are perhaps only a few of the factors that need to be considered: (1) Social service–oriented clergy have made up the bulk of those—and their numbers have been substantial in all faiths—who have left the ministry, apparently feeling that they could "do their thing" better in a secular setting. Moreover, the departure of such ministers may itself indicate that the salvation emphasis is still dominant. (2) Financial pressures have forced denominations to eliminate some of the administrative positions that formerly served as sources of and encouragement for dissidence. (3) The halt of growth in church membership (see Table 15–1) has tightened the job market for clergymen. Not only are clergymen less horizontally mobile within the denomination, but the job market outside is also less open. Such a constriction may have prompted some clergymen, perhaps quite unconsciously, to accommodate themselves to the attitudes, both expressed and unspoken, of the congregations they serve. (4) In some denominations controversy has shifted to more traditional theological issues —a matter we'll take up in the following section of this chapter. (5) Some laymen who objected most strongly to what they defined as at best a dilution and at worst a perversion or betrayal of the proper purpose of the church have left their denominations for more conservative ones that still emphasize salvation and personal goals—another subject we shall deal with later in this chapter.

As indicated earlier, it appears that the first flush of the most recent salvation–versus–social action controversy is past. There is some indication that the interest in social concerns has fallen victim to the mood of the nation, as people have become more concerned with such urgent personal goals as keeping a job when others are losing theirs, maintaining financial solvency while inflation forges ahead, and staying healthy as new dangers from cancer-inducing agents are made public constantly. Further, the stridency of many of the victims of social inequities who shout "Black Power," "Gay Rights," and "Women's Liberation" has tended to encourage some of the faint-hearted do-gooders to withdraw—they didn't intend to go to "war," but only to help the helpless.

Exactly how the salvation–versus–social action issue will finally be resolved is not easy to predict. Disappearance of the salvation emphasis in the wake of social action becoming the central concern of organized religion in the United States appears highly unlikely. On the other hand, neither are social action concerns within American religion likely to disappear. Obviously the adherents of neither side of the issue will be completely happy. Yet such is the nature of large groups and institutions. Internal diversity is universal as various subgroups jockey for power and influence. Clear winners and losers in such competition are rare indeed.

THE CONTINUING TRADITIONAL THEOLOGICAL CONTROVERSY

What we intend to discuss now is of course related to the discussion just completed in the sense that the question of salvation versus social service is clearly a theological issue. After all, defining the purpose of religion and of religious institutions is a central theological concern. Here, however, we wish to look at what can probably best be termed the *traditional theological question*—that is, what is true doctrine? In a real sense, then, what we observe happening in several denominations in the United States at the present time is a reenactment of the fundamentalist-modernist controversy that began around the turn of this century and culminated in 1925 with the debates between Clarence Darrow and William Jennings Bryan in the Scopes "monkey trial" (discussed in Chapter 12).

Actually the issue exists at two levels. First, some denominations that either did not face the question settled by fundamentalists to their own satisfaction fifty years ago or faced them and came down squarely on the fundamentalist side of the fence are now facing these questions anew and finding themselves arguing internally about the nature and authority of the Bible, the virgin birth and resurrection of Christ, whether Jonah really lived, whether the miracles recorded in the Bible really happened as described, and so on. These are old battles, to be sure, but within some denominations they are being fought for the first time.

The second level at which doctrinal controversy is occurring is in a real sense more basic, and to some degree it affects all of American

Christianity—and of world Christianity, for that matter. This is a crisis of basic faith—what Hadden calls the "crisis of belief."[11]—by which is implied the posing of questions about the fundamental nature and basis for the Christian religion. These are *not* the ancient, enduring questions such as the proper mode of baptism (whether to immerse, pour, or sprinkle) or whether the relationship of the bread and wine to the body and blood of Christ in the Lord's Supper (Holy Communion, Eucharist) is one of transubstantiation (Catholic), representation (Reformed), or real presence (Lutheran): these we might call superficial issues, even though protagonists for various points of view would object to such a designation. Today the issues seem more fundamental. That is, the kinds of questions frequently raised are whether God in fact exists (regardless of how you define the concept of the Trinity), whether baptism is valid and necessary in the first place (regardless of how much water is used), whether Christ really lived and died and rose again—not whether wine or grape juice should be used in the Lord's Supper. In other words, at this second level are questions about the reality of God, as well as assumptions about the relationship of God with man, that have been essentially unchallenged until now.

Returning to the first issue or level of theological dispute, we observe that even denominations which appeared to resolve the fundamentalist-modernist issue years ago by camping on the liberal side of the fence do not evidence the internal unanimity today that one might expect. Thus although a majority of Congregationalists, Methodists, and Episcopalians cannot accept without reservation that Jesus was born of a virgin, or that miracles actually happened just as the Bible says they did, some of these people do. On the question of Jesus' virgin birth, for example, 21 percent of Congregationalists, 34 percent of Methodists, and 39 percent of Episcopalians accept the doctrine without reservation. Similarly, 28 percent of Congregationalists, 37 percent of Methodists, and 41 percent of Episcopalians accept the biblical account of miracles as completely true.[12] That is, although such denominations may have essentially resolved the fundamentalist-modernist controversy (if only in the sense of tolerating a diversity of views and beliefs), some of their members still hold to traditional beliefs and might even feel reasonably comfortable in another, theologically more conservative denomination.

Of even greater contemporary relevance are those groups which have continued to maintain an official position supporting traditional beliefs and interpretations of Scripture, and in which (according to survey data) members have consistently expressed high levels of concurrence

---

[11]Hadden, *The Gathering Storm*, pp. 15–26.
[12]Charles Y. Glock and Rodney Stark, *Christian Beliefs and Anti-Semitism* (New York: Harper & Row, 1966), pp. 9–10.

with these doctrinal formulations, but in which an erosion of doctrinal solidarity appears to have begun. Two prime examples are the Southern Baptist Convention and The Lutheran Church—Missouri Synod. Both groups have long proclaimed their adherence to a conservative version of Christianity and continue in an official way to subscribe to traditional doctrine—essentially what we have referred to as fundamentalist doctrine. However, voices throughout both groups appear increasingly to be challenging or at least questioning their official traditional positions. For example, in The Lutheran Church—Missouri Synod, there has been an ongoing "battle" between the president of the denomination, who holds firmly to a traditional, conservative theological position, and the denomination's major seminary, Concordia Seminary in St. Louis. A majority of the seminary's faculty have urged adopting a more open-ended approach to many historical definitions and understandings of Christian doctrine without necessarily denying them. There is no doubt, however, that the doctrinal position of these faculty persons, and of many of the graduates they turn out, is less explicitly traditional, less narrowly defined as such, than that of most leaders in this denomination in the past. The denomination's president, J. A. O. Preus, and many laymen and clergy recognize this and object. They request that those who deviate either reaffirm the traditional positions of the church or leave it. This position was made explicit in the church's July 1973 convention in New Orleans (waggishly called the "Second Battle of New Orleans"), in which the assembled delegates accepted as binding on all clergy and seminary instructors a highly specific and conservative statement of faith, approved the censure of dissident faculty members at the St. Louis seminary, and set in motion procedures for purging theological deviates. The latter process proceeded to the point in early 1974 of a majority of the seminary faculty being relieved of their positions.

Quite clearly, those who oppose such deviance and diversity do not recognize the sociological realities that any large group faces, particularly as it grows larger. Any such group will inevitably have greater deviance and will find itself tolerating more deviance. In fact, we would suggest that the appearance of diversity and controversy in such groups is not nearly so amazing as the fact that these were forestalled or at least kept hidden for so long. The point is that unanimity does not exist, cannot exist, and that diversity will only increase, unless, as now appears likely in the particular case described above, one faction accumulates sufficient power to essentially split the group formally into two groups or force out the deviates.

Let us now proceed to the second level at which the doctrinal issue or crisis of belief is operating—in terms of questioning, or, perhaps more accurately, appearing to question, the basic understanding of God him-

self—his nature and reality and his activity in the world. As indicated before, various theologians within both Protestantism and Catholicism seem
at least superficially to be characterizing fundamental religious presupposi-
tions, such as the reality of God and how he has chosen to relate to man,
as problematical. Certainly great numbers of both clergy and laymen interpret what these theologians are saying as direct challenges to the very
foundations of Christianity. Whether they are in fact such challenges
is more difficult to determine and is certainly beyond the province of the
sociologist and outside the scope of this volume. However, it should be
noted that all such theologians—whether demythologizers such as Ru-
dolph Bultman, or "theology of hope" proponents such as Wolfhart Pan-
nenburg, Jurgen Moltman, and Hans Hoekendijk, or foundational theologians, or "death of God" theologians, or popularizers such as Harvey
Cox and John A. T. Robinson—all seem primarily concerned with "God-
language," not just with God himself. For example, when Church of
England Bishop John A. T. Robinson says that our image of God must
go, he is not denying the existence of God or proposing that somehow we
banish him from the universe; rather, he is challenging our traditional
conceptualization of God, a conceptualization that he regards as inadequate for today. Whether other, related theologians are similarly inclined
or whether they are going farther and in fact proclaiming or even cele-
brating the "death" of God is a matter for theologians, not sociologists,
to decide. That such suggestions have disturbed, even shocked, people in
the church is, however, an understatement. That such statements and
discussions have cut some people loose from "the faith" is a possibility.
That such issues leave the future of Christian theology and conceptualization wide open is a certainty.

Quite clearly, then, the future of religion in the United States promises to hold excitement, whether one is inside or outside the church,
whether one is a theologian or a sociologist, for there is no doubt that
new concepts, formulations, and approaches to theology are still emerging, stirring up hornets' nests of controversy and discussion. For the sociologist, following these controversies will be fascinating and assessing
possible new directions for religion will be challenging to say the least.

MOVEMENTS TOWARD ECCLESIASTICAL RENEWAL (AGGIORNAMENTO)

So far in this chapter we have discussed, among other things, the conflict between the personal-salvation and social service emphases within
organized religion and the traditional conservative-liberal theological controversy that is very much alive in some denominations today. As already
suggested, these two issues are interrelated, a fact clearly seen in another

important relatively recent religious development, the call for the renewal of religious institutions from within. Such *ecclesiastical renewal* or reform is being proposed and is occurring at a number of levels—at the level of religious behavior, both institutional and individual; at the level of theology, in the sense of changes in official doctrinal formulations and policy; at the level of interaction of the two issues we have already discussed. That is, the entrance of religious groups into the arena of social reform and action is accompanied by readjustment of theological position. Also, theologians' reassessments of official denominational positions and interpretations of Scripture have had implications and repercussions concerning the action and application side of religion. Quite clearly, we are back to the central, unifying theme of this book—that religion as an interactional phenomenon moves and is moved, initiates action and is also acted upon, suggests and is suggested to. Thus when the Roman Catholic church speaks of *aggiornamento* (literally, "modernization") in the papal encyclical *Progressio Populorum* and in the documents that came out of the Second Vatican Council, or when observers speak of reform and change going on in the church, one sees both a conscious and unconscious awareness of changing social conditions that religion should speak to, whether for the first time to something new or in a new way to changed and changing social conditions.

Certainly the civil rights movement stimulated religious groups in the United States to reassess what they were teaching about race. For example, while thirty years ago it was not uncommon to find in the literature of many denominations an account of the "curse of Ham"—how Ham and his descendents (identified somewhere along the line as the Negro race) were cursed by God and destined forever to be slaves and servants—one reads this sort of thing very seldom now. In other words, social change can be seen in this case to have had an effect on theology and the interpretation of Scripture.

Similarly with anti-Semitism. In the wake of worldwide revulsion following Hitler's murder of 6 million Jews, and in positive response to an active educational campaign by American Jews, Protestants and Catholics have removed some of the more blatant anti-Semitic statements and implications from their educational literature. It is questionable whether the official theological positions of Christian groups with regard to Jews have changed much, however, for many positions still hold that eternal salvation requires faith in Jesus Christ and that those who do not profess such a faith—whether they be Muslim, Buddhist, Jewish, or adherents of any of a host of other non-Christian, "pagan" religions—are beyond the pale. In any event, at least the conversion attempts of Christian denominations now seem less strident and intense. And certainly not all Christians personally believe or accept the official theological position of their denominations in this matter. For example, the proportion of those who feel that belief in Jesus Christ as Savior is absolutely necessary for salvation ranges from 38 percent of Congregationalists to 97 percent of Southern Baptists and Missouri Synod Lutherans.[13] Similarly, the proportions who agree that "the Jews can never be forgiven for what they did to Jesus until they accept him as the true Savior" range as follows: 10 percent of Congregationalists, 11 percent of Episcopalians, 12 percent of Methodists, 14 percent of Catholics, 20 percent of the Disciples of Christ, 31 percent of Presbyterians, 37 percent of American Lutherans, 40 percent of American Baptists, 70 percent of Missouri Synod Lutherans, 79 percent of sectarians, and 80 percent of Southern Baptists.[14] That is, although in some Christian groups a majority hold to Christianity's historic theological view of the Jews and their prospects regarding eternal salvation, a significant proportion of Christians either disagree or are uncertain.

While a substantial majority (70 percent) of Missouri Synod Lutherans in Glock and Stark's study (cited above) agreed that Jews need to believe in the divinity of Jesus in order to be "forgiven," data published by Lawrence Kersten, gathered in the Detroit area approximately five years after Glock and Stark conducted their survey in the San Francisco Bay Area, show a significantly lower proportion of Missouri Synod Lutherans subscribing to this view (53 percent of laymen, 60 percent of clergy).[15] Whether such modestly dramatic differences in proportions from one date and location to another are indeed a function of change over time or simply reflect regional differences (or perhaps a simple vagary of sampling error) is impossible to determine and hazardous to guess. Actually, we do not have to resolve which is the "correct" proportion or whether change has in fact occurred over such a short time period. The point of the data is that in a denomination that has traditionally held strongly in its official theology that Jews need Jesus to be "forgiven," not nearly all members, even clergy, subscribe to this view today. Thus it is highly intriguing that in a recent survey of a large national sample of Lutherans, Merton Strommen and associates found that although approximately 75 percent said that belief in Jesus Christ is necessary for salvation, an equal proportion said that all religions lead to the same God—implying (though not stating) that belief in Jesus is not necessary.[16] Such an apparent inconsistency is enough to cause one to pause and

[13]Ibid., p. 23.
[14]Ibid., p. 62.
[15]Lawrence K. Kersten, *The Lutheran Ethic* (Detroit: Wayne State University Press, 1970), p. 82.
[16]Merton P. Strommen, Milo L. Brekke, Ralph C. Underwager, and Arthur L. Johnson, *A Study of Generations* (Minneapolis: Augsburg, 1972), p. 169.

think for a moment. The authors' suggestion that what 75 percent of Lutherans are saying is that belief in Jesus Christ is necessary for *me*, but not necessary for others, is a most likely explanation.

The example of change, both in practice and in theology, that could be classified as reform could be extended at length. Changes in religious views with respect to birth control, marriage and divorce, the function of sexual intercourse (procreation and/or pleasure combined with ultimate communication), homosexuality, and capital punishment are but some of the more obvious. For some, the motivation for change is an imperative growing out of their theological and biblical studies. For others, it is a desire to be "relevant" and to maintain one's religious institution as an attractive affiliation for people, youth in particular. For all who advocate change it is a willingness to change and modify present patterns within institutional religion. For some this means allowing greater latitude in theological definitions and understandings. Certainly some of this was evidenced in the deliberations of the Second Vatican Council (1962), in which there was discussion of such theological issues as the diffusion of ecclesiastical power, birth control and abortion, the status of Jews, the marriage of priests, liturgical reform, and so on.

What all discussions of ecclesiastical renewal seem to have in common, however, is a willingness to amend organizational forms and to experiment with various new structures and organizational life-styles. At one level we observe the emergence of the ecumenical movement in the early 1900s that has culminated in a number of organic mergers in the last decade; in the formation of the Consultation on Church Union (COCU) by twelve Protestant denominations for the purpose of expediting their joint merger; and in the legitimation of both formal and informal theological discussions among a great variety of groups who have explicitly expressed their desire to discover what common grounds exist for greater cooperation and sharing. Although our own sociological assessment of the long-range success of the ecumenical movement is pessimistic (for example, the original twelve participants in the COCU have been reduced to nine and will probably never result in organic union of more than two or three groups), one cannot ignore that some mergers have come about and, above all, that a great many groups are willing at least to discuss the possibility of such mergers—that is, about changes in their organizational form.

Renewal attempts are also being discussed and effected at the local level of individual congregations or parishes concerning their structure. Although there have been many different specific proposals and experiments, they can all be grouped into three major categories. First and oldest is the attempt to improve the utilization of existing large congregations or parishes by developing specialized ministries and services within them. This may involve establishing specialized assistant ministers each in charge of youth, music, counseling, social services, education, and the like. Or it may involve sponsoring specialized services to people within the congregation and in the surrounding community—services such as legal aid, medical and dental consultation, and assistance in securing welfare rights. This concept is one of the local congregation serving an umbrella function under which a great variety of activities take place and specialized services are rendered. The congregation in a sense becomes "all things to all men," offering services that would not be defined by everyone as religious, strictly speaking.

Another approach is that of redefining the traditional congregation, seen as a single worshipping unit, into a set of special-interest groups ranging from Bible study groups, to work cadres that devote their time to analysis and criticism of governmental structures, to service agencies for people requiring social welfare benefits, and so on. That the participants may all be members of a particular local congregation is almost incidental to their subgroup cohesion around a specialized interest or activity. In many cases the congregation and the physical facilities themselves serve essentially as a locus of organization and point of departure. For example, Glide Memorial Methodist Church in San Francisco serves various groups—blacks, the poor, people recovering from mental illness, homosexuals, and others who experience problems of social adjustment and acceptance—not by trying to absorb them into the church but by offering them leadership and facilities for meeting and sharing and planning together.

A third approach involves forsaking altogether the idea of a local congregation meeting in a building in a specific geographic location and instead sends the church out to where people work, play, or reside. In such "nongeographic ministries" a clergyman might find that his "congregation" is not "Fifth Avenue Protestant Church" at Fifth Avenue and Sixty-first Street, but is jazz musicians, or motorcyclists, or weekend skiers on the slopes, or summer campers in Yellowstone, or homosexuals in midtown gay bars, or residents of high-rise apartments, or businessmen in the financial district. The clergyman serves as a convener of people with similar interests and as a counselor on a one-to-one basis.

It is of special sociological interest concerning the second two approaches to restructuring local congregational life discussed above that what they are really attempting to do is revive the sense of community and human interrelatedness that growing cities and geographic mobility have tended to inhibit if not entirely destroy. Although one continues to hear nostalgic talk about the friendliness and warmth and sense of fellowship and community to be found in the old rural, small-town, or ethnic neighborhood church, an important sociological fact is overlooked in such glowing accounts—namely, that the local church was only one among several cohesive, unifying elements in such communities. The people referred to likely grew up together, went to school together, married within the community, interacted daily in the course of business and commerce, and found in their church what amounted to a reinforcement of social relationships that existed on many other levels. As such communities grew and people became geographically mobile, many urban and even small-town congregations became collections of strangers whose paths crossed only for an hour on Sunday. Therefore, although the restructuring of congregations around specialized interests and needs is not about to replace traditional congregational forms, and although a majority of congregations and certainly a majority of individual members of religious groups continue to work within traditional organizational forms and participate in traditional religious activities, the experimental forms described above have successfully met the needs of at least some for whom traditional patterns had proven less than satisfying.

NEW RELIGIOUS MOVEMENTS AND CULTS

If the proverbial "man in the street" knows anything about current developments on the religious scene, he is likely aware of new groups that appear and behave in somewhat unusual if not bizarre ways. He may see members of the Hare Krishna movement with their shaven heads and saffron robes. He sees notices and advertisements about this or that guru touring in the United States to extol the benefits of his Eastern religious philosophy. He may encounter young people in his neighborhood who talk freely about being really "turned on" to or by Jesus and take pride in the semiderogotory designation "Jesus freaks." He may know of someone in a traditional mainline Protestant or Catholic church who talks about his fantastic experiences with the Holy Spirit and how he has the gift of "speaking in tongues."

While one might be tempted to observe that offbeat and unconventional religious expressions are certainly nothing new, such an observation would not do justice to the proliferation of "new" religious expressions in the United States today. Although there is probably nothing in the "new" religious expressions and forms that has not appeared in another age or culture before, much of it is new to the American religious heritage. That the new religious expressions and forms are predominantly youth-related is fairly clear. We shall treat the phenomenon of religion and the American youth culture at some length in the next chapter. In a real sense, what we discuss here is an introduction to that chapter.

That American society—world society, for that matter—is in a changing, fluid, uncertain state is a truism that is obvious to most and that appears incredibly trite on the printed page. Yet this observation is fundamental to any discussion of new religious movements and cults. As modern man has begun to sense the serious, perhaps disastrous, repercussions of his past and present actions upon the future, he has become extremely discomfited. Unplanned and unlimited procreation appears to be leading to unbearable population pressures. Uncontrolled and expanding use of natural resources portends not only their disappearance but also a polluted, potentially unviable environment. Securing a college education and specialized academic training has produced a surplus of labor in a host of career fields. Blind faith in a political system and entrusting national leadership with virtually limitless power has resulted in the scandal of Watergate. The cultivation of suburban lawns and the accumulation of gas-powered engines to traverse winter snows and summer waters has resulted for many in less satisfaction and fulfillment than was confidently expected. Managed economies have on the average produced little more personal economic security than unmanaged ones. The unresponsiveness of governmental bureaucracy to personal cries of anguish, whether over undeclared wars or impoverishment and discrimination, has provoked both rebellion and cynicism, both strident assertiveness and navel-contemplating despair.

Both as a consequence and as a concomitant of these and other factors, traditional religious forms, answers, and solutions have for many become unsatisfying, even empty, and certainly quite irrelevant. Even the "civil religion" that Bellah cites as having been a unifying factor in American society almost from the founding of the nation has broken down.[17] As we have suggested earlier in this chapter, one consequence of the dissatisfaction with traditional religious forms that many people have expressed has been that religious organizations have made attempts at restructuring and reforming themselves. Yet another consequence has been individual and small-group experimentation with new religious forms, ideologies, and structures. Most of the "new" religious activity centers around personal quests for meaning, purpose, and roots in an unsettled and quavering if not fractured social environment. Who am I? Where am I going? Where do I—and my whole world, for that matter—fit vis-à-vis not only the history of this planet, but the cosmos itself? These are fundamental religious questions of personal identification and relationship with forces that affect both personal and societal destinies. One result of trying to answer them has been increasing experimentation with new and reborn or rediscovered religious forms and emphases.

17Robert N. Bellah, "Civil Religion in America," *Daedalus* 96, no. 1 (1967); 1–21.

Neopentecostalism

At the moment we shall focus on two general types of new religious form, and expand the list a bit in the final chapter as we focus on religion and the youth culture. The first, which appears to be as much an adult as a youth phenomenon, is the *charismatic* or *(neo-)pentecostal movement* that has emerged within both Catholic and mainline Protestant denominations. The quest for special experiences with the Holy Spirit and his special gifts in the form of glossolalia ("speaking in tongues"), trances, miraculous healing, and bodily expression in dancing and "fits" is not at all new. A solid tradition within Protestantism that goes back to the latter's beginnings in the fifteenth and sixteenth centuries has developed parallel to the dominant denominational Protestantism. The healing evangelists of the type of Oral Roberts and scores of other contemporary exemplars are known to most everyone. The "snake cults" in Appalachia in which the special spiritual gift of handling poisonous serpents and quaffing poisonous strichnine without harm periodically hit the public press. But middle-class denominational Catholicism and Protestantism have habitually dismissed such activities out-of-hand as appropriate only for lower-class persons in need of some bizarre form of escape in order to adjust to their life situation, but hardly satisfying behavior for middle- and upper-class types.

Thus what is new and from certain perspectives surprising is the emergence very recently of pentecostal subgroups in the traditional Christian denominations. Not that anything approaching a majority of these denominations are becoming charismatic or pentecostal or that such a majority will appear in the future. But enough have emerged not only to elicit concern and censure from denominational authorities but to merit sociological interest. Although the numerical strength of those practicing this neopentecostalism is not overwhelming, estimates have been as high as five hundred thousand persons spread throughout the major denominations in the United States.[18] The *Seattle Times* reports that among Lutherans alone in the Pacific Northwest the charismatic movement has become a network of about fifteen hundred families and one hundred clergymen.[19]

Although the neopentecostal (now commonly called "charismatic") movement can trace its genesis back to isolated cases in the 1950s, it first gained public attention in 1960 when Dennis Bennett, an Episcopalian

[18]*St. Louis Post Dispatch*, October 29, 1972.
[19]*Seattle Times*, November 11, 1972.

minister in Van Nuys, California, resigned his office in an effort to stem incipient divisiveness over pentecostal practices by himself and some members of his congregation. Apparently publicity of this episode served as a catalyst to bring to the surface other instances of charismatic activity in nonpentecostal churches. In 1961 support was added from the academic community when nineteen students and one faculty member at Yale University reported receiving the baptism of the Holy Spirit. Similar reports came out of Dartmouth and Princeton soon after. A decade later the movement had been established in all mainline Protestant denominations and among Roman Catholics and Eastern Orthodox as well.

In most cases, regardless of denominational affiliation, charismatics emphasize that they do not wish to separate from their parent churches, but simply to aid in revitalizing their congregations, their denominations, and Christianity itself by testifying to the extraordinary work of God brought into their lives through the power of the Holy Spirit. Not that such experiences are for everyone, they feel; but they are to be seen as a viable option for those who are touched.

Watson E. Miller sees a possible source of this new emphasis in traditional Christian churches in the fact that "glossolalia (the ability to speak words and phrases of a language unlearned and unknown to the speaker) may ... be a loud protest against the cold impersonality that sometimes characterizes institutionalized worship."[20] If we add to Miller's suggestion the observation that, except for the occasional conventions of charismatics that attract hundreds and even thousands of people (such as the annual meeting of Catholic charismatics at the University of Notre Dame), charismatics tend to meet in small groups where one observes interpersonal warmth, openness, trust, and emotional support, sometimes even without "speaking in tongues," we may be explaining some of the attractiveness of the movement. Amid rapid social change, the uprooting of many traditional institutional moorings, the breaking of contact with families and friends through job mobility, and other concomitants of contemporary American life, many people are especially receptive to opportunities for open, trusting, intimate contact with others. In very simple sociological terms, they are seeking primary groups and relationships to replace those they have lost.

All such comments remain for the present essentially hypotheses, however, as little research data are yet available. It is nevertheless interesting to observe—although such observations are not quantified or validated—that some standard demographic variables do not, on the surface at least, seem to apply to charismatics: that is, they are of both sexes, of a

[20]Watson E. Miller, "Glossalalia: Christianity's 'Counterculture' Amidst a Silent Majority," *Christian Century*, September 27, 1972, p. 951.

full age range, both urban and rural, of a wide variety of occupations and levels of education, and of a diversity of religious backgrounds (e.g., from both liturgical and nonliturgical denominations). Whether any of these or other factors are significantly related to receptivity to or participation in the charismatic movement is not yet clear.

It is significant that whereas denominations at first attempted to discourage the movement by censuring congregations and particularly clergymen who participated, much of that opposition has been modified. Thus the movement today, though not necessarily encouraged, is increasingly tolerated. In a sense, this growing tolerance undermines one source of growth for charismatic groups, according to Gerlach and Hine. These researchers found that among important growth factors for the groups they studied was the "psychology of persecution." Ridicule, nonacceptance, and rejection by traditional denominational churches served to stimulate growth, whereas in those instances where local denominational officials did not oppose the movement, recruitment was more difficult.[21]

From the perspective of the host institution (churches) within which the charismatic movement is occurring, such activity would normally and naturally be resisted because it is by definition beyond the control of the host organization. Charismatic activity and authority is a challenge to traditional, organizationally legitimated authority. Who knows what such open-ended authority from outside the organization (the Holy Spirit moving as and where it wills) will produce? The only apparent explanation for the relative tolerance of the movement on the part of the denominations is that most within the movement insist that they are not out to destroy the organization or even to withdraw themselves from it, but want to offer an internal, optional form of religious experience and worship: they desire simply to enrich what institutional religion already has to offer.

The Cult Movement

While the charismatic or neopentecostal movement in American religion is new by virtue of its development within standard denominational religion, pentecostalism is nonetheless an old tradition in Christianity that has attained a considerable measure of legitimacy in its own denominational forms. Other recent developments in American religion, however, do not fit within standard denominational forms and are in fact alternatives if not challenges to such standard forms. We are referring

---

[21]Luther P. Gerlach and Virginia H. Hine, "Five Factors Crucial to the Growth and Spread of a Modern Religious Movement," *Journal for the Scientific Study of Religion* 7, no. 1 (1968); 36.

to what can fairly properly be called the proliferation of cults in American religion.

Cults in general are of course not at all new to American religion. They abounded in the nineteenth century, when they were represented by such religious utopian communities such as the Shakers, the Oneida perfectionists, and the Amana community, as well as by such cults as Christian Science, the Theosophical Society, and Divine Science. The first half of the twentieth century also witnessed the emergence of many cults —the Church of Truth Universal–AUM, Psychiana, and the Fellowship of Divine Truth, to name just three.

What seems new in cult development in the second half of this century are two features: (1) a change in the origin or base of the belief and practices system, (2) a probable increase in the number of followers, though numbers are impossible to substantiate with assurance. Before we offer some tentative evidence in support of these observations, we must admit to the difficulty of making generalizations of any kind in the area of religious cults in the United States. In the first place, they exhibit a great diversity in focus and message. Thus comprehensive generalizations regarding all cults must of necessity be very broad. Secondly, consistent with our emphasis on the informal structure of cults as discussed in Chapter 7, they are likely not to have much in the way of printed material or creeds for an observer to analyze. They have fluid memberships and usually no hard membership statistics—or at least none that they are willing to publish or otherwise report publicly. Further, they are often localized and virtually unknown beyond a given locality or region.

Having acknowledged these methodological difficulties and the consequent tentativeness of our observations, we shall return to the two general features mentioned above. First, there is evidence of a strong Far Eastern religious influence in many American religious cults today, although not all contemporary cults by any means. Hinduism and Buddhism particularly serve as points of origin and orientation for many of them: Zen, Subud, Vajrayana Buddhism, Sufism, Meher Baba, I Ching, and scores of others. In most cases, these groups and their messages offer something dramatically different from most of Western religion (with the possible exception of some of the Catholic and Eastern Orthodox contemplative and eremitic monastic orders). Cults that arose during the last century and during most of this century were built strongly on either Western philosophy and Christianity or, at the farthest extreme, on Near Eastern religions such as Egyptian Rosicrucianism—but to very little extent on religions from the Far East. The exceptions to this were the New Thought and Theosophical cults that emerged seventy-five to one hundred years ago. Most modern (within the last twenty-five years) American cults share with them quite distinct strains of Hinduism and Buddhism—

themes of meditation and getting right in your mind and body with the cosmic forces and fluids of the universe. It seems, however, that Far Eastern Hindu and Buddhist influence in American cult religion is more conscious and explicit than before.

The second point we want to make about modern cults, regarding the numbers of their members, is, as already indicated, impossible to document—and we're on even less solid ground when talking about the past. Our impression is, however, that there are more people attracted to religious cults in the United States today than were in the past. Estimates of membership numbers for some of them, made by Peter Rowley, will be instructive at this point:[22]

Scientology	600,000	Association for Research	
Nichiren Shoshu	200,000	and Enlightenment	13,000
Spiritual Scientists	150,000	Meher Baba	7,000
Transcendental		Gurdjieff	5,000
Meditation	125,000	Witchcraft	5,000
I Ching	125,000	Satanic Cults	5,000
Yoga	125,000	Zen	2,000
Nation of Islam		Subud	1,500
("Black Muslims")	100,000	Hare Krishna	1,500
Bahai	100,000		

If these estimates are anywhere nearly accurate, and if we add those followers of older cults that still persist, there are over a million and a half Americans in the cult movement today.

Another observation about contemporary cults that we might expect to make, given the new age in which we live and the apparently greater Far Eastern influence on cults—namely, that the content of the cult message or gospel is different today—should not be made at all. Certainly the Power, or Force, or Spirit, or Method, or God is different from one group to another. But the central idea inherent in cults both past and present is strikingly similar: a technique of "getting your mind together," of putting mind and body in closer harmony by getting in tune with the energizing or central power or force in the universe. It is truly striking, after listening to members of various contemporary groups and reading their publications, to realize that what each group defines as the problem to be overcome and what each offers as the method for resolving that problem resemble so fundamentally every other group's definitions as to be essentially identical. The problem to be solved is typically a highly integrated pair of issues: (1) Who am I and where do I fit into the world? (Identity)

[22]Peter Rowley, *New Gods in America* (New York: McKay, 1971), pp. 3–4.

and (2) How can I find peace and unity of mind and body, of the spiritual and the material within me? The solution is typically a technique involving, on the one hand, meditation (perhaps using yoga or related postures and exercises, or perhaps by repeating key words and phrases), and, on the other hand, small-group encouragement, support, and reinforcement. It appears to be crucial for this purpose that the cult be small and that members be capable of close contact on a one-to-one basis or with at most a handful of others. In this sense cults resemble, and perform functions similar to, the charismatic groups within traditional denominations discussed in the previous section.

It is not at all surprising that such religious cults flourish today. This author is personally surprised, not by their numbers and their followings, but by the fact that there aren't actually more people involved in them. Amid the defilement of our natural environment, the violation of the integrity and freedom of people by all manner of exploitation, enslavement, and discrimination, the hypocrisy and self-centeredness of one's fellow men, the failure, as many young people see it, of science to solve our problems, and the overarching threat of planetary self-destruction, it is small wonder that many people seeking a way out find an answer in what religious cults offer.

Whether such an answer is a "copout" or indeed a way out we may not be certain. Is Charles A. Reich correct when he sees in the new "consciousness" typified by (though not found exclusively in) the new religious cults the great hope for America and the entire Western world?[23] Or do the ideas and strivings of these groups represent the end of the line, a last-ditch attempt by the misfits and the unloved to find peace and security? We certainly cannot say.

But we can say that the new American cults are asking religious questions and posing religious solutions and that in many senses their members are more profoundly religious than many in standard religious organizations who have submerged the great religious questions and participate only perfunctorily and halfheartedly in ritual activities. In fact, Jacob Needleman strongly suggests that the "great value of this new 'religiosity' is that through it our young people are able to *entertain great ideas.*" In other words, part of the crisis of our civilization is that the great transcendent ideas that once dominated and defined people's lives have become choked to death by an impatient pragmatism that seldom thinks carefully before it acts.[24]

We would also suggest that the "success" of the new religious cults, in combination with the middle-age vitality of some standard religious

23Charles Reich, *The Greening of America* (New York: Random House, 1970).
24Jacob Needleman, "Winds from the East: Youth and Counter-Cults," *Commonweal,* April 30, 1971, p. 189.

organizations in the United States, indicates clearly that religion in our society, whether as an institution or as an absorbing quest for truth, is certainly not dead, nor about to die soon. Concern with this question of the future of religion, which will return us to the fundamental question of the function of religion, will constitute the first part of the next and final chapter as we consider some of the contributions of important contemporary theorists in the sociology of religion.

DECLINING LIBERALISM, EXPANDING CONSERVATISM?

We earlier referred to the possibility that some people have been leaving the so-called liberal denominations and affiliating with conservative denominations partly as a protest against the social service emphasis of some of the mainline liberal Protestant denominations. Certainly this is a ready conclusion one might make after reading the early chapters of Dean Kelley's recent book *Why Conservative Churches Are Growing*.[25] Kelley points out that such prominent denominations as the Episcopalians, Methodists, Presbyterians, Congregationalists, and Lutherans have been declining in membership, some for several years, while other religious groups have been growing by substantial proportions, certainly exceeding the net rate of population growth for the nation. Among the latter Kelley lists the Southern Baptist Convention, the Assemblies of God, the Churches of God, Mormons, Jehovah's Witnesses, the Salvation Army, and Seventh-Day Adventists.[26] What do these observations mean? Is religious conservatism making a comeback? And if so, is it at the expense of religious liberalism? Is our prediction early in this chapter of a continuing decline of institutionalized religion so soon to be contradicted? These are significant enough questions addressed to significant enough empirical data to demand our serious consideration.

What, then, can be said? That conservative churches are growing and liberal churches are not is clear. That some of the growth of conservative churches consists of defectors from liberal churches is assured. That continued growth for the one category and decline for the other will mark the immediate future is also very likely. Yet we dare not ignore that some people are leaving conservative churches for liberal ones. Moreover, some are leaving liberal churches and not going to conservative ones, but are proceeding in the altogether different direction of total disaffiliation from all organized religion.

We should note at this point that Kelley rejects all that he calls

---

[25]Dean M. Kelley, *Why Conservative Churches Are Growing* (New York: Harper & Row, 1972).
[26]Ibid., pp. 1–25.

simple explanations—such as reaction against the social action emphasis of liberal churches, or the growing secularization of the liberal churches, or the centering of authority in liberal churches in the clergy and a subordination of laity to passive roles. Kelley's own hypothesis is that the growing religious organizations are the strict ones—the ones that demand firm allegiance, tireless devotion to proclaiming the Gospel, obedience to authority, stoic acceptance of ridicule from outside, and so on.

In a similar vein is the explanation for conservative growth and liberal decline proposed by George LaNoue, who notes that the conservative churches offer people a scare commodity for which religion is the nearly unique source—namely, salvation—while the liberal churches have been trying to offer a panoply of goods and services that are also available from a host of other sources—entertainment, intellectual stimulation, and discussion and activity centering around social issues, for example. Because many secular groups can often do a better job of delivering such goods and services within their areas of specialization, liberal religious groups are likely to lose out in the competition. Small wonder, then, that conservative groups that promise delivery of a scarce commodity should grow, and liberal groups that must compete with numerous secular groups in the same business, so to speak, should be shrinking.[27]

Inately appealing as these hypotheses concerning the differential growth and decline in conservative and liberal religious groups may be, we must introduce a couple of studies that trace the changing religious affiliations of people. The reason is that a distinct disadvantage of both Kelley's and LaNoue's work is that their data represent total membership figures only, and thus cannot be used to trace the movements of individuals from one religious group to another. In fact, we can't necessarily infer from these data any movement at all. For example, if the birth rate were higher among members of the more conservative religious groups (which is quite likely, in fact) then the growth of these groups through natural reproduction alone might conceivably account for their increasing numerical advantage over the liberal denominations. Or again, perhaps the conservative groups are gaining strength by picking up the nonaffiliated person with little or no religious background, not necessarily the dropouts from liberal denominations.

As for studies tracing changes in religious affiliations, in Stark and Glock's San Francisco Bay Area study nearly half of the Protestant respondents (46 percent) reported having changed denominational affiliation at some time in the past.[28] In seeking patterns away from and toward

---

[27]Cited in ibid., pp. 92–93.
[28]Rodney Stark and Charles Y. Glock, *American Piety* (Berkeley: University of California Press, 1968).

certain denominations, Stark and Glock conclude that the general tendency for those who change religious affiliation is to move from more conservative bodies to those that are more liberal theologically.[29]

Samuel Mueller, analyzing the same data, reached different, though not diametrically opposed conclusions. Through the application of factor-analytic techniques he found that switches of religious affiliation occur essentially without reference to the liberal or conservative stance of the groups involved, but are made in such a way as to preserve similarity among as many dimensions as possible. That is, people tend to affiliate with a religious group similar in a sociological sense to the one they are leaving. The relevant similarities do not seem to be so much doctrinal or creedal as they are related to such factors as social status and liturgy. That is, people seem to look for another religious group that has members like themselves and which has a form of worship similar to what they have known and practiced in the past. Some of these religiously mobile people wind up in more liberal denominations, but usually for other than theological or doctrinal reasons or motivations. Similarly for those who move to more conservative denominations.[30]

Where does this leave us, then, with regard to the issue of the relative growth and decline of conservative and liberal churches? And at an even more general level, where do these trends fit into the observation with which this chapter began—namely, that there has been a recent general decline in denominational religion in the United States?

For one thing, the analyses offered by Mueller and by Stark and Glock cast some doubt on Kelley's hypothesis. Since we do not know the source of the new members in the conservative groups for which Kelley gives data—whether defectors from liberal denominations, converts from irreligion, or simply above-average natural-reproductive increase—we cannot infer the doctrinal motivations for the discrepancy between liberal and conservative denominational growth rates that both Kelley and La-Noue at least implicitly suggest. In fact, Stark and Glock's data, as well as National Opinion Research Center data that they also examined, suggest that denominational mobility proceeds in both directions between liberal and conservative groups—and proceeds, moreover, according to Mueller's analysis, in a nearly random fashion insofar as theological stances of the gaining and losing denominations are concerned.

We should also mention what in some senses is probably the most crucial factor in this entire issue—that is, that the groups with the highest rate of increase are relatively small groups. Except for the Southern

---

[29]Ibid., p. 187.
[30]Samuel A. Mueller, "Dimensions of Interdenominational Mobility in the United States," *Journal for the Scientific Study of Religion* 10, no. 2 (1971); 76–84.

Baptist Convention, the total number of new members of conservative religious groups in this country is not large in absolute numbers, particularly when the natural-reproduction factor is taken into account. We mention this not because we wish to discredit conservative theology or somehow translate conservative growth out of existence through slippery argumentation. We simply feel that although the growth of some conservative denominations and the decline in some liberal denominations are important phenomena well worth airing, both trends fit within the larger context of overall incipient decline so far as organized religion is concerned. So although we can observe differential rates of growth and decline when we consider individual denominations, the overall effect is a net loss so far as denominational religion is concerned—not only presently but as we are predicting, in the future as well. Thus we can expect current rates of growth for conservative groups to level off and even begin showing net losses twenty years or so from now.

SOCIOLOGICAL
PROJECTIONS

Part **V**

16

The Future of Religion

In the preceding fifteen chapters we have run through many of the major topics that have been subsumed by social scientists under the heading *sociology of religion*. Much of the time we have been descriptive of the religious scene and have done much of what sociologists are prone to do —categorize behavior and attach labels—always trying to explicate and understand the world around us. We have also introduced some theoretical perspectives and discussed attempts to show relationships among variables—all in an effort to explain religious behavior and its impact on other types of human behavior. We have deliberately tried to produce a summary of relevant contemporary research and thought in the sociology of religion upon which one can build. We now wish in conclusion to introduce the reader to some of the major theory building that has been going on within the sociology of religion—not so much in the hope that we can summarize in one short chapter the theoretical developments under way in the field, but with an eye on suggesting to the reader some of the directions of thought and research that provide wide-open possibilities for development. In a sense, we shall be implicitly considering in this chapter the question: Where do we or might we go from here? In that sense we are here trying to prepare the reader for the next level— perhaps a second, higher-level course, but in any event certainly the next level of thinking in the sociology of religion.

Our specific point of departure is the observation made near the end of Chapter 15 to the effect that religion in its fundamental sense of seeking answers to questions of ultimate concern and of seeking some order in chaos has not disappeared from society and does not appear about to do so, at least not very soon. This observation brings us back to our concerns, early in this book, with the definition of religion and its purpose or function in society. These are continuing concerns of contemporary theorists in the sociology of religion, continuing in part because of the observed continued vitality of religion—how to explain it? —and also in part because theorists attempt to project the future of religion and its relationship with society.

Our procedure in this chapter will be first to summarize some of the theorizing being done by sociologists and sociologically oriented theologians regarding the future of religion and its potential forms of adaptation. Second, we shall present a brief analysis of the "Jesus movement," both because of the theoretical insight into contemporary religion it provides and because of its practical interest and descriptive value for students of the sociology of religion. That is to say, the Jesus movement is a relevant and interesting contemporary topic for anyone with an interest in religion, whether as an academic, scientific observer or as a traditional or even a "new" believer. But further, the sociological themes inherent in the Jesus movement provide an appropriate ending to this introductory text in the sociology of religion.

SOCIOLOGICAL THEORIES ABOUT THE FUTURE OF RELIGION

Berger's Proposal

The first theorist whose thought we shall examine is Peter Berger, who has dealt extensively with the place and function of religion in society. One of his fundamental points is that society by virtue of its order and predictability protects the individual from the terror of chaos and meaninglessness.[1] It tells him who he is, where he's from, what he's a part of, and what he can expect. When the society is most successful in providing a predictable framework for its members and staving off the nightmare of meaninglessness and anomie, it has convinced its members that what they and their society understand and know to be true is actually "in the nature of things." People's understanding of reality is then neither arbitrary nor limited to their experience and understanding. It

[1] Peter L. Berger, *The Sacred Canopy* (Garden City, N.Y.: Doubleday, 1969), pp. 22–24.

is neither historical nor temporal. It is universal. It is cosmic. It is truly the way it is—in the universe.

At this point Berger introduces religion. The ultimate authentication for the societal reality, as members of a society see it and know it, derives "from more powerful sources than the historical effects of human beings. . . . Religion is the human enterprise by which a sacred cosmos is established."[2] The neat thing is that although this sacred cosmos far transcends human beings, it also includes them and helps give man a meaningful place within the ordered universe. Above all, it protects man from the terrible alternative of chaos and tentativeness. Berger is careful to point out that such *"cosmization"* need not be sacred or religious. It may alternately be attempted, even achieved, by science. Originally, however, all cosmization had a sacred character.[3]

Once such cosmization has been established, a potent legitimating force has been unleashed within the society. The leader can then say: "These are not just my ideas or merely the conclusions of our wise men; these are cosmic laws, universal principles, 'God's will and design.' " The citizen may go against and challenge such cosmic authority, but only at the risk of plunging into chaos and anomie. He risks moving into negative reality—an antiworld of darkness as opposed to light, of devil as opposed to God.[4]

Onto this account of what appears to be, on the surface at least, a well-wrought argument for the proposition that man has a universal need for religion, Berger proceeds to impose a series of historical developments that in fact seem to undercut this argument. One of these is the secularization process, which we introduced in Chapter 15. In defining secularization as "the process by which sectors of society and culture are removed from the domination of religious institutions and symbols,"[5] Berger proceeds to show that in modern society religious definitions of the world have lost much of their plausibility not only for intellectuals but for a broad range of citizens. Science, technological development, and new political and economic structures have posed alternatives to religious world-views and have proved capable of functioning on their own, independent of religious influence or even legitimation. Add to secularization the development of pluralism and privatization—actually part of the secularization process—and old religious foundations are now "on the ropes," so to speak. *Pluralism* meant not only that there were alternative explanations of where the world came from and how it was maintained, but also that other religious alternatives were available. Religion had two prob-

2Ibid., p. 25.
3Ibid., p. 27.
4Ibid., pp. 39–40.
5Ibid., p. 107.

lems: it no longer had the official support of the state, and it was fragmented into many groups, each competing with the others for members.

Privatization or *individualization* of religion refers to the growing concept of religion as a matter of individual choice; it is therefore closely related to pluralism, as well as being an adaptation aid for the individual psyche. Further, religion became a family rather than a societal phenomenon, a matter of private morals that was not particularly relevant for conduct in the economic and political institutions "out in the world."

The result corresponds with what we described earlier in terms of the breakup of the church-type of organization and the emergence of denominational society—not only religious competition for members in essentially a free market system, but accommodation and change and adaptation on the part of religious systems to appeal to people and to be "relevant" amid changing social conditions. Thus Western religion has produced, in essentially chronological order: pietism, social gospel, neo-orthodoxy, religionless–death of God–existential Christianity in efforts to adjust, communicate, and be relevant to changing conditions in society. But there has been reaction formation also—a resurgence of fundamentalism and a few membership shifts out of liberal denominations to conservative ones, plus neopentecostalism and the cult movement.

The conclusion one might draw from both such a theoretical perspective and such accumulations of data is that religion is in trouble. Actually, Berger regards the dramatic changes within Protestantism as a prototype of changes one would expect not only in other Western religions, but in religious systems everywhere as they face secularization, pluralization, privatization, industrialization, and political change. It is essentially very simply the problem of maintaining plausibility in the face of social change.

As a partial antidote to conclusions such as those noted above, Berger published *A Rumor of Angels* (1970) as his own reflection and reaction to what he had written in *The Sacred Canopy* (1969). In the preface to the sequel he says of his earlier book: "The analysis of the contemporary situation with which it ended could easily be read ... as a counsel of despair for religion in the modern world."[6] He goes on to point out that from his personal perspective—and he trusts from a sociological perspective as well—religion need not, perhaps cannot, be excised from man. Religious understandings and definitions may change, institutional forms may come and go, but fundamental religious questions and, for that matter, even religious answers will remain.

Although (he notes) traditional Western institutional religion has been undergoing a serious "plausibility crisis" for some time, and al-

---

[6]Peter L. Berger, *A Rumor of Angels* (Garden City, N.Y.: Doubleday, 1970), p. ix.

though we can observe serious crumbling of its walls, superstition and interest in astrology abound—to which we might add the significant up-surge of interest in the occult and, of course, all manner of flirtations with cults as noted in the preceding chapter. Berger cites research in England which reports that nearly half of the respondents had consulted a fortuneteller, one in six expressed belief in ghosts, and one in fifteen claimed actually to have seen a ghost.[7] That is, despite rationality, em-piricism, relativism, and conclusions about the implausibility of tradi-tional religious answers and formulations, many people presume the supernatural and participate in quests to find and explore it.

But Berger goes beyond what we may conclude after a moment or two of reflection are apparent contradictory bits of evidence to anyone's predictions about the imminent demise of religion. It is very likely people are more than genes and cells and that the world is more than black earth, blue sky, turquoise water, and green foliage. In an effort to find what else there is—the stuff of which religion is made and on which it is based—he suggests a theological quest for "signals of transcendence within the em-pirically given human situation."[8] By *signals of transcendence* he is refer-ring to phenomena that occur within the natural domain and experience of man but seem to point beyond that particular realm of validity.[9] He mentions such things as the desire and propensity of man for order and predictability and the universal experience of man we call play, in which time becomes suspended or redefined—e.g., as the second act, the ninth inning, the third quarter, or the off-beat. Or, there is the argument from damnation—"experiences in which our sense of what is humanly permis-sible is so fundamentally outraged that the only adequate response to the offence as well as to the offender seems to be a curse of supernatural di-mensions."[10] No human punishment is enough in the case of the sexual murder of a five-year-old child or the wholesale gassing of millions of European Jews. Or, there is the argument from humor, humor being viewed essentially as the recognition of the comic discrepancy of being human, and then relativizing it. At least for the moment the inherent tragedy of man (progressing ultimately toward death) is suspended or "bracketed," and we become convinced that death will not have the only laugh, perhaps not even the final one.

At this point Berger is suggesting that the human touches the tran-scendent, perhaps the supernatural, and has a taste of what might exist outside rational, empirical, sensate experience. At the base of it all is the usually unconscious desire and attempt by man to obviate death, to avoid

[7]Ibid., p. 25.
[8]Ibid., p. 52.
[9]Ibid., p. 53.
[10]Ibid., p. 65.

chaos, to see purpose and future in his mundane stumbling and mumbling. That is, there may be more to this than that man has some kind of religious need: some kind of nontemporal reality that transcends and eludes the grasp of empirical measuring devices may, in fact, exist. Berger is suggesting that man at least has some models for such ideas from his everyday experiences. These may be not only "signals of transcendence"— hints of a supernatural world that really exists—but most important so far as our focus in this final chapter is concerned, we may be pointing toward understanding not only why religion in its multitude of forms has persisted so long but why we might expect it to continue. This is not to say necessarily that man is a religious animal, but suggests that there is a "religious" element in the world or universe that man senses and tries to apprehend. It's a possibility. Certainly Berger himself is careful to point out that his is a quest and an encouragement for others to engage in quest, not a system of answers and discoveries. That what we might call the religious quest is still embarked on with varying degrees of intensity by so many people certainly suggests at the very least that if a supernatural world does not exist, man has an abundance of experiences that would make him think it does. What is particularly intriguing about Berger's theorizing is that one does not need to rely on a charismatic leader or special divine revelation or even deep mystical introspection to pick up "signals" of the transcendent. Although such signals of course do not "prove" its reality, the search for that transcendent will not require much rationalizing or justification for many people.

Luckmann's Proposal

Thomas Luckmann pursues a theme that we barely alluded to in our above discussion of Berger—namely, that change in contemporary religion centers in the individuation and privatization of religion. Actually, Luckmann develops a theoretical framework for understanding the status of religion in contemporary Western societies that is parallel to that of Berger. Luckmann accepts as an empirical observation the process of secularization, defined essentially as a growing irrelevance of traditional religious forms in contemporary society. The symbolic reality or universe of traditional church religion, Luckmann says, "appears to be unrelated to the culture of modern industrial society. It is certain, at least, that internalization of the symbolic reality of traditional religions is neither enforced nor, in the typical case, favored by the social structure of contemporary society."[11] Luckmann's definition of religion centers in the concept of "symbolic universes of meaning" that groups create to inter-

11Thomas Luckmann, *The Invisible Religion* (New York: Macmillan, 1967), p. 37.

pret their experiences. He defines *symbolic universes* as "socially objecti-
vated systems of meaning that refer, on the one hand, to the world of
everyday life and point, on the other hand, to a world that is experienced
as transcending everyday life."[12] The key distinction between religion
and other systems that also provide meaning and interpretation of individual experiences is that religion refers to a transcendent dimension of
reality that the others do not have. Another way of saying this is that
only religion provides the society with a sacred cosmos and an encom-
passing world-view, in which everyday, mundane activities that make up
individual biographies and social history are subordinated to levels of
significance and meaning that transcend that everyday life.[13]

Articulating the relationship of mundane activities within the context of the sacred cosmos tends to become a specialized function on the
basis of which religious institutions emerge. Although this is not necessarily implied when a society first recognizes a sacred cosmos, increasing
complexity and specialization within the society makes religious specialization almost inevitable. In a literal sense, the process of secularization
begins when religion becomes a specialized function along with education, economics, and politics. The institutionalization of religion implies
both a growing gap between laymen and religious specialists and a tendency to freeze religious understandings and definitions into doctrine.

Because the individual is socialized into the religious system, for the
typical citizen, according to Luckmann, "matters of 'ultimate' significance
are, therefore, those that are designated as religious by the specialized
religious institutions in their 'official' model."[14] The individual is socialized into a religious organization with doctrines, liturgies, and traditions
which hopefully he will adopt as his own. Successful accomplishment of
this process of course presupposes that the official model is "subjectively
plausible."[15]

It is unrealistic to expect a perfect congruence, and certainly that
has not happened historically. Certainly it is possible that religious specialists by virtue of their specialization get out of tune with the life situations and concerns of laymen. But equally crucial is the fact that the
religious institution of necessity finds itself involved in "secular" activities
(see Chapters 7 and 9): it becomes bureaucratically organized; it becomes
a part of the larger economic system of the society; it engages in internal
and external political activity. In a sense, religion becomes contaminated.
But further: in complex societies characterized by religious diversity,
competition among symbolic systems that are at least somewhat different,

[12]Ibid., p. 43.
[13]Ibid., p. 58.
[14]Ibid., p. 73.
[15]Ibid., p. 74.

friendly though that competition may be, tends to undermine the universalistic claim that is endemic to religion.

Add to this the aforementioned tendency of religious systems to "freeze" their system and, even if willing to adapt, to not quite know which direction of change to choose. Consequently, the religious institution is in an awkward situation. The result is that the individual member and citizen confronted with not only an increasingly implausible symbolic system but also a wide range of alternative explanations of reality begins to lose his attachment and commitment to the religious system.

The citizen lives in a world that changes at an increasing rate and he sees fathers who do not practice what they preach. But not only is there a generation gap. People also find themselves in differing social situations by virtue of occupational specialization, social class, place of residence, and so on. The degree of incongruency between the "official" model and the experiences and priorities of individuals only increases as a consequence.

The upshot is, as Luckmann states: "The norms of traditional religious institutions—as congealed in an 'official' or formerly 'official' model of religion—cannot serve as a yardstick for assessing religion in contemporary society."[16] Another way of saying this is that if religion persists in modern societies, we will not expect to find it residing solely in the traditional religious forms, institutions, or expresssions.

As mentioned before, one of the crucial elements in the process of the declining influence of institutional religion that occurred over a long period of time, back at least to the Renaissance, was the formation of religion into a specialized institution. Luckmann states that "the long-range consequences of institutional specialization of religion as part of an over-all process of social change resulted, paradoxically, in the loss of what institutional specialization originally accomplished in the 'pluralistic' religious context of the Hellenistic world and the Roman Empire: monopoly in the definition of an obligatory sacred cosmos."[17] Religion became one among many institutions in society. It became restricted to its "proper" sphere. Its proper sphere increasingly became that of private life. The individual or privatized citizen now confronts the traditional religious model essentially as a consumer. The traditional religious model is thus lined up with other thought systems, institutions, "packages," and life-styles from which the consumer chooses to provide himself with "ultimate" meanings and satisfactions. Luckmann suggests that syndicated advice columns, "inspirational" literature ranging from books and tracts

16Ibid., p. 91.
17Ibid., p. 94.

on positive thinking to *Playboy* magazine, *Reader's Digest* versions of popular psychology, the latest philosophy embodied in popular songs, and so on, offer options as to models of "ultimate" meaning and satisfaction.[18] Traditional religious forms and expressions continue to be an option, of course—but only one among many from which the privatized citizen selects what he wants for himself.

Without explicitly saying it, Luckmann is implying of course that the fundamental religious questions of personal identity, of how to confront the vagaries of life, and of how to face the ultimate terror of death are still there. As the citizen faces them he is very much alone. He is still "religious." But clearly it is not religion in a traditional sense to which he subscribes. In the trend toward the privatization and individualization of religion there are two possible consequences, and the two are intimately related. One consequence, the progression from privatization and subjective autonomy to anomie, is likely a short step. The second is that the liberation of the human consciousness from the constraints of social structure may lead to mass withdrawal into the private sphere "while Rome burns."[19] Luckmann is definitely suggesting that the "triumph" of secularization and individualism over traditional religious constraints and the creation of an "invisible" religion may constitute a hollow victory indeed, as people become anomic and indifferent to societal norms, or as they lose a sense of responsibility for the society of which they are a part.

The Civil Religion Hypothesis

One resolution of the problem implicit in both Berger's and Luckmann's analyses—the decline of traditional religion in the face of secularization and the resultant privatization of concern over the Ultimate—a resolution which some regard as having a firm historical base and others want to encourage whether firmly based or not, is what is generally called *civil religion*. In the analyses of both Berger and Luckmann there are three dimensions or types of religion that are considered. First is what we might call the *church pattern*, built on the primary religious pattern, in which there is one unifying religion for all and which is intimately related to the state. Second, there is the *denominational form*, in which individual religious groups vie for members. Third, there is the *privatized religion*, which may be most anything, including extensive borrowings from denominational forms. In fact, the individual will likely be formally attached to a religious denomination, though he may make

[18]Ibid., p. 104.
[19]Ibid., pp. 116–17.

it clear it is of his own volition, with certain personal reservations, and that he has other alternatives and other ingredients in his symbolic universe.

Is that all there is? Not according to several theorists. There is another dimension or form of religious participation in the United States that we need to understand before essaying to make any predictions about the future of American religion—namely, the phenomenon of "civil religion." Robert Bellah has been the prime stimulater of thought on the subject, though others, frequently using different terms to describe the phenomenon, have also recognized it and discussed it.

The central idea of civil religion is that despite denominationalism, despite the successes of secularization at the expense of traditional religious forms, expressions, and beliefs, despite the internalization of religious definitions alternative to traditional ones, there is a superstratum or substratum (as you prefer) of common religious understandings that are quite pervasive in American society. As Bellah says:

> *Although matters of personal religious belief, worship, and association are considered to be strictly private affairs, there are, at the same time, certain common elements of religious orientation that the great majority of Americans share. These have played a crucial role in the development of American institutions and still provide a religious dimension for the whole fabric of American life, including the political sphere. This public religious dimension is expressed in a set of beliefs, symbols, and rituals that I am calling the American civil religion.*[20]

Bellah goes on to point out that America's civil religion is certainly not Christianity in anything like the specific sense such as would necessitate belief in Jesus Christ and the Atonement, but is rather more "unitarian," in the sense of regarding God as a sort of single supernatural being. But this God is not to be understood simply in the deistic tradition of an aloof Maker who set the world in motion and then left it to shift for itself. No, "he is actively interested and involved in history, with a special concern for America."[21] At the heart of civil religion is the idea that America is the promised land that God has led people to—out of the land of bondage (Europe). Thus this nation is to be dedicated to order, law, and justice as God would have them carried out. Bellah quotes extensively from Washington and Jefferson as well as from John Kennedy and Lyndon Johnson, pointing out the idea of America as charged with a divinely ordained mission to fulfill in bringing about God's will for

---

[20]Robert N. Bellah, "Civil Religion in America," in *Religion In America*, ed. William G. McLoughlin and Robert N. Bellah (Boston: Houghton Mifflin, 1968), pp. 5–6.
[21]Ibid., p. 9.

mankind. Out of the trauma of the Civil War emerged new themes of sacrifice and rebirth. Lincoln's Gettysburg Address was replete with Christian symbolism without being specifically Christian ("that those who here gave their lives, that the nation might live"). Lincoln's own "sacrificial" martyrdom enhanced the concept. Memorial Day ceremonies and to a lesser extent the ceremonies of the Fourth of July, Veterans' Day, Thanksgiving Day, and Washington's and Lincoln's birthdays provided ritual vehicles for the civil religion.

Coleman formalizes a definition of civil religion and lists three central characteristics of American civil religion. He defines *civil religion* as "the set of beliefs, rites, and symbols which relates a man's role as citizen and his society's place in space, time, and history to the conditions of ultimate existence and meaning."[22] Three characteristics, according to Coleman, typify American civil religion: (1) The nation is the primary agent of God's meaningful activity in history. This belief gave rise to the doctrines of manifest destiny and world obligation. (2) The nation is the primary society in terms of which individual Americans discover personal and group identity. Like the historic church, through the doctrine of the melting pot, America was called to be "catholic." (3) The nation also assumes a churchly feature as the community of righteousness.[23]

In the 1950s and 1960s many writers, most with a strong theological orientation and commitment, reacted strongly against what Bellah subsequently called civil religion and which seemed to constitute much of the so-called religious revival of the 1950s. Martin Marty's criticism of what he calls the "religion of democracy" or "state Shinto" is typical. Marty states that in American state Shinto, "democracy becomes the ultimate, religion the handmaiden."[24]

Whether critical of such a religon of democracy as a perversion of Christianity or not, most who have analyzed the phenomenon would agree that civil religion in America is differentiated. That is, neither state nor church is in charge of it. Coleman sees this as a new development. He suggests that much of the furor in the 1950s over a sellout of Christianity to secularism and the substitution of a new American Shinto was implicit recognition that control over civil religion had fallen out of religious hands. His view is that such differentiation is "healthy for both the state which does not place itself in opposition to the church and the church which remains free to perform a prophetic religious function."[25]

Others have suggested quite a different perspective—the rejuvena-

---

[22]John A. Coleman, "Civil Religion," *Sociological Analysis* 31, no. 2 (1970); 76.
[23]Ibid., p. 74.
[24]Martin E. Marty, *The New Shape of American Religion* (New York: Harper & Brothers, 1958), p. 78.
[25]Coleman, "Civil Religion," p. 76.

tion and encouragement of civil religion and the active involvement of organized religion in that process. A writer such as J. Paul Williams sees this as the future task of religion, although he does not use the concept *civil religion* and his proposals predate Bellah's introduction of the concept. Actually, Williams blends, in a most interesting way, a couple of sociological ideas: the idea of religion as an integrating, functional entity in society, and the Berger-Luckmann view of the decline of institutional religion and the rise of pluralistic choices for the symbolic universes of individual citizens. Williams would probably agree with both Berger's and Luckmann's analyses of the situation and the problem. But he would propose how to bring together the problem of the religious institutions, the needs of the individual, and above all the needs of the society.

Williams calls the integrating factor *"societal" religion*. This is distinguished from *"private" religion*, which an individual shares with only a few other intimate persons, and "denominational" religion, which is simply the denominational phenomenon we have discussed several times before. Williams points out that although denominational religion has changed in response to social change, societal religion has remained quite uniform over the decades. Its essence is commitment to the democratic way of life. He quotes A. Powell Davies's description of the democratic faith or way of life, which posits that man was meant to be free, that he can improve his level of life through the power of reason and discussion, and that human rights such as liberty and justice are by their nature universal. In final summation, Davies states: "God and history are on the side of freedom and justice, love and righteousness; and man will therefore, be it soon or late, achieve a world society of peace and happiness where all are free and none shall be afraid."[26] The central idea here is that the core values of America, which are almost by definition nearly universally accepted by Americans, are essentially religious values that in turn constitute the societal religion.

Since Williams deeply believes that American democracy and the societal religion that undergirds it face threats of various kinds, they need buttressing. Such support, he feels, ought to come from denominational religion. "Americans must be brought to the conviction that democracy is the very Law of life."[27] To accomplish this, "democracy must become an object of religious dedication. Americans must come to look on the democratic ideal (not necessarily America's practice of it) as the Will of God or, if they prefer, the Law of Nature."[28] Williams's proposal is simply this: "The churches and synagogues should not only promulgate their

---

[26]Quoted in J. Paul Williams, *What Americans Believe and How They Worship* (New York: Harper & Row, 1969), p. 481.
[27]Ibid., p. 491.
[28]Ibid., p. 484.

own denominational values, but in addition should support those broader values which are essential to the continuance and betterment of society as a whole. ... In America the churches and synagogues should teach faith in democracy as one item of their creed."[29]

Implicitly Williams is suggesting that all would be better off if religion in America would lose much of its denominational character and get on with the important business at hand of creating and maintaining a true democracy—that is, if religion would return to its true social purpose of enhancing the integration of society. It hardly needs pointing out, however, that his proposal has not caught on in a particularly striking fashion. Many religious groups would reject it out of hand—conservatives because of its tendencies to dilute traditional religious tenets and because of a tendency to blur the distinction between church and state, liberals because it appears to them too uncritical of existing political arrangements and of the manner in which democratic principles are expedited. Certainly many secularized Americans would raise serious questions about Williams's proposal in this day of political and intellectual dissent and criticism, when many can find no honest way to give democracy (as it obtains in the present, at least) unqualified support.

Lest the reader begin to think we have strayed from our point, we should mention it again. Our intention in this first section of this chapter is to introduce the reader to some of the theoretical perspectives that speak to the future of religion in the United States and other industrialized societies. Berger and Luckmann speak of the decline of traditional institutionalized religion (see also the first section of Chapter 15), but with a lively residue of essentially religious concerns that become privatized and involve a choice from many available forms. The concept of civil religion as a viable religious form quite apart from institutional religion was presented as a form of religion that already exsts in American society but that may continue to embody religious concerns irrespective of what happens to organized religion. Although some decry this possibility, others call for its wholehearted encouragement.

Greeley's Analysis

We now want to examine another theoretical perspective, one which begs to differ with much of the preceding. In essence, it says that organized religion as it has developed in the United States is not only obviously not dead (as all the preceding theorists would also readily grant), but it is also not even dying. This position is forthrightly advanced by Andrew Greeley.

[29]Ibid., p. 488.

Although Greeley foresees a great many changes in American religion in the next fifty or a hundred years, he does not see them as being what we might call fundamental in nature in the sense of a significant decline of present institutional patterns of American religion. Although there will be an increase in democratic forms of organization to tolerate greater internal diversity within denominations, more meaningful dialogue with the social sciences, and more emphasis on the nonrational, both in the ecstatic and in the contemplative and mystical sense—to mention only some of Greeley's expectations—religion, in forms quite familiar and recognizable by us today, will persevere with little if any loss of adherents.[30] Quite specifically, he says that in the United States, membership, church attendance, and doctrinal orthodoxy will persist at the levels reported in 1952–1965 surveys.[31] Denominations as well as local congregations will remain and will be a force in the community and the nation. Greeley amasses a wide variety of data in which he sees no sign of significant incipient decline. Further, he feels that the concept and process of secularization has been greatly overrated both as to its pervasiveness and power.

At the base of Greeley's argument are a couple of implicit assumptions that we would single out particularly. One is that man will continue to have religious needs—or more properly, will continue to face problems for which he needs religious answers. The second is that people who are affiliated with groups (in this case, religious groups) that seem to be satisfying them at least fairly well are not likely to withdraw totally from the group. This would be especially true as they observe the organization adapting and "improving" a bit over time. The net result is definitely not the demise of religion; it is, in fact, organized religion hardly disturbed at all.

Greeley's position, though admittedly a "conservative" one, is no more easily dismissed than those of the other theorists to whom we have referred in this chapter. He has developed a respectable theoretical framework, and he has more data to substantiate his position than many others do. In fact, the attempt here is to try not to evaluate his perspective in a final way or attempt to reach closure, any more than has been done earlier in this chapter. This is because this chapter will hopefully open some doors and present a sampling of the kinds of sociological thinking going on concerning the future of religion. The purpose of this chapter—more than that of most others, which have covered material in the sociology of religion about which there is considerable agreement in

---

[30]Andrew M. Greeley, *Religion in the Year 2000* (New York: Sheed and Ward, 1969), pp. 171–73.
[31]Ibid., p. 168.

the field—is to introduce the reader to some of the ambiguities and the differences in perspective that exist.

Before we move into the second part of this chapter, however, the reader deserves to be given a couple of leading observations. One is essentially the observation we made at the end of the last chapter—namely, religion in the general sense will likely not disappear or lose much of its present volume of appeal and interest, although religion as embodied in organizations and institutions might. Actually, Greeley doesn't adequately, to this author's taste at least, distinguish between the two senses of religion. Whether intentionally or not, Greeley tends to identify religion with organized forms that religion has adopted—forms such as congregations and denominations. Not that he isn't well aware of the difference, but he simply doesn't make much of it in the particular book we have been citing. Certainly his approach makes some sense when we realize that religion must always get organized—it is, after all, first of all a group phenomenon. But present forms or only slightly modified versions of those forms need not be the only options.

The second observation is that Greeley perhaps does not differ so greatly as he thinks he does from Berger and Luckmann—if we could put the following words in all of their mouths: "There will be greater flexibility in religious form and content as religion evolves in the future."

Greeley sees membership remaining at recent levels. Perhaps. But one suspects it will be membership with a different meaning and greater casualness about it. Very likely more people will be saying, "My church doesn't give me all my meaning. I have other options also. I have other groups I belong to and other sources of knowledge to which I refer." Therefore, people may retain membership yet feel less guilty when they miss a few worship services or when they direct financial contributions to other causes. Secularization enters here, too—perhaps not secularization "all the way," but secularization at least in the sense of less total, "blind" commitment to a religious institution, doctrine, or tradition, in the sense of finding some satisfaction of one's "ultimate concerns" from sources other than traditional religion.

It would seem that such a possibility or view combines Greeley's projection of "business as usual"—in the sense of continuing existence and strength of the organization, but also with the open-endedness of Berger and Luckmann's analyses—with good old civil religion running down its own set of tracks in the middle of the highway as usual. Greeley is undoubtedly correct in asserting that American society is not nearly so secularized as many have been saying it is. Yet secularization has progressed, has made some inroads on traditional religious patterns and forms, and will have other influences in the future.

RELIGION AND THE YOUTH MOVEMENT

In an attempt to bring together some of the ideas floating around from the first section of this chapter, as well as to close this text on a contemporary note, we shall now introduce some sociological reflections on religion and contemporary youth, particularly as evidenced in the widespread attraction of young people to Far Eastern mysticism and the emergence of the Jesus movement. Actually, the cults with a Far Eastern religious flavor and the Jesus movement can quite legitimately be considered together despite their differences so far as theological content is concerned. Sociologically their similarities outweigh their differences in terms of the kind of group that forms, the attraction each poses, the kinds of people that approach and join them, and the questions they are asking.

In general terms, both the Far Eastern cult religions and the Jesus movement clearly have emerged out of the American youth counterculture of the 1960s. At the heart of the counterculture, its motivation, so to speak, has been the desire of young people for two things: (1) to find personal identification—to know oneself—who I am and where I fit into the world and the cosmos; and (2) to find open, honest, meaningful interaction with at least a few other people.

The many analysts of the emergence and development of the counterculture essentially agree that many young people have been caught in an uncomfortable if not intolerable situation. As Roszak describes it, they are turned off by technocrats who counterfeit or machine-tool youth to the needs of the overarching bureaucracy while calling it education, by government representatives who interpret public opinion polls to fit predetermined policies while calling it democracy, by media managers who stage encounters between noncommittal candidates while calling it debate.[32] In short, many feel shortchanged, duped, betrayed, and unsatisfied because the answers they receive don't fit the questions they are asking.

As a consequence, some have gone the political-activism route in an effort to reform the system, whether in the area of education, the military, presidential-selection procedures, environmental protection, or whatever. Others have withdrawn from the system and devoted their energies to finding and knowing themselves. The latter goal seems implicit in the turning of some to hallucinogenic drugs that promise not only a form of escape but a clarification and deepening insight both into oneself and

---

[32]Theodore Roszak, *The Making of a Counter Culture* (Garden City, N.Y.: Doubleday, 1968), p. 16.

the problems that surround us. Others have taken the route of religious exploration, some after following the drug route, some contemporaneously with drugs, some without such experimentation at all.

Two major religious avenues have opened up to youth and have been developed by them. The first we referred to in the preceding chapter—the Far Eastern religious cult scene. Far Eastern religious imports, as well as indigenous American groups that have borrowed extensively from Far Eastern religious thought, emphasize one of the major characteristics of religions in the Far East, particularly of Buddhism in its many variations—that is, methods and techniques of introspection and self-discovery and achievement of inner peace and harmony. Amid external chaos and change a person makes peace with himself. Such subjectivity is in great contrast with Western religion's "objectivity"—bodies of doctrine to be believed, God's objective grace there waiting to be grasped, atonement achieved for me by another. Certainly youth who are characterized by the "hang loose" ethic as described by Simmons and Winograd,[33] particularly the characteristic of pursuing personal experience ("Don't tell me about life—let me live it and experience it myself") and the characteristic of spontaneity (being able to "groove with the scene that's happening" at the moment), will find the Far Eastern religions' emphasis on subjectivism quite compatible with their needs and perspectives.

Although superficially quite different, the so-called Jesus movement exhibits many basic similarities with the Far Eastern religious cult movement. Although it is obviously different both terminologically and conceptually to talk of Jesus than of Meher Baba, and although there are obviously different connotations to saying "Jesus saves" and chanting "Hare Krishna, Hare Rama . . .," the problems to which each movement speaks, the motivations for immersion in the group, and the effect on participants are all similar. Although the evidence from systematic research is still insufficient, the clear indications are that the young people that are drawn to the Jesus movement as to the Far Eastern religious cults are troubled young people—troubled in the sense of finding it difficult to establish their personal identity in the world, of defining the middle-class American values and behavior patterns of their parents and of the authority figures around them as empty and unfulfilling, yet searching for a meaningful alternative, or needing love and acceptance and openness, yet lacking it in family relationships.

In a study of "Jesus people" in California, Peterson and Mauss see a common core of ethical and psychic deprivation in the youthful participants. They express their ethical deprivation in their biting criticism

[33]J. L. Simmons and Barry Winogard, *It's Happening* (Santa Barbara, Calif.: Marc-Laird, 1966).

of establishment churches in the United States and the latter's failure to attain their goals and change people while all the time supporting the status quo. They are convinced there must be a better way; they latch onto "The Way." Psychic deprivation is more a matter of the emotions —the person does not *feel* satisfied. He may have food and shelter and conveniences in abundance, but does not feel satisfied. The Jesus people thus seek and find a "new birth."[34] Peterson and Mauss point out that quite commonly the followers of the Jesus movement are middle- and upper-class (we might note here that you can't feel truly unsatisfied by money and conveniences unless you've first had some). Many of them have had an unsatisfactory family life. They have not enjoyed good communication and rapport with their parents for much of their lives, and they are seeking love, understanding, and authority. In fact, in the communal living arrangements that are common in the Jesus movement members seem to find "family" relationships that they had not found with their real families at home.[35]

Enroth, Erickson, and Peters found among the Jesus people a high proportion of dropouts from the drug culture. In fact, the genesis of the Jesus movement dates back only to 1967, not getting seriously under way until 1970, with its earliest beginnings in the hippie drug scene in the Haight-Ashbury district of San Francisco when this was the center of the counterculture. Some hard-drug-using hippies became converted to Christianity and began spreading the word. They established a coffee-house ministry and over a two-year period established contact with thousands of young people.[36] The movement grew and now is scattered nationwide.

Many of the Jesus people are in their late teens and early twenties who have dropped out of the drug culture and seem to have latched onto the Jesus movement as a way back into society. It is highly interesting to note that the experience of feeling close to Jesus seems to be a substitute for a drug experience. A very common expression in the Jesus movement is "being high on Jesus." Adams and Fox have drawn three parallels between the drug experience and the Jesus experience: (1) Both are outside the normal, average American life-style, and are antiestablishment. The drug culture rejects traditional American middle-class values; the Jesus movement rejects traditional denominational religion as being

---

[34]Donald W. Peterson and Armand L. Mauss, "The Cross and the Commune: An Interpretation of the Jesus People," in *Religion in Sociological Perspective: Essays in the Empirical Study of Religion*, ed. Charles Y. Glock, (Belmont, Calif.: Wadsworth, 1973), pp. 261–79.

[35]Ibid., p. 274.

[36]Ronald M. Enroth, Edward E. Erickson, Jr., and C. Breckinridge Peters, *The Jesus People* (Grand Rapids, Mich.: William B. Eerdmans, 1972), pp. 12-15.

"phony as it can be." (2) Both the drug and Jesus cultures are highly subjective and experientially oriented. Recall one of the characteristics of the "hang loose" ethic mentioned earlier was that first-hand experience is a desperately sought-after virtue. (3) The nature of the religious experiences in the Jesus culture is very similar to previously experienced drug highs. "To come to know Jesus is a rush like speed." "I haven't had a 'down' day since I came to know Jesus."[37]

Theologically the Jesus people appear quite fundamentalistic and lay great stress on the Bible, though many of them don't seem to pay a great deal of attention to most of it. They portray a simple Gospel and proclaim "Jesus saves," in a very simplistic way. They are basically anti-intellectual and prefer not to discuss abstract theological questions. They are strongly apocalyptically oriented and emphasize that these are the last days and we'd better get prepared for the end of this present world and the Second Coming of Jesus. Most of them are into pentecostalism and look for the special gifts of the Holy Spirit such as "speaking in tongues." Clearly such an emphasis fits perfectly with their stress on experience as a prime ingredient in their life-style.

In a study of the Christ Commune, a self-supporting agricultural group of Jesus people comprising some six to eight hundred members in several locations throughout the United States, Harder, Richardson, and Simmonds found that members were most likely to have come out of a Baptist or Roman Catholic background, though many were Methodists, Lutherans, and Pentecostals. Most came from fairly affluent but unhappy homes. Eighty-six percent had engaged in premarital sexual relations and 90 percent admitted to experimentation with drugs, mostly "harder" than marijuana, though this group as well as nearly all others in the movement are now quite puritanical insofar as sex and the use of alcohol and drugs are concerned. The men and women are quartered separately; the women wear body-masking clothing; "dating" is carefully supervised; and the announcement by a couple of their intention to marry necessitates a forced six-month period of separation to test the durability of their attraction and love for one another. The researchers found them to be non-competitive, antiintellectual, otherworldly, and alienated from the society around them and essentially disinterested in it.[38] Yet they also observe: "The members had been transformed from purposeless, cynical, and self-destructive persons into loving, concerned, productive individuals with a sense of mission."[39]

[37]Robert L. Adams and Robert J. Fox, "Mainlining Jesus: The New Trip," *Society* 9, no. 4 (1972); 50–56.
[38]Mary White Harder, James T. Richardson, and Robert B. Simmonds, "Jesus People," *Psychology Today* 6, no. 7 (1972); 45–50, 110–13.
[39]Ibid., p. 110.

CONCLUSION

As we conclude this chapter on the future of religion with a discussion of transplanted and transposed Eastern religious cults and the Jesus people ("Jesus freaks"), we must point out that we do not mean to suggest that either or both of these religious forms or perspectives will be the religion of America's future. The membership in both movements is fluid and the dropout rate appears high. This seems particularly so as each group performs its function for society of helping citizens through times of trouble, quests for identity, and perhaps drug withdrawal and then sends some of them home, or back to school, or into a job. On the other hand, neither is likely to disappear overnight, if ever. Harder, Richardson, and Simmonds observe that groups such as the Christ Commune, with its stable economic base, nearly self-contained community, and abundance of mutual support, could go on indefinitely.

Actually, predicting either the phenomenal success or the ultimate demise of such groups would be in error—and beside the point, anyway. Our purpose in drawing attention to both the Far Eastern religious cults and the Jesus groups is to suggest some of the diversity of religious expression that we can continue to expect in American society, and worldwide as well. Neither form is particularly acceptable to much of traditional Christianity. But that's the point: *diversity* is the key word.

A second reason for focusing attention on these two movements is to emphasize once again the functional relationship of religion to society. Not that dysfunctional aspects are not also present there. To the extent that such cults and groups withdraw citizens from what the society sees as its task and isolates creative talent, they may be societally dysfunctional. On the other hand, to the degree that they provide meaningful relationships for people who have been isolated, perhaps desperate, perhaps destroying their brain cells and genes on bad trips, and generally being nonproductive members of society in the first place—in that way such groups perform societal functions.

And a third point, made several times before, is that people, young people particularly in these cases, are seen continuing their religious quest. That is, religion in some form or other continues. Its form changes, but the questions and problems and situations that seem to have generated it in the past continue to enervate it and send people out on religious quests. Religion has a future to the extent that humanity has a future, because religion is an expression of the confrontation of people with their environment, both physical and social, and with each other. It is a reflection of the precariousness of human existence and of the imperfection with which man relates to man. As such, religion in some form —or rather, in a variety of forms—not only is a part of society but will remain so.

Index